PORTRAITS OF
AMERICAN PRESIDENTS
VOLUME IV

THE KENNEDY PRESIDENCY

SEVENTEEN INTIMATE PERSPECTIVES OF JOHN F. KENNEDY

EDITED BY
KENNETH W. THOMPSON

UNIVERSITY PRESS OF AMERICA

LANHAM • NEW YORK • LONDON

University Press of America,® Inc.

4720 Boston Way
Lanham, MD 20706

3 Henrietta Street
London WC2E 8LU England

Printed in the United States of America

Co-published by arrangement with
The White Burkett Miller Center of Public Affairs,
University of Virginia

The views expressed by the author of this publication do not necessarily represent the opinions of the Miller Center. We hold to Jefferson's dictum that: "Truth is the proper and sufficient antagonist to error, and has nothing to fear from the conflict, unless by human interposition, disarmed of her natural weapons, free argument and debate."

Library of Congress Cataloging in Publication Data
Main entry under title:

The Kennedy presidency.

(Portraits of American presidents ; v. 4)
1. Kennedy, John F. (John Fitzgerald), 1917-1963—Addresses, essays, lectures. 2. United States—Politics and government—1961-1963—Addresses, essays, lectures. I. Thompson, Kenneth W., 1921- . II. Series.
E176.1.P83 1982 vol. 4 973'.09'92 s 85-18023
[E842] 973.922'092'4 [B]
ISBN 0-8191-4873-3 (alk. paper)
ISBN 0-8191-4874-1 (pbk. : alk. paper)

Dedicated

to

those who lead

by inspiring confidence

and

restoring hope and faith

in

mankind

TABLE OF CONTENTS

V. KENNEDY AND THE PRESS

VI. KENNEDY AND FOREIGN POLICY

VII. KENNEDY AND VIETNAM: TWO VIEWS

VIII. KENNEDY AND DEFENSE

IX. KENNEDY AS LEADER: HISTORY'S JUDGMENT

PREFACE

A pattern has emerged in the course of organizing Miller Center Forums which has led to the present volume. We have discovered that the leading authorities on particular presidents have helped the Center to draw others with common background to the University of Virginia. By "word of mouth advertising," they have encouraged their friends to come to Faulkner House. Their help has been of inestimable value to a fledgling public affairs center. It has enabled us to further presidential studies through the contributions of distinguished visitors to the understanding of contemporary presidents.

Partly by accident and partly by design, we have discovered our guests were turning the spotlight on certain American presidents. They were viewing particular administrations with shared values but different perspectives. They helped us to understand the President they knew best. The product is a portrait, not a photograph; it helps us see the character and spirit of a leader, not the more or less important details a photograph tends to convey. It tells us what was central to his life and works, not what was peripheral. The photograph reveals what can be seen with the naked eye. The portrait shows one thing the photograph cannot reveal: the human essence of the person portrayed.

With this volume, we continue a series of Miller Center publications, *Portraits of American Presidents*. We are grateful to the University Press of America for making volumes in this series available to a wide audience. We have embarked on similar inquiries into the presidencies of Lyndon B. Johnson and Richard M. Nixon. We plan to complete the series with volumes on the remaining postwar presidents. In the Introduction which follows, the editor traces the history of the Center's interest in the presidency of John F. Kennedy.

INTRODUCTION

The year 1983 marked the 20th anniversary of the death of John F. Kennedy. November 21, 1963 remains a day much like April 12, 1945 for Americans who remember where they were and what they were doing when they learned of President Kennedy's and President Roosevelt's deaths. Americans are not alone in possessing such memories. In cities and villages around the world, ordinary men and women mourned the loss of a world leader. In 1945, it had been a leader who stood at the helm of the Grand Alliance and with Churchill and Stalin guided free men to victory. In 1963, it was a younger leader who also had brought hope who was cut down by an assassin firing on a presidential motorcade from an abandoned floor of a Dallas warehouse.

Beginning in 1983, the Miller Center invited some twenty of President Kennedy's close associates to come to Charlottesville to discuss the Kennedy presidency. Among those who responded were Charles Bartlett, Theodore C. Sorensen, C. Douglas Dillon, Nicholas Katzenbach, Orville Freeman, McGeorge Bundy and Arthur Schlesinger, Jr. Their Forums which were conducted at Faulkner House, the home of the Miller Center, proved memorable and instructive for local scholars, retired public officials and respected community leaders who joined in the discussions. While each associate of President Kennedy had the opportunity to edit and revise his text, we have tried in the printed version to retain the spontaneity and directness of the questions and answers of the Forums.

The choice of the main themes and the organization of the book reflects the responsibilities, interests and experiences of those who participated and at least some of the dominant concerns of the Kennedy administration. Civil rights, the economy and foreign policy stood out in the Kennedy presidency. The volume concentrates on these areas drawing on leaders who played important roles. In the organization of the volume, discussions were organized under nine headings: Kennedy the Man; Kennedy and Civil Rights; Kennedy and the Economy; Kennedy and Foreign Policy; Kennedy and Vietnam; Kennedy and Defense; Kennedy and the Departments; Kennedy and the Press; and Kennedy as Leader: History's Judgment.

In addressing the first topic, we were fortunate that a member of the Miller Center Council, Charles Bartlett, was available. Bartlett was one of two or three newspaper men who were close to Kennedy, enjoyed his confidence and saw him frequently. His "Portrait of a Friend" is sympathetic, straightforward and remarkably detached. Arthur Schlesinger, Jr., is not only a leading biographer of President Kennedy but someone who helps place the President in historical context. Apart from relations with Kennedy, Schlesinger's powers of analysis and expression make his contribution noteworthy. Senator George McGovern was the first director of the Food for Peace Program and from that vantage point and later from the Senate provides a political perspective of Kennedy the Man.

The field of civil rights proved an especially rich source for exploring Kennedy's moral and political values. Initially, the Kennedy administration had not considered civil rights a significant area for engaging the full powers of the federal government. By 1963, however, the President defined civil rights as a moral issue. One of the merits of the four contributions on Kennedy and Civil Rights is in tracing the shift in the President's thought and action. Nicholas Katzenbach was the first deputy to Attorney General Robert Kennedy and observed the change at first-hand. Burke Marshall was an anti-trust lawyer recruited at the initiative of Byron White, who was President Kennedy's only appointment to the Supreme Court. Louis Martin worked within the Kennedy administration and the Democratic National Committee to advance the cause of the minority which he represented. John Seigenthaler participated in defending civil rights in the trenches being himself a victim of the violence against Freedom Riders in Alabama. However, he survived to become the publisher and editor of the newspaper, *USA Today*. Taken together these four essays offer some unique and remarkable insights into the unfolding of Kennedy's civil rights policies.

It is generally agreed that the two most influential figures responsible for economic policy in the Kennedy administration were Secretary of the Treasury C. Douglas Dillon and Chairman of the Council of Economic Advisors Walter H. Heller. Secretary Dillon conducted a Forum at the Miller Center. Professor Heller made available an interview on his role in the administration conducted by Professor Erwin C. Hargrove of Vanderbilt, sometime scholar in residence at the Miller Center. While viewing the economy from decidedly different perspectives, Dillon who is a moderate Republican and Heller who is a liberal

Democrat reenforce one another's viewpoints. Their consensus illustrates one of the strengths of the Kennedy administration, the President's success in drawing on leaders of different outlooks and backgrounds without their engaging in open political warfare.

Orville Freeman served as Secretary of Agriculture in both the Kennedy and Johnson presidencies. His contribution centers on the Kennedy administration's organization and policymaking from the standpoint of a Cabinet member's perspective. It also provides insights on the organization of the White House under Kennedy contrasting it with the Johnson White House.

Charles Roberts discusses President Kennedy's relation with the press framing it in terms of image and reality. He was in the first press bus in Dallas at the time of the assassination and was one of two reporters to return on Air Force One to Washington. It would be difficult to find a news writer who offered a more independent critique of Kennedy's relations with the press.

Foreign policy is remembered as one of President Kennedy's "success stories." His American University speech is present in almost every collection of great foreign policy speeches. His commitment "to make the world safe for diversity" is often quoted as alternative to "making the world safe for democracy," Woodrow Wilson's axiom. Two of his closest associates were his Secretary of State and National Security Advisor. Dean Rusk has visited the Miller Center on several occasions and his contribution is taken from some of his reflections on foreign policy, including the Kennedy foreign policy. McGeorge Bundy is engaged in a monumental study of the history of the nuclear problem. His assessment of the Kennedy foreign policy is focused on this issue.

A section follows on Vietnam. Frederick Nolting who was Ambassador to Vietnam early in the administration discusses the shift in support for Diem and the military coup. While Nolting is critical of the change in policy, William Bundy, a longtime public servant who served in Defense and the Central Intelligence Agency, supports the case for change.

General William Y. Smith was a deputy to General Maxwell Taylor, who was Chairman of the Joint Chiefs of Staff under Kennedy. General Smith offers his reflections on Kennedy and Arms Control and Defense.

Appropriately, the concluding essay in the book is by Theodore C. Sorensen who qualifies, if anyone does, as an intimate of President Kennedy. Sorensen looks back at the main characteristics of the philosophy and policies of the Kennedy presidency. He looks ahead to the legacy transmitted by that administration to future presidencies and its fate. He reflects on his own relationship with Kennedy and their contrasting backgrounds and traditions. Because of the intimate ties that bound them together in carrying out the mandates of the administration, a portrait of enduring value emerges.

It is our hope at the Miller Center that these essays will provide concerned Americans with a better picture of the Kennedy presidency and historians and scholars with source materials to deepen their research and supplement the written records.

I.
JOHN F. KENNEDY: THE MAN

PORTRAIT OF A FRIEND
Charles Bartlett

NARRATOR: Charley Bartlett is a Pulitzer Prize-winning national reporter. He was a reporter and Washington correspondent of the *Chattanooga News Times* which is the newspaper published in the city of the donor of the Miller Center, Burkett Miller. He went on to become a columnist for the *Chicago Sun Times* and the *Chicago Daily News*, and editor of the News Focus. Mr. Bartlett is a graduate of Yale, an ex-naval officer and co-author of *Facing the Brink*. He is a member of the Gridiron Club and well known in Washington circles.

Recently he has taken the lead in examining the nature and structure of the American political system. Almost every group concerned with public affairs expresses itself with fervor on the question of taking another look at the system, one group saying that there are basic systemic problems in the American system of government with others taking the opposite view that we have to operate within the constitutional system as we have it (and appearing nervous about the whole process).

A wry humorist, to whom I mentioned that we were hoping Charley Bartlett would speak in our series on the Kennedy presidency, remarked, "Surely that is appropriate. You knew, of course, that he introduced Jackie to John F. Kennedy. But an equally serious qualification is Charley's knowledge of the Kennedy presidency. In planning the series, Ambassador Bill Battle advised if you can get two people to participate in the Kennedy series the program will be a success. He said if it is possible to recruit Ted Sorensen and Charley Bartlett you will have perspectives on the Kennedy presidency that no one else can give.

So with all of this in mind we are proud that our good friend and Council member Charles Bartlett will reflect on memories of JFK and then open the floor to discussion. We regret that Senator John Sherman Cooper's illness made it impossible for him to be with us this morning. With all there is to say about President Kennedy, perhaps we are fortunate though in having Mr. Bartlett for a "full hour plus" to offer us his recollections.

MR. BARTLETT: Ken's introductions are always more eloquent than what comes after them. He was nice enough to mention the Jefferson meetings which some of you may want to take a look at. What we are doing is trying to get Virginians who are interested in such constitutional questions as the six-year term for the President or limitations on service in Congress to look at various proposals that have been made to make the government more efficient from the constitutional structure standpoint. That excludes issues like abortion, birth control, school prayer, etc. We're not getting into those matters.

What we are going to do in Williamsburg is bring together about one hundred fifty Virginians who are interested in these issues. We will see how people feel about the Constitution and whether it does need to be updated. We formed the Jefferson meetings because Thomas Jefferson said that every generation ought to take a look at the Constitution to learn if it is meeting the needs at that particular time. We are going into the third century of the Constitution and this has never been done. The Jefferson meetings are an effort to discover if citizens have thoughts about the structure of government.

If the meeting goes well in Williamsburg we are going to do it all over the country. The idea is to have every state hold one before the bicentennial celebration in 1987. At that point we will have had a reasonable facsimile of what you would call a solid echo of the ratification process. People will have developed their own thinking and maybe even have some new ideas. There is supposed to be a sort of native political genius in Americans, but it's been rather dormant of late. As Madison said, the purpose of the Constitution is to serve the public happiness and if you can enhance the public happiness through some provision of the Constitution then we should talk seriously about it.

I'm sorry John Cooper couldn't come down today because he is one of the great men of Washington. He is elderly now and there are times when he doesn't feel as well as he should. But he is a great figure and an old-fashioned man operating in a modern environment. I remember back in 1952 after he'd run for the Senate and been beaten, he was going to run again. We had a little dinner and there were John Cooper, Jack Kennedy and Albert Gore from Tennessee. Each of them was getting ready to make a race for the Senate. Gore and Kennedy were talking about the preparations they were making for their announcement. Gore said he was going to charter a plane and start flying in Tennessee. He would stop at Bristol, Knoxville, Nashville, and Memphis and make an announcement in each place and go on TV in each place. He said by the end of the day he would have pretty well covered the state. Then he asked, "What are you going to do, Jack?" Kennedy said he was going to go on television for thirty-six hours in Massachusetts and have people phone in. It would be one of the first telethons and people would be asking questions and getting a chance to know him. He asked, "What are you going to do, John?" Cooper said, "I hadn't really thought much about it. I thought I would just go down to Somerset and announce." But that's John Cooper. He kept his courtly Kentucky ways and was a great moral influence in the Senate over a long period. We will have to be sure to get him down here because he was a very, very good friend of Jack Kennedy.

Ken asked me to reminisce a bit about my recollections of JFK. It is interesting for me because he taught me how fast a person can grow. He was extraordinary. I met him in a nightclub in Palm Beach right after the war. I was just getting into the newspaper business and he was just going out of it. He came back from the war wounded and had gone to work for Hearst and covered the United Nations conference in San Francisco. He said, "I've loved the newspaper business but the fact is you get a feeling of frustration because you write about these things and you are really not doing much about it. I figure if I get into politics I might get a chance to do something about the system. I really would like to weigh in a little heavier." So I went to Chattanooga for about a year and a half and he went to Washington. We resumed our friendship up there.

Looking back on his experiences in the House, I must say that Jack Kennedy was a very different member of the House than John Adams and some of the other Presidents that served in the House. It totally failed to fascinate him. It really never grabbed him. I think his father may have made one mistake which was to give him an air travel credit card so that he was on the plane to Palm Beach every Friday night during the winter and of course up to the Cape in the summer. He seemed to me to stay pretty much on the periphery of House life. I remember he told me he had gotten very fond of George

Smathers who was a congressman from Miami. He said, "I like George because he doesn't take it very seriously." I don't know what the record is but I remember reading somewhere that he introduced no more than four or five bills during the entire time he was in the House.

He lived in Georgetown with his sister Eunice. They had friends like Scoop Jackson and Joe McCarthy and Torby McDonald. I remember the lady who lived on Lafayette Square, Mrs. Beale, had him to dinner one night and of course he was late. His habits were very casual in those days and I remember he told me they were seated when he came in. There were about thirty people at the table in black tie. Mrs. Beale looked at him coldly and said, "Congressman, your seat is down there!" He wasn't a great social success in Washington. He didn't work at it. He was always casual.

In Washington I came to know Jackie Bouvier. She was an extraordinary and attractive girl, and knowing something about him, I thought she was the kind of person he would like. I did arrange for them to meet, first at my brother's wedding in Long Island, where they met in passing, and then later at a dinner in Georgetown. They were attracted to each other but his concentration at that point was on getting elected to the Senate. Jack was gone for a year and a half but the romance caught fire when he came back.

I'm not sure looking back that I would make a practice of introducing interested young ladies to politicians to marry. I think marrying a politician is a very dubious exercise for anyone. It's strenuous. Politicians are interesting if you can watch them. It's a form of acting. The sense of self unfolds as they mature. Politicians don't really become more endearing as they get older because they are so wrapped up in themselves. The sense of self grows stronger with time.

Kennedy was always very critical of the older people in the House and Senate. He found great character flaws in the people he had to deal with as seniors in the system. That has been my experience as well in Washington. I'm amazed at how many young men go through this process; they go from being very bright, aggressive young men trying to get into the Senate and having the personality and ability to put a campaign together and get the money—to sort of losing something as they go on. Somehow a philosophy of life doesn't develop in that environment. They are dealing with so many factors and so many people that it's kaleidoscopic. He didn't really enjoy the legislators. He didn't want to hang around the legislative life.

The Senate was a great career at one point, certainly in the early fifties and before. I felt then that the members had a sense of each other. They enjoyed each other and respected each other and exchanged philosophies. Many of these men seemed to be complete human beings. What you feel today is that these people face such tremendous pressure, are torn in so many directions, and are expected to be in so many places and on so many airplanes that you really wonder if they have time to develop richness of spirit, even to relish the experiences they have. You feel it is just one trip after another, one hearing after another. And I don't think the Senate fascinated Jack Kennedy very much. I never felt that he was intrigued by it.

I never felt Jack had any sense of a mission in the Senate. I think the dramatic episode for him was the censure vote on Joe McCarthy. This was a hard vote not only because of the Irish in Massachusetts but also because Joe had been a friend of the family. Jack had had a very bad back operation and was ill at the time of the vote. Later he felt as if he had walked away from it a little bit. I don't know whether he could have voted or not but it was a tough one. That was what caused him to write the book *Profiles in Courage* about the senators who had cast very courageous votes.

But he was never mesmerized by the personalities in the Senate. I think he was, like all of us, fascinated by Lyndon Johnson. I must say I don't think he ever stopped being intrigued by that amazing personality. I don't think he had any really good friends in the Senate except George Smathers. And that was about it.

In this period, father Joe Kennedy was clearly pushing Jack. I believe that left to his own instincts, he probably would never have girded himself up to run against Henry Cabot Lodge for the Senate in 1952. That was a courageous thing to do. It was a big gamble because Henry Cabot Lodge was running the Eisenhower campaign. He was an enormously attractive fellow. He had done a very good job organizing Ike, getting him back to the country, and getting him on the road. He appeared to be tremendously popular. Of course he didn't campaign at all in Massachusetts and this was the opening that Jack exploited. The Kennedys went to work. They gave tea parties in every little town in Massachusetts and they brought out the family silver and put on a tremendous show.

Jack at this point was not a prepossessing speaker. His voice was rather thin. I went around the state with him some and he had a quick nervous way of talking. He was especially interested in the intellectual aspects of foreign policy and I'm not sure how many of the people in Massachusetts really reacted to that. I think that what they liked was the Kennedy thing, and the glamour and good looks and boyishness, and probably the Irishness, too. If you looked at Jack Kennedy in 1952, I don't think you would have said that this is a man who is going to be President of the United States. It never occurred to me. He was fascinated by foreign policy, not at all by domestic issues, and as I say not particularly in love with the legislative life.

But the maturation process began with his election to the Senate in 1952. It has always been my belief that at this point Joe said, "Now look, you start behaving like a man who is running for President of the United States because that's what you're doing.'' I think that somehow the possibility of that moment dawned on him because I did notice that he became more political in talking about people in the Senate. We used to have fun discussing the foibles of a Sam Rayburn or a Lyndon Johnson. But after he was elected to the Senate, Jack became diplomatic. He began to say nice things about these people who had powerful positions in the Senate. That was a change that I noticed clearly.

I brought him down to Chattanooga. He had never really been out of Massachusetts politically. He made a speech which was interesting to the people of Chattanooga because at that point Massachusetts was very resentful of the Tennessee Valley Authority and even the liberals in Massachusetts were voting against the Tennessee Valley Authority in Congress. So he came down and made a very good speech to the Rotary Club in Chattanooga. At that point he hired a fellow from the TVA called Lee White who turned out to be an enormous asset in the White House and in the Senate office.

He had a marvelous way about him and of course people responded to his charm. This charm made itself felt more slowly in Washington than anywhere else. There a lot of people who didn't like Jack Kennedy. He was controversial socially and politically. This really wasn't Venus springing full blown out of the shell. It was an emergence. The emergence developed in the Senate.

The 1956 convention gave him his first assurance that a potential for national leadership might really be there. As you remember, Adlai Stevenson threw the convention open for the choice of a vice-president. He declared that he wasn't going to pick a vice-president so that they should compete for delegate favor. I went back to the Hilton Hotel from the stockyards with Jack. I think Joe had worked very hard on Adlai to try to persuade him, and Eunice (Shriver) had worked very hard on Adlai. Every pressure had been applied to get him to pick Jack as his running mate. Adlai was caught between these pressures and the fact that Estes Kefauver had done very well in the primaries around the country. There were a lot of delegates who were strong for Kefauver and Adlai just didn't want to take the chance.

It is amusing to me to remember how shy and diffident Jack was about the whole business of mounting a convention fight. He had only one night to go out and see how many delegates he could get. As we went up in the Hilton elevator there was a third person aboard and it was Carmine DeSapio of New York. He was an aloof figure who had enormous power at that point. He controlled the New York delegation. We all got off the elevator together and it was obvious that Kennedy hadn't recognized him. I said, ''Jack, that's Carmine DeSapio. You really ought to say something to him.'' I'll never forget the timidity in his voice because it was so ironic in light of subsequent history. He was like a little boy going to the headmaster of his boarding school. He went up to Mr. DeSapio and said, "I'm Jack Kennedy. I thought I might run for vice-president and if you would think about supporting me. . . ." It was a highly tentative approach to a powerful, cynical political leader.

Anyway they gave it everything they had. It was a good try. The climax came at a moment when Kennedy had been taking a hot bath in the Stockyards Inn. He had this constant back problem so whenever he was having trouble he would crawl into a hot bath. The inn was about a hundred and fifty feet away from the convention floor and he was over there relaxing. He was invited to the floor to concede to Estes Kefauver. If there was a moment that made Jack Kennedy this was it. His charm did come across and it was at that moment the country caught the sense of a young, very attractive fellow, very graciously acknowledging that he had not won this race. Somehow it was electric. It really wasn't anything he said, it was his charm. And that is what put him on the road, I think.

After that we had some very interesting talks about whether he should run for President and I was very much against it. I said, "You're young, you're Catholic, and you've never really had any experience with the leadership role. You don't have great standing in the Washington community. It's going to be very tough for you." I urged him to pass it up for eight years arguing that he would make a better presidency if he made it to the White House eight years from now. The discussion was at times rather testy because his point always was, "In politics you have to take the moment that comes. If this seems to me to be my moment, I've got to do it."

The outcome was surprising because the Eisenhower administration had by my lights done a pretty good job. I don't think anybody was at all crazy about Richard Nixon but you had to give it to Ike; they'd fought against inflation and ended the war. It seemed to me that the Democrats were going in without many cards. But it's interesting how a lot of the partisanship in politics is generated by young people who come to work for these senators and want to go all the way to the White House. Their ambition is to be in the White House because they know that's where the payoff is for them. They are the ones that hone the issues and sharpen the divergencies and create the excitement. Kennedy was very temperate and he was not a boiling liberal by any standpoint. I always regarded him as a sort of middle-of-the-road person. He could have been a progressive Cooper-type Republican just as easily as a Democrat. There was no bitterness or passion in him of a partisan nature. And yet he started boiling up against the Eisenhower administration, saying these people have done a terrible job and they've left the country in a stalemate. You could see the ammunition being fed to him by these young fellows fresh out of college.

Every once in awhile Jack's picture would suddenly appear on the cover of *Life* magazine. He hadn't done anything particularly to get on the cover of *Life* magazine. I think Mr. Joe Kennedy had hired an astute public relations man named Sonnenfeld. He didn't tell Jack who was pleased but surprised by the publicity windfalls.

Another interesting thing about Mr. Kennedy. Red Fay told me about being down at Palm Beach for Christmas of 1959 just after Jack had announced. Mr. Kennedy was looking at the TV news and Ike came on with an announcement about something, some development that had been resolved fairly satisfactorily. Old Joe shook his head and said, "You know, these guys are just going to murder Jack. He's going into an impossible situation." He said, "They have got a pretty good story to tell the country." But when Jack came in the room about five minutes later, Mr. Kennedy's line completely changed. He said, "Jack, you're going to really crucify these guys." It was a complete flip. There was that sort of fascinating aspect about it. In the presidential campaign you felt the hand of Joe Kennedy all the way.

We have a lot of people looking at the selection process and how it works in this country. The Lord knows it's long and awkward and expensive and people get bored with it. But I'll say one thing for it; it has an enormous capacity to make the candidates grow because it does rub their noses in every corner of this country.

The most phenomenal growth that I've seen in any human being in my lifetime occurred in Jack Kennedy between about 1958 (when I was urging him not to run for the presidency) and 1960 (when he was reaching for the nomination.) He had really been out there and met a lot of people and learned a lot about what this country was all about. He became deeply baptized in American life. This was a tremendous change. This was the first time I began to feel passion in him and to hear him express a deep sense of what this country is all about. A lot of that was reflected in the speeches that he made in the campaign in 1960. That passion in those speeches is what made him President. He became for the first time something more than a diffident, intellectual politician talking intelligently and sensibly about foreign policy. There are moments when I've thought we've got to do something about the nominating process because it's an ordeal, but the ordeal is really part of a tremendous educational process.

The primaries demand a lot of judgment. That was when I began to see Jack did have unusual political judgment because of the people that he picked to be his leaders in these states. This is an important part of the test. In other words, when you go into a state and you are looking at five men and you pick the wrong one to be your campaign manager in that state, it costs you and it costs you badly. And if you make the right choice and you pick the right person for the right reasons, you will probably win in that state and that makes a difference. When people talk about amending the primary system and making it a popular vote you have to be careful. The present system is too long but it is a superb test of the candidates. Jack survived the test and he did it with considerable grace and enjoyment. His back hurt him all the time but he was a darned good sport. He never complained about being tired. He always was kept alive and peppy by his sense of humor which saw characteristics in people that amused him. He had an air of gaiety about him all the way.

I remember one telling instance. Going to Wisconsin for the first time, I said I would fly out with him because I wanted to write some stories about the Wisconsin primary. We had dinner at his house. As we were leaving the house he pointed to some overcoats hanging on the wall and said, "Which one shall I wear?" I said, "I don't know, I suppose the tweed one looks more like Wisconsin than anything else." He said, "Now you see you are wrong. I've got to take the black one because that's the coat I always wear and the most important thing when you are in one of these things is always to be yourself."

That's a very important thing that I think a lot of politicians forget. You don't change your personality to match the situation. Adlai Stevenson used to wear a sort of shooting cap when he went up to Minnesota. He looked as if he were on a pheasant shoot or something. Jack always had that black coat. I don't think you'll ever find a picture of him on any campaign poster when he wasn't wearing the black coat and no hat. That was Kennedy. And he stayed himself through the presidency, I'm proud to relate. I don't think his personality was ever really affected by anything that happened to him.

He had another gift which became apparent to me at this point. That was an ability to discern quickly what people had to say that would be important to what he was trying to do. In other words, he didn't make conversation with people about things about which they knew very little. His effort was always to try to find the area of expertise and to keep the dialogue in that area. He had a very keen sense of what somebody might know that might be very useful to him.

Another change occurred, more after the election than before. He became much better mannered. The Kennedys have never been noted for politeness, but I noticed after the election he became almost courtly. He developed a gracious personal style. It was fun to watch somebody grow under your eyes. At no point after he got elected did I feel that he was inadequate for the job or that he was too light for the job or that he hadn't had the background for the job. Somehow he did grow into the job in the process of getting there.

QUESTION: Would you have any light to shed on the relationship between

Jack Kennedy and Lyndon Johnson, especially the choice of Lyndon Johnson for vice-president?

MR. BARTLETT: That's a good question. I was told as a friend and a newspaper man several days before the climax of the convention that Jack was going to take Stuart Symington as the vice-president. I was told that it was set and to go ahead and write it, which I did. At this point the relationship between Kennedy and Johnson was very bitter. Johnson, of course had been in the Senate and thought that he ran the world from the Senate. He believed that as soon as he flew to Los Angeles, the delegates would line up behind him. He regarded Jack as an opponent whom he could brush aside.

I remember flying out with Jack on a trip after the West Virginia primary. Kennedy was very anxious to have the support of Adlai Stevenson. He said, "I'm going to stop in Chicago because Adlai Stevenson said he would support whoever wins the West Virginia primary. So I'm going to pick up my marbles." We stopped in Chicago and I went my way and we met back at the airplane. I said, "Well, how did it go?" He replied, "Well, I learned one thing today and that is that Adlai Stevenson will never be my secretary of state. I'm used to being turned down. I ask a hundred people a day if they will support me and about ninety-eight of them are still saying they are going to wait and see how this thing develops. Adlai did make this statement earlier and I reminded him of it and he said, 'Jack, I've decided I'm not coming out for you now. I'm going to hold back because I think that it's important and because I can serve as a bridge between you and Lyndon Johnson.' " Jack said to me with a laugh, "I don't think Adlai realizes that Lyndon Johnson thinks that he's a fruit. The idea of Adlai Stevenson as a bridge between me and Lyndon Johnson is a joke. If he were a great diplomat, he would have been able to come up with a better one than that."

There was bitterness in the Kennedy-Johnson relationship at that time. Johnson had made some rather ugly remarks about Mr. Kennedy and also about Jack's illness. The Addison's disease thing was going around. Bobby Baker started working the corners. It was getting ugly. They had a sharp encounter before the Texas delegates in the Ambassador Hotel.

Joe Alsop and Phil Graham had the idea that Johnson should be on the ticket. They were both very fond of Johnson. And they persuaded Jack that he should go down first thing in the morning after he had been nominated and offer the second slot to Johnson. They said, "He'll turn it down and you can go back and have breakfast but you will have done a great thing because you will have shown appreciation for Johnson. He will have had his ego way and you will have cooperation instead of an antagonist in the leadership of the Senate." I'm really quoting Jack on this. So he said he went down and was amazed when Johnson said, "I want to think about it."

Jack was absolutely appalled at the thought of running with Lyndon Johnson. His idea was to run a fresh face campaign. He had developed a lot of respect for Stuart Symington who had gone around the country and made a lot of friends. Stuart was the kind of person he wanted to run with. He represented the sort of spirit he wanted to reflect, middle-road Democratic policy. He was genuinely shaken by Johnson's decision to accept this offer. Later he said to me, "You know I didn't offer the vice-presidency to Lyndon Johnson, I just held it out there."

So he sent Bobby down to tell Lyndon Johnson he couldn't have it. Bobby was always the one who got the dirty jobs. So Bobby went down and the first person he encountered was Sam Rayburn. As soon as Sam heard what he was after he got all red in the face and said, "You tell your brother if he wants to talk a man's business he ought to send a man to do it!" So Bobby got nowhere and came back. And they realized at that point that they were stuck with Lyndon Johnson. Of course, at that moment the liberals went into a fury, particularly Mennen Williams and the Michigan delegation. It was gloomsville in the Kennedy camp for the rest of the day.

I well remember that night. It was at Marion Davies' house which Mr. Kennedy had hired for the proceedings—a great big baronial Spanish thing with a fountain in front. I'll never forget the scene. The sun was going down over the green trees and Bobby Kennedy's kids were slopping around in the fountain. Jack was reading the *New York Times* on the front of a car that was parked out in front of the house. Bobby was lying on the floor of the front seat dictating to the convention on one of those telephones to tell Larry O'Brien how to get Johnson nominated. Bobby said, "Yesterday was the best day of my life and this is the worst day of my life." And Jack was gloomy. His head was down. He looked beat. He had no animation in his face at all. And I remember old Joe Kennedy in his velvety dressing coat and slippers with foxheads on the toes. He was looking out at the sunset and said, "Jack, in two weeks they will be saying this is the smartest thing you ever did." It was the most valid observation of the evening.

I also remember sitting with Jack and Bobby to watch the process on television as they nominated Lyndon Johnson. There was a black congressman called Dawson from Chicago. Of course the blacks had been screaming all day about this racist Texan on the national ticket and they were very angry. But Dawson had been persuaded to get up and make a seconding speech for Lyndon Johnson. I remember Kennedy sitting there puffing his cigar as Dawson urged the delegates to support Johnson. He smiled and said, "It's a great system." About that time the telephone rang and Jack picked it up and said,

"Yeah, I'd like to see you. Come out tomorrow morning and we'll have a little coffee about nine thirty. That will be fine." Bobby said, "What was that?" He said, "It was George Meany." Bobby said, "Does he want to see Dad?"

QUESTION: I met John Kennedy several times. Then I went to Turkey in 1958–9 and he wrote to me. In one of his letters he said, "With friends like George Meany, I don't need any enemies," that kind of line. I later checked that with Frank Thompson who was active in the House in those days and very close to Kennedy as a personal friend. He thought Kennedy started to grow up, or do his homework, during the period of the conference committee's work on the Lanham-Griffin Act.

MR. BARTLETT: Yes, that was a very maturing experience, trying to pull those pieces together. That was the biggest legislative effort that he ever was involved in. He got into that very deeply. It could have destroyed him so he had to deal with it very carefully. That's a good point. That was part of the maturing process.

QUESTION: If he didn't work terribly hard, how did he master the details? I had a similar experience. The foundation I worked for was trying to deal with Hungarian refugees. I happened to sit next to him on a plane and he asked me who I was and what I was doing. I thought I had the facts and figures about Hungarian refugees and Polish refugees but he had mastered every last detail. He seemed to know everything. It was after the Hungarian revolution in 1956.

MR. BARTLETT: I think that he was fascinated by these foreign policy issues and I think he read the same books that you have. He did a tremendous amount of reading. What he didn't get into was the legislative pulling and tugging. He always read tremendous amounts and always discussed it. That was one of the great things that Mr. Kennedy did. He created an environment in which the kids talked constantly about these issues. He and Jackie stayed home a lot after they got married and they read a lot of books. Both worked to pull out quotes that you could use in speeches. There was a lot of that kind of homework done. His background was deep. There's no question about that.

QUESTION: You keep saying how amazed you were at his growth. What do you think prompted his growth? What about his faith? Did his Catholicism play a part in that or his vision of the American dream?

MR. BARTLETT: No. I think he always had the basic character. I think the talents he had were not triggered until he started running for President. He had a busy life and was fully occupied and did the things that interested him. When he started putting the talents to work, he began to grow. He needed to use his perception to make judgments about strategy. The real Jack Kennedy just came out in the pressure cooker.

QUESTION: What about the character of President Kennedy compared with that of his father, Mr. Joe Kennedy? You have referred to the operations behind the scene on the part of the father to get him elected; he was opportunistic in order to achieve his objectives. The President certainly knew the character of his father. To what extent did the influence of the father go beyond making arrangements and providing finances into influencing his son on the philosophical front?

MR. BARTLETT: I can tell you an interesting story that bears on that. The campaign began on Labor Day in Michigan. I was covering it as a newspaper man. Kennedy campaigned in all those United Auto Workers' cities across Michigan. The group got in a couple of planes late in the evening and flew to Pocatello, Idaho to spend the night. I was in my room writing and I got a call from the candidate who said, "Well, I just got a call from the old man down in Palm Beach. He says that if I keep talking the way I talked today that they are going to bury me six feet under. I'm not going to listen to Dad anymore on this campaign because he doesn't understand what a Democrat has to do to get elected. In this country a Democrat can only win if he excites an awful lot of people to believe that their lives are going to be better if he gets into the White House. If he doesn't generate that sense, there is just no chance for a Democrat."

QUESTION: His father then did help him in a sense because he would listen to his father and do the other thing!

MR. BARTLETT: He concluded this conversation by saying, "I'm just not going to talk to Dad about the campaign anymore."

I think Joe Kennedy understood an element of politics which was crucial at that point and that was the role of the Dick Daleys in Chicago, the Crangles in Buffalo and the Dan O'Connells in Albany. There were at that point still some very powerful Irish figures in these big cities. The old man's greatest value was working with them plus of course the resources that he brought into the campaign.

QUESTION: What's your opinion of the theory that Daley delivered that election?

MR. BARTLETT: Well, I think you have to give him some credit. I wasn't out in Chicago at that point so I don't know how it worked, but I was sure that Daley was going to carry that state for Kennedy and he did.

There was one other incident which bore on his character at this point. It is an interesting story that tells you something about Kennedy. We were out walking one Sunday before the election when he said, "I had the damnedest meeting in New York last night. I went to this party. It was given by a group of people who were big money contributors and also Zionists and they said to me, 'We know that your campaign is in terrible financial shape!' [Which it was, they were deep in debt]. The deal they offered me was that they would finance the rest of this campaign if I would agree to let them run the Middle Eastern policy of the United States for the next four years if I were elected. I will probably never be elected President but as a citizen I thought this was outrageous. If I do get elected President, I promise you this. I will do everything I can do to get federal subsidies for presidential elections because we've got to protect any man who may be elected to President of the United States from that kind of pressure."

I talked to Roger Stevens about this. He was the finance manager for Adlai Stevenson in 1956. He told me that the same proposition had been put to Adlai at a country club in Los Angeles in 1956. So it shows you've got to have men of character as candidates because these groups are moving in and wielding their financial influence.

Jack was in an elated, creative world after the election, and particularly after the inauguration. A person who has just been elected and installed as President is an invigorated personality. He thinks of all the good things he wants to do. The Kennedys thought about Thomas Jefferson and of all the things they might do that would put them in the footsteps of the great Presidents. He was determined to be a great President and Jackie shared his excitement.

On every front there was a challenge and they were exhilarated by the chance to do some constructive things. I think it is saddening from that point to watch the President as he confronts the fact that he is up against grave odds in trying to do these constructive things because of our system of divided powers. The euphoria lasts a very brief time. But it is the finest hour of the presidency. There is no question about that. It's straight downhill from there.

From that point it was tough all the way. It is not hard work in the usual sense. The staff system has been built up to a point at which the President deals only with the important things, the key people. He said to me once, "I hope Mike Feldman is honest because he is handling our entire domestic policy.'' The public doesn't understand how the President is protected from many pressures that the rest of us feel. Kennedy once said to me, ''I don't think there is any amount of money that could buy the level of living that they give you in the White House. It is not just the food and the house. It is just that there are so many people who are so darn bright trying to do all these things for you.'' I think we do create a court atmosphere which is probably a mistake. It would be a wonderful thing if our President could be preserved in a simpler environment, if he could be kept closer to the simple realities of life.

I remember the night the inauguration took place. He said, ''Hey, you wouldn't believe it but there were four maids running in and out of the bathroom. I had to kick them out.'' I think there is too much of this. I think it is spoiling. It is one of the things that worries me, not in terms of an imperial presidency, but simply because I don't think people function as well when they are being spoiled.

I remember we went over for dinner on the second night after he had been there and he said, ''You know what I did last night? I slept in Lincoln's bed.'' I asked, ''Did anything strange happen or did you have any unusual dreams?'' He said, ''No, I just jumped in and hung on!''

It is a rarefied atmosphere. You never get over the fact that you are in the White House in the sense that you are looking out on Pennsylvania Avenue on one side and it is a fish bowl. You don't feel any sense of privacy. Jackie put in a lot of rhododendrons around the edge trying to get a little area where the kids could play. Some people got after her on that. There is so much going on that the President's mind is being constantly diverted. Questions like: What kind of party are you going to give for the Shah of Iran? The atmosphere is not conducive to the clearest thinking.

I feel so strongly about a single six-year term for the President. I don't think most of us realize how much the desire to be reelected is on the mind of the President. There was no conversation that I had with Jack Kennedy, and it was on a purely personal basis, that did not involve how this or that would effect the election in 1964.

About three weeks before he died, Kennedy and I took a walk in Arlington Cemetery. We began talking about where we wanted to be buried. He said, ''I suppose I'll have to go back to Boston because that's where my library is going to be.'' And then his face darkened and he said, ''But of course I'm not going to have a library if I only have one term. Nobody will give a damn.''

An influential aide, of course, understands that a first term President is usually preoccupied by his political interests. The result is that the President depends more and more on the White House aides who are politically loyal to him. They are people who went through the campaign with him. His election has made these people and he commands their loyalty. The result is that these White House aides get relied on more than they should be. They usually don't have much expertise in government and they are spread pretty thin. Frankly, I worried a lot about the power of the Irish mafia, the group that came in with him. A President is excessively reliant on his aides because of his tremendous desire to be reelected.

I don't think the public realizes the degree to which that second term is meaningful to a President. I've had to laugh about all the speculation about whether Ronald Reagan would run again because if you have the job, you realize that your one chance of being memorable is to get the second term. In other words you've got to become one of the twelve Presidents—and there have only been twelve—who have gotten elected twice. We've made this the test of our system. If you talk to Presidents who have had only one term—if you could go down and talk to Lyndon Johnson as I did in Texas or Jimmy Carter—they have a sense of defeat.

This is one of the reasons that I feel so strongly about the six-year term. As Bob McNamara said to me the night that Jack Kennedy was killed, "The tragedy is even a greater one for the nation than most people realize because all the good things that the Kennedy administration was going to do were put off until the second term." I think if you talk to the Reagan people you would be amazed at the number of things that they have put off until the second term. They put off those things that are hard to do politically in the first term.

This is the way it works under the system that we have and I felt this very much with Kennedy on Vietnam, for instance. He used to say to me very frankly, "We don't have a prayer of staying in Vietnam. We don't have a prayer of prevailing there. Those people hate us." He added, "They are going to throw our tails out of there at almost any point. But I can't give up a piece of territory like that to the Communists and then get the American people to reelect me." That was why the first fifteen thousand men went to Vietnam. I've always thought that this was the reason why five hundred thousand men ended up there under Lyndon Johnson. He didn't want to cave in before his reelection and of course it kept getting harder and harder to stay.

I remember one time he got into a fuss with Adlai Stevenson. Stuart Alsop and I wrote this article for the *Saturday Evening Post* about Adlai wanting to give up our missile bases in Turkey and Italy in exchange for getting the missiles out of Cuba. There was a great deal of shock in the administration that this should be the entering proposal. They felt you don't negotiate with the Russians by giving them something. And there was a flap when this article appeared in the *Saturday Evening Post*. A lot of people thought that Kennedy had been trying to do in Adlai and there was a great fuss about it. I remember

Kennedy calling me in New York. I was hiding out in New York and Kennedy called me and said, "Lyndon Johnson doesn't have a cult, I don't have a cult, how does Adlai get a cult?"

I never had the feeling that he had a great sense of his countrymen's esteem while he was in the job and I think that it was day-to-day, constant, issue by issue. I think he was growing in office. He would have been a very good second term President when he had that election behind him. He would have done a lot to make people think about what the country means because he was intensely patriotic.

QUESTION: You mentioned earlier that Senator Kennedy was quite astute in his choice of campaign managers in various states. I'm very puzzled why he chose two people, one of them being Dean Rusk for secretary of state. Was he afraid? Did he not want a too powerful secretary of state? And why did he choose Bobby Kennedy for attorney general?

MR. BARTLETT: Well, the answer to the second question was Papa. I was in the middle of that one and I didn't think Bobby should be the attorney general. I didn't think he had the experience. I told Bobby, "You could go as high as director of CIA or something in the Pentagon but not the attorney general. It's going to be tough with this racial segregation stuff." Bobby asked me to call his father and tell him that. I refused. And then I got a call from Jack a little bit later and he said, "Charley, lay off this thing. It's all settled. Don't get into it anymore." I think that the father said, "You've got to do this. We all worked for you. Now you take a few rocks for us." This was one of the great ploys of the father. Bobby was the price that Jack had to pay for the efforts that the family had put into his election.

I remember he told a funny story at a dinner at the Alfalfa Club about two weeks after he was inaugurated. In the course of his speech he said, "I don't know why all of you are being so critical of me for wanting to give my little brother some legal experience before he goes out to practice." Everybody laughed and at the end of the meal Bobby came up and his face was blue and his fists were clinched and he said, "Jack, you shouldn't have said that." Jack said, "Bobby, you don't understand. In politics you've got to make fun of your vulnerable points in order to make people laugh with you. If you poke fun at yourself then you get the people on your side." Bobby said, "Yeah, but you weren't poking fun at yourself, you were poking fun at me."

As for Rusk, I think the search for secretary of state was a very complicated thing and his inclination was towards Senator William Fulbright. There is no question about that. But Fulbright had the problem of Little Rock, that racial problem in Arkansas, and the fact that he had cast a couple of segregationist votes. Despite even that, I think Kennedy would have gone with it. There was terrific opposition, though. I remember at the christening at the chapel at Georgetown Hospital I was talking in favor of Fulbright and I thought Bobby was going to hit me. He was vehement.

Everybody was getting into the act and I think it was a very hard decision. Rusk presented himself as a substantial man who was noncontroversial. He was respected. He came from a good background, knew the State Department. My impression is that they were not chemically well matched, that they never acquired an easy rapport. Kennedy respected Rusk as a man but he was disappointed that he didn't speak up more strongly against the Bay of Pigs invasion.

QUESTION: Had he thought of Robert Lovett?

MR. BARTLETT: Mr. Lovett was pretty old at that point. He had the greatest respect for Bob Lovett. He had him down a lot and talked to him but I think that Bob Lovett and John McCloy at that point were a bit too old.

QUESTION: You commented quite freely on your belief in a six-year term for President. What is your thinking about the two party system versus the necessity for a coalition?

MR. BARTLETT: Clinging to the two party system would be my thinking. What coalition are you talking about?

QUESTION: Well, I mean have more parties in which we would have to negotiate. You believe in the two party system?

MR. BARTLETT: Absolutely. I think that is the strength of our system. One party in, one party out, changing them as often as you can.

QUESTION: I read somewhere that Jack Kennedy was reckless and craved excitement, which could have been the reason why he had his PT boat accident and why he couldn't wait to get into the Bay of Pigs. Would you consider that a facet of his personality?

MR. BARTLETT: I'd say that was true of almost every Irish friend I have.

NARRATOR: This is the proper season, whether we are Irish or not, to wish you all a happy holiday season and to thank Charles Bartlett who certainly has enlivened our sense of history on a great President and his own relationship to him. Thank you very much.

A BIOGRAPHER'S PERSPECTIVE

Arthur Schlesinger, Jr.

NARRATOR: I would like to welcome you to a Forum in the series on the John F. Kennedy presidency, appropriately this morning to be conducted by Professor Arthur Schlesinger, Jr. Professor Schlesinger was born in Columbus, Ohio. He graduated summa cum laude from Harvard where he was a member of the Society for Fellows. Later he was a Henry Fellow at Cambridge University. After serving in the OSS in World War II, he returned to become a permanent member of the Harvard history faculty from 1946 to 1961. He served as special assistant to President John F. Kennedy from 1961 to 1964. He became Schweitzer Professor of Humanities at the City University of New York in 1966 and continues in that position to the present time.

I brought along my notes because he makes life difficult for anyone who is to introduce him by the number of major prizes he has received for his scholarly work. He has received the Pulitzer Prize for history, the Frances Parkman Prize, the Bancroft Prize, the Pulitzer Prize for biography, the National Book Award, and the National Institute of Arts and Letters Gold Medal. His books are too numerous to mention as are his honorary degrees but one might simply call attention to *The Age of Jackson, The Vital Center, Crisis of the Old Order, The Coming of the New Deal, The Politics of Hope, The Thousand Days, The Imperial Presidency,* and many other significant works.

He has sought and established relationships of intellectual trust and confidence with such leading American figures as Reinhold Niebuhr, Hans Morgenthau and George F. Kennan. While they agreed on many points they disagreed on others. None of the differences kept these friendships from flowering, growing and reaching fulfillment in the last years of these remarkable men.

We are especially pleased that Dumas Malone is with us this morning. Nothing goes further to assure an intellectual feast in our discussion of John F. Kennedy than to have Professors Schlesinger and Malone together in one room. It's an honor to have you both with us.

MR. SCHLESINGER: Thank you, Ken. I must say how very pleased I am to see my old friend, and my father's dear friend, Dumas Malone, here with us in his marvelous vitality. As the years rush by, it has occurred to me that I have only a finite number of book-writing years left, but when I get discouraged I think of Dumas and feel better.

I might begin by saying a few words about President Kennedy's operating style, discuss its advantages and disadvantages and then consider the uses to which it was put. There are several salient characteristics from the viewpoint of one working with Kennedy. The first was intelligence. He was a man of very high and very quick intelligence; it was an intelligence accompanied by inexhaustible curiosity. He was an unusually skilled questioner. Isaiah Berlin after meeting him was reminded of what someone said of Lenin, "He exhausts you by listening." He could drain people with great skill and speed, and sometimes he forced them to think anew about problems with which they had lived for a long time and presumably knew more about than anyone else.

He joined with this an exceedingly retentive memory. This was sometimes disconcerting. You might say something to him, and he would remind you that you had taken a different view on the same subject three months earlier; or he would remember things he had asked you to do and for one reason or another had not been done. He had curiosity, memory, the instinct for the critical question, and a talent for concentration. When reading a document, for example, he would seem almost physically to absorb the document as he looked at it. He had these intellectual qualities under perfect control, yet everything he did was done with a slightly ironic tone. That helped distance him from problems and also facilitated the conduct of business.

In the technical realm of administration, Kennedy had a preference for flexibility. In this respect he was more in the tradition of FDR than he was of his immediate predecessor, President Eisenhower. Eisenhower, coming out of a military background, was used to rather elaborate staff work; and his White House reflected that concern. He liked committees and channels. Kennedy didn't like working that way. His experience had not been one of large organizations. It had been rather the experience of running the office of a legislator, which is much more ad hoc. However, by temperament the Kennedys were not planners; they were improvisers. And Kennedy, like Roosevelt, was determined not to become the prisoner of any single information system. He liked to pit information he got through official channels against information he got from newspaper friends or from foreign visitors or from his own extensive reading; he read the British weeklies for example. In that way he protected himself against exclusive dependence on the information the bureaucracy below saw fit to send up to him.

He also liked to have official information directly from the people on the desk. Instead of accepting information from the State Department that came up from the desk to the assistant secretary, to the under secretary, and then was transmitted in suitably diluted form to the White House, he would often call the person at the working level. This, too, was part of his reaching out for information and checking various versions of the same problem. Particularly after the Bay of Pigs, he developed an extreme skepticism about what the Joint Chiefs of Staff or the CIA might say about any situation. He felt that one of his great mistakes in the Bay of Pigs was not checking, for example, the CIA theory of the state of public opinion in Cuba. In order to avoid that in the future, he was determined to get the information at the source as much as possible.

Another of his qualities, in addition to intelligence and flexibility, was a tendency toward activism. You'd tell him about something, and he would listen carefully and then say, "O.K., but what do you want me to do about it?" The relationship between information and remedy was in his mind close and urgent. This was partly produced by his temperamental optimism. He really believed that with goodwill and reason and steadiness of purpose you could surmount, if not solve, a lot of the problems that were assailing us. He communicated that optimism to the people around him. I think he communicated it to the nation and to the world, so that there was an insistent search for a remedy and an insistent pressure to do something about problems.

Every President works out the White House system that serves him best. Kennedy's personal characteristics led him to prefer a small staff. The senior people had direct access to him. People talk these days about White House chiefs of staff as if this were a routine necessity. The question of having a chief of staff never arose in the Kennedy White House because the White House staff was too small to require a chief. Ted Sorenson had seniority in domestic affairs and McGeorge Bundy in foreign affairs but other top assistants had access to the President and did not report to anyone except him.

The modern White House staff was created by the Government Reorganization Act of 1939. When FDR signed that act, he laid down standards for the appointment of special assistants. He said he didn't want the special assistants to interpose themselves between the President and the heads of departments and agencies, that he did not want more special assistants than he could deal with personally, and that he did not want his special assistants to set up staffs of their own. He wanted a collection of generalists who would serve as his personal eyes and ears.

Of course the FDR ideal has long since disappeared. Today special assistants interpose themselves all the time between the President and heads of departments and agencies—and often create a cleavage between them. Unless you are secretary of state or defense or the President's brother, Cabinet members sometimes find it hard to get to see the President. The President now has far more senior staff in the White House than he can deal with personally. Some people on the White House staff count themselves lucky if they see the President once a month. And of course the tendency of the White House assistants to build up staffs of their own has become uncontrollable. The quantum leap in the size of the White House staff came with Nixon. But Nixon's successors, Carter and Reagan, in spite of all the time both spent wailing about the size of government bureaucracy, did nothing to cut down the size of the White House staff.

The Kennedy senior staff and the Johnson staff were about a third the size of the Nixon staff and the post-Nixon staffs. Arthur Link argues that there is is a relationship between the size of the presidential staff and the President's personal sense of security. An insecure President like Nixon obviously wanted a praetorian guard to shield him from people he didn't like. On the other hand, Ford and Reagan both seem reasonably secure men, and they also liked large White House staffs. So I don't know to what extent the relationships between insecurity and large White House staffs can be maintained.

At any rate, Kennedy had the kind of staff he wanted. Through the erosion of time most of his generalists acquired one or another specialty. There was always the danger, if you happened to be in the President's office when something was on his mind or on his desk, he'd lift the paper up and say, "Would you do something about it?" You'd look at it and know this was something that someone on Bundy's or Sorenson's staff had been handling. So the assistants themselves often passed on assignments they were given by the President in order to maintain administrative order in the White House.

Unlike Roosevelt, Kennedy did not pit people against each other by deliberately asking them to do the same thing. In that regard he was a kinder man than Roosevelt. He would often ask a couple of people to look into the same thing. But it was a relatively harmonious White House staff; we were all on moderately good terms with each other, so we'd inform each other when we were doing something which bore on something we knew had already been assigned to someone else.

As this whole recital has suggested, he was a very accessible President. If there was something of importance to communicate, it was relatively easy to get to him. One could always reach him in short order on the telephone. Very often at the end of the day he would leave the door open between his office and Mrs. Lincoln's office, and the assistants could stick their head in; he'd generally be reading documents but then he'd beckon you in. Sometimes he was in a talkative mood and liked to chat about the experiences of the day. As I read about subsequent Presidents and the difficulty their own staff had in getting to see them and having to make appointments weeks in advance and so on, I do think that in this respect Kennedy, and certainly FDR before him at least until we got into the war, represent a quite different and, in my mind, a far more valuable model for the presidency.

One advantage of the Kennedy approach was an openness to ideas from whatever source. He was always interested in finding out what were problems and in talking to people who might have new ideas. This flexibility in strategy and response was exactly, it seemed to me, what you require for a rapidly changing world.

There were disadvantages too. Probably, Kennedy was too impatient with systems. I think he was quite right to dismantle the Eisenhower national security apparatus; that had become a means by this time not of exploring problems but of papering them over. But I think he did not use the Cabinet as well as he might have done. Of course, all Presidents become impatient with Cabinet meetings, and all Cabinet secretaries feel that Presidents don't appreciate the Cabinet as a body. If you read the diaries of Treasury Secretary Henry Morgenthau during the Roosevelt administration, you find constant complaints about the uselessness of Cabinet meetings. Yet in retrospect I think Roosevelt used Cabinet meetings as a wise President would use them. He met with the Cabinet quite often—twice a week. Cabinet members were often disappointed because they did not get a full discussion of their particular interests. In fact, after a while they stopped bringing up their particular interests because they were afraid they would expose themselves to attack by other Cabinet members. But Roosevelt wanted a kind of national sounding board. The members of the Cabinet were relatively experienced men—these were the days before we appointed faceless clerks to the government—and represented broad constituencies. FDR often threw them general topics. The second Cabinet meeting, for example, discussed our relations with Japan.

I wish Kennedy had used his Cabinet this way. He had some very able men in his Cabinet. But he would say, "The secretary of the interior, the secretary of agriculture, what do they know about Laos? What can they contribute to that?'' In point of fact, his secretary of agriculture (Orville Freeman) and secretary of the interior (Steward Udall) were both experienced men whose judgment on Laos and later on Vietnam was a lot wiser than the judgment of his secretary of state. Foreign policy particularly is not so arcane a subject that people with experience and intelligence and some knowledge of the world can't have as good judgment as people who spend their lives on it. I think Kennedy should have taken his Cabinet more seriously as a general sounding board. This would not have satisfied members of the Cabinet, but it might have given him a better sense of some of the national opinions on some of the problems.

Kennedy's habit of skipping channels and going down to the people at the desks had both advantages and disadvantages. It was rather disruptive of the sense of security of the upper bureaucracy, of the levels that were skipped. I don't think the secretary of state liked it much when Kennedy talked directly to his subordinates. On the other hand, it was enormously stimulating for the people at the desk. It also made Kennedy's presence felt through the executive branch in a much more direct way. This is a perennial problem in the relationship between the presidential government and what I called in *The Thousand Days* the ''permanent government.'' Kennedy's direct contact with lower-level bureaucrats was one way of making a permanent government more responsive to presidential purpose.

Did Kennedy get involved in too many things? FDR veterans felt that one of Roosevelt's strengths was a certain detachment from detail, a willingness to give his people their head, and then, if they went out on a limb, not to hesitate to saw the limb off. He was prepared to let problems take shape to a certain degree before he got too closely involved himself. Averell Harriman used to comment in the Kennedy days on how the State Department had changed since Roosevelt's days. He didn't blame this development on Kennedy; he blamed it on the general evolution of the bureaucracy. Roosevelt's instructions were general and flexible. Roosevelt gave his emissaries much more responsibility—responsibility which he knew was accompanied by accountability if things went wrong. By the 1950s and 1960s—and I'm sure it's worse today—people abroad were bound by the most minute instructions from the State Department. Since the people in Washington knew less about the situation than the people who receive the instructions, this is not necessarily the most profitable way to run things.

I remember lunching one day with Tom Corcoran and Ben Cohen and they made the same kind of comment from another angle. They felt that Kennedy was keeping too tight a grip on his administration, that he got involved in things too early. Kennedy, on the other hand, felt that if he didn't get involved early, then the bureaucracy would determine the choices. Cohen and Corcoran thought that Roosevelt's competitive theory of administration preserved the President's capacity to make the final choices but did not get him involved in details and therefore committed to particular approaches or remedies at too early a point. Ben Cohen used to say that Kennedy in this respect was more like Wilson, that Wilson's fault was trying to run too many things himself.

Now the besetting sin of the New Frontier as I look back was the addiction of activism. I think in retrospect that there is much more to be said for the policy of leaving things alone. The notion that every problem demands an instant remedy can get you into a lot of trouble. It is especially dangerous in foreign policy. I now think that the commitment on the part of professional diplomats to restraint, slowness, and caution probably had more wisdom than we understood at the time. A certain amount of activism was necessary to awaken the State Department from the stagnation of the Dulles years, but I think that the tendency to move in, for example, to the internal affairs of countries, to press our ideas of reform, created problems—unless handled with great tact, as indeed ambassadors like Galbraith in India, Reischauer in Japan, and Murat Williams in El Salvador did. In retrospect I place a higher value on the State Department. I must confess, though, that State could be extremely exasperating in its resistance to anything new. For example, long after it was evident to every child that the split between China and the Soviet Union was deep and probably irreparable, the secretary of state and high officials continued talking about the Sino-Soviet bloc. Probably the balance between a State Department that hated to do anything differently from the way it had been doing it and Kennedy activists who wanted to change the world overnight came out not too badly.

These were, as I saw it, salient features of Kennedy's operating style. He was operating against a historical perspective, and it was a perspective of which he was well aware. The perspective was the one set forth by my father in an article in the *Yale Review* in 1939 about the cyclical fluctuations of American politics. Kennedy had read it, and we talked about it, and he gave some speeches when he was running for the presidency saying that the time had come for a new epoch of forward motion: "Let's get America moving again."

If you look at the political history of the twentieth century the first two decades were decades of action, passion, idealism, reform; two demanding Presidents trying first to get the American people to democratize their political and economic institutions at home, and then to make the world outside safe for democracy. After two decades of this, the nation was worn out and entered into a period of drift and "privatization," as sociologists say, hedonism and cynicism. That went on for a decade, and then you had the thirties and forties: FDR and the New Deal, the Second World War, Harry Truman and the Fair Deal. Again two decades of action and passion left an exhausted nation. Thus the Eisenhower lull in the fifties—and Kennedy felt that this was coming to an end and the country was ready to get moving again.

This kind of thirty-year cycle ran from Theodore Roosevelt in 1901 to Franklin Roosevelt in 1933 and was ready to resume again in 1961. Kennedy believed that there was a reserve of idealism and a generous energy in the American people which had been repressed during the Eisenhower years and which was ready for release. He thought that Presidents like FDR and Wilson with their belief in the latent idealism of the American people were right and that the time had come to give this pent-up idealism expression again. Kennedy used to describe himself as an idealist without illusions. He was a tough experienced politician, as FDR had been, but like FDR he also had faith in the ultimate generosity of the American people and their desire to do things for less fortunate people at home and abroad.

Getting America moving again meant in part an intellectual breakaway from a stagnation and complacency, as it seemed to us, of the Eisenhower years. In domestic policy in particular it meant an effort to reduce the disparities of power and opportunity existing in the country. People complain a lot about primaries and I think we probably carried the primary system too far in the years since. But I felt, in observing Adlai Stevenson in 1956 and Kennedy in 1960, that there are great educational values in the primary system. Primaries not only show the candidate to the country, they show the country to the candidate. Both Stevenson in 1956 and Kennedy in 1960 had to go into parts of the country they hadn't known particularly before. They had to acquaint themselves rather intensively with local problems. It was a valuable experience for both of them.

Kennedy was struck by what he saw in West Virginia. This gave the problem of poverty a great reality for him. Poverty remained a constant concern throughout his presidency. He got through the Area Redevelopment Act and the Appalachia Program. When the tax reduction bill was sent to Congress in 1963, he insisted that this be accompanied by a program to help those who would not benefit directly from tax reduction. Twenty or thirty percent of the American people were, after all, too poor to pay income tax. He then initiated the studies that eventually came to fulfillment in Johnson's war against poverty. Walter Heller remembers Kennedy saying to him, "All right, when you get your tax reduction program, I'll get my expenditures program." The result was the poverty program.

Kennedy did have a chronic problem when it came to legislation. Like every progressive President since 1938, he lacked a working majority in the House of Representatives. Roosevelt lost that working majority in the 1938 mid-term elections. Truman never enjoyed it and Kennedy never enjoyed it. Kennedy recognized that the best he could do in certain areas, like Medicare and federal aid to education and to the cities, was to start a process of education. Introducing bills and holding hearings were a means of planting seeds that, with care and nurture, might yield a harvest in his second term. He expected in his second term to have a working majority in the House, and then these things would be enacted. He used to console himself with the thought that Theodore Roosevelt got more legislation passed in his second term than in his first.

In fact, this is exactly what happened. In 1964 the Republicans did the philanthropic act of running Barry Goldwater, thereby presenting the Democrats with thirty-nine extra seats in the House of Representatives. Lyndon Johnson was the first Democratic President since FDR before 1938 to have a working majority in the House. That enabled Johnson to pass the notable legislation enacted in the great sessions of 1965 and 1966. Then, in the 1966 mid-term elections, Johnson lost most of that majority and the Great Society petered out.

Johnson was a man of formidable skills in dealing with Congress. Still, had Johnson been elected President in 1960 and Kennedy been vice-president, and had Johnson presented the same program that Kennedy did to Congress in 1961, I doubt that he would have gotten further than Kennedy did, perhaps not so far because he wasn't as effective as Kennedy in appealing to national opinion. Had Johnson died in 1963 and Kennedy succeeded to the presidency, he would have beaten Goldwater in 1964 and gotten those thirty-nine lovely extra votes in the House of Representatives. Then he would have passed all that legislation and the pundits would have contrasted the finesse with which Kennedy handled Congress as emphasis on personal sorcery when what is really decisive is parliamentary arithmetic. It was the forty extra seats, mostly northern Democratic liberal seats, that made the real difference in the legislative records.

Let me say a particular word about civil rights. Kennedy, like most white politicians, underestimated the moral passion behind the civil rights movement. If anybody asked him in 1960 about racial justice, he would have said, "Of course we must move toward a desegregated and multi-racial society. And will—but it is an explosive question and therefore we have to do this prudently." But he was soon educated by events; and his brother, as attorney general with direct responsibility, was educated even faster. But for a long time civil rights legislation was simply not feasible. In 1962 Kennedy had trouble in getting a new Department of Housing and Urban Development because legislators were afraid he was going to appoint Robert C. Weaver, a black economist, and they didn't want a black Cabinet member. That suggests the primitive state we were still in in the early sixties.

What changed the balance of opinion were the outrages of 1962 and 1963, beginning with the University of Mississippi and then particularly Bull Connor and his police dogs in Birmingham, Alabama. I was present when Kennedy met with Martin Luther King and other black leaders. Someone mentioned Bull Connor, and Kennedy said, "We shouldn't be too tough on Bull Conner." This caused a stunned reaction. Kennedy continued, "After all, Bull Connor has done more for civil rights than any of us." This was true because the photographs of Bull Connor's police dogs lunging at the marchers in Birmingham did as much as anything to transform the national mood and make legislation not just necessary, which it had long been, but possible.

The Kennedys finally threw themselves, belatedly in a moral sense, realistically in the sense of getting congressional legislation, into the civil rights fight. It was one of the President's less popular acts. In January 1963 his approval rating was seventy-six to thirteen percent, which is an astonishing figure when you think of Presidents in recent times. By November, mainly as a result of the civil rights fight, it was down to fifty-nine approval, twenty-eight percent disapproval. This is still good enough by contemporary standards but suggests the political cost of the civil rights battle.

Kennedy was less dependent on congressional action. In economic management, he did very well. He had the very able assistance of Douglas Dillon, secretary of the treasury, and Walter Heller as chairman of the Council of Economic Advisers. Dillon and Heller were men of very different experience and originally of considerably divergent views. They grew to like and respect each other and worked with Kennedy to produce virtually a balanced and remarkably successful economic policy. The growth rate in the Kennedy years was 5.6 percent; unemployment was reduced to five percent; and the inflation rate was 1.3 percent.

Though inflation was not the issue it became in later years, Kennedy was keenly aware of the vital relationship between inflation and productivity. He knew that wages, prices, and profits had to have a stable relationship with productivity if prices were to remain stable. An increase in wages beyond the rate of increase in productivity would lead to an increase in prices. So Kennedy sought to relate wage, prices, and profits to productivity through the wage-price guideposts of 1962—our first experiment with incomes policy and a successful one. Kennedy and Arthur Goldberg, the secretary of labor, persuaded the steel union to accept a noninflationary wage settlement in 1962, after which U.S. Steel raised prices in violation of the guideposts. This led to Kennedy's explosive reaction: "My father always told me all businessmen were sons of bitches, but I didn't realize it until now," he was said to have said. He claimed he had said, "My father always told me all steel men were sons of bitches."

In foreign policy, the administration overreacted to a very tough speech that Khrushchev gave two weeks before Kennedy's inaugural. The speech had two main themes: one was the impossibility of nuclear war between the superpowers; the other was the inevitable victory of Communism through wars of national-liberation in the Third World. Looking back, one can infer that Khrushchev was probably attempting a rather complicated thing. He was trying to persuade Washington that the Russians believed in nuclear coexistence and he was trying to persuade Peking that the Russians believed in world revolution. Inevitably each capital read the message intended for the other. The Chinese thought the speech meant that Khrushchev was selling out the revolution. The Americans read it as meaning that he was going to promote revolution, especially in the Third World. Kennedy had the speech xeroxed and circulated. Everyone read it. Kennedy's own inaugural, with its extravagant language about helping any friends, supporting any foe, and so on, was a response to this speech of Khrushchev's. Actually the distinctive note in the Kennedy inaugural, and the one that the press commented on most at the time, pointed in another direction. That's when Kennedy said, "Let us never negotiate out of fear, but let us never fear to negotiate." This was much closer to the heart of Kennedy's concern in foreign policy.

The overreaction to the Khrushchev speech led to some mistakes. The Kennedy people, when they came in, honestly believed in the missile gap. It wasn't until we put up the Samos satellite and later when the British spy Penkovsky began to report that it became evident that the missile gap was fiction. The "missile gap" idea originally came out of the Gaither Committee during the Eisenhower administration. Many liberal scientists had been on the Gaither Committee staff, and they believed in the missile gap. This experience has led me not to take seriously any military gap ever promulgated by the Pentagon thereafter. The military are always seeing gaps because it's the best way to increase their own budgets.

The Air Force bitterly fought the new intelligence findings about the missile gap because it meant a reduction in their budget. By this time, we had already gone ahead on a missile program which McNamara later said was inordinate. That was one mistake.

A second major mistake was the overreaction to the problem of national-liberation wars. This led Kennedy for awhile into the fantasy of counterinsurgency. As conceived in Washington counterinsurgency was, in a phrase of Robert Kennedy's, "social reform under pressure." The Green Berets were supposed to win the hearts and minds of the people and encourage them to democratize, promote land reform and so on. It never worked out that way. The kind of people who got involved in counterinsurgency were men of violence. "If you get people by the balls," the Green Berets used to say, "you don't have to worry about their hearts and minds."

Counterinsurgency was a terrible business. Americans were not adapted to fighting that kind of war. Nor should we have trained other people in counterinsurgency, because, while we never actually taught torture, people whom we taught other things used torture. It was a horrible thing to encourage in any way, however indirectly. More than that, counterinsurgency nourished the notion that we had a right and a duty to intervene in the inner lives of other countries. This is obviously not a healthy way for any nation to see itself.

Kennedy, contrary to the revisionists, was not *macho* by temperament. He'd seen war. He had fought in a war. He didn't have to prove his manhood by sending a new generation of men out to kill and to be killed. He was by temperament a conciliator, not a confrontationist. He always believed that you could work things out whether it was with Governor Ross Barnett or with Khrushchev. He also had a clear understanding of the limits of American power. His essential view of things was expressed in a speech he gave at the University of Washington a few months after the inauguration in November, 1961. He said then: "We must face the fact that the United States is neither omnipotent nor omniscient, that we are only six percent of the world's population, that we cannot impose our will upon the other ninty-four percent of mankind, that we cannot right every wrong or reverse each adversity, and that therefore there cannot be an American solution to every world problem."

He added to the sense of limits of American power an ability to refuse escalation. Before the Bay of Pigs, a project that he inherited and let go forward with some misgivings, he stipulated that American troops would not be involved. As the exile invasion was failing, he was under great pressure to send in the Marines. He refused to do that.

In his last meeting with Kennedy, the day before the inauguration, Eisenhower had told Kennedy that the exile invasion of Cuba should be accelerated and supported. He also said we must be prepared to fight in Laos, unilaterally if necessary. Kennedy thought Laos was not a part of the world that was worth a war between the superpowers. He enlisted Harold Macmillan to exploit Macmillan's wartime relationship with Eisenhower and write Eisenhower to urge the futility of American intervention in Laos.

Similarly in the Berlin crisis in 1961, when Dean Acheson and others wanted to run an armored brigade into Berlin, Kennedy opposed that. When Maxwell Taylor and Walt Rostow came back from Vietnam in 1961 asking for combat troops to be sent to Vietnam, he refused to do that. During the missile crisis he refused, under great pressure from the Joint Chiefs and Dean Acheson and others, to take out the missiles by a sneak surprise attack.

It is odd how our values have changed. Robert Kennedy turned the group against a sneak attack by saying that a sneak attack by a great power like the United States against a small island was antithetical to one hundred seventy-five years of American tradition. He made a very moving speech to this effect. Two weeks ago we made a sneak attack, without authorization by Congress, without advance warning to the people, against an island of 110,000, without an army, without a navy, without an air force, and we saw it as a glorious victory. No one remembers the point that Robert Kennedy made so forcefully during the missile crisis. Grenada was Pearl Harbor in reverse. We regard Pearl Harbor as a day of infamy—except when we perpetrate Pearl Harbors ourselves.

At any rate, Kennedy did show repeatedly this capacity to refuse escalation. I think he would have done the same in Vietnam. One of the revelations of the Pentagon Papers was a disengagement plan Kennedy asked the Defense Department to prepare in 1962. It was finally approved in the spring of 1963 and called for the complete withdrawal of American advisers in 1965. Under that plan the first 1,000 advisers were recalled by Kennedy in October 1963. There were then 16,000 advisers. Pierre Salinger tells in his book how Kennedy said, when McNamara was going out to make the announcement, "And tell them that means all the helicopter pilots, too." Helicopter pilots were the advisers who were most directly involved in combat.

Kennedy did increase the number of advisers to 16,000, of whom seventy-five were killed in combat during the Kennedy years. But he also had the withdrawal plan. I find it hard to think he would ever have sent in combat units because he had been in Vietnam as a young congressman when the French were there; and he came away from that experience deeply convinced that sending a white army into Asia would only rally all the forces of nationalism against the intruder.

Mike Mansfield has said that Kennedy told him his intention of getting out after the 1964 election. That shocks some people who say, "Why should the election make the difference?" But in 1952, only a decade before—one of the things used to defeat Stevenson was the claim that Democrats had "lost China." This was much in our minds. Kennedy didn't want to fight an election on the ground that we had "lost" Indochina. An election fought and lost on that ground would have inevitably resulted in an expansion of the American involvement in Indochina. He was prepared to give the Saigon government a run for its money through the election, and then it was his intention to pull out in 1965.

He did not believe in a world organized on the model of America. He believed in a "world of diversity," in a world composed of nations diverse in their politics, their economic systems, and so on, but living together within an international framework. When he gave the American University speech in 1963, he said, in a deliberate revision of the famous Wilson line, that our goal was to make the world "safe for diversity." This was his concern.

His other great concern in foreign policy was nuclear war. In the 1961 General Assembly at the United Nations, he said, "Mankind must put an end to war, or war will put an end to mankind." This was a constant preoccupation. I rarely saw him more depressed than the day when we received news in the autumn of 1961 that the Soviet Union had resumed nuclear testing. He was depressed not only because they had resumed but because he knew the pressure from our military would be so great we would have to resume testing, too, which we did after a delay the next spring. He felt the deepest concern about the irrationality of a world with nuclear weapons lying around and no adequate form of control. So after the Cuban missile crisis he forbade gloating and recrimination and began moving as expeditiously as he could toward some form of nuclear arms control.

There were points at which he developed a kind of sympathy with Khrushchev. He told Norman Cousins, the editor of the *Saturday Review* in the spring of 1963, "Khrushchev and I occupy approximately the same political positions inside our governments. He would like to prevent a nuclear war but is under severe pressure from his hard-line critics who interpret every move in that direction as appeasement. I've got similar problems. The hardliners in the Soviet Union and the United States feed on each other." That was the case then, and it is the case now.

The American University speech was a deliberate effort to get Americans as well as Russians to rethink the cold war; to reconsider this cycle of suspicion and counter-suspicion, the vicious cycle in which weapons beget counter-weapons; and to try to figure out where it's all leading and how to stop it. Had Kennedy lived, Khrushchev might have survived. Between them they might have made great progress on the control of nuclear weapons. Khrushchev must have felt the same thing. He wrote in his memoirs, "I had no cause for regret once Kennedy became President. It quickly became clear that he understood better than Eisenhower that an improvement in relations was the only rational course."

Why is Kennedy out of fashion these days? Well, there is the historiographical rhythm. All Presidents' reputations decline in the period fifteen to twenty-five years after their death. When I was in college in the 1930s, I was taught that Theodore Roosevelt, who died in 1919, was a bullying, adolescent jingo and that Woodrow Wilson, who died in 1924, was a Presbyterian fanatic. Both those views have been revised in the years since. Today Kennedy's ideals are out of sync with the historical cycle. It seems somewhat exotic and old-fashioned to call on Americans to think about the poor and the dispossessed, or to think about the control of nuclear weapons, or to ask not what your country can do for you but what you can do for your country. But if the cyclical rhythm holds, the thirty-year cycle should renew itself by 1988 or 1992; and we should have a period equivalent to the ones ushered in by Theodore Roosevelt in 1901 and FDR in 1933 and Kennedy in 1961. At that time I think the ideals and concerns of Kennedy will seem less exotic and less out of fashion and more to the point. At that time we will be able to get a fairer picture of his accomplishments as President.

NARRATOR: Who'd like to ask the first question? Dumas, would you like to open our discussion?

MR. DUMAS MALONE: Well, I don't know whether any of the rest of you have seen the latest issue of *The New Republic*. It contains a magnificent article by Arthur Schlesinger on Kennedy. I regard it as judicious and balanced and admire it very much. I did my homework promptly. I had my wife read it to me immediately.The cyclical theory, this thirty-year business, brings us to 1988 and 1992. I wish you could shorten that.

MR. SCHLESINGER: So do I.

MR. MALONE: I don't expect to be around to check up on that particular prophesy but I think nobody knows what the situation in the world is going to be then—whether force will have taken over to a greater extent than it has. But granting a relative degree of rationality, I think the vast body of American historians will strongly approve the position you've taken in this article.

MR. SCHLESINGER: Thank you very much. I hope I didn't repeat too much of the article today.

QUESTION: I'm told that President Kennedy dismissed the entire National Security Council staff immediately after he was inaugurated. If that is true, why did he do it, and secondly, what effect could that have had on American foreign policy?

MR. SCHLESINGER: I don't think Kennedy quite dismissed the entire National Security Council staff. He brought in his own special assistant for national security, McGeorge Bundy. But he retained the secretary to the National Security Council. Kennedy and Bundy wanted their own people in there, but the entire staff was not dismissed.

QUESTION: Did Kennedy's resistance to escalation of military activity over the advice of his military heads reflect in part his practice of going below them to minor agencies' heads? Or was it the result of his experience with fighting wars himself?

MR. SCHLESINGER: I think more of the first. He did hope to find in Maxwell Taylor a liberated military man who would give independent advice. He underestimated the extent to which Max Taylor, though an able and decent man, was in the end a military man, and he consistently rejected Max Taylor's recommendations that we send combat units to Vietnam. I think that he felt that it was the military's job to insist on military remedies, but because it's what you expect you don't pay all that much attention.

It was Kennedy's view that the military force must always be a weapon of last resort and not of first resort. The more advice he got from the Joint Chiefs of Staff the less respect he had for it and them. Roswell Gilpatric, the under secretary of defense, tells stories of Kennedy's real fury after a talk with someone like Curtis LeMay. LeMay had an extremely primitive view about policy, but people like LeMay and Arleigh Burke, who was chief of naval operations, were very popular on the Hill; their terms were running out so it seemed simpler to replace them in the normal course of events than to cause a great furor by dismissing them.

QUESTION: Arthur, would you say that Kennedy's program for Latin America, had it continued as he designed it, would have averted the troubles we are having now?

MR. SCHLESINGER: I think it would. If the Alliance for Progress had been pursued we would have averted a good many of the troubles we have now. The Alliance for Progress had three components: economic assistance; land and tax reform; and political democratization, that is, supporting regimes, parties, leaders, who believe in democratic processes. These were not ideas imposed by the United States on Latin America. They came out of Latin American proposals. Latin American economists played the crucial part in the original thinking that led to the Alliance for Progress.

The Alliance for Progress depended for its success, however, on the existence in Latin America of political parties and political leaders that believed on their own in the need for economic reform and for political democracy. It also required American representatives in Latin America who would support such leaders against their own oligarchies and their own military and give them the sense that they weren't endangering the American relationship by pursuing this course.

Where such parties and leaders existed, as in Venezuela, the Alliance for Progress was successful. If Murat Williams's policies had been continued in El Salvador, El Salvador would not be the tragedy it is today. But one of the first Kennedy policies to be reversed after his death was the Alliance. The new administration dropped the reform and democratization emphasis of the Alliance, transforming it into an aid program which was soon put into the service of American business. When Robert Kennedy went to Latin America in 1965, he had a briefing at the State Department. He listened to what they were doing and finally said, "Look, we stopped aid to Peru because they nationalized an American oil company; and we're giving more aid to a military dictatorship in Brazil. Is this what the Alliance for Progress has come down to?" The assistant secretary of state said, "That's about the size of it."

The Alliance for Progress under Johnson was very different from the one under Kennedy. I think that we are going to have to come back to something like the Alliance in Latin America today.

QUESTION: Mr. Schlesinger, I believe that Dean Rusk was President Kennedy's third choice for secretary of state. Do you know who was his first choice?

MR. SCHLESINGER: Yes. Kennedy's first choice was Bill Fulbright, but his brother Robert Kennedy thought Fulbright would be a great mistake—a view Robert Kennedy later repented. He was opposed because Fulbright had signed the Confederate Manifesto in 1956 on civil rights, and Robert Kennedy thought this would make him unacceptable to the non-white world. In retrospect the man Kennedy should have appointed as secretary of state was Averell Harriman, but the reason he didn't was that Averell Harriman was thought to be too old—seventy years. Averell Harriman, like Dumas Malone, is going to have his 92nd birthday next week, and like Dumas Malone he is still going strong. Averell Harriman, I think, would have made a great secretary of state.

QUESTION: Can I ask you to talk just a minute on the question of Kennedy's relations to staff departments? For the Cuban crisis he established a special ad hoc crew. My impression is that he did something of the same in Berlin. You mentioned Dean Acheson. Was this his general policy in managing a crisis? To go outside the government, let alone below the standard heads, shows a certain amount of what he thought about them, the heads. Could you comment a little more on how he used his staff? Did he do the same thing with Vietnam?

MR. SCHLESINGER: Yes. He preferred ad hoc groups and he did have a task force on Vietnam. I should have mentioned, because I think it's a useful thing, the extent to which he occasionally brought in people from outside. Dean Acheson did not play, in my view, a helpful role during the Cuban missile crisis. Still, the principle of consulting 'wise men' in times of crisis is a good one. Kennedy also occasionally brought in senators, as he brought Fulbright to one meeting before the Bay of Pigs. Fulbright made by far the most sensible speech that anyone made in all of those meetings. Unfortunately his advice was ignored.

Kennedy found the National Security Council, as constituted by statute, not too useful a forum, partly for a trivial reason. One of the statutory members was the head of the Office of Civilian Defense Mobilization, Frank Ellis of New Orleans, and he talked a lot to no point. This made National Security Council's meetings trying for Kennedy. In general I think he believed that to bring together the representatives of the departments involved in a particular crisis was the most expeditious way of doing it.

QUESTION: Would you say that Roosevelt helped nurture the Democratic party and brought it along and that President Kennedy tended to ignore it and helped harm the party process? Is that a fair judgment?

MR. SCHLESINGER: I wouldn't have thought so. The national committee generally languishes when the President is of the same party, but I think that Larry O'Brien and Kenny O'Donnell of the White House were in close touch with John Bailey, the national chairman. I hadn't heard this view. What did you have in mind, particularly about Kennedy's neglect of the party?

QUESTION: Well, I'm not sure, but it seemed to me that the whole process in the way he won the election showed that he intended to make it a personal contest rather than a party contest.

MR. SCHLESINGER: I would have said that was true of Roosevelt, too. You must remember that the party machinery in 1932 was in the hands of Al Smith's people. Both Roosevelt and Kennedy took over against the existing party organization and brought in their own people. But both were experienced practical politicians and recognized the role of the party. I've never understood the argument that Eugene McCarthy used to make that Kennedy in some unique way "personalized" the presidency. I don't think he did so any more than FDR did or more than Theodore Roosevelt did. Any vivid person in the presidency personalizes it in some way.

QUESTION: I wonder if I could ask a follow-up question about Latin America and the collapse of the Alliance for Progress. Some analysts of American policy keep insisting that no American President should have supported Allende or should have collaborated in the overthrow of Somoza. Do you think it would have been possible for Kennedy to have brought about a situation in which, for example, undercover CIA aid was given to such movements as those?

MR. SCHLESINGER: I don't see any problem about co-existing with a regime like Allende's. Allende created his own problems by trying to do too much on the basis of a thirty-two percent popular vote. In Bolivia, for example, the revolution of 1952–53 nationalized the mines; even the Eisenhower administration accepted that. The problem of nationalization is now, in a certain sense, a dead issue. Any country that wants to nationalize and will go through some compensation process can do so. No one is going to send in gunboats.

The harder question is: could or would or should the United States support subversive movements directed to the overthrow of dictatorship? In the Kennedy years this was done to some degree in Africa. We had relations with African nationalist groups who were opposing colonial rule. Some support was given to them in Angola, in the Congo and Mozambique. The leaders came to Washington, they would meet Robert Kennedy, the CIA would give them money and so on.

In Latin America we used to talk about how we would like to get rid of Duvalier, and the CIA was in contact with Haitian exiles. Nothing much was ever done about it. I was never sure in my own mind about the ethic of it because in general I am an anti-interventionist in the affairs of other countries. I think other countries should be able to pursue their own historical logic. I believe if we hadn't intervened to overthrow Mossadeagh in Iran we wouldn't have Khomeyni today. Our intervention in Chile to save it from Allende produced Pinochet. Most interventions rebound against our interests.

I can never forget a meeting over the Congo in 1961 when Adlai Stevenson was very anxious to send a UN force to the Congo to put down a civil war there. The argument was made that, if we don't act in the Congo, the Congo will become a Soviet bastion in the center of Africa. This was before we used to talk about the Soviet-Cuban bastion. We called it then a Sino-Soviet bastion in the center of Africa. None of that really impressed me very much, but the British and the Americans agreed to support the UN in its efforts to stop the civil war in the Congo. I walked out with the British ambassador, a very intelligent man, David Ormsby-Gore, now Lord Harlech. He had been silent during all this, and I said to him, "You seem somber. Are you out of sympathy with the decisions that have been reached? He said, "Yes, I believe that every country has a right to its own War of the Roses."

The struggle for national identity is very difficult and often bloody. It sometimes involves civil wars. To adopt the notion of the present administration that every civil war has Soviet origins is madness.

QUESTION: Can I raise a question about the whole matter of the vice-presidency, which is often debated? I bring to bear a little story I heard many years ago about FDR's reaction to John Nance Garner. He asked him how he felt about this man sabotaging him on the Hill and so forth, and FDR had his own sense of perspective because he said, "Whenever I think of Garner I think that McKinley put up with my cousin."

MR. SCHLESINGER: I think a vice-president is not only useless but a dangerous office and should be abolished. We should adopt some other system of arranging a presidential succession, like the French system for example. They just hold a special election. I've argued this in detail; I won't go into the argument here. I think the vice presidency is *not* only not a training job for the presidency; it's a destructive job for people to hold. The vice-president has only one job, and that is to wait around for the President to die. This is not ordinarily the basis for an enduring relationship. Presidents don't like vice-presidents; they are reminders of their own mortality. And Presidents think up excuses to send them to state funerals and so on. Lyndon Johnson was a very loyal vice-president, but at immense psychic cost—so much so that by 1963 he seemed in a state of permanent depression. He always felt that he was never being used enough; he thought he should be used more on the Hill. In the first place, the Senate Democrats did not want him on the Hill. When he tried to come back as vice-president and sit in the Democratic conference, they voted him out. In the second place, the President did not wish to give control of his legislative program to Lyndon Johnson. But Johnson was a loyal vice-president.

Hubert Humphrey was practically destroyed by the vice-presidency. Johnson treated Humphrey far worse than Kennedy treated Johnson. I think Carter made a gallant effort to try to find a function for the vice-president, and probably Mondale had more responsibility given him than any vice-president since FDR made Henry Wallace head of the Board of Economic Warfare. But I still think it is a useless office. It's not a real preparation for the presidency because the man has to suppress his own views. Now Mondale is explaining all the time how he shouldn't be held responsible for things the Carter administration did because he disagreed with them. It is a demeaning job for a man to have. I'm against the whole thing.

QUESTION: Professor Schlesinger, in your *Foreign Affairs* essay you talked about the need to move away from an emphasis on ideology and back towards a foreign policy based on national interest. Then today in *The New Republic* article you talked about this movement between periods of idealism and periods of disillusionment. I'm wondering if you might elaborate on how a President can maintain a prudentially conceived foreign policy when having to deal with this other element of the American political character.

MR. SCHLESINGER: That is a question I've thought about and haven't reached any satisfactory resolutions. Idealism in domestic policy may lead to crusading in foreign policy, and that can be a source of mischief. This was true of Wilson who refused to concede the balance of power reasons which justified our entry into the First World War, and instead tried to put it on other grounds. Both Roosevelts were basically national-interest, balance-of-power men, though Franklin Roosevelt also had an admixture of Wilsonianism. Kennedy, I think, was basically a balance-of-power, national-interest man. But there is no guarantee that affirmative government at home may not lead to crusading abroad. Nor is there any guarantee that periods of negative government at home will lead to abstention abroad, which is clearly not the case today. So I can't quite fit foreign policy into the cycle, except insofar as foreign policy projects abroad the values that are decisive at home—private enterprise under Reagan, for example.

NARRATOR: Next Thursday at this time Louis Martin who is a close friend of several around the table will pick up the theme of Presidents and their approach to civil rights. He served in the Kennedy administration, the Johnson administration, and more recently the Carter administration. He's not a figure who was in the public limelight but those who were well informed consider him one of the most knowledgeable people about Presidents and their approaches to civil rights.

MR. SCHLESINGER: May I say a word about Louis Martin? I've known him for years and worked with him closely and he's one of the shrewdest and most interesting men, a very careful and detached observer of the process, and he is fascinating. I wish I could be here myself.

NARRATOR: I'm sure that our experience today has taught us a great deal about President Kennedy, and also about the breadth and richness of Professor Schlesinger's thought. I hope very much that this will be only the first of a number of visits for him and perhaps a longer stay. Thank you very much.

A SENATOR'S VIEW

Senator George McGovern

MR. THOMPSON: Senator McGovern, you are kind to participate in a brief interview on President John F. Kennedy. The one thing we've asked everybody is where and when they met Kennedy and how they got involved in the Kennedy administration?

SENATOR MCGOVERN: I first came to know him during the labor reform battles in the Congress. You'll recall that in the 1950s Kennedy led the fight in the Senate for labor reform that was aimed specifically at the Teamsters Union because of the abuses under Hoffa and Beck. Kennedy was on the investigating committee that looked into those abuses. He teamed up with a Republican senator by the name of Ives. The Kennedy/Ives bill called for certain reforms to end abuses on the part of some of the unions. I was active on the House side in that effort. That would have been in the late 1950s and I worked rather closely with Kennedy's office on that bill and had visits with him personally about it. I also got to know Robert Kennedy who was then working for his brother. That was my first introduction to both Bob and Jack Kennedy.

Following that initial contact with them, I got John Kennedy to come to South Dakota to speak in 1960 when he was running for President and I was running for the United States Senate against Karl Mundt. Kennedy had a particular dislike of Mundt. Their styles and philosophies were so different that he did what he could as a presidential contender to help me in 1960 but he was shrewd enough to know that his running as a Catholic in South Dakota for the presidency would probably do me in, which in a sense it did. I never said that publicly at the time; I just said I got beat. But it was quite clear that losing South Dakota as overwhelmingly as he did against Nixon in 1960 made the difference in an otherwise close race that I had with Mundt. I only lost by about one percent of the vote.

I came to appreciate during that time Kennedy's wit and his capacity to stand back and look at a campaign or look at issues somewhat detached from the kind of emotion that characterized other politicians. I always found him a cool, thoughtful individual. It wasn't that he was free of emotion, but from the earliest contact with him in maneuvering on the labor reform bill, then the way he handled himself against Nixon in 1960, and the little bit that I saw of him in South Dakota where he made a couple of appearances during 1960, I came to the conclusion that here was a rather cool-headed, detached man who was capable of laughing at himself and yet at the same time a determined figure who would be a very difficult antagonist. Of course he was and did go on to win that election.

MR. THOMPSON: Most people didn't feel in the beginning he had much chance, did they?

SENATOR MCGOVERN: That's right. Nixon had much more experience, was better known, and had been around longer. But I've always thought Kennedy won that race in 1960 partly on sheer nerve. The steadiness he had, the capacity not to get flustered under intense pressure—in a sense he outwitted Nixon in the 1960 campaign.

I felt at the time and still do even more so in retrospect that knowing that he was running against a hard-line anti-Communist—in a sense Nixon had made that his trademark—that Kennedy probably made some mistakes by trying to outflank Nixon on the right, on issues of national security and foreign policy. As you look back on it, it is regrettable that he ran on a missile gap which didn't exist.

MR. THOMPSON: The Gaither Report of course had said there was a gap. He picked it up.

SENATOR MCGOVERN: He picked it up. He was listening to those Pentagon generals who were critical of Eisenhower for refusing to go along with a lot of their plans. Other members of the Senate, Jackson and Symington and others, were pounding on the same theme so Jack picked up on that and converted it into a major campaign issue. Also he suggested that the Eisenhower administration might be a little weak for not invading Cuba. This prompted Nixon to explain how irresponsible it would be for us to do something like that. I think Kennedy is the only candidate who ever ran against Nixon as a Democrat who was able to outflank him on the hard-line anti-Communist stand; maybe it took that to win.

MR. THOMPSON: Senator McGovern, one of the other things we've asked each of our participants in this portrait of the Kennedy presidency is what were your initial impressions of Kennedy as a leader, of his style of leadership, his political assets, his limitations, if any? And then did any of that change as the administration went on and you saw him, first, as special assistant to the President for the Food For Peace Program, and later from the vantage point of the Senate?

SENATOR MCGOVERN: The very first thing that impressed me about Kennedy was his wit and coolness. Just those two things. I also thought he had a very graceful style of operation, just the way he moved and the way he handled people. It wasn't particularly warm and ingratiating. It was more a kind of a gallant, graceful type of thing that he had. I didn't feel that he was a powerful speaker when I first met him or a particularly effective communicator. He didn't always speak in complete sentences and he wasn't a powerful orator but that is one thing that changed rather dramatically in the 1960 campaign. He came to speak with greater force and power. He carried that over into the presidency where I thought he was steadily improving as a speaker and communicator. He always did use television well and that was perfected with the passage of time.

There was another quality that Kennedy had that impressed politicians and that was his capacity to draw good people to his staff. You saw very few ineffective and clumsy people around Kennedy. Rather there was a Ted Sorensen in an absolutely key role. People like Arthur Schlesinger and Walter Heller and others that he brought into the administration, I thought, were a mark of political imagination.

I think on the weakness side that sometimes maybe he was a little too expedient in the things that he did. I remember being somewhat disappointed, and I still am, that his first announced appointments were to keep J. Edgar Hoover in the FBI and Allen Dulles as director of the CIA. I know that was done to reassure the right wing in this country but it didn't seem to me a very wise step for a liberal Democratic President to do as his first act. The decision to pass over people like Adlai Stevenson and Chester Bowles for secretary of state disappointed me greatly, not that I have any quarrel with Dean Rusk as a person. But I didn't feel he had the breadth of vision in the 1960s of an Adlai Stevenson or Chester Bowles. I think it might have been less likely that we would have become involved in Vietnam and in the Bay of Pigs fiasco if the secretary of state had been somebody of that stature and wisdom.

I also felt that Kennedy was too quick to buy the arguments of the military and that he needlessly expanded American military spending and American military involvement during those nearly three years that he served in the White House. He felt that Eisenhower was too weak and soft in his approach to the world. Kennedy was much more energetic and forceful but I think that it is not an accident that after he ended the Korean War, Eisenhower presided over eight years when not a single American soldier died whereas under Kennedy very quickly we went through the Bay of Pigs invasion and then, shortly after, a deepening involvement in Vietnam.

MR. THOMPSON: Do you think the phrase in his inaugural address on defending liberty, fighting any battle, defending any people, bearing any burden had any connection with his efforts to work militarily to support regimes that were threatened?

SENATOR MCGOVERN: I do. I think that he psyched himself into thinking that this country could do anything in the world and that there was nothing too big for us if we just had the will to do it. And of course as it turned out there are limitations on what even a very great power can do. Our involvement in Southeast Asia reminded us that we are not all-powerful and that will is not enough, you also have to have a certain degree of wisdom and sense of limits and those things were missing in the Kennedy administration. I think one of the great tragedies is that he was killed before the learned wisdom of those early years had a chance to ripen into a different kind of policy that I think we would have seen in a second term.

MR. THOMPSON: You don't think that the *gung ho* attitude of some of the people around him, who were extraordinarily able but also had this *gung ho* attitude, pushed him on.

SENATOR MCGOVERN: Well, I think they did push him on but I think they thought they were pleasing him. He set the tone and then the tough-guy mentality was something that was easy for others to manifest. They didn't do it because they thought Kennedy had to be pressed in that direction. They did it because they thought this was the way to manifest the President's will. But I remember in those early months of the Kennedy administration that it was considered quite *chic* if you were reading Mao's books on guerrilla warfare and studying the writings of Che Guevara. If you were going to be a tough-minded intellectual you had to know how to win battles. You had to know something about warfare. It wasn't enough to be a student of international affairs. You also had to be willing to take up a machine gun and to know how guerrillas survive in the jungle. So there was a lot of that nonsense going on at that time that I think John Kennedy's inaugural address set the keynote for.

MR. THOMPSON: I remember some of the ambassadors around the world, Ken Young in Thailand and others, pushed for the development of anti-guerrilla activities. They had a very strong aggressive attitude toward what should be done.

SENATOR MCGOVERN: And then there was another factor. In all fairness you have to remember now that Kennedy won that election by a margin of one hundred and twenty thousand in the popular vote. It was a close call. I think he was trying to demonstrate, at least in his first term, that the conservatives and the hard-liners in this country could trust him. He wasn't going to give away the store.

Early in the administration I got a call from Bob Poage, a Democrat from Texas who was the chairman of the House Agricultural Committee, and he urged me to propose to Kennedy that he announce that American ships loaded with wheat had just been dispatched to China, even though we had no relations with them. There was a great famine going on in China at the time and the Chinese desperately needed the wheat. All they had to do was to accept it. No strings attached. And Poage, a conservative Democrat incidentally, said this was not only going to help the American farmers by finding an outlet for surpluses but it might help improve relations between the two countries. I thought it was a good idea and I went to Kennedy and talked to him about it and he said, "Well, George, it is a good idea, frankly." But he said, "I just can't do this in the first term. We may be able to do something on China in a second term. But it's the kind of thing we can't do in the first term."

MR. THOMPSON: What about your area? Was he sympathetic to the idea of using food in a creative way to help starvation?

SENATOR MCGOVERN: He really was. I mean he understood that during the campaign. I don't think he understood a lot about the farm problem in 1960. He spoke somewhat mechanically on things like parity, price supports, and set-asides. That was all Greek to him and he didn't believe it all that much, either. He didn't really believe in the government being so actively involved in agriculture but when it came to feeding the hungry, both here at home and abroad, Kennedy was there.

His first executive order as President was to call for an increased distribution of surplus food in hungry areas like West Virginia, which he had seen during the primary campaign. And the second executive order a few minutes later was to create the Office of Food For Peace and to ask me to chair that office. Those two things were both done without congressional authorization. They were done by executive order of the President. So we had an immediate step-up the first day he was in the White House of food distribution in this country and a few minutes later the creation of the Office of Food For Peace where he called for a maximum effort that, in his words, would "narrow the gap between abundance here at home and near starvation abroad." And in every quarrel where there was a question of how much we were going to do, he backed me.

MR. THOMPSON: Where would he have fallen in the little discussion you and Senator Humphrey had at one stage with Earl Butz and with Henry Kissinger when the question of using food as a weapon came out? As I remember, you and Senator Humphrey took the broader view and said that it ought not to be a weapon but it ought to be a means of helping people.

SENATOR MCGOVERN: Kennedy would have come down on the side of using food as a humanitarian instrument to reduce hunger and suffering. One question he considered as President was how much were we going to do to get a world food program started. We needed the approval of the Department of Agriculture, the Department of State, and the Budget Bureau to make any kind of an offer to the first World Food Conference I attended in 1961. I was a delegate to the World Food Council, the head of the American delegation, and we didn't really have any authority to do anything except to say we were sympathetic to the idea. While we were flying over there, there was an official from the Department of Agriculture with me by the name of Ray Ioanes. He is still at Agriculture. I said to him, you know if we could just get through to John Kennedy I think we could get an authorization at the White House-level to go ahead and make an offer to start this world food program and I said why don't we call Ted Sorensen when we get to Rome and, even though it's a weekend, see if we can't get clearance to do that. Ioanes was a very well-informed intelligent man but he said, "Who is Ted Sorensen?" Now this is the first time I saw the gap between the bureaucracy and the politicians. This well-informed, longtime career man didn't know who Sorensen was.

Anyway, after I explained who he was I said, "What should we ask him?" He said, "Why don't we ask him if we can start the world food program with a hundred million dollars in cash and commodities, with the United States contributing the first forty million with the understanding that that will have to matched by the rest of the world, sixty percent." It seemed a reasonable proposal to me so I called Sorensen. It was a Saturday afternoon and he cleared that thing within a few hours, obviously through the President. I made the offer the next Monday morning and it absolutely staggered the whole World Food Conference. They hadn't expected anything to break that quickly and they recessed to figure out what to do. They came back that afternoon and voted to accept the offer and that's how the World Food Program got started.

In later years after Kennedy was gone and Johnson was gone and Nixon came into office and we had Butz there, there was an effort to expand that operation and Butz was very skeptical of that.

MR. THOMPSON: In a way you were more in an agency than a department. However there is a recurring debate about the relationship of the White House to the departments. Did Kennedy do it about right, do you think?

SENATOR MCGOVERN: I think so. He struggled with it, though, and we went through several reorganization experiments, particularly on foreign aid. Kennedy always seemed to me to be somewhat impatient in his attitude toward the federal bureaucracy. He wanted things done faster than he was able to get them done working through the regular departmental machinery. On the other hand he had good people in key spots. He had Dave Bell running the Budget Bureau and Bell was a superb administrator and expediter. He had good Cabinet people who were eager to get things done and he imbued the whole government with a sense of urgency and eagerness and inspiration that I think has been missing a good part of the time since then. But I think he handled his relations with the department heads about as well as a President could.

President Kennedy always had a very well-developed political sense. While he was President of the United States, he never forgot for one minute that he was going to have to face the voters again and he took a great interest in politics while he was in the White House. It's ironic that that's really how he was killed. He was on a political mission to patch things up in Texas between the Yarborough factions and the Connally factions. He was very much interested in what I was going to do. If I could be forgiven a personal observation, I had told him I was thinking about running for the Senate in 1962 and he always had told me that he had beaten me in 1960 inadvertantly by losing the state by such a big margin. I never admitted that to him. I always denied it.

But in any event when I was thinking about running in 1962, I went in to get his advice and he said, "Well, if you can win, do it. If you can't win, the hell with it. Don't go out there just to be brave. If you can win, fine. But unless you are pretty sure you are going to make it, I wouldn't attempt it again." So I told him I thought it was uphill but I was going to do it in any event. And he said, "Okay, if that's what you want to do I'll help you every way I can." And he did. He came to the state. He came out there early. He would have been glad, obviously, to help more. He did everything he could. He finally sent Bobby out to help and did various other things that helped us win a very narrow victory.

MR. THOMPSON: Thank you, Senator McGovern, for the light you have thrown on John F. Kennedy and the Kennedy presidency.

II.
KENNEDY AND CIVIL RIGHTS

ORIGINS OF KENNEDY'S CIVIL RIGHTS

Nicholas deB. Katzenbach

NARRATOR: Nicholas Katzenbach needs no introduction to many of you here. He has lectured at the Law School and has many friend in the area.

Mr. Katzenbach is senior vice-president and general counsel of IBM Corporation. His life can be divided into three parts. After graduation from Princeton in 1945, he went to Yale Law School from which he graduated in 1947, and he was a Rhodes scholar from 1947 to 1949. So he moved through the educational phase of his life with dispatch and efficiency. In the fifties, in addition to being admitted to the bar in New Jersey and Connecticut, he also taught law, first at the Yale Law School and then at the University of Chicago Law School, and served in various capacities in his law firm. The sixties, as many of you know, was his period of public service: first as assistant attorney general, then as deputy attorney general, then as attorney general, and finally as undersecretary of state. All these appointments took place in the Kennedy/Johnson period of our history. He played a central role in the civil rights movement and in events that took place in the Kennedy administration and after. He was active in the educational field, as a member of the American Law Institute, the American Judicature Society, and the American Bar Association. He published a book on *The Political Foundations of International Law* with Morton Kaplan in the early sixties. He has continued to participate in scholarly groups and discussions on the law and on foreign policy. In many other ways he has served his country in the fields of education, foreign policy and civil rights, with great distinction. We are privileged indeed that he will speak to us today.

MR. KATZENBACH: Thanks very much. I thought I'd just talk a few minutes at the beginning about President Kennedy and civil rights, in part because it provides a chance to see a rather unusual relationship that existed in that administration between the two brothers. There was no question at all that Bobby Kennedy was the most trusted adviser that President Kennedy had on any subject whatsoever. They were very close and worked very well together. That doesn't mean that President Kennedy always took Bobby Kennedy's advice because he didn't, but they were very, very close. He had a number of advisers who were close, but Bobby was the one who was, I think, the closest.

Almost the first contact I had with President Kennedy was with respect to civil rights. We were in the process of drafting an executive order on employment and government contractors that he wanted to get out in a hurry. Bill Moyers had been working with Lyndon Johnson on that. I took it out to Bobby Kennedy's house on a late Saturday afternoon and the President was there which I hadn't realized when I went out there. The difficulty that I was having was that Bobby didn't know anything at all about the executive order and the President had obviously followed it very closely. So as Bobby's subordinate I was in the position of not being able to tell him what was in the piece of paper while the President kept asking questions about it and was very interested in it. Whether it was because of his interest in civil rights or because of his desire to do what Lyndon Johnson wanted in an effort to start building a closer relationship—since it never really had been very close in the past—I don't know. But he was on top of a lot of details of an executive order, which is unusual.

When you look at Kennedy and civil rights, I think it must have been a terrible pain in the neck for the President. He was very aware of the closeness of the election, I think too aware of it, and it tended to make him rather cautious in a number of areas in the beginning of his administration. He did have some civil rights legislation that was prepared but there wasn't a chance in the world that he was going to get any civil rights legislation through. So whatever his desires about civil rights might be it was nothing but a problem for him. Bobby tried his best to take that problem on his own shoulders just as far as he could and keep the President as far away from it, in appearance at least, as he could.

There were two different kinds of problems. One was that the President had a lot of other things that he wanted to do which he thought were possible, but he didn't have much in the way of a majority in the House or Senate and you needed coalitions in each case to do this. Civil rights was a problem in getting help from southern Democrats. So that was one area of difficulty that he had, simply the politics of it. The other part was really entirely on the other side. You had Dr. King and others being very active, being joined by lots of well-known liberals who would come down for the day and go home. They were constantly putting pressure on the government to do more.

There was very little that the government could do. Bobby tried to do everything he could in the Department of Justice to try to ease those feelings but what you had were legal suits that took a lot of manpower and a lot of time and were very difficult to get any results. In fact, in my judgment, they never did get any results until the 1965 Voting Rights Act was passed. You could not deal with it by lawsuits. And there were the problems in school desegregation where you could bring suits, but again it took forever with all the appeals. Once you got all the appeals done and won the case five or six years had passed, and then they would say the circumstances are different, you really ought to try all over again. Bobby was trying to do it that way and it didn't work very well. Not a great deal of progress was made. No legislation was passed, and he was getting constant criticism from liberals and from the blacks. The situation was quite tense and quite dangerous.

In many states the Freedom Riders were not a joke. They were beaten up and they wanted federal protection. And if you stop to think of it, providing some kind of protection of that kind is very nearly an impossible thing for the federal government to do. Furthermore, it was very much against the philosophy that President Kennedy had and that Bobby had—which I think was totally right—which was that you did not solve a civil rights problem in the south if you did things for people. They had to do those things themselves. Local police had to be responsible for law and order. You didn't do it by putting the military in. The resolution of those problems had to be resolutions at a local level. The difference between the University of Mississippi and the University of Alabama was the difference in the administration of the two universities. Frank Rose did a job of integrating Alabama which was superbly done. You had to have that kind of local initiative to make it work. Nevertheless, you kept getting these pressures to use troops, which was always resisted.

We did some rather strange things. One of the things that we discovered in the law was that you could swear in marshals about anywhere you wanted to. So we began to build up and train marshals. The people we used for the Freedom Riders and later in Mississippi and Alabama and other places—until we had to use the military—were not really U.S. marshals in any real sense. Most of them were from the border patrol sworn in as deputy marshals. They had fairly good law enforcement training. The FBI would have nothing to do with it, predictably. We would swear in prison guards as marshals. We also had some alcohol and tax people. Then we tried to give them all special training. When people would say, "Send down a hundred marshals, or five hundred marshals," they had no idea what this involved. It meant dropping every federal prisoner at the local jail, leaving the Mexican border wide open, and putting prison guards on twelve hour shifts when you did this. It was a constant effort to use palliatives that really never worked.

Now that's not the way it was perceived. Bobby Kennedy was perceived as evil by those who believed in white supremacy in the south and as an activist. But, he was seen by the civil rights people in those years as not doing nearly enough, and the President was seen the same way. Bobby tried to take it in his own hands, and there was very little that they could do. We did try to put the Department of Justice where we could on the side of the civil rights groups. This was possible largely because Dr. King did observe the law and there was constitutional principle involved.

We went down to Mississippi. We had to send the troops in and that was regarded by both President Kennedy and Bobby Kennedy as a great failure. They both, and particularly the President, had a real conviction that it was very wrong to send troops in, that they had to be a last resort, and that it would be a failure if troops were sent. Anything that could be done by civilian law enforcement should be done. He really didn't mind sending four hundred "marshals," but he didn't want to send troops. He felt that Little Rock was a great failure in the Eisenhower administration, and it was the last thing they ever did, because they sent troops. He saw that if they had to send troops to accomplish this then it couldn't really be done. The resentment which built up for it was so great that he was determined never to do it. And of course he ended up doing it very early in his administration at Mississippi. But, he did regard it as a failure.

With that activity and George Wallace at Alabama, we began to feel that it was absolutely essential—although I think in lots of ways the President resisted that it was essential—to get some civil rights legislation. So with a good deal of fanfare the Civil Rights Act of 1964 was introduced. And I might just take a few minutes to talk about that because it will give you an idea of how the Kennedy administration functioned in a rather unusual way.

The drafting of the Act was an effort to solve problems that we were facing, primarily the sit-in problems and the problems of public accommodations. We had a lot of sessions over in the Department of Justice on just what the law should involve. These sessions involved a lot of people: political people, Louis Martin from the Democratic National Committee, and others trying to say what kinds of proposals would satisfy whom. Lyndon Johnson was involved. He was big on wanting something on employment. He felt that that was a very important thing to put in. That was also politically what seemed really the most impossible to get through, but he wanted it in there so some of it was gotten in.

Then the way in which we worked on this was legislation. President Kennedy didn't really like to work on that all that much and really left it to Larry O'Brien, which was quite a contrast with Lyndon Johnson, who loved to do it himself to the extent that he could. He liked to keep playing majority leader but President Kennedy didn't like it all that much. And Larry O'Brien and his people were very good. I worked a lot with O'Brien and then we would go and talk to the President and with Bobby on this.

To get a Civil Rights Act through we knew we had to have Republicans and that it could not be done without them and therefore we had to do something to get Congressman McCullough, who was the senior Republican on the House Judiciary Committee. He had to be persuaded to support that legislation. If we had him, we thought we could get Charlie Halleck. If you had the senior Republican on the committee you normally could bring along the Republican leadership for a bill that he would support. We could not get it any other way. Then the way in which those people worked—O'Brien, Manatos, Simpson, and so forth—was that we as the department were responsible for the substance of the bill. They would not do anything, would not talk substance with any congressman or senator. They would get referred to us.

After that, with a lot of our help, they took over the responsibility for the whole House and the whole Senate to pick up the votes there that were necessary. We ran all that over with the President and became persuaded that we could indeed get that legislation enacted. But McCullough, first pulling for us, said he would support a reasonable civil rights bill, that he thought it was important to the country that this be done. But we had to agree with him that we would not give away any provisions in the Senate to get it enacted. He said the House had walked that plank before and he wasn't going to ask people to do that. So that was the deal that was made.

Then in the committee, Congressman Celler just totally lost control of the thing. Congressman Celler was a long-time chairman and very liberal and he took it in his own subcommittee. He had the votes in that subcommittee to do anything. He could have amended the Constitution in that subcommittee if he wanted to! Because he was liberal, Congressman Celler would vote for every liberal suggestion that was made by anybody. So would the other Democrats on that committee. The bill that we had submitted just got everything that anybody could think of put in. Of course McCullough was sitting there saying, "I'm not going to vote for this bill. You've got to get that bill back in the committee." So Celler kept saying, "Well, you'll get it back in the committee." But the problem was that Celler himself didn't want to vote against any of these liberal amendments.

So we then had to have another hearing—and I think this was fairly typical—where Bobby took all the heat for removing all of the very liberal provisions and testified that they were not wanted by the administration, which did not do him any good politically. It certainly didn't help him any with the people who were opposed to any civil rights bill, and it made all of the civil rights people angry, although it was the only way a bill was going to get through.

To get that bill through, we had to hold that bill and not allow any of these amendments. That meant a lot of people had to stand up who did come from very liberal constituencies and vote against a lot of liberalizing amendments. We had to do it first in the committee and President Kennedy—a rather unusual thing—got the Democrats on the committee plus some others over to the White House before the vote was going to come up in the committee that morning to ask for their support and tell them that this was what he wanted and would they please do it his way. He had Kenny O'Donnell on the phone to Mayor Daley to get him to be sure that Congressman Libonati voted correctly because we couldn't get it through the Congressman's head which was yes and which was no. And he made a mistake and he did not come back. He did not choose to run again in Chicago. Halleck was there and just as Halleck was leaving he said, "Well, you know Mr. President, I'm not committed on the fair labor part," and the President said, "Yes, I know Charlie." Then he turned and said, "He is committed, isn't he? and I said, "Oh, yes he is," and he did in fact vote for it and did stay committed. I found out about two years later my notes said, "Halleck not committed."

A lot of people have asked whether that bill would have been enacted if Johnson had not become President. They assumed that it had something to do with Johnson and the Senate. Johnson worked very hard for that bill and I don't mean to take any of that away. But, in my judgment that bill would have been enacted by exactly the same process that it was enacted with

Johnson, although I think it's clear that Johnson had more influence than Kennedy.

I'll have to tell you a little anecdote about the communication satellite legislation, and then I'll stop on this note. Early in the administration the FCC had decided that when we get satellite communications they should all be given to the carriers, or substantially at that point, the Bell Company. Kefauver thought it ought to be all government run. I had suggested to Bobby Kennedy, who then suggested to the President, why not just sell the stock, create a company and let the Bell system control it and not have it government owned? President Kennedy thought that was a good idea. So that was the legislation he put up. I testified all day on that. Senator Kerr was opposed to that and he was the most powerful senator I think I've ever seen. After I testified there all day in opposition to him the President called me up and said, "Can you have lunch tomorrow with Bob Kerr?" and I said, "I can but I doubt he wants to have lunch with me," and he said, "No, he does. He said you were the first witness up there who knew what he was talking about." So I had lunch with Kerr and made one of the few political deals I think I ever made. He said, "I'll support it if you give half of it to the carriers and half of it to the public. My reason for that is that I don't think it will succeed without the carriers. I think they have to have an involvement." So that happened.

Now the relevance of this to civil rights is that Kefauver continued to fight carrier control; he wanted public ownership. And it got a lot of people irritated and they voted for cloture. We went over all of those votes for cloture on that Communication Satellite Act when the Civil Rights Act came along. It was enormously helpful because it was very difficult for senators who had voted for cloture because they were angry at Kefauver to say that they would not vote for cloture on a matter as important as civil rights. That vote, I think, was the key. And one of the reasons that I said we would have gotten the legislation with or without President Johnson was really because of the communication satellite connection. But I think I'll stop there and then have a more general discussion.

NARRATOR: Who would like to ask the first question?

QUESTION: This concerns Bobby. From the time he worked for McCarthy to the time that he was running for the presidency, he seemed to do a complete flip-flop on his view of civil rights. He seemed to be very highly regarded by the blacks, and he seemed to be very sincere. Why would you think that took place?

MR. KATZENBACH: Maybe he grew up and got educated. It is almost that simple, really. He had a little bit of Boston Irish in him and a little bit of the fighting temperament. And he was certainly interested in putting Mr. Hoffa in jail if he could do so. That was a carry-over from when he was on the staff of the Senate labor committee. But I think he began to get interested in civil rights in the sense of equal rights for blacks. He believed in it. Equal rights for women he believed in principle but I don't think emotionally.

I remember getting a note on a piece of paper where President Kennedy had written something, urging that something be done for women. Bobby sent it down to me with a note that said, "I think a woman's place is in the home." I think he was old-fashioned in that way.

Then I think on the civil liberties side of it, wiretapping and so forth, he really had a change of position as things went along and he saw more and more how it could be abused. I think it was just a growing up process and an educational process with him.

QUESTION: Was this true about Jack too?

MR. KATZENBACH: I think it was true of them both really. I don't think Jack Kennedy was particularly liberal when he came in. I don't have any doubt that he did in fact believe in equal rights for blacks. But I don't think he would have put it as high on an agenda of things that he wanted to accomplish when he came into office as it in fact came to be as a result primarily of Dr. King. He was always fiscally very conservative, which I always assumed he got from his father. I don't think we've ever managed the economy better than it was managed in the three years of the Kennedy administration.

QUESTION: I was thinking of an area you know so well. The New Jersey Constitution of 1947 was the first state Constitution that provided for opening up public accommodations to the blacks and so on. New Jersey and Princeton were way behind in terms of being open about these matters. I think probably for Jack Kennedy, who had come from a comfortable environment, it was awfully hard to make the big change emotionally and otherwise.

MR. KATZENBACH: I think that's true. I think that Bobby had more contacts than the President and he began to have much more understanding and much more appreciation of what was involved in the civil rights movement than he had when he first came in.

I'm interested that you raised the New Jersey Constitution because I take a particular piece of pride in the fact that my mother was vice-president of that. She was the chairman of the group that did the civil liberties part of it, the part that would correspond to the first ten amendments.

QUESTION: "The stroke of the pen" was also another little slogan that Jack Kennedy couldn't do much about. It was a question felt very deeply by some political groups. They were putting the heat on the President to deliver on that promise but it was awfully difficult, I think, to start moving on it.

MR. KATZENBACH: It was very difficult to start. It was very difficult politically to do it when you are in a close election. It's not even clear who got the most votes and he just didn't feel he had the clout.

QUESTION: Following the Bay of Pigs, there was an exchange of a thousand or more prisoners for drugs that drug companies contributed to Cuba. What was the role of the attorney general's office in that transaction?

MR. KATZENBACH: We put the whole thing together.

QUESTION: Whose idea was it?

MR. KATZENBACH: The idea came from Jim Donovan. He was an outside lawyer who had some connections with Castro, and I've forgotten now just how and why this was, but he thought that could be done. Bobby and the President felt an enormous obligation to those Cuban Prisoners. The President felt they were in prison because he goofed and therefore he wanted to do something about it. So when we had this possibility of doing something about it, Donovan went back down to Cuba and I think he took along with him on his first or second trip John Nolan who became an executive assistant to the President. He was a young attorney in Washington and later succeeded John Seigenthaler as Bobby's executive assistant. The first thing we had to get was three and a half million dollars in cash, and of course the temptation was to get it from the CIA because they always seem to have small change in petty cash. Then Bobby said, "No, we just cannot do that." We had to raise that money, and how it was raised was very funny. A lot of people were out working to get that money and they got donations.

We were determined, in terms of those donations, which were charitable contributions by the drug companies, not to bend any rules of the Internal Revenue Service at all. The only thing we were doing was giving them an opinion in an awful hurry, which was done by the head of the tax division, Lou Oberdorfer, now a federal judge in Washington, and some others. But, from the drug companies' point of view this was a kind of bonanza because it was acceptable to Castro and it was all the stuff they couldn't market. Nutritionally it was fine, and it was what they wanted down there. I mean it was usable. They had some of this diet stuff you used to drink instead of eat meals; I've forgotten what it was called but it was very nutritious. And that was fine for children and babies down there. They were having difficulty marketing it so this was a way of doing it.

But, back to the money thing. Bobby called me up once and he asked me how it was coming and then he said, "You're going to get a call from the Cardinal in Boston." He said, "I don't want to talk to him but you see what you can get out of him." So I called and the Cardinal said he'd be happy if he could contribute a million dollars. And I said, "Well, right at the moment what we need, because we've only got about forty-eight hours left, is the ability to use that as a guarantee with the bank. If you will guarantee it, we can get the money advanced by a bank." He said he would do that, and Cardinal Cushing did. I'm sure that cost Joe Kennedy a million dollars.

Anyhow, subsequently, maybe a month later, Bobby called me up and said, "The representative from the Cardinal and a lawyer are coming down and they want to see me. Will you meet them at the plane and take them to lunch?" At lunch I kept saying, "Won't you check your briefcase here?" Neither one would check his briefcase. When they got up into the attorney general's office afterwards, they went over and said they had come about the million dollars that the Cardinal promised. They had brought it with them. I opened up their two briefcases and there in small bills was one million dollars. Bobby said as they left, "What do I do with a million dollars in cash?" and I said, "The only man I know who is capable of knowing what to do with a million dollars in cash is Clark Clifford. I'll find out from him what you can do." I knew he was a director of the Riggs bank. We could put it in the Riggs bank.

QUESTION: You said something very interesting about the civil rights legislation and the role of Lyndon Johnson. Kennedy and Johnson were hardly bosom pals but in a way with this narrow majority it would seem that here was the possibility of bringing Lyndon Johnson closer by using his abilities. Would you talk to us a little bit more about the relationship of Lyndon Johnson and the Kennedys in this early period in this context?

MR. KATZENBACH: I think in the Kennedy administration the relationship with Lyndon Johnson and Jack Kennedy was quite proper and really not all that bad. Bobby, he couldn't stand. He admired Bobby in that funny kind of way, but they were oil and water; they could not get along together. I think

Jack got on with him fairly well. The problem was that you kept forgetting him. I think that must be the problem of every vice-president.

QUESTION: I'm sure that's the case.

MR. KATZENBACH: You'd have a meeting and obviously he should be there but nobody had thought to invite him. Then you would invite him at the last minute, which is, in and of itself, sort of insulting. Obviously he knows about the meeting; he's going to hear about a lot of other people who are going to be there. I do think that President Kennedy tried very hard to remember the vice-president and tried to create something for him that would use his abilities. I do think they grew to have a lot of trust and confidence in each other even though they were very different people. I think that Lyndon Johnson was a superbly good vice-president in a situation that must have been enormously difficult for a man with his energies and his ego. To play number two to a younger person from a very different setting and background must have been very difficult. And I think he did it very well.

Civil rights? I think the only two things that I am absolutely sure that Johnson believed in were civil rights and education. I never was sure about anything else, how much of it was really conviction or not. But those things were real convictions.

QUESTION: Perhaps for some others who have never been in government, what are the parameters of an executive order? You mentioned it a couple of times. Is that something that doesn't involve the Constitution? Does that go through the attorney general's office for clearance?

MR. KATZENBACH: It goes through the attorney general's office for clearance. An executive order is in essence just what the name indicates—that is, it is an order from the President of the United States to all of the executive departments and agencies, people that he controls.

There may be parts of the executive orders that are classified. That's possible. You can have parts of an executive order that are classified.

QUESTION: Have executive orders ever been declared unconstitutional?

MR. KATZENBACH: Sure.

QUESTION: They're making it out of whole cloth, is that it?

MR. KATZENBACH: Well, very few Presidents underestimate their authority.

Sometimes they overestimate it, but when you issue an order of that kind, it has to have a basis in law somewhere.

We tried to solve the busing problem by persuading the Interstate Commerce Commission to issue an order to the bus companies that they could not discriminate. Well, the Interstate Commerce Act uses the word discrimination. It's quite clearly referring to rate discrimination but we brought a very unusual action. I don't think it had ever been done before. The attorney general brought it in the Commission and asked for the order and used that as a statutory basis. And the Commission went along with them, which didn't surprise me too much. The courts went along with it and upheld it as being consistent with the Act. I think for anything less powerful than the Civil Rights movement, the judges would have looked a little more carefully at what kind of discrimination the Congress was talking about back when they created the Interstate Commerce Commission.

QUESTION: Mr. Katzenbach, I was in and out of Washington occasionally during the period you were there. Before the assassination of President Kennedy there was a very strong rumor in the State Department that Bobby Kennedy was going to take the secretaryship of the state. I wonder, was this the way it worked?

MR. KATZENBACH: Not to the best of my knowledge. I know there were those rumors. There was a frustration on the part of President Kennedy and perhaps more so with Bobby with respect to the department, and to some extent with Dean Rusk. Dean was not particularly an activist secretary of state. He wasn't full of new ideas on how you might do this, that or the other thing, and I think Kennedy was very anxious to have that. Dean also felt that it was terribly important to know what the President was thinking before you gave him advice so that you wouldn't give him advice that would be embarrassing. I have an enormous affection for Dean Rusk, and a good deal of admiration, but I think he was not the kind of person that worked very well with Jack Kennedy. I think their personalities were too different. But I doubt very much that Bobby would have gone over there. I think it would have been too much of an exposure to administration for him to have done that.

QUESTION: It seemed to me that Jack Kennedy relied on his brother on foreign policy matters, such as the Cuban missile crisis, more than he did with the Department of State or anybody in the Department of State.

MR. KATZENBACH: On foreign policy matters he did rely a good deal on Bobby. He had, after the Bay of Pigs, I think, a lot of confidence in General

Maxwell Taylor and he had a lot of confidence in Averell Harriman. But in a crisis situation he would have relied more on Bobby than he would on almost anybody else. But he didn't always take Bobby's advice. It was not a blind reliance. He thought that he would get from Bobby, and I think he did, something that was absolutely straightforward, something that was brother to brother and not from attorney general to President or from cabinet officer to President. I think that's what he wanted from Bobby. Some of the stuff that Bobby thought of was not bad. Ignoring the letter at the time of the Cuban missile crisis was Bobby's idea. It was a good idea.

QUESTION: How did the two brothers manage to keep old Joe Kennedy out of the picture, or did they?

MR. KATZENBACH: Yes, they did, although they had enormous respect, affection and even awe, I think, for their father. I remember one conversation. One of the few things that Joe Kennedy really wanted was to have Frank Morrissey appointed a judge in Massachusetts, and Frank Morrissey had no qualifications. I remember Jack was talking to Bobby and said, "What do I do? What do we tell Dad?" And Bobby said, "Just tell him you are President, not him," which I don't think was the most helpful advice to John Kennedy.

QUESTION: Mr. Katzenbach, following the resolution of the Bay of Pigs problem, did President Kennedy give any indication he might change direction from the Eisenhower approach to Castro through the Alliance for Progress or that he might open up a dialogue with him? Or, did he have the time?

MR. KATZENBACH: I think that might have happened eventually in a longer Kennedy administration because there was more interest in Latin America. But that again was an area that he had no confidence at all in the State Department, and I think that it was probably a mistake that he did not. I think to some extent it got messed up as a result of three amateurs over in the White House creating the Alliance for Progress. But I think that it would have been very difficult for some time to have had any dialogue with Castro because you had the Bay of Pigs and, then you had the Cuban missile crisis. You would have had to have three or four years go by before you could do very much on that, I think.

Also, Bobby used to have all those Cubans out to the house all the time. I'm sure that these were the exiles who had been prisoners down there. They were always out at the house, and I'm sure that what they were telling him was not that he ought to go down and be friends with Castro.

QUESTION: The increased reliance on White House staff and exclusion of departments or cabinet personalities is concentrating power without institutional depth. How do you look at that as the presidency is evolving and the difficulties it presents in running the country?

MR. KATZENBACH: I agree that that is happening, and I think it is a very unfortunate thing to happen. I think that the nature of the problem is that the President does not feel that the members of his administration, the cabinet officers running the departments and government, have a total and complete dedication and loyalty to him. That was why Bobby was so effective. There is a tendency to put into the White House and to surround oneself with loyal people who have worked through the campaign. You feel that their loyalty is of the highest order and I think that's why this happens.

I think it's very unfortunate because it doesn't provide the institutional depth. If you are going to serve the President's interests well, you have to be aware of how the Congress is going to react to things within your area of responsibility and how the influential part of the public is going to react to those things. Now this will vary from one department to another. The Treasury Department cannot ignore the banking or the investment community. It cannot ignore their views. It doesn't have to follow their views but can't ignore them. There has to be a feeling of responsibility. The Department of Justice can't ignore the views of various organized bars or, just pay no attention to them. The Agriculture Department is dependent to a large extent and probably pays too much attention to outside views, but that's what it was intended to do.

Now, the fellow sitting in the White House who doesn't have to face the chairman of the Agriculture Committee, doesn't have to testify time and time again and doesn't have to deal with farmers can come up with a very smart idea of how you are going to do this and get the President committed to it. But it doesn't serve the President's interest. I think there has to be a way of making the government work through departments. Those people ought to be, and I think today they can be, people who are going to be committed politically to the President.

I even feel that way about the Department of Justice, not that you should have politics involved in one sense, but I do think that if the attorney general is not close to the President then why should the President take his advice? If anyone of you here has a lawyer, you have one because you get along with him and because you have some confidence and respect in him. That same relation ought to exist between the President and the attorney general.

QUESTION: Mr. Katzenbach, how did the administration handle the congressmen and the senators whose political power depended on white supremacy? Did they ignore them? Did they write them off? How was it handled?

MR. KATZENBACH: In various ways. For one thing, I think there was a major effort on the part of both Kennedys, and the administration generally, to have a lot of civility as far as relationships with those people were concerned. I think that, with the exception probably of Strom Thurmond who was still claiming to be a Democrat at that time, the relationships were pretty good. Certainly the relationships were good with Jim Eastland and the Judiciary Committee. Bobby's relationship was very good and so was mine. I think Jim Eastland didn't care about civil rights, he cared about money. It was politically useful for him to take the views that he took in the state of Mississippi, but it wasn't because of any deep conviction and passion on his part at all. He had told me, "If I were a young person in the Senate today I would not take the views that I've been taking." He then said, "You know I'm a hundred miles to the left of George Wallace and the University of Alabama."

But I think that really it was civility. You invite them to White House occasions, you deal with them on other matters, probably with more deference than you would to a lot of other senators. Although they were fairly conservative as a group, they were important and would go along and would be helpful. It is always important in relationships with the Congress to remember: no matter how mad you get at somebody today you may need his vote tommorrow.

But Eastland was funny on civil rights. I'd say, "When am I going to get that bill out?" and he'd say, "You know better than to talk to me about the civil rights bill. It will be about a month."

QUESTION: How did you become undersecretary of state? You were my back door neighbor at that point. I never asked you, but I always wondered.

MR. KATZENBACH: I volunteered. I volunteered about six months before it happened.

QUESTION: Because of the position of your predecessor who was clearly phasing out, was that it?

MR. KATZENBACH: No, the President wanted somebody who would replace George Ball and asked me if I had any thoughts about it. I said, "Well, if you're really looking for somebody why don't you offer the job to me, I'll take it," and he said, No, he didn't want to do that. Then a lot of time went by, and the next thing I heard was, "I'm going to appoint you tomorrow." In part, I think Dean Rusk wanted it and George Ball thought it was a good idea.

NARRATOR: One last footnote that our speaker may or may not be willing to share with you. This is a solution to the problem of the vice-president. What should we do with the office? Do you want to try that one out?

MR. KATZENBACH: I can see both pros and cons. I had suggested that the vice-president be made secretary of state.

QUESTION: Wilson did that once. That was a disaster. Presidents don't like to repeat disasters.

MR. KATZENBACH: The difference is that vice-presidents are selected rather differently today than they were back then. Today you haven't got anything for the vice-president to do, and it's very irritating to a vice-president. And yet you select today, I think, a man who you wish the American public to believe would be capable of being President. Then you give him nothing to do. If you made him secretary of state it would solve some problems around the globe.

QUESTION: If I were President I would never do that. You cannot have a secretary of state with any power base in the country at all unless you happen to have a secretary of state who is from Guam.

MR. KATZENBACH: I think that's the problem. The difficulty is that he is hard to remove; you could remove him as secretary of state, but take a political risk in doing it. But if you were Reagan, you wouldn't be very nervous about George Bush as secretary of state.

NARRATOR: We're terribly grateful. We know that this has been a sacrifice in a busy schedule and we certainly look forward to the next time you can visit us.

MR. KATZENBACH: It has been a pleasure to be with you.

CONGRESS, COMMUNICATIONS AND CIVIL RIGHTS

Burke Marshall

NARRATOR: Professor Burke Marshall, the John Thomas Smith Professor of Law at the Yale Law School, served as assistant attorney general from 1961 to 1965. He is a graduate of Yale College and the Yale Law School; he was admitted to the bar in 1951; he became an associate and then a partner of Covington and Burling in Washington, D.C.; he was named to the Kennedy administration at its inception and continued in government for two years after the death of the President. He became senior counsel and ultimately senior vice-president of IBM where he served from 1965 until 1970. He has been a law professor at Yale Law School since 1970. He is the author of the book *Federalism and Civil Rights* and coauthor of the book on the Mylai incident and its coverup. He has been chairman of the board of various bodies including the celebrated Vera Institute on Justice in New York City and chairman of the Center for Community Change Board in Washington. It is a privilege to welcome him to the Miller Center. Following the presentation he has kindly consented to answer your questions. Professor Marshall.

PROFESSOR MARSHALL: Thank you. You have total recall. The Center provided me with a list of ten questions, and reading them I thought that I would touch on them without addressing each one of them specifically. What

I've done is make some notes and the notes are organized by function rather than in terms of these questions. As a backdrop I should note—this affects everybody who talks about the Kennedy presidency—that I was in the Department of Justice and therefore I worked for Robert Kennedy. So the whole view of the Kennedy administration is colored for me by the very special relationship between the President and his attorney general.

The way that I've divided up these functions are by executive action, that is the internal management of the executive branch by President Kennedy, and I include in that, as you will see, relationships with state and local officials, because from my point of view civil rights matters were the main part of that work. And secondly, the relations with Congress and thirdly, President Kennedy's role as a public leader on the issue of civil rights. Fourthly, his particular relationships with the civil rights movement and civil rights leadership during that time. Then I have some personal comments about him as a man as I saw him.

With respect to the first of those, that is the running of the executive branch of the government with relationship to the civil rights matter, I think it is fair to say that the Kennedy presidency started with the notion that civil rights matters would not be dealt with as executive action in the transition period before President Kennedy took office but after his election. The working groups that had to deal with this kind of a problem focused on that: how you would organize the executive branch rather than whatever else the President might do in this area. It was partly for that reason, but not totally for that reason, that Robert Kennedy, I think, was appointed attorney general. The Department of Justice was intended to be and became the focal point of civil rights matters in the Kennedy administration. You will remember, I'm sure, some of you who have paid attention to such things, that Senator Ribicoff, who was very close to President Kennedy in the election campaign, turned down the job as attorney general because he perceived what that part of the government was going to be involved with. Senator Ribicoff didn't want to do that, he said later, because of being Jewish. He didn't want himself to be the focal point for the intensity of feelings and emotions and the political intensity that revolved around civil rights problems.

So it started as a Department of Justice thing and the President was not—at least from my point of view—personally involved in it. The Department of Justice was given a free rein to do what it could do under the law, vigorously. And what we could do under the law vigorously was mainly initiate and press as hard as we could voting rights litigation. That was the job that the Department of Justice was given under the 1957 and 1960 Civil Rights Act. The Department also inevitably became involved, although we could not initiate a school litigation, in school litigation from the point of view of making effective court orders that started the implementation of the Brown decision. The implementation of the Brown decision did not really commence until the beginning of the sixties.

I will refer to the cases; I'll come back to them if anyone has any particular question about it. But the type of cases that I have in mind that were school cases, which we didn't start but which we took over the management of, included the case in Prince Edward County where the schools were closed; the New Orleans school litigation which was the focus of a tense, political struggle in Louisiana; and the two university admission cases at Alabama and Mississippi, both of which involved great difficulties.

So that's a piece, that's sort of a two-year piece you might say, of Kennedy administration business that was not personal to the President but was delegated by the President to his brother in the Department of Justice to be done there with the White House being separated from it.

Now nothing is that neat, and particularly civil rights aren't that neat. So the second thing I want to mention about the running of the executive branch during this period is that the Department of Justice in the front line, and the White House and the President personally, became deeply involved in the control of violence. That started with the first incident. It was, incidentally, the first time I ever met President Kennedy. The need for control of violence occurred during the Freedom Rides that took place in May of 1961. The Freedom Riders were an integrated group that rode buses through the South in order to prove their right to ride buses in an integrated group. And there was an enormously violent reaction to that in the state of Alabama, in Anniston first and Birmingham second and Montgomery third.

The control of the violence that was associated with those buses was enormously important. It was perceived to be important by the United States generally, in the South, and even internationally. And it was important because it did have to do with the movement of people freely among the states, so it wasn't just a local eruption of violence. It was an eruption of violence that interrupted things that were of direct national concern and national responsibility. So the President had to get into that because the federal government can't control violence basically, having no police force, without presidential action. Presidential action involved in that time the sending of marshals to Montgomery—I call them marshals, they were just federal people who were deputized formally as marshals, a lot from the Immigration Naturalization Service—and briefly involved the nationalization of the Alabama National Guard. So that was the first time the President became involved with the control of violence.

The President got personally involved in the control of violence, as I'm sure you all remember, at the University of Mississippi in October of 1962.

He got personally involved in the control of violence in Birmingham in the spring of 1963. Although federal troops were not used at that time, they were moved around in a gesture like sending the fleet to Lebanon or something like that. He got involved in the control of violence on lesser occasions and, although there was no violence in fact, got principally involved in the confrontation with Governor Wallace in Tuscaloosa, Alabama in June of 1963. These are examples of specific control of violence. The general problem which I want to discuss at length was much more difficult.

The general problem was the protection of individual people, especially young people who were participating in the civil rights movement, both blacks and whites. And the problem of protection was that the local and state law enforcement officials in some places wouldn't protect them and in fact were coordinated with violent groups, elements of the Ku Klux Klan that intended to hurt them, even kill them, and did. The question of federal protection of such individuals was a policy question as well as a logistical question of great importance. The position of President Kennedy and the Department of Justice, basically, was that we couldn't do it. It was not the business of the federal government, even though these people in a way were on a federally protected constitutional mission. We had no legitimate constitutional way of mobilizing a national police force and policing the areas in which these people were working.

So there were two things: one was the outbreaks of violence that had to be dealt with by force, including military force. The other was a continuing problem of danger to American citizens, American college students in many cases, who were down promoting voting rights registration, racial integration, and civil rights progress that was highly unpopular in some areas. I'm speaking specifically of parts of southwest Georgia, parts of Alabama, parts of Mississippi, parts of eastern Louisiana mainly, but to some extent some other localities.

There was a presidential decision on that and a presidential policy, and it was highly controversial and well noted by the civil rights workers but it was invisible except from time to time to the rest of the country. It was a decision of constitutional dimensions.

I mentioned dealing with the state and local officials. On all of these matters, on the voting rights litigation, school integration, and on these outbreaks of violence—both sporadic and very public as well as continuous and nonpublic, both kinds—it was the policy of President Kennedy implemented through the Department of Justice by me personally to try to persuade state and local authorities, governors, mayors, police chiefs and sheriffs, to deal with these matters, even if they wouldn't accept the law part of it in terms of racial integration, at least with the problems of order.

I traveled a lot in the southern states myself for that reason at the direction of Attorney General Kennedy. That was a rather specific policy of the President that was most publicly noted, I suppose, at the time of the Freedom Riders when the President sent a representative to try to arrange matters with Governor Patterson of Alabama so that the state of Alabama would take over this problem of violence rather than having it end up in the hands of the federal government.

The third thing, and this is the last thing on executive branch administration, was that there was a certain amount of lawmaking that the President did and that he promised to do. One was on housing—he said in the campaign of 1960 that the proper President, meaning himself, could end racial segregation in federally supported housing at "the stroke of a pen." When he became President people started sending him pens and so he had to do something. Let me speak about the politics of that. It was a matter of internal executive organization but there were political aspects to it. The first time that he considered seriously signing that executive order was in the fall of 1961 about eight months after he had become President. But he didn't do it then. He was getting a lot of flak from Congress and civil rights leaders for that failure. The reason he didn't do it was that in his mind quite clearly it was connected with his desire to form the Department of Housing and Urban Development and his desire to appoint Robert Weaver, who is black, as the secretary of that new department. And of course housing would have come under that department. He believed and his congressional advisers told him that if he signed this housing order that would adversely affect congressional action on both of those matters. So he deferred it. Well, there was adverse congressional reaction on both of those matters anyway since they knew perfectly well what he was doing. And he finally signed the order.

At the time he signed it there was debate over its scope. The debate was technical and he took the conservative and the only lawfully proper view as to its scope; that's a technical matter which I won't go into unless somebody wants me to. In any event, he stuck to the limits of his constitutional legal authority rather than responding to a lot of public pressure, which he could easily have responded to in order to broaden the order.

The other executive action was the President's Committee on Equal Employment Opportunity which had had roots in the Eisenhower administration when Vice-President Nixon was chairman of the committee. In fact it went back to the Truman administration. Vice-President Johnson was the chairman of the President's Committee on Employment Opportunity which had two jurisdictions: one was in the employment of federal people in the federal bureaucracy and the other was in the enforcement of the contract provisions whereby people who had contracts with the federal government were required not to discriminate in their employment practices. Those two matters were under this interdepartmental committee chaired by Lyndon Johnson. There's a lot of detailed history but what I wanted to mention was that it was an example of a mutual difference between the President and the vice-president. The President personally would get impatient sometimes with the activity going on in the vice-president's committee, but he didn't want to tell the vice-president what to do. On the other hand, the vice-president had strong expansionary notions about what that President's committee should do but he didn't want to ask the President for authority to do it.

As far as relations with Congress are concerned, until 1963 President Kennedy's policy was, as I stated, basically not to turn to Congress for civil rights legislation. His congressional relations on civil rights matters accordingly up until 1963, which I'll come to, was basically a defensive relationship. The Republicans, northern Republicans from New York and the Northeast especially, would put in legislation. And then northern Democrats would be required to support it and then everybody would turn to the White House and say, "Mr. President, is this part of your program this year, 1961–1962 and the beginning of 1963?" and he had to say no. Why did he have to say no? He had to say no because he knew perfectly well that what was going on was political posturing and that there was no chance, given the cloture requirement in the Senate at that time and the lack basically of national public support, that any of these bills would pass. So that if he said yes then he would do one of two things: he would either engage himself in the political posturing or he would get himself involved in a terrible fight in the Congress that would consume a whole year of Congress without anything coming out of it. Now I think he was very conscious; he was very aware; he was very intelligent about that problem and that's the way he dealt with it up until 1963. So as I say the relations with Congress on this matter, on civil rights matters, were all defensive against a group of Republicans and Democrats mainly from the Northeast, not confined to the Northeast but mainly from the Northeast.

The President did not—and therefore I did not and the attorney general did not—try to deal with Congress at all with respect to the consequences of the executive action that was being taken by the Department of Justice. There was no attempt to get senators or congressmen to agree that a voting rights case should be brought in the middle of their district or in their state or to agree that schools should be integrated in the middle of their district or in the middle of their state. So there was no conversation about that subject between the President or the attorney general or me with, say, Senator Eastland who was chairman of the Judiciary Committee. It simply was not a subject of conversation. The deliberate policy from the beginning in the White House was a protection of the Department of Justice in doing its work and a protection, in my judgment, to the members of the Senate and members of Congress who would otherwise have been involved. That's not a custom that has been followed since then so much.

Now in 1963 in the spring, President Kennedy—and I was deeply involved in this so I could see that it was happening—came to the conclusion that the country could not continue to do business without facing up to the civil rights problem. That was, in part, a consequence of enormous outbreaks, street outbreaks, protests—justified protests in the mind of the President and my own mind—against racial oppression, racial segregation in many cities, north and south. We counted one hundred and sixty of them in the space of two or three days going on constantly. He concluded over the space of a few weeks, in May to the beginning of June in 1963, that this had to be dealt with, and the only way it could be dealt with was through a comprehensive civil rights bill. So he decided at that time to send one down to Congress which he did in early June of 1963.

From that point on his relations and the administration's relations with Congress were very different because this was not political posturing; this was something that he had committed himself to politically and historically. Despite the advice from the vice-president, from Senator Mansfield, from Bobby Baker who was supposed to be the great vote counter in the Senate at the time, that it could not pass, the President was determined that it would pass. He thought he had no choice but to stake his presidency on it and he sent it down.

Unlike the previous behavior of the administration, at that point there was intensive consultation with members of the Congress. The President met with congressional leaders before and during the time that he sent down this bill although it was all quite rapid. The attorney general and I met personally with every senator, including senators who were going to be dead set against this bill, and every member of the House—not individually—but every member of the House who was not from a state that is simply impossible, every member of the House, for example, from the border states. That was to explain that the President was truly committed to this, to explain what the bill was all about and to answer substantive questions. One obviously could not deal with the politics of it with senators from the south who were politically incapacitated, no matter what they thought, from voting for it or from doing anything except voting against cloture when that came.

The President, from that time until his death, was deeply involved with Congress and made efforts to put together this piece of legislation, deferring things that he thought were enormously important, especially the tax bill. It was finally enacted in 1964.

Most of the lobbying, day-to-day lobbying on behalf of the administration, he delegated not to his own staff, which was Larry O'Brien, but to the Department of Justice. So lobbying was done mainly by the attorney general, by Nick Katzenbach, by me and by members of our staffs. That lobbying was bipartisan. The very first thing that I did personally was go to Ohio to visit with Congressman McCulloch, who was a Republican congressman, and the senior minority member of the House Judiciary Committee, to make sure that he understood the bill and that he, who came from a district without a black voter in it, was ready to support it. Everything that was done by the President and by the Department of Justice on its behalf was of a bipartisan nature.

In September towards the end of the summer, there was a vote by a subcommittee of the House Judiciary Committee that deserted that consensus. It was a vote that was engineered by a combination of northeastern Democrats, northeastern liberal Republicans, and southerners who wanted to defeat the bill. So the next step was to determine whether or not the full Judiciary Committee, despite great political pressure on the Democratic members, would go back to the consensus. The President personally lobbied on that with the members of the Judiciary Committee and with the House Republican leadership—all of whom were invited to the White House on two or three occasions—with the commitment that the administration would stick with the bipartisan bill, despite liberal Democrat opposition to some parts of it, not only through the House and not only through a vote in the House Judiciary Committee, but through a fight on the floor and on through the Senate. So the administration and Lyndon Johnson stuck to this and were committed to what was the bipartisan consensus bill in the House.

The attention during that period was focused on the House because the legislative strategy was to put the bill through the House first. The President also paid a great deal of attention to Senator Dirksen and the Republican members of the Senate. You could count votes. You had to count sixty-seven votes and there were some senators that you knew were among the twenty-three that you couldn't count, so that you had to count some Republicans. You had to count about sixteen Republicans who did not come from constituencies where this was of political importance to them. So that negotiation, especially with Senator Dirksen who was the minority leader in the Senate and very influential, started with President Kennedy personally and continued with President Johnson until the passage of the bill in 1964.

In terms of public leadership, which is of course related to congressional work, the President's public statements, his public position on civil rights until 1963 was, I would say, one of conciliation and understanding. That was his personal attitude, it wasn't just his public position. When he was called upon to speak in news conferences and other occasions on civil rights matters, what he wanted to do was understand the civil rights movement and at the same time understand the trauma that the Brown decision and the implementation of the Brown decision and the whole change in political, social, and economic fabric entailed. It was something that he appreciated. So if you look at his public statements—I think the first one was made at the time of the Freedom Ride, there were some made at the time of a dispute going on in Albany, Georgia, there was a speech he made at the time of the riot at the University of Mississippi—they were all statements that I would classify as being understanding and conciliatory.

When he decided that this problem had to be dealt with nationally by means of a comprehensive bill, he called the matter a moral question. You can look up that speech of June 1963. It was a very eloquent speech, virtually extemporaneous, there was so much going on. I was in the White House, where I watched him give the speech from notes. He called it a moral question, and of course as soon as you do that you make some comment in a way about the opposing sides and morality. So he took sides, and he was committed to taking sides from that point on in asking Congress to pass a comprehensive civil rights bill that covered all aspects of the problem in education, voting, the Title VI bill for federal programs, and so forth.

That was not just a speech, because President Kennedy was an activist and an organizer and not just a preacher. At the time he made that speech, it was immediately followed by a lot of non-public speeches. They were organized mostly by the Department of Justice but not entirely; he had meetings in the White House almost daily for a period of several weeks, certainly two or three a week, of nationally prominent people—regardless of party, regardless of geography—who were businessmen, educators, university people, church people, lawyers, publishers, the leadership of the American society. He had these people, leaders of that sort, in groups. Maybe they would vary from one hundred to three hundred. And he would talk to them and Lyndon Johnson would talk to them, and sometimes, depending on who the group was and how much they disliked him, the attorney general would talk to them. Sometimes he would get other members of the Cabinet who had a special interest. If they were farm leaders, Orville Freeman would talk to them. So there was that speech and then there was a concerted, almost frenetic effort to communicate with the American public through its leadership but not its political leadership, its leadership outside of politics, about the urgency of this problem and the moral dimensions of the problem and especially the national need to have the problem dealt with and gotten over with.

Those speeches, that effort at communication with the American public through its leaders, was followed up actively by other people. The effort was to try to get a commitment out of some members of each group to do something, whatever it was, in the future so that they organized themselves around some action.

The fourth thing I want to mention involves relations with the civil rights leadership. I would say that President Kennedy did not have a close personal relationship with the civil rights leaders. There were six groups basically that were the six civil rights organizations. When the President met with civil rights people, it was usually with all the heads of those six groups. (The students were left out sometimes.) Those meetings were very down-to-earth. The ones that I remember best were at the time of the March on Washington. It was a great national outpouring, a great moment, where the President talked to them about this bill and how they were going to get votes for the bill, who could support the bill, who couldn't support the bill. He was trying to move them from just a speechmaking mood into some mood of political action.

There was one person in the White House—he actually was at the National Democratic Committee but he worked in the White House—who was the most important black adviser, a man named Louis Martin.

NARRATOR: He was one of your predecessors in our Forums.

PROFESSOR MARSHALL: Well, he's been here. He was a person I had an enormous respect for myself and President Kennedy had a great deal of respect, too, for he gave practical, far-seeing advice.

There was a notion about the civil rights leaders—this affected the President's relationship with them—of Communist infiltration of some of the civil rights groups. That was not true. There is a special problem with that allegation. The Southern Christian Leadership Conference was Dr. King's group and as you probably know—it has since become public—the President tried to deal personally with Dr. King so that Dr. King was not subject to that kind of attack. There were really just two people whom Dr. King shouldn't have been involved with.

Now I'll mention briefly my personal relations with the President. I did not know President Kennedy when I went into the government nor did I know Robert Kennedy. I was one of these people who was brought into the government on grounds other than personal or political relationship. So I didn't know President Kennedy at all, at least personally, to talk business with him until the Freedom Rides, which were in May of 1961. That was four months after I came there and a couple of months after the Senate finally confirmed me. I saw a lot of him before his death, especially in 1962 and 1963. My impressions were of a man of extraordinary intelligence, ability to grasp and understand things so that one always felt that one was talking to a mind, communicating with a mind that was listening and responding intellectually with extraordinary detachment about problems that were just awful. From his personal and political point of view, he always seemed to have detachment and a long-range view and that extraordinary composure. I never saw him angry; I never saw him upset no matter what was going on. I remember specifically a whole night that I spent in the White House when these riots were going on at the University of Mississippi. The problem wasn't just the riots at the University of Mississippi; it was the behavior of the military which concerned the President. He talked about it. The military would say our men are here when they were in fact three states away. They're in the air when in fact they were in their bunks in some barracks. And so the behavior of the military was something that, had I been President, would have driven me wild. But he faced that with detachment, with composure and with action. It was shortly before the Cuban missile crisis. During the three weeks between the Oxford riots and the Cuban missile crisis, the military did all sorts of things to shape itself up so that it knew where its troops were and could move them. They had to move a lot of troops during the Cuban missile crisis down to the southeast. It was their experience of being unable to do that kind of thing quickly and accurately and efficiently at Oxford that sparked that reform.

And then finally he had extraordinary ability, I think, to persuade, partly by charm but mostly by just appeal to reason, and reason appealing to other people's reasoning. He thought everybody had reason. So with the civil rights leadership in one hour and with people that were just dead set against the civil rights leadership in the next hour, on both occasions he would appeal to them as reasonable people and exerted, as I say, an enormous ability to persuade on that basis.

NARRATOR: Somebody who visited President Kennedy and asked about a problem came away saying, "I've been in the presence of a mind at work." We're also this morning been in a similar presence and won't soon forget the progression of thought and analysis in what Burke Marshall has told us. Who would like to ask the first question?

QUESTION: I'm fascinated by the picture of you as an Ivy Leaguer and as an Easterner and lawyer going down and riding the circuit, dealing with these red neck sheriffs who had their own constituency. Regardless of what their personal feelings may have been, they had a constituency that they had to appeal to. Could you give us a couple of anecdotes maybe of what you said to these people when you went in to talk to them one on one?

PROFESSOR MARSHALL: Well, "red neck sheriffs," that's a wrong description. I didn't try to do anything with people who were not capable of being reached. For example, in Birmingham, where I spent a lot of time because it was such a difficult city and was inevitably going to be visited with disaster, I wouldn't try to deal with Bull Connor, who was the superintendent of public safety there. But I did see the editor of the newspaper, the publisher, even the mayor (who wouldn't let anyone know that I was seeing him but who was interested in his city and in the future of his city), and the businessmen, who were also interested in the future of their city. No matter what they might have to say publicly in that climate, there were people who wished to avoid disaster by making a little movement. I saw people in public office and people outside public office who influenced people in public office. I didn't try to preach to them by moral exhortation or anything like that. But I could tell them in a way that would be true, and therefore persuasive, the consequences of not acceding in an orderly way to what was inevitable anyway.

QUESTION: Professor Marshall, did you find more latent sympathy with the civil rights movement in the South than you anticipated? Was it there to begin with and just need to be helped?

PROFESSOR MARSHALL: You mean among the whites?

QUESTION: Yes.

PROFESSOR MARSHALL: It was awfully difficult in the early sixties for any white person in a public position to come out and publicly support the civil rights movement. There was this business that there were outsiders. I mean in some places you would get white people, white leaders who would say, "If we didn't have the outsiders then I could have something to work out." But of course you always have the outsiders; the outsiders were the civil rights movement; so that was an unrealistic kind of condition to put. There were some white people of course who ruined their lives by associating themselves with the civil rights movement. There were some lawyers who did that and some people in the clergy who did that. But it was unusual. Now if you are talking about an underlying understanding of it, I think that was quite widespread among the educated people. But the time wasn't right; I mean they didn't think it was right to go public on it in any way.

QUESTION: You must have done a fabulous job, as everybody knows. I had the occasion to fly to Birmingham the day before Martin Luther King's funeral. My wife didn't want me to go but I flew over Washington as it was burning, and in the Atlanta airport there was intense excitement. In Birmingham there wasn't a thing going on. At that time the University of Alabama at Birmingham had the largest number of black students of any major university in the country, so some of those leaders must have responded to you other than Frank Rose.

PROFESSOR MARSHALL: Well, I don't know quite how to respond to that. I don't want to say responded to me but I think they responded to the situation.

QUESTION: Well, you laid the groundwork for it.

PROFESSOR MARSHALL: No, it wasn't just Frank Rose. Frank Rose was publicly isolated but he wasn't really isolated at all. In fact the person who was really isolated was the governor in that situation and the governor behaved accordingly in the end. The way that he conducted himself at Tuscaloosa, I think, was responsive to the fact that most of the people who were important to the governor (important personally and politically) as well as important to the state, were on Frank Rose's side. They wanted to get the thing over with. I mean, why have a war over having two black students in the University of Alabama? It's preposterous. Most people realized that. They thought about it and read about it, but there was a strong political base that they didn't understand.

QUESTION: You talked about this groundwork of talking with leaders outside of political office. I assume that includes a number of business leaders who had enterprises in the South, the so-called "big mules" of Birmingham. What was their response? Was it U.S. Steel? There are a couple of other companies that were down there.

PROFESSOR MARSHALL: Well, in Birmingham specifically, that's what the term was, "the big mules," and they included the steel companies especially. In a way the steel companies were outsiders. I'll just tell you briefly how it went in Birmingham.

Martin Luther King started street demonstrations, and these street demonstrations caught hold, they gained enormous national attention, so that Birmingham was in chaos. When the President sent me down there, it was in chaos and nobody would talk to anybody. There were some businessmen who wouldn't talk to the outsiders, but they would talk to some local black people by which they meant the local lawyers, Arthur Shores and so forth. And so we had a meeting like that, and then we'd have another meeting with Martin Luther King, and then the local businessmen who would meet with Arthur Shores (so there would be a biracial meeting) would go meet with local businessmen who wouldn't meet in a biracial setting. So there was a whole layering of meetings going on.

The way that ended up—they let me in to all those meetings—was with the "big mules." The local businessmen, the store owners who were just being driven out of business by this chaos and wanted it ended, didn't think that they could do what they had to do, which was hire a few people or open their lunch counters, unless they had the support of "the big mules." So there was a meeting with an organization whose name I've forgotten but it wasn't the Chamber of Commerce; it was something at a higher level. I went to that meeting of "big mules." After complaining a lot about the federal government and President Kennedy specifically, they agreed to stand behind the department store owners. The department store owners went back to those members who would deal with the local blacks, and the local blacks went back to the "outsiders." And the process ended up in a compromise. The "big mules" did it for good business reasons; they varied in their personal commitments, I'm sure.

The President did what he was accused of doing then: he personally called, and had members of his Cabinet call, a lot of business people, including Roger Blough, for example, who was chairman of the board of U.S. Steel at the time (the biggest plant in Birmingham was U.S. Steel). They called business people in Alabama who didn't have any personal stake in whether or not black people ate at lunch counters or didn't eat at lunch counters, but who did have a personal stake in the future of Alabama and in the economic viability of their enterprises.

QUESTION: Did he at any time feel that he wished he hadn't made that statement about businessmen being sons of bitches?

PROFESSOR MARSHALL: Probably many times, I'm sure many times. That was in a different context, as you remember.

NARRATOR: We'll have a couple more questions.

QUESTION: Mr. Kennedy once defined a liberal as an idealist without illusions. Mr. Katzenbach pointed out that Johnson had passions about two things: civil rights and education. Did you feel that Kennedy himself had some passion in certain areas where he might feel the moral issue and the human side of the problem? Would you share your thinking about how Kennedy operated on these big major crises that were felt deeply by the masses or by the leadership in some cases?

PROFESSOR MARSHALL: "Passion" is not a noun that you would use to describe his behavior in government. What he felt personally about some matters, I can't tell. He had a deeply religious background, for example, which he had to overcome, disassociate himself from in the campaign, in order to get elected. In everything that I saw of him, the way that he dealt with crises, the way that he dealt with people, "passion" isn't at all the noun that you would use. Detachment, intellect, organizational ability, persuasion—all of those things but not emotion. Now when he argued that this is a moral problem, I think that he believed that. I've heard him express exasperation, but the exasperation was at other people's passion overcoming their sense of reason. For example, he couldn't understand Vietnam soldiers taking off their uniform, and then being refused a hamburger at a local lunch counter. He thought it was irrational, and it exasperated him to have people come into his office and preach to him about it. From his point of view, their passion overcame their intellect.

QUESTION: You alluded to the relationship of Bobby Kennedy to the civil rights movement. As I understand, at its inception President Kennedy delegated the responsibility in civil rights matters to Justice. And the impression one gets, not from your modest remarks, but my recollection of the period, is that Bobby in turn delegated that responsibility to you and that you were the active leader in that front. I'm curious how active was Robert Kennedy, the attorney general?

PROFESSOR MARSHALL: The attorney general? Of course he was a very active fellow. You mean in his personal relationships with leaders of the civil rights movement, is that what you have in mind?

QUESTION: Yes. In support certainly, but otherwise active in himself.

PROFESSOR MARSHALL: Well, it would be unusual, not impossible, but it would be unusual that they would talk to him directly. Most of the routine conversation or argument, it was often argument and not something else, was with me, as in the case of Dr. King, for example, or in the case of the legal actions with Roy Wilkins. But on some matters Kennedy was very active, and when he felt strongly about something he would call up the leaders involved. He got to be more engaged with them as time went on.

At first, because the protest movement was a problem for his brother, he looked at it a little bit as a problem for himself. In the Freedom Rides, for example, he could understand perfectly well, he could understand passionately—passionately is a word you might use for him—how if he were just a private citizen he might be a Freedom Rider himself. But from his point of view as his brother's agent and bearing a responsibility for the success of his brother's presidency on these things, he thought it was one thing to have a Freedom Ride and it was another thing to continue it and to have all these celebrities go down there. So he was angry at the celebrities and he was angry at the civil rights leaders who invited the celebrities. So he would feel differently on different occasions, and when he felt strongly no matter what it was about, he would be apt to pick up a telephone and communicate directly without consulting me or anybody.

QUESTION: It is probably obvious to everyone but me here but I was wondering what there was about your past that made them select you for this job?

PROFESSOR MARSHALL: I have been asked that question before. It is pure accident in a way. I told Mr. Thompson before that I think the common thread connecting people that went into the Department of Justice was Byron White more than anything else. Most of the people that were recruited at my level of assistant attorney general into the Department of Justice were picked by a lot of list making and calling for recommendations by Justice White. I didn't have any civil rights background, but I was a Washington lawyer so that my name came up in that talent search.

QUESTION: Had you had experience in being a conciliator between opposing groups, for example?

PROFESSOR MARSHALL: No, I was just in practice at Covington and Burling. I was mainly an antitrust lawyer. In fact I taught or participated in a seminar at the University of Virginia Law School for two or three years in the late fifties before I took that job in antitrust.

QUESTION: Do you have any comment on Clarence Mitchell who just died?

PROFESSOR MARSHALL: Yes, I saw that.

QUESTION: Did you have some dealings with Mr. Mitchell?

PROFESSOR MARSHALL: Yes, I did. Clarence Mitchell worked for the NAACP, as you know. He was primarily a lobbyist. He dealt especially in the House of Representatives but he had some senators he dealt with all the time—Senator Phil Hart and Senator Clark from Pennsylvania. He was a very good lobbyist; he was very successful. He was sort of a cantankerous fellow.

he was not the policymaker, he wasn't the public leader that Roy Wilkins was. He worked for Roy Wilkins. He was in a way a technician but he was very good at it and he knew everybody. He was a fine man.

NARRATOR: For those who teach, whether in a classroom or in the community or in their own family, I think we've had an example today of pedagogical excellence. We can only hope that there may be a chance to hear Burke Marshall again. Thank you so much.

ORGANIZING CIVIL RIGHTS

Louis Martin

NARRATOR: We are pleased to welcome you to a Forum in a series on the Kennedy presidency and civil rights. Louis Martin is a graduate of the University of Michigan. He's received honorary degrees from such institutions as Harvard, Wesleyan, Atlanta University, and Howard. He has been a university trustee of universities such as DePaul. He was publisher of the *Michigan Chronicle* in Detroit and editor of the *Chicago Defender.* He was vice-president and then president of the *Sengstacke Newspapers* in Chicago. Since 1981 he has been assistant vice-president for communications at Howard University. He's been a director of important financial institutions including Chicago City Bank and Trust, the Riggs National Bank in Washington and the Amalgamated Bank in Chicago.

His political life, which brings him to the subject we want to discuss today, began during his service as a member of the Wayne County Board of Supervisors from 1942 to 1944. He served as deputy chairman of the Democratic National Committee from 1961 to 1969 and as special assistant to President Carter from 1978–1980. In his capacity as deputy chairman of the Democratic National Committee, he was in effect an assistant on minority affairs to both the Kennedy and the Johnson administrations, moving in and out of the White House in that and other capacities.

He has received a number of important awards for his work. About the time our Faulkner House was built, the first black newspaper in the country was founded in the state of New York by Mr. Ruswurm who was a graduate of Bowdoin College. The Ruswurm Award is one of the most distinguished awards in journalism and Louis Martin is a recipient. He has also received equal opportunity awards, honors from various publishing associations, and was president of the National Newspaper Publishers Association. He was a member of the American Society of Newspaper Editors and of other groups concerned with public affairs in Washington.

What makes this discussion especially noteworthy for the Miller Center is that given all that Martin has done and all that he knows about public affairs, one would have thought that he would have been on the front page of every newspaper. However, much of the important work in public affairs is done by people who respond to the task at hand rather than seek public attention. What the Miller Center hopes to do more and more is to identify those who have done the nation's public business, in whatever area and on whatever front, and seek to learn from them and draw on their experience in public affairs. I am especially pleased that we have to speak with us this morning Mr. Martin who knows as much as any living American about the relationship of Presidents and civil rights. It's an honor to have Louis Martin with us.

MR. MARTIN: It's a great honor for me of course and I'm so happy that my wife is here to hear that introduction. I've been trying to impress her for a long time.

But seriously, when I got the invitation and my friend, Nathan Scott, who I knew in Detroit, insisted that I come, I began to think how to approach this, relate some of my experiences and then try to field some questions. I thought of three telephone calls. I got a call in the summer of 1944 from Congressman Bill Dawson of Illinois who was the lone black member of the Congress. I got another call in 1960 from Sargent Shriver's associates to come to a meeting in Washington and that was an interesting eight years. And then I got another call from Ham Jordan. It seems to me there's a program on TV that I'm sure you don't see, the Rockford Files. He's always getting telephone calls from some big operator, and it seems I get these telephone calls.

But I was a little concerned because I didn't know Bill Dawson. I was a publisher of a new newspaper and we'd just got it off the ground. And what I had heard was that Bill Dawson was a ward healer from Chicago and in those years politics in Chicago had an unsavory reputation. As a matter of fact, I was told a joke that if a black didn't vote twice on election day he was an Uncle Tom. So I had some concerns. But Dawson said, I am now vice chairman of the Democratic National Committee and how would you like to handle the advertising and publicity for the 1944 campaign of President Roosevelt and Senator Truman? He asked me to spend three months in DNC headquarters at the Baltimore Hotel in New York. And I was absolutely thrilled but I thought about it and wondered how I could possibly do that. I had no national experience. I had been active in local politics in Detroit, Michigan. He said, "Well, I don't have any national experience either so we'll learn together."

Anyway, I was very thrilled for another reason as four months before the call I had had an opportunity to meet Roosevelt. Blacks rarely were in the daily newspapers in any major city, save for a few criminals here and there. So the black press was a rather important force at that time. We were invited into the White House and we were very disturbed young men and very angry. As a matter of fact, we were anxious to set forth a list of grievances that we wanted the government to redress, and most of them focused on the treatment of blacks in the armed forces. Our newspapers were full of stories of terrible injustices meted out to black servicemen, and we were very upset. And as we walked to the Oval Office I can never forget the picture of Roosevelt sitting in that wheelchair and I was struck with the fact that he was handicapped. But when he stuck out his hand as each of us came up and said to me, "Louis Martin"—you know, just the sound of his voice was something else. He had that New England accent and I'm a southerner from Savannah, Georgia and, like other blacks from down South, when we heard that New England accent we used to think it was a symbol of something very liberal. Anyway, I was thrilled.

But before we could get our list of grievances out he started telling stories. And he said, "You know, in Casablanca when I met Churchill and Stalin we talked about the war and so forth. But on my way back, I stopped in Gambia and I discovered that the British had taken ten dollars out of Gambia for every dollar they invested. And so at the next meeting with Winston (he didn't call him Churchill) I told him: Winston, the first thing I'm going to do after this war is have an international body investigate your colonies, and I cited the situation in Gambia. And I've got the data on you. And Winston turned to me and said, 'Look, the first thing I'm going to do after the war is take that same committee down to Mississippi and find out how you're doing.' " He was an absolutely exciting human being, and to be in his presence was exciting.

So naturally when I got the call from Bill Dawson I accepted his offer and went to New York, and I found out my title for the campaign was assistant publicity director of the Democratic National Committee. And my boss was a young lawyer out of Kentucky whose name was Paul Porter. He was new to the national scene, too. You may remember him because subsequently he founded a major law firm in Washington, Arnold and Porter. Porter was not a newspaper man as I was, but as publicity director he had a number of flacks around and I was among them. It was a fascinating experience and I learned a great deal about national politics. I learned the major characters and there were some great names in American life associated with us in the DNC at the time—oil men like Ed Pauley and Oscar Ewing who had owned the Aluminum Company of America, some real wheels. But the committee was dominated by Truman's men; Bob Hannagen was the chairman. So it was said that we were working for the Truman gang.

Anyway, I think that experience led ultimately to the second call I got in 1960 to work on the campaign of John Kennedy and Lyndon Johnson. I had just returned from a year in Nigeria where I was a part of a nine-man British team sent to work on preindependence communications in Nigeria which was still a colony. Some of my associates were very able people. Among them were those who set up the first TV network in Africa in Ibadan in 1959. I was with the print media working in Lagos for the Amalgamated Publishers Limited headed by S. O. Shonibare. So when I got that call in 1960 I had no idea of the political trends, not only nationally but even in the black community. But I came down to Washington for a meeting. We met in the LaSalle Hotel on Connecticut Avenue, and Sargent Shriver had assembled a lot of nationally known black leaders, not necessarily politicians. In the course of that day-long discussion on how to mobilize the black vote and support for JFK and LBJ, we got down to some practical things—how do you budget this, how do you do that and so forth. It turned out that my experience in 1944 stood me in good stead. And, although I went there thinking I was going to stay for one day, I stayed for eight years.

One of our early problems was that when LBJ was nominated for vice-president, many liberals including some of my associates in the labor field whom I knew well were aghast that this conservative—they called him "reactionary"—was on the ticket. And they thought that JFK for all his liberal notions betrayed them by having a vice-president like LBJ. I had an immediate problem. How were we going to sell this when many blacks shared the sentiments of the liberals? So this was one of our first tasks and I took a simple measure first. Having been in the black press so long, I knew practically all the editors and publishers around the country. So I called them and told them of a meeting LBJ had with a group of black delegates he called together at the Los Angeles convention. Frank Reeves chaired that meeting and LBJ said, "I know what you think about me and I know what they're saying about me. But I'll tell you I'll do more for you in four years than anybody's done in a hundred." I thought we did a fair job of convincing them to give this guy a chance and not to lynch him verbally in the newspapers until we could see what he was like. Anyway, they gave us a pass which was very good news for me because I'm a publicist and that meant that at least my copy would get a fair shake in the newspapers. And that's the way it worked out.

Well, we won the election and of course you are familiar with those stories about JFK's calling Martin Luther King's wife during the campaign to express his outrage over King's imprisonment. One of the interesting things that I think has not been too well reported is that Harris Wofford and some of us agreed that we should protest the jailing of Martin Luther King on a traffic charge shortly before the election by having JFK intervene in some way.

I was asked to go to Bobby Kennedy and tell him about it the day that we learned all this. Everyone was sort of afraid of Bobby but I didn't know him well and therefore wasn't afraid of him. I had to figure how in the world I was going to get him to take some action. So I told him, "You know, Jackie Robinson (who was supporting Nixon) is trying to get Nixon to call a press conference and they're going to blame the jailing of King on Democrats because that judiciary and everybody down there are Democrats and I think you've got to do something about it." He looked at me and asked, "Four months for a traffic violation?" I said, "Wait a minute, don't talk about that. He's black, this is what I'm talking about." I knew right away Bobby was aghast at the sort of sentence King was given but at first he didn't seem to really register the race relations aspect. I wasn't sure when I left whether I had any effect on him at all. But about three o'clock in the morning I got a call from Bobby, waking me up: "I just called that judge (Judge Mitchell) and I told him to get him out of there or I'll take care of him and I gave him hell." "Well," I said, "you are now an honorary brother."

I ran over early in the morning to our office where I got word they were holding a press conference on channel 1. I asked why do they want to hold a press conference? They answered, "Well, they're trying to deny that report on the wire that Bobby called Mitchell." I said, "Well, he did." "No, he didn't," they responded, "They're going to have a press conference and deny it." So I ran over to Channel 1 and caught the press secretary and said, "For God's sake, don't call any press conference. Cancel this thing. Bobby did call him." His reply was, "No, he didn't." I said, "Listen, Bobby called me and told me he called him. We'll be embarrassed." So they cancelled the press conference. That was one of the unusual incidents in the campaign.

Winning the election was, of course, very tight. We won it by one vote at a precinct in Illinois. And having come from Chicago I got extra credit for that fact. But Daley got most of the credit and, of course, Nixon said he stole it but I didn't believe that. Chicago politics had quite an unsavory reputation. Anyway the task, once elected, was to pick the Cabinet and do necessary things to mobilize your forces to govern. And I had assumed, reading a little political science at Ann Arbor, that there was a real difference between governing and campaigning. Well, I found out there's really no difference. You never stop campaigning. However much you govern you've got to campaign year in and year out, day in and day out. It doesn't matter whether your man is in or out, you're still campaigning.

At that time I didn't know that I was really going to stay with the administration. After we won I went back to Chicago and then got another call saying you'd better come on back down here. In fact, Bobby told someone, "That guy told all those lies during the campaign, he'd better come down here and make them come true." Anyway, we started working immediately to figure out how to keep intact that great force and support we had assembled in the campaign. Blacks are rightly skeptical, they are critical; they watch every move. We had made promises about civil rights legislation; we had made promises about black appointments and many other things. And there was that "stroke of the pen" reference. Those of you who are familiar with the housing situation in 1960 probably remember that JFK said that Nixon could have removed all the federal housing discrimination with a stroke of a pen. So I assumed that if JFK was elected he would follow through on this.

At the very beginning JFK said he didn't have any muscle. As a matter of fact I confronted him after an argument with Kenny O'Donnell saying "I've got to save face, we've got to have some action on housing." Kennedy took the position, "I'm not going to just play at this business. We can't get any civil rights legislation through at this point, we don't have any muscle over there and until we get some political muscle I'm not going to engage in just token show business." And there we were.

The only recourse I had at that moment was appointments, with a promise that we would take some positive action on civil rights legislation as we developed more muscle on the Hill. Then I ran into the problem of how do you move on appointments, and the most important job that seemed possible was in the housing field. We had a distinguished black New Yorker, Bob Weaver, who was head of the housing commission in New York and was very well known. He had another great advantage: he was a Harvard graduate. So we got all of the Harvard clique on our side—Arthur Schlesinger included. I had no problem selling Bob, but then I had a problem with some black political leaders who said that Bob isn't really straight on this issue. He isn't as straight as he ought to be. He's an upper-class, elitist type and we've got to have somebody who's really going to do something for blacks. I said listen, we've got to be practical. Bob is qualified and I can get him in. I called a meeting at the Hilton Hotel in D.C. and invited our labor supporters from Detroit and others. I convinced them that we were going to move on civil rights legislation but right now we had to move on appointments and I had a candidate for the housing agency I was sure we could get in.

This was the first appointment of a black to an independent agency of government. (At that time housing was not a Cabinet level department as it is now). And it was a landmark appointment. Earlier, I should have said, I had asked Judge Irvin Mollison, a friend from Chicago who had been appointed to the customs court by President Truman to help me compile a list of "superblacks." So I had about 750 black Ph.D.s in all areas. I didn't even know they gave Ph.D.s in such subjects as agricultural economics. My theory in making the list was that it's difficult to get blacks in, and one of the first things you face is the question, is he qualified? Everyone argued about qualifications, and I had well-qualified blacks on this list. Bob Weaver was among them. But then I had to proceed down the line. Every morning at ten-thirty we met in the White House. Kenny O'Donnell organized it but Dick McGuire presided. I had a White House pass and I was in and out every day, anyway, because we had no civil rights action going on in the White House. We had Harris Wofford who was over there temporarily; Frank Reeves was there for a very short time. Since I was in the political apparatus, they depended on my knowing the mood of the country and getting the best candidates for positions. So we met every morning at ten-thirty and I used that list. Whatever job was available I had a black candidate for it.

You must remember that when we won, Larry O'Brien came in with a little blue book with three thousand or so positions listed in it—three thousand or so spots. And we thought we're going to change this thing completely. Then we found out that at Health Education and Welfare (HEW), which had the largest number of bureaucrats, there were only four spots. Abe Ribicoff, who was picked to head HEW, had only three other people to depend upon. You've got to understand the picture in Washington at that period. You could cut southern accents with a knife in any agency in the government and in those years the bureaucrats controlled everything. Further, despite the argument of separation of powers, practically all of the wheels in the bureaucracies were somehow cousins of somebody over in Congress. I found out that the chairmen of congressional committees that control budgets had so intimidated the heads of the various agencies that the personnel offices would employ Senator So and So's cousin and the same thing on the congressional side. And so we, coming in with a whole lot of idealism and reform concepts, wishing to move America forward, were running up against a brick wall in the bureaucracy itself. As a matter of fact, Ribicoff never got control of HEW, and I remember the day he walked into our office and talked to John Bailey. He said, "I'm quitting this job. I'm so tired of these goddamn social workers."

I had very difficult times with JFK because I had to carry water on both shoulders. I had to assure my constituency that we were going to move forward. And then I had to fight the administration leadership to do something. So it was a terrible position to be in. But we were able to do one thing, to make some major appointments. We broke a lot of new ground. Incidentally all this had to be done without the benefit of the daily newspapers because they didn't carry any black news. They just started that after the civil rights revolution. The line that I used in the releases and in my communications to the black leadership was this—and it was true—that up until JFK, blacks serving in the government, even the blacks in FDR's so-called kitchen cabinet, were simply advisors. They sat at the elbow of a white administrator and whispered in his ear, but under JFK they were decisionmakers. So I said this is what we wanted; we must have black decisionmakers. And I never will forget in one of those patronizing meetings we called in those Democrats who were supposed to find out what jobs were open, and we had Paul Dixon who was a southerner and in the Federal Trade Commission (FTC). When we came into power they switched Paul Dixon to chairman. I was the only black guy in this room and he looked over at me and said, "Incidentally, I'll hire one of your boys, too, if he's qualified." So I remembered him. The reason I bring that up is Leon Higginbotham was recommended highly for the judiciary. JFK had promised to do something about the federal judiciary. There was only one black judge on the Appeals Court in the United States. Bill Hastie was appointed by Truman. But there were no district judges. The district judge actually hears the cases for trial. The appellate court hears the appeals.

One of the campaign issues that JFK had made a great deal of noise about was that there was not a single black district court judge in the United States. He appointed Jim Parsons as the first one in Illinois, so now we had one. But the reason I mention this is that Higginbotham had such a fantastic resumé—Law School and great honors, great scholar and great lawyer. Politically any way you looked at it he was good. I got him down to Washington and introduced him to Bobby, and Bobby said this guy is great for a federal judge. The only problem was that just as we were about to get JFK to send over the nomination papers we discovered he was thirty-four years of age. Federal judges must be thirty-five, so we had a problem. Then I thought of Paul Dixon so I told Bobby what Dixon told me in the patronage meeting, and I suggested we put Higginbotham on the FTC. So he called Dixon and Dixon said okay and that's the way he got the first black member of the Federal Trade Commission. It was a landmark appointment. He remained there until he was thirty-five, and then he became a judge.

But I had another problem because Michel Cieplinski headed what we called an ethnic operation during the campaign. Michel didn't want to be a politician or campaign worker; he wanted a State Department job and there was an opening and Michel got the job. But that left a vacuum. Who is going to handle the foreign-born? John Bailey was chairman of the Democratic National Committee and I was his deputy. One day Bailey announced that if anybody comes in here with a funny name give them to Louis. John Bailey was state chairman but he couldn't have cared less about the national politics. All he really wanted was to be boss of Connecticut. So I inherited the foreign-born. So this was a real problem.

One of my first experiences of riding in a car with JFK was when he addressed Delta Sigma Theta, a black sorority, at their national convention in Washington. I had written a memo for him with all the statistics, the history of the association, how powerful it was, etc. I was over in the Oval Office trying to get it in his hands when the time came for him to leave. So Kenny O'Donnell said for me to get in the limousine, ride over there with him, and tell him what he should do as we rode. I went out the side door of the Rose Garden and jumped in the limousine. The first blunder I made was that I sat on the right side. Kennedy looked out and saw me, and someone ran out and asked if I didn't know that the President sits on the right side in the back of a limousine? I didn't know that was the protocol. So I got over to the other side and JFK finally came out. I had this little concise statement written up beautifully, I thought, in a little folder. When he was seated in the car, I said, Mr. President, here's the statement. He looked at it, then gave it back to me. I thought, My God, after all the work I did on this, he didn't even concentrate on the memo. I was terribly frustrated. When we arrived at the hotel, cameras were flashing and I thought, now if he pulls a boo-boo I'm in this car with him and people will think this black guy screwed the whole thing up. There were wall to wall brothers and sisters when he went up on the dais. He did a magnificent job, but what absolutely floored me, he remembered the dates, all the statistics, he remembered everything—the quickest study I've ever seen in a human being.

I couldn't believe it. On the way back he asked me how I was doing. I told him I was having trouble with the Italians. He said, "Well, what's the problem?" I said, "Bobby is raising hell over there because they're voting Republican. We've got two million Italians in New York. We're getting our brains beat out." He said, "They're no real problem. Let me tell you something. I ran against an Italian and beat him in the Italian district." I said, well, I didn't say it was impossible, I said it was difficult. But he was very proud of the fact that he had breached the ethnic wall in his own campaign and had captured their votes despite the pull of those ethnic ties.

In many respects, it's my view that JFK was the first really "ethnic" President we've ever had. I don't know whether you realize it or not but the first Italian American ever to be a member of the Cabinet was Anthony Celebreze. The first Polish American to ever get in the Cabinet was John Gronouski. It was JFK who made those appointments and I believe JFK was sensitive and understanding of ethnic needs and aspirations because of his own background. He was from Boston and, as you know, the Irish Catholics were looked upon with some scorn by the Brahmin WASPs of that period. And as a matter of fact the first story I heard about the Kennedys was that Ambassador Joseph Kennedy moved his family to New York to get away from WASPs who were socially ostracizing his children. That may not have been true but that was the story we heard.

JFK was very conscious of that and of course there was the campaign fight about JFK being a Catholic. Incidentally, I omitted it earlier, but that was one of my big jobs. Along with others in the campaign organization, my job was publicity. There were some efforts by the Republicans to sow dissension among black preachers about the business of this Roman Catholic candidate building a tunnel from Washington to Rome. Anyway, I was fortunate to have some friends like the Reverend J. H. Jackson who headed the National Baptists U.S.A., Inc. which claimed six million members. He was a very strong supporter. Jackson was very conservative and later he was regarded as a reactionary, but he issued a good statement on this issue which we published in a pamphlet and distributed it nationally, especially to all the black preachers in the United States. Then we had speakers who went out through the Speakers Bureau. One of the most eloquent was the Reverend Marshall Shepherd from Philadelphia. He'd make the rafters ring anywhere. I never will forget. We sent him down to North Carolina where we sponsored a big black church group meeting. The local religious leaders were there and Marshall Shepherd tore the place up. So the Catholic issue did not cut into us too deeply in the campaign.

Coming back to JFK, he was an exciting, sophisticated, charming man and, having worked a little bit in the 1944 campaign and having met FDR, I had a framework for comparison. I often wondered, is JFK smarter than FDR? I do think his reactions were faster and he was a quicker study but I don't think he understood politics the way FDR did. I think FDR was the supreme politician in American history. One of the problems we had with Kennedy was that we couldn't move him on the civil rights legislation until all of the civil rights demonstrations and marches and trouble began. And I never will forget that following Birmingham—some of you are too young to remember—there was great TV coverage of the terrible treatment blacks were receiving in Birmingham.

On June 1, 1963 I got a call from Kenny O'Donnell telling me to come to the Cabinet room at eleven-thirty. I walked in and there were LBJ, JFK,

Bobby, half the Cabinet, representatives of the FBI, and Justice. Bobby told me to sit on his left; he sat on JFK's left. The issue was how to cool the civil rights tension in the South and avoid more violence. This was the first time, sitting in a group like that, the President looked at me and asked: "Louis, what's the mood of the country and what should we do about it?" I had already been communicating the black leadership views with regard to economic help, jobs, etc. But one of the things I said now is that the administration must make some dramatic move to assure black America that it meant business on civil rights. I said the unrest in the South is not confined there. I told them that they were concentrating on Birmingham and what was happening there but they also had to worry about the possibility of riots in Chicago, Detroit, Pittsburgh and New York.

LBJ, who was sitting in his usual place across the Cabinet table from JFK, spoke up and said, "Louis is right." That evening when I went home I told my wife, "Do you know what LBJ said? He said I was right."

Suddenly all of them began to focus in on the problem. They were all frightened by the stories they heard about the black Muslims who were then at the height of their membership at about a hundred thousand. These people said little and because they said nothing nobody could find out what they were doing.

Several of the whites who were authorities on black life tried to figure out the Muslims and couldn't, so they asked me. I said this is a potential problem that is unlimited. I really felt that while the South was on fire, the South was not the sole concern of this government because blacks were angry all over the United States and in the major cities. Of course, I pointed out to them that in many of these major cities the black ghetto was contiguous to the business district. I said now if we have an outbreak nothing is going to be safe. And I saw the wheels turning.

So I mentioned the figure—one billion dollars. I said, we've got to put a billion dollars into jobs and development. I said, you've got to understand that in all these cities we are worried about we've got a tremendous number of young unemployed kids who have no hope for the future. We have got to do something. FDR had WPA and other programs to combat poverty. And whatever the jokes about WPA, it was a constructive program which made a great contribution to the society. I emphasized the importance of these issues, in addition to standing firm on civil rights issues. I must say that all of them agreed that from a moral point of view they had to say the right things in their speeches, but what I was calling for was some positive action. We had agreed earlier on ultimately coming down with a voting rights act. There had been voting rights acts in 1957 and 1960. The concern for voting rights has been a continuous thread in the thinking of civil rights leaders. So I think I didn't have to sell that issue too much. But I *did* try to sell some other programmatic approaches to this problem.

That was the day, I believe, that the administration made up its mind that the time for delay was over: they had to move on civil rights legislation. About a week later I was called to Bobby's office where his advisers were talking about what the provisions of the civil rights bill should be. For some reason someone tried to knock out this business of public accommodations. I went into an absolute rage. Bobby was sitting there looking hard at me and he asked, "What are you talking about?" I said, "Listen. You are worried about unrest. You're worried about civil anarchy, but what is the trigger? One of the triggers is this business of public accommodations. That was the thing in North Carolina when the students sit in whenever blacks are refused service. That immediately causes anger and there is absolutely nothing we can do with a civil rights bill if we don't address it."

Then I made the statement which Harris Wofford has in his book: "I have a daughter and there is an Italian restaurnt not too far from my home. I understand they don't want any black customers. If my daughter is turned down by that guy I'm going to take a gun and shoot him. And as old as I am if I feel that way about it, what do you think about young blacks?" Everybody started shuffling because the tension in the room was tangible.

I have a memorandum from one of the participants in the meeting who said, "That broke it up and there was no question about public accommodations being in that bill." I said I felt it was a self-serving statement but I feel that it was something that really registered.

Anyhow, we began to move in working on the provisions of the Civil Rights Act of 1964 and the cardinal tenet, as far as I was concerned, was this business of public accommodations. Then, of course, you know what happened—before we could get anywhere President Kennedy was assassinated.

After the assassination when I began to think about where to go from there I never forgot what LBJ said at that meeting. I had come to know him much better as vice-president because he called meetings once a month in his office, and I was among those who came from the political apparatus to talk about politics and everything else. I was convinced that LBJ was a master of the Congress, and that had been our problem—JFK had no muscle on the Hill. Despite the great efforts of Larry O'Brien, his legislative assistant, and some of the others on the White House staff, he just didn't feel he had the support on the Hill. And we got those judgeships through only because Bobby would give Eastland a southern reactionary for every black. They had a scheme for working that out.

Anyway, LBJ succeeded to the presidency and immediately the picture changed. For one thing, during JFK's years the White House access was easy.

You'd walk through all those adjoining rooms and right into the Oval Office. Now under LBJ they brought carpenters in and had them build all kinds of little structures and change the entire first floor plan. Even though Kenny O'Donnell was still there, access was not the same. When I had wanted to talk to JFK, I would tell Kenny, "Look, I've got to see him on this issue." Kenny would say, "Well, sit here and when the next guy comes out, put your head in and if he says come in, go on in." So that's the way I used to see him. You never made an appointment. And fortunately when I showed up I usually had something serious to discuss and JFK would say, "Come on in."

But when LBJ took over, the Oval Office became a formal office. He brought in Jack Valenti and he had a different way of operating. But LBJ recognized one thing immediately, that the national mood following the assassination of Kennedy was the moment to strike for legislation including civil rights that had been stalled on the Hill. In fact, he told me once, "You know, we don't have much time." He was aware of the mood of the country and that mood could change. And he moved vigorously on both those pieces of legislation, the Civil Rights Act of 1964 and the Voting Rights Act of 1965, completing what Kennedy had begun in 1963.

There were a lot of funny incidents in my experiences and I was embarrassed on many occasions. First of all, I had to maintain a low profile because the one thing I felt blacks would not stand for was some black sitting in the White House assuming that he had power and telling the President how he should run the country for blacks. One thing I did was make certain that Whitney Young and Roy Wilkins and other black leaders had access to the President or the top aides on any issue. Not only that, I brought them in to meet the speechwriters, from Ted Sorensen on down. In fact, as Vernon Jordan said, I always kept the gate open and I always argued for getting the gate open.

If you remember, in the beginning the White House was upset over the 1963 march on Washington. His aides were telling JFK, "These guys are coming down here and it is going to be a horrible political blunder. They are going to attack the administration, etc. The Washington business community is upset about all the blacks coming and they think they are going to tear up their buildings. It is going to be a horrible thing." We worked for at least four months to turn that thing around. We weren't trying to co-opt the operation but we made it clear that as far as JFK and the administration were concerned we were together on the basic issues for which the march was being called. Bayard Rustin and I met with the chief of police and that's the way I got to know Joe Califano who was over in the Defense Department. Anyway, I got a call to meet with Joe in the West Wing and go over to the police superintendent to talk about the coming march. Rustin was an old friend from my newspaper days. We insisted, among other things, that this be a national demonstration and not solely a black nationalist demonstration. Bayard was certainly on that wave length, and that is why Walter Reuther and several others were participating and helping to organize the march. As a matter of fact, every sign carried by the demonstrators in the 1963 March on Washington was printed by the United Automobile Workers. The truth is that Reuther and a number of those in the labor movement who were sympathetic literally bankrolled a number of civil rights operations. Coretta King is only one of the black leaders who still remembers that because she still gets contributions from labor groups.

I must say out of the Presidents I've known, none of them had any real knowledge of black life *except* Jimmy Carter. When you had JFK, you had two Presidents—JFK and Bobby. They had no real contact with blacks. They didn't know the infrastructure of the black community. In fact that is one of my big arguments with the politicians. Blacks are treated as though they are something foreign. These politicians never go to our black churches; they don't go to black weddings or black funerals. They have no feeling for the life of a black community. To me this is the kind of knowledge you must have when there are thirty million blacks who constitute a large segment of our society.

A large part of the job of anyone in a liaison position is bringing the leadership in to meet the President and other administration figures. The story was that the first black to have dinner in the White House was Booker T. Washington who had a meeting with President Teddy Roosevelt that ran late and he was invited to stay for dinner. The business of social acceptance was a crucial issue among blacks. You might admit that blacks might have some sense; they can learn to read like anybody else. But to have them in your living room and to eat with them, those things were still taboo. So in 1963 we were thinking about how we might strengthen our hold on black Americans. I suggested that we invite all the black leadership to the White House on Lincoln's birthday. I chose Lincoln's birthday because it had been considered a Republican day. Arthur Schlesinger, by the way, voted with me on this in a small meeting we had. Letitia Baldridge, who was social secretary, almost died. It was a fantastic performance event with eight hundred persons present. JFK came downstairs with Jackie and it was a real thrill to see distinguished writers like Langston Hughes, Arnno Bontemps and other black notables there in the East Room.

We broke up this whole concept of social acceptance and now a lot of people say, "Well, that's only symbolism." But there are times, I believe, when symbolism becomes substance and I think this event made a difference in black thinking about whether they are acceptable or not. One of the problems blacks have always had was with the white racist propaganda as well as white racism. My wife and I come from Savannah, Georgia where we were told in everything we could see, feel, or hear that white was right and black was not. So we always had to rise above that. I think the greatest contribution of Martin Luther King was psychological—he removed fear from the hearts of blacks.

These are the kinds of things you have to think about and those of us who are in the political arena have to be sensitive to the moods, views and forces at work. We have another responsibility and that is that all our planning be in the national interest. In everything I have ever worked for I've maintained that it was not just good for blacks, it was good for America. This was the clincher. And that's the way I feel about it.

QUESTION: Mr. Martin, the brilliance of your observations today, it seems to me, are founded in the absolute candor you have demonstrated about your experiences which makes me emboldened to ask a more general question. You mentioned two things, one the mood of the country and then I think you used the term "minority sensitivities." If you put those two things together and mix in with it progress and political responsiveness, is there going to be, on a long-term basis, a political conglomeration based on minority interests? Is it going to solidify groups of blacks? And will there be a counterforce, is there going to be solidification of white perspective on this? Is there going to be choosing up sides that can result from aggressive moves on the political front?

MR. MARTIN: I don't know whether I can respond adequately to your question but I just want to point out one thing that is most encouraging to me. A survey was made by the Joint Center For Political Studies in 1982. They studied ninety-five of the most populous cities with black mayors. Thirty-five of those cities had populations in which over sixty percent were white. Even in the South, fifteen of the southern cities with black mayors had white majorities. In fact, eighteen of those cities had populations that were over eighty percent white. What I see is, and I may be completely wrong on this, a diminution of this business of color emphasis in the long run.

But you take Mayor Goode in Philadelphia. Goode did not want Jessie Jackson there. Goode did not want a racist campaign. Charlotte, North Carolina has a black mayor. You look at Dutch Moreal in New Orleans. You look at Tom Bradley in Los Angeles. I think that black leadership is beginning to see that whites will accept intelligent, even-handed leadership if it is presented in the right way. As long as that's true I think we're on the way to having a different view about race. While it's a fact right now that it is very important and you can't neglect it, look at the Irish and look at the other ethnic groups and their political progress, and we're taking the same route. I think it's taken us a long time to get around to it.

QUESTION: As you indicated earlier, it was a problem with the Italians.

MR. MARTIN: The Italian problem is still very severe. You wouldn't believe it but I had more trouble making an Italian judge than I had making a black judge at that period because the FBI would not provide clearance. The black guys, they would look them over but unless there was some criminal activity they would let them through.

If you think about how Hollywood portrays Italians, it's been all stereotypes—every time you turn around they're gangsters. Italian contributions to this culture and civilization are fantastic. I would be very aggrieved myself as a young Italian at the propaganda against Italians in this country. I think it may be changing slowly; it will take some time but they will beat it.

The Irish were in that same position a long time ago. As a matter of fact it was very instructive to me that Richard Daley and some of the other Irish politicians didn't want Jack Kennedy to run. The first state chairman who came out for JFK was John Bailey of Connecticut. The mayor of Pittsburgh, David Lawrence, and Daley were afraid because this Irish/Catholic prejudice was so strong and they feared a reaction that would affect them. But they didn't count on JFK's supporters. When I first got back to America in 1960 I asked someone what was happening? The answer was, "Well, I'll tell you. A bunch of Irish micks are up there at Hyannisport and they are going to take over the United States." But I think no one feels this way anymore about the Irish Catholics.

It is difficult to project the future but I do think it is very instructive that eighteen of the cities that now have black mayors have populations that are over eighty percent white. That is a very instructive thing to me. It doesn't mean, however, that black nationalism and white racism aren't going to still be with us. We are going to be bothered with all that for a long time.

I think more and more of these young people, particularly the intellectual types who stay in school, will see the national interest and I think that is where ultimately we are going to win out. It is in the national interest to play fair.

Let me tell you something; just take the Defense Department. What are we engaged in today? The greatest concern for power, global power, confronting this colossus Russia. One of the greatest resources we've got is blacks. Because if you look at the people in our military the blacks are there in numbers disproportionate to whites. The same was true of casualties in Vietnam. I don't want to say this as a truism but I do think that a whole lot of middle class white boys don't want to fight. We found in Vietnam that a lot of them went to graduate school and professional school to escape it.

There is something happening in America and I may be too optimistic but I think positive forces are at work. I think the black political movement is going to strengthen the hands of the best elements in those society. From what I've seen of government, I think we have a problem. We do not have the best minds, the research minds, in many areas of government and particularly in the intelligence divisions. It is just absolutely scandalous to me.

Under Jimmy Carter we had a big embassy in Iran full of people and only three of them could read the signs out there. Only three of them knew how to read Arabic. It's crazy that our foreign service is so weak. To tell you the truth it was the same with the Grenada invasion. You mount a billion dollar gigantic invasion and don't have the G2 to know how many Cubans are on the island. Yet there aren't but a hundred thousand people on the whole island. To tell you the truth I don't understand it. Maybe somebody can explain it but we didn't even know there was a hospital over there and we bombed that. That is just unbelievable.

When a corporation decides to issue a new product they have a feasibility study. They send people out, they research it and they know everything about it. The corporate people approach their problems properly. They know what they are doing. They might fail but they've certainly done all of the intelligence work. Now I think that is one area we need to shore up despite the vaunted reputation of the CIA.

QUESTION: Earlier in your talk you used the phrase "hot minute"—for a "hot minute" someone was in the office. Is that right or did I hear you wrong?

MR. MARTIN: I don't want to say that LBJ would quote Chairman Mao, but he said, "Seize the moment" all the time, if that is what you are talking about. Because he said that the mood of the country was at the point where you could get some action out of the Congress and if you notice that was the theme of his speech—continue, continue, carry on for JFK. And so he said we've got to act fast. Now he was talking about civil rights in addition to other things.

You've got to understand the mood of the country. For instance when we got caught in Iran, for the first two months the political stock of Jimmy Carter went up. But the more ineffective it became, the more horrible that thing developed and we had no way out of it, the polls began to reflect frustration, depression, and so forth.

NARRATOR: The only good thing about coming to the end of a session like this is that we recognize there are many other questions that we would like to ask and would like to hear about. Now that Louis and Gertrude have found the Miller Center, we hope very much that they will come back. There is much we have learned today but so many things that we could be taught tomorrow. The best way to close our Forum is to say that we hope there will soon be another session with Louis Martin.

CIVIL RIGHTS IN THE TRENCHES

John Seigenthaler

MR. SEIGENTHALER: I first met the Kennedy brothers as a result of their service on the Senate Select Committee on Labor-Management racketeering, the McClellan Committee. As you know, President—then Senator—Kennedy was a member of that committee. And Robert Kennedy, his brother, was chief counsel of the committee.

My initial reaction to Robert Kennedy was very negative. I thought he was abrasive. I thought he was short-tempered. I thought he was not congenial. He was almost unfriendly to me personally the first time I met him. Had he not been in the position of chief counsel of that committee, I think that after my first encounter with him in New York City in 1956, I would have been just as happy with the idea that I would never see him again.

I found his brother, on the other hand, to be congenial, relaxed, easy, witty and responsive. I really didn't get what I wanted from either of them, initially. My first meeting with Robert Kennedy was at the federal courthouse in Foley Square, New York, where he was investigating racketeering in the garbage industry. My first meeting with then Senator Kennedy—Jack—was in Washington a few weeks later at the Senate Office Building. I came away with a totally different perception. I felt the information that I had developed as a reporter was compelling. And ultimately it became important to the work of the committee. For weeks after my initial contact with Robert Kennedy, I heard nothing from him. Then suddenly one afternoon, I was at my office in Nashville and I received a call from Robert Kennedy. Finally, he had read and digested the material that had been published in The Tennessean. During the period of the next several months after that call, I came to know him better, then quite well, then quite intimately. I came to think highly of him. I always had admired his brother. By the time the Kennedy administration came to power I was much much closer to Robert Kennedy than I was to the senator who was to become President. They had different personalities. They shared many values. In different ways they had the appeal to attract the loyality and respect of people like me.

I developed a continuing, close relationship with Robert Kennedy. Even after I returned to journalism we had almost routine weekly conversations, wherever we were. If we were able to talk to each other, we did. We came to be close friends and I enjoyed the relationship. I think that he also enjoyed it. I suppose that once you are in the pressure cooker of the public life it is difficult to break away and tear your focus of attention from the demands of public office and the demands of constituencies and deal with people on a very personal level. It is difficult to have friends with such pressures on your time and on your resources. We managed to do that and I look back on that initial abrasive meeting with a good deal of humor. I told him about it very early on and he repeated it, to my embarrassment, in public many times thereafter. It amounted to his needs to set priorities. At the time of our first encounter he had other priorities. When I tried to interfere with them, he refused to let me do it.

Back in 1957 that committee literally reached out and grabbed the attention of the entire country. There were almost daily televised hearings that focused on the work of the committee. Senator John McClellan, the Arkansas Democrat, John Kennedy, and Robert Kennedy were constantly in the spotlight of public attention. The hearings resulted, some of you will remember, in the downfall of Dave Beck and his replacement by Jimmy Hoffa. The television encounters between Hoffa and Robert Kennedy were, during the period of 1957, watched by a percentage of audiences that I suppose watch today's soap operas. It was high drama.

Then in 1958 when I was a Nieman Fellow at Harvard, President Kennedy was running for reelection in the United States Senate and that campaign was preparatory to his presidential campaign. He had decided in his own mind, as had his father Joseph Kennedy, and brother Robert, that he would indeed make an effort to become the Democrat nominee in 1960. The campaign was relatively easy. His 1958 opponent was an unknown, an Italo-American. The Republicans had put him up simply because they did not want to give Kennedy a free ride in Massachusetts that year. They felt an unknown who got a respectable vote would shake him. Kennedy treated it as if it were a life-or-death political struggle and campaigned constantly. My own schedule at Harvard in 1958 was such that it was possible to spend a good deal of time around that campaign observing its structure. I was particularly interested in Jack Kennedy's relationship with the press but also with Irish politicians whose reputation for corruption was widely known. It was interesting to see a son of wealth and affluence relate to politicians who even then represented a cross-section of the ethnic makeup of this country in a unique way.

He was running against, as I said, an Italo-American but his appeal with Italian-Americans was enormous. It was recognized in Massachusetts that year that this campaign was really to be a springboard for him to a national campaign. That knowledge had a magnetic effect on my own personality. I found myself, not unwillingly, being drawn closer and closer to the man who was to become President and to his brother who managed that 1958 campaign, The gave me access to them and I enjoyed watching them work together. Already, Robert Kennedy demonstrated a willingness to become his lightning rod.

The following year his brother Robert asked me, after I finished the year at Harvard, to work with him on a book he was preparing to write. It was a book that ultimately came to be known as *The Enemy Within* which analyzed the work of the McClellan Committee. It went to the top of the *New York Times* best seller list in early 1960 and stayed there for a couple of months.

I extended my leave of absence from the paper after Harvard to work on the book. Then, I went back to Tennessee and worked as a reporter covering politics during 1959 and early 1960. I covered some of the Humphrey/Kennedy primaries in Wisconsin and West Virginia. I had been an old admirer of Hubert Humphrey. I felt that he was a dynamic figure. He was a friend of Estes Kefauver whom I knew well. None of us really thought Hubert Humphrey was going to be President. I think many people saw him as a surrogate for Lyndon Johnson in 1960. I went to the Los Angeles convention and on the first day I was at the convention Robert Kennedy asked me if I would give up journalism for the rest of that campaign. He knew that first day that it would be a first ballot victory in Jack. I had only been back in journalism for about a year. I thought it would be a great, novel experience. So after the convention, I went to work as his administrative assistant in the national campaign. Initially, I told him I wanted to think about his offer at the convention. After the convention, I agreed to become his campaign administrative assistant. I did so with the full intention of going back to journalism after the November 1960 election.

The problem was that during the course of that election he found himself creating political bonds with all sorts of people all across the country—bonds that had to be severed once he agreed to become attorney general. He needed somebody to help him gently cut those bonds. He then asked me if I would take on that responsibility for another six months in 1961 and I agreed. That six months became fifteen months. And it was April of 1962 before I went back to journalism where I have happily remained since. That is not to say for a moment that I did not love every hour of every day that I was in government. I certainly did.

Being involved in what was then called the New Frontier was an exciting experience. It was an experience that was important to those of us who were identified as part of the New Frontier. We thought that we were dedicated to changing dramatically the course of human history. I think those who join every administration feel that way in its early days. The fact was that the need was not as pressing as we had convinced ourselves it was. The dawning knowledge of that didn't alter our enthusiasm at all. The fact that the bureaucracy works and is working, and the bureaucracy is not shaken tremendously by the dynamism or the personality or the charisma of a new President or attorney general, didn't dawn on us until we had been there for awhile and had an opportunity to evaluate who these people were who had been running the government a long time before we got there. We did not accept at face value their competence.

Looking back on it, one of the great values to me and to many of us was that we came to understand that—to borrow David Halberstam's title—the best and the brightest are attracted to government. There is within many of the important divisions of the federal government a sort of ongoing establishment that seems to transcend partisan administrations and keeps the country and the workings of the government on a relatively even keel. People, for example, who were part of the Civil Rights Division in the Justice Department before we arrived stayed on after we left. Many of them were there long after I had gone. The work of that department which had been important in the Eisenhower years took on more importance largely as a result of the pressures of the civil rights movement created by the leadership of Dr. Martin Luther King, Jr. and continued on into the Justice Department of Lyndon Johnson and beyond to the administration of Richard Nixon. Because of the commitment of the bureaucracy, the thrust of it is difficult to blunt *even* when an attorney general with a different ideology may seek to do so—as I think John Mitchell sought to do in the early Nixon years.

With that background, let me talk just for a few minutes on the Kennedy's and civil rights. It seems to me that in the 1960 campaign it was obvious to us that civil rights was going to be an important area for the incoming administration. But none of us envisioned that it was not an area that would be impossible or difficult to manage. Sure, we expected crises. Certainly, we anticipated that court decisions would evolve that might force the Justice Department into confrontations not unlike Little Rock which had been terribly difficult for the Eisenhower administration.

I don't think we fully appreciated, however, what was going on inside black America, or Negro America as it was then called. The power of Martin Luther King's personality was recognized, but the depth of its pull was certainly not appreciated by any of us. In 1960 we had, within that Kennedy campaign, a Civil Rights Division. I worked closely with those who were involved in it. Sargeant Shriver was the person who picked black and white leaders and put them together in the formation of that campaign division. The members of that group included people like Louis Martin, Harris Wolford, Frank Reeves (a black lawyer in Washington), and a half dozen other black leaders from across the country, most of them involved in local groups of the NAACP. They came in from time to time and worked with the core group in Washington. Basically, the conversation of that group involved organization and registration and getting out the vote and how much money it would take in a given organization to produce the vote. It went along like that until the moment when Martin Luther King found himself incarcerated in jail in Alabama and the pressure began to build on the political establishment to respond to the unjust incarceration of Dr. King.

Well, the story you all know. President Kennedy, at the urging of Harris Wolford and Sargeant Shriver, ultimately acted. "Ultimately" is the accurate word. It was not an easy thing to get done. The President was busy. He was campaigning. One telephone call hardly seemed worth pulling him off the campaign trail. There was a fear inside the campaign that a call would cost him the entire society. At any rate, he made the call to Coretta King. It made news. It demonstrated concern. A few days later Robert Kennedy did what was unheard of: he called the judge who had incarcerated King and gave him a verbal blistering which made more news and created more controversy.

Suddenly, civil rights was a crucial part of that 1960 campaign and we were flooded in the campaign headquarters with calls from governors and state party leaders from all across the South. Write off South Carolina, said Fritz Hollings. Write off Florida, said George Smathers. An anecdote: Mississippi was not written off. As a matter of fact, I remember well that Sen. John Stinnett was asked if he would endorse Senator Kennedy on statewide television and he agreed to do it. We had a chance in Mississippi. There were a series of television commercials that had been prepared during the course of the campaign. Politics was not that different in some ways from this year. But there were differences. For example, back then both sides thought it was possible to have regional television tapes. In other words there was a theory that you could have a tape that was prepared for dissemination in New York and it wouldn't get telecast to Mississippi. And, there was one tape in which Harry Belafonte endorsed Senator Kennedy during a walk through Harlem. It is hard to appreciate why Harry Belafonte's endorsement was damaging anywhere—but it was in the deep South. It was a one-minute tape. There was limited distribution for a relatively few political leaders, one of whom was Gov. G. Mennen Williams—Soapie Williams—of Michigan. When Governor John Bell Williams of Mississippi called the office where these tapes were kept in reserve, he asked for a copy of the tape. He said simply that Governor Williams was calling. He was told that he could get a copy for $6.95 and the cash came over via his secretary. So John Bell Williams, the governor of Mississippi, took home that tape. That one-minute tape played immediately precedent to and immediately after the endorsement by Senator Stennis of Mississippi and we lost Mississippi by five thousand votes—Sen. Stennis would say today as a result of the Harry Belafonte tape.

But in that campaign I think from the time of the telephone call to Coretta King on there was great interest in the area of civil rights. What came afterward was not much of a surprise because from that point on, while we anticipated that most confrontations would evolve through court suits, it was obvious that Martin Luther King was going to continue to press in every way he could, and in unconventional ways. That is to say, to press outside the courts and the legal framework, to dramatize the plight of blacks, particularly in the South.

Let me move to the administration. The first meeting between the attorney general and Martin Luther King and King's subsequent meeting the same day with President Kennedy is interesting because King talked with the President very briefly and not substantively. It was a "get acquainted" meeting in which each was courteous with the other.

The meeting earlier in the day with Robert Kennedy went almost immediately to the heart of what was to be thereafter an unspoken disagreement between them. Robert Kennedy urged Martin Luther King to take on as part of his movement the registration of voters in southern states. He pointed out to him that there were many states in the South where registration of blacks was not prohibited by state or local law and was allowed by custom. He said that blacks in those areas were under-registered simply because there had not been a very active campaign waged to get them to register. He had gleaned that fact during the course of the campaign, as a result of the work of Harris Wolford and Sargeant Shriver and Louis Martin and others. And he urged King to take that on. He said during that conversation, "Jim Eastland won't be so fresh if half the people registered to vote in Mississippi are Negroes."

King said, "I think registration is the job of a political organization and I urge you to do with the Democratic National Committee exactly what you are urging me to do. I have another agenda; the Southern Christian Leadership Conference has another agenda and we will be calling on you from time to time for help because what we will be doing to pursue our agenda may create dangers."

That difference of approach was the first indication Robert Kennedy had, or the President had—and Bob told Jack of that conversation the next day when they compared notes—that the movement was going to become more aggressive, more assertive, more challenging, more demanding, and that the federal government would need to provide an umbrella of protection as best it could for the movement. And sometimes that was very difficult to do.

President Kennedy picked, upon Robert Kennedy's recommendation, a man named Burke Marshall to head the Civil Rights Division. Burke Marshall was an anti-trust lawyer with Covington and Burling. I strongly favored Harris Wolford for that job. He had a record in the field. Burke Marshall did not. Wolford was an advocate. I thought he would be a doer. I thought Burke Marshall was sort of a mousey little fellow who had a squeaky voice and I really didn't think there would be much leadership. I was wrong, of course. He had a constitution of iron. He was an innovative and creative lawyer and he found ways to make the Justice Department's presence felt in a variety of areas. As a result of his work, everyone came to feel that the Civil Rights Division of the Justice Department was its most creative and innovative arm.

The civil rights movement established links in the Justice Department with a number of people who were interested in and concerned about denial of civil rights in the South. Burke Marshall was the point man for that. But I think others, John Doar for one, Louis Oberdorfer, the head of the Civil Division, for another, me for another, Berl Bernhardt who was director of the Civil Rights commission was still another—many of us found ourselves being called upon constantly, I mean weekly and sometimes daily as the demonstrations gained momentum. We found ourselves being called constantly by those involved in the movement and asked for advice and support. Sometimes at night calls would come from people who were seeking to desegregate public facilities in places like Macombe, Mississippi. They would be in trouble, under threat, sometimes under attack. They often sought protection from federal authorities.

The Klan was very well organized throughout the South in those days, and was violent. The Justice Department's law enforcement was viewed in those days as limited. There were strict jurisdictional lines that limited federal authorities. In addition, the FBI had a tradition of dealing with local law enforcement officers and letting them enforce the local law. The local police helped FBI agents with federal crimes, auto theft and bank robbery. Because the Klan had infiltrated many law enforcement agencies in the South, it was a perilous situation. It was frustrating to be on the receiving end of those phone calls which would come to your home at night and know that human life might be in the balance. You call, then, to the FBI asking for help for a civil rights activist might not be passed on, or if it was, it probably would be passed on to a local law enforcement officer who didn't care or was hostile to the idea of providing help to blacks who were considered to be outside agitators, because many of the people who joined King came from outside the South.

My own involvement really related to the work of Burke Marshall and the Civil Rights Division. I was the attorney general administrative assistant and may desk was located just outside his door. I constantly found myself being called upon to work as a liaison with the Civil Rights Division, to travel from time to time with Burke Marshall to different parts of the South to try to help resolve potential problems before they developed. As we were moving in one direction, there was a constant feeling that the FBI was reluctant to move. A great part of that had to do directly with that traditional relationship with local law enforcement officers. Mr. Hoover did not view his mandate as including his ability to take over local law enforcement and he resisted that. His view was that local laws called for segregation and local police enforced those laws.

An anecdote: the attorney general, after he had been with the Justice Department about six weeks, began to roam the halls one day a week to meet lawyers in the bureaucracy. He and I would travel, division to division, and visit Bill Orrick in the Tax Division and Louis Oberdorfer in the Civil Division and Ramsey Clarke in the Lands Division and Burke Marshall in the Civil Rights Division.

One day after we visited the Civil Rights Division, Bob Kennedy said: "Do you realize that we've seen our first Negro lawyer today? We've been visiting these offices now for weeks. Will you conduct a study and see how many Negro attornies there are among the twelve hundred lawyers in the Justice Department?" And so I started the survey and there were three among twelve hundred. One of them had been employed since we came in and the other two had been there under the Eisenhower administration, both in the Civil Rights Division.

Orrick and Oberdorfer now are federal district judges—Orrick in San Francisco and Oberdorfer in the District of Columbia. Ramsey Clark served as attorney general in the Johnson administration.

There was a problem. Mr. Hoover did not respond to the survey and I was called upon to enter into dialogue to get him to respond. It was difficult. I would send a memo and I would get a memo back: We do not, in accordance with the federal law, log the race of employees in the FBI. To do so might be construed as encouraging discrimination. So I would write a memo asking if it would be possible to conduct a head count? Well, he would answer, we have so many people on the road, we are a very mobile organization and it is very difficult to get all FBI staff together for a head count. But I perservered. I insisted.

Finally, when it came in that the number was three blacks—total—in every other discussion of the Justice Department, he responded with a memorandum saying that there were two black FBI agents. I then wrote back and asked him to identify them because the memo had not said who they were. And we went through another period of memo juggling about that. Halfway through I went to see a man named Sal Andretta who was department administrator for the bureaucracy—which meant he ran the business of the Justice Department—and I said, "Sal, could you help me? I'm not having much luck." He said, "Yes, I can help you. I know who they are. They drive for Mr. Hoover and they have rank because they've been faithful employees and he's given them the rank of agents. But they are his drivers. They serve as his bodyguards as well."

But the statement that Mr. Hoover was reluctant to get into that civil rights field is accurate. A great deal of the television docu-dramas that have been written are revisionist and they make J. Edgar Hoover appear to be a malevolent, evil figure that, I think, is totally out of character and grossly unfair to him. It is fair and accurate to state, though, that he was reluctant to get into this area and, beyond that, he sought to make us believe tht the civil rights movement was really an extension of the Communist party in the United States. He went so far as to falsely identify a man named Stanley Levinson, who was a financial and moral supporter of Dr. King, as a Communist. And later, after I left the Justice Department, there were memoranda that identified Levinson as a KGB agent. All that was false. All that was created out of whole cloth.

Beyond that the whole effort by the FBI to start the cointelpro movement, which was calculated and designed by some officials of the FBI to undermine the civil rights movement. That was something that Hoover, if he was not the architect of it, certainly did put his imprimatur on it. And so from the outset there was a great split inside the administration of Justice over civil rights.

On the one hand there was a President who was a politician, whose brother was in charge of the Justice Department, who wanted the very best for his brother, the President, and understood—as politicians would—that this was a very volatile area of public life and also understood that practice and history *and* the local law imposed limits insofar as the federal government was allowed to act. And on the other side, the law enforcement wing of the administration—

the FBI—was lethargic, and at times hostile to the idea that it should respond to need.

Most often we found ourselves nudging and pushing the bureau to move them. And usually there was a feeling that Mr. Hoover was not easy to push. Finally, the attorney general pushed very hard indeed.

My most direct involvement came during the Freedom Rides. That's when James Farmer of CORE initiated a demonstration to demonstrate CORE's competitiveness with the Southern Christian Leadership Conference. The idea was to put together a group of people, an interracial group, who would travel from Maryland to Mississippi by bus, riding in front of the bus which, as many of you know, was against not only national tradition but southern Jim Crow law. The notice of that ride came in a press release which was sent to the Justice Department. Reflecting on it afterward, the only other notice we could find was a visit by a black reporter from *Jet* and *Ebony* who was going along to accompany them and he met briefly with the attorney general on the day before he left. We asked him to let us know if there were problems along the way. And there were occasional problems. They were arrested or removed from restrooms and restaurants, in a couple of bus stations along the way, but there was no serious incident until Anniston, Alabama where the Klan met the bus, bombed it, burned it, and beat the Freedom Riders.

The President was getting ready for a meeting with Charles De Gaulle. He had heard from Harris Wolford very early on that there had been a confrontation in Georgia. He had asked Harris Wolford if it would be possible to end the ride. Wolford told him that he was in contact with the riders and he thought not.

The first time we heard in the Justice Department directly about the serious trouble was when this black reporter, Simon Booker, called from Anniston and asked for help. They were being moved from Anniston to Birmingham. They were taken to Birmingham, hospitalized overnight, and then put in the airport terminal. But each time a plane landed to take them out, there was a bomb threat. That had gone on for about eighteen hours when I was sent down. The President and the attorney general talked and decided they needed to send somebody who could get them out of there and get them to Mississippi. And I was asked to take that on. I convinced them they should fly to New Orleans on the first plane. They agreed. They were badly moved and were frightened by them.

I went down and worked out with the airlines details of how to get them out. The strategy worked. We got them to Louisiana by air.

An anecdote: One of the great ironies came in New Orleans. There was almost as large a mob waiting for them when they got off the plane in New Orleans, as there had been in Birmingham when we got them out of there.

But, at any rate, one friendly face in New Orleans was Sen. Barry Goldwater who suddenly burst out of the crowd, welcomed us with open arms, and was very congratulatory and very laudatory to me personally for going in and getting them out. It was very nice to have a Republican senator for the opposition say such nice things and we felt we were lucky to have such a man there on the scene. It made our arrival in New Orleans a little easier. When Goldwater later opposed the civil rights legislation, I remembered and reflected on his presence at the airport.

About two o'clock the next morning the attorney general called me and said another wave of Freedom Riders had started now from Tennessee headed for Birmingham and would I go back to help them through. I did and when I got back to Birmingham they had been jailed by Bull Conner, the police commissioner. For three tough days of negotiations I worked to get them out of jail. Bull Conner, as police commissioner, was difficult if not impossible to deal with. Gov. John Patterson was making terrible statements about outside agitators and would not meet with me for those three days. Finally he did. I negotiated safe conduct and the bus went from Birmingham to Montgomery where the Klan, with the cooperation of the local police (while the FBI looked on and took pictures) assaulted those people who were on the bus, including the administration's representative. That was me. I spent some time in the hospital as a result of that and stayed in the hospital until Martin Luther King came in a week later to preach in a church. The same commercial flight number 736 that brought him in took me back to Washington.

That incident marked the first time that the administration was forced into positive action. After the assault on me the decision was made by the President to send in U.S. Marshalls. By nightfall the hospital where I was being kept, or I can almost say was being held, was surrounded by marshalls and by state troopers who were very unhappy at being there. There was a great deal of abuse aimed at the marshalls from, among others, the local police.

That confrontation succeeded in getting the state of Alabama to recognize its obligation to protect citizens with interstate commerce without regard to race. It was said at the time that I was the crutch on which the marshalls walked into Alabama. It was an unpleasant role. The President's representative was laid out flat in the street of Montgomery with an iron pipe and left for a half-hour without help. All ambulances were elsewhere on "emergency call". And all local police were elsewhere on "emergency call". That was enough of an incident to make the marshalls welcome to most who were antagonistic to racists. And so it was assumed, from that point on, that the marshalls would be the answer when a state refused to protect citizens and crisis developed.

Of course, when James Meredith went to Mississippi two years later I was, by that time, out of the administration and back in Tennessee. But the effort to use marshalls then failed. After retired General Walker heated up the crowd there, and the marshalls were fired on, the result was that federal troops had to be called in. The great confrontation that took place there later when Gov. Wallace stood in the schoolhouse door made it clear that the law enforcement establishment and myself were not going to be adequate in the Kennedy administration to break down barriers of segregation and indeed that military force would have to be threatened and used if change was actually going to take place.

I would like to say just about three or four sentences about the attitude of the Kennedy brothers, a changing attitude, in this area. It has been said, and I think accurately, that they understood the problem but did not understand the depth of it. They looked upon it as a political problem that could be dealt with politically. Throughout the 1960 presidential campaign they looked at it that way—as a political problem. Throughout the early days of the administration they looked at it that way. It was a political answer to say that the problems could be solved in the courts. It couldn't. The action was in the streets, not in the courts. From the outset, they had anticipated that the challenge would come through court suits. They felt that if that was the case, they could avoid the trap that the Eisenhower administration had been drawn into when there was the confrontation at Central High School at Little Rock. They were confident that somehow they would be able to use the influence of the government with politicians and business leaders, labor leaders, and educators—leaders in all institutions in southern society—to bring about peaceful change. The courts would play a part. They did not want to fall back on the Eisenhower solution—federal troops. They never allowed themselves to think that they wouldn't be able to bring change peacefully. Nor did they understand, as I said earlier, the potency of the movement that was building inside black America. They didn't understand the full power of Dr. King and those who followed him. And because they underestimated that and because they had the natural instinct to deal with a problem politically when it became a crisis, it was impossible to avoid the hostility that ultimately developed. Once it was clear that the administration simply could not wait for events, then the administration's approach was much more reasonable. It was more direct.

For example, in early 1962 Burke Marshall evaluated every school district in the United States that would have desegregation during the course of that year. He and I and others, in teams, visited city after city to negotiate months in advance a peaceful resolution of the problem. Indeed, desegregation that following September 1962 was almost without violent incident. There were occasional outbreaks but nothing serious.

It is fair to say, I think, that both the President and the attorney general in the face of crisis responded to it in Montgomery and in Oxford. I think they they responded well—better after that first confrontation in Montgomery when it was clear that local law enforcement authorities would not uphold the law. From that point on it was just a question of where the next crisis was going to develop and how to best handle it.

Some of what has been written and much of what has been said in the docu-dramas since then I think inaccurately characterize the response of the administration. Some of what has been written and much of what is part of those docu-dramas indicates that there was almost a hostility on the part of the President and the attorney general toward the movement. I never felt that. I never heard that. I never sensed that. On the contrary, I had the impression that there was great sympathy for it. Sure, it was a problem. All of us would have preferred not to have to deal with it, but it was a reality and it dawned on us that it was a reality that had to be faced. As the movement's momentum grew, the administration became more and more activist.

On the political side, it was very mean and ugly and at times almost vulgar. Some political jokes and slogans that developed across the South are not heard today and not read in anything that is written and the depth of hostility for the administration somehow has been missed as a result of what I call revisionist history. I think both of them grew intellectually and emotionally as crises evolved. The conviction was there from the outset but the commitment grew as the challenge grew.

NARRATOR: Two people I know have tight schedules. Ambassador Battle is fitting this meeting in between two other meetings so he ought to have the chance for the first question.

We are pleased to have Louis Costello, candidate for the Democratic party in the ninth congressional district, with us and he has a tight schedule.

We are glad to have one of our standbys who has been gone for a year, the deputy chairman of the English Department, Austin Quigley with us and he ought to have stored up questions for about a year. So he ought to have a right to ask a few.

QUESTION: I just noticed the other morning in your newspaper that Jessie Helms has gotten the right to have access to the FBI tapes on the wiretapping of Martin Luther King and I'm sure he will use it in his present campaign. What is this going to reveal?

MR. SEIGENTHALER: From everything I know about it, it is an unintelligible series of conversations at the Woodward Hotel in Washington in which

King and some of his associates are talking about a number of things, including women. I think no more. That is heavy on my part. I based that largely on the effort that was made by some people in the FBI a good while back to get those tapes out. At the time, Hoover made the statement about King being the most notorious liar in America. To reinforce that, some agents of the bureau then floated around with the media and tried to peddle those tapes. I don't think they are going to show very much beyond that. You might hear some profanity, a good deal of laughter. I haven't heard them but people who have heard them say that that is about the extent of it. It is my understanding that a copy of them was sent to Coretta King about that time as part of the Cointelpro Project and either she dismissed them or couldn't understand what was being said.

AMBASSADOR BATTLE: I remember when we were in Australia the Communist party down there was aboveboard. It wasn't pushed underground. They had newspapers. In one of the news issues was an article with appreciation to Martin Luther King for a financial contribution that he had made to the newspaper. Well, just out of meanness I clipped that out and sent it to Bobby Kennedy. I got back a very interesting and very nice letter from Burke Marshall which led me to believe that maybe there had been some disaffection between the attorney general and King because it said in effect there is a hell of a lot wrong with King and we know a lot about him but we don't think he's Communist and then he thanked me for this and asked me to keep him posted.

MR. SEIGENTHALER: About a week before that first meeting Hoover sent memoranda to the attorney general of which Burke and I both received copies. And that memorandum said there were two people who would be in King's party who were Communist. One was somebody named Odell—and this has all been written—and the other was Stanley Levinson. When I left the department, we were still getting memos about Levinson and his relationship with King and after I left, he began to identify Levinson as a KGB agent. I think that without question was false. But I left the Department of Justice believing that Stanley Levinson was a Communist. I believed it at the time I left the Department of Justice and I think Burke probably believed it too.

QUESTION: He obviously didn't believe that King was.

MR. SEIGENTHALER: Absolutely not. I was given the assignment to bring the subject up with King long before the wiretaps. This would have been about the time of the first meeting. I was asked to tell him that there was information that some of the people close to him were members of the Communist party. I was speaking directly about the memoranda on Levinson. Incidently, before Levinson died I wrote him a letter. I said, "there is no way for you to ever know that I ever said or thought this about you, but I feel that I owe you an apology." I'm glad I wrote that letter just looking back on it. There was a campaign to brand him as a member of the Communist party. I can't remember all of the evidence, but it seems to me that it went so far as to maybe have a number or a card or a card number, but at any rate it was pretty persuasive. I said to King, standing on the sidewalk outside the Justice Department, that just as a confidential matter I wanted to alert him to the fact that there were some people who felt that there was a strong effort to infiltrate his movement with Communists and that I felt, just as one person, knowing the South, that that would undermine his movement. His response to that was direct. He in effect said, "I take people at face value. I don't worry about what organizations they may have belonged to as long as their first commitment is to the movement." He said, "I know what some people have said, but I also know that until somebody violates my faith in them I'm not going to doubt or question them." I think he felt a lot better about himself after that statement than I felt about myself. I reported that back to the attorney general and I think he felt that we had both done what we had to do and all we could do.

But I think Burke was certainly reflecting the feelings of everybody, including Hoover, at that point. King was not, indeed, a Communist, nor was there any evidence of massive amounts of money that were being fed in from any source. They had money, but not massive amounts of money. And, certainly, there was no indication that any money they received was coming from the Communist party. Although by identifying Levinson, who had money, as a Communist, that suggestion was right there. Hoover's memoranda suggested that tie.

QUESTION: It is always something of a surprise to anyone who comes over to the United States from Europe to find the degree of hostility there is in parts of the United States for the Kennedies and the Kennedy administration and particularly for the Kennedies personally. It is an odd phenomenon, but it is there and I'm sure you know of it. They seem to inspire a great deal of love and affection and some deep-seated hatred in certain parts of the country.

I've often tried to explain this to myself. One of the things that I have leftover from memories of that administration is the kind of politics of personal confrontation where it's John Kennedy against Khrushchev in Vienna, John Kennedy against Khrushchev again in Cuba, and Robert Kennedy against

Jimmy Hoffa in Washington. This politics of personal confrontation seems to be around and seems not to be precisely duplicated by any administration since. The kind of people who feel very hostile about the Kennedies because of the desegration problems don't seem to feel the same hostility for President Johnson who in fact passed the civil rights legislation. He obviously was in power at that time.

I wonder in terms of your own recollections of that administration whether you think that the appointment of Robert Kennedy, the brother of the President, as attorney general in any way made the civil rights movement more difficult, in any way exacerbated the problems of dealing with certain entrenched beliefs in the old South by making them somewhat personal issues between the Kennedy family, at least the two brothers, and the people in the South who were perhaps feeling they weren't dealing with the U.S. Government but with a particular family and in a particular set of attitudes?

MR. SEIGENTHALER: I was in Washington throughout the campaign as well as during that first year of the administration. I think that while I felt it when I would go into the South as a representative of the administration in an effort to negotiate, those were all relatively quick trips and, except with some confrontation around the Freedom Riders, I met with friendship. Most politicians would say, "Look, we don't really need any help and we know you'll send in the marshalls, but we can handle this matter locally. We'll ease through this. Sure, don't pay any attention to what we say, just watch how we act. I may be very critical of the attorney general but tell the President not to be mad at me the way I talk about him because I'm going to have to say what I say. We'll get through it." So most of the responses that I got were political responses that were not unfriendly and not hostile. John Patterson and Bull Conner were exceptions to that.

In the heat of Freedom Rides confrontations, John Patterson and Bull Conner were demagogues. Aside from that and occasional telephone calls, I was somewhat removed from a great deal of that hostility. We would read about it and listen to what people would say and occasionally it would show up on television. I guess no place in the South was completely devoid of that sort of demagoguery. Of course, Bill Battle would have been in a position to pick up a good deal of that.

AMBASSADOR BATTLE: I think Bob Kennedy was definitely a lightning rod for Jack. No doubt about it. My judgment of Bob Kennedy was at that time that he was probably the most misunderstood public figure that I had ever seen in a significant place. I think once he got one on one with any of these people the attitude changed. I remember bringing him together with

Howard Smith and that was like oil and water and yet they turned out to be working together wherever they turned and became very good friends. But for a long time Bob was in the hot seat and I think you are right that a lot of people in the South did view it as the action of a Catholic family from Massachusetts telling them what to do down there. But I think that was to be expected.

MR. SEIGENTHALER: There was no other way to bring about change.

AMBASSADOR BATTLE: Harry Byrd supported Lyndon Johnson because he was "from the South." Yet Lyndon Johnson was so much more liberal than some of the people that Harry Byrd opposed, it defies comparison. I think it was regional, but I don't doubt that Bob was a real lightning rod and his name didn't bring many cheers in the South in those days. I think he would have carried the South if he had lived.

MR. SEIGENTHALER: I think he would have. The first civil rights speech he made was at the University of Georgia at Athens on Law Day. He refused to make a speech from the time of the election in November until Law Day, May 1961. He decided he wanted his first speech to be a civil rights speech and he wanted to be in the South. A young man named Jay Cox who was a law student at the University of Georgia came up and asked him if he would come. Jay Cox said, "I'm chairman. Some students may not want you, but I do." And Jay Cox later came to work in the Justice Department. But I remember the attorney general laughing to me one day. He said, "Call Griffin Bell and tell him he can be excused that day." Griffin Bell was chairman of the party in Georgia. Bob was saying, "Tell our old friend who carried that state for us that I'm going to make some statements that will be highly unpopular and I don't want any of that to rub off on him so he can be excused that day." So I called Griffin Bell on the telephone and said, "The attorney general wanted me to have this conversation with you and I hope you'll take it in the spirit that it is meant. You are excused on Law Day from coming back to your old alma mater at Athens." He said, "I know all about that. I expect to be with him and I hope he'll ask me to introduce him." I think Griffin Bell served on the court by President Kennedy's appointment because his reaction was always like that. He said, "I want to be there." Jay Cox insisted on introducing him but Griffin sat on the platform with Bob and, in effect, gave his sponsorship to that appearance and applauded, although many people did not.

It is really interesting how they were blamed for things. Charlene Hunter Gault was a student at the University of Georgia then. And some people told the attorney general it would be better if she didn't see him, that there might be trouble if he saw her. And so he said, "Obviously, I've got to see her. I'm not going to go on campus and not see her, so go find her and make sure that we have a chance to meet because she may feel intimidated." Then to jump ahead, I guess the next year she married a young white student there. There was a wave of protest. The flood of mail came in blaming him for the interracial marriage of Charlene Hunter Gault who now is a TV reporter on McNeil-Leher.

I certainly agree with Bill that he was the lightning rod. I have never really understood that sort of fanatic fringe response that he evoked. And, it was more than a fringe during a great part of that period of confrontation. There were some very sick jokes at that time. And some of it still continues. I think Ted Kennedy continues to suffer from a great deal of it although Chappaquiddick earned his measure of it.

QUESTION: Was it a shock technique that made people react? He came to visit us one time. We had been giving fellowships for fifty years in Asia and he lectured us and others on the fact that you've got to help young people. Ninety percent of the staff who heard it were angered to the core because we thought we were helping young people. He had a point, we were helping them within a framework, but he didn't gain any friends that day and yet I wondered whether this was his method.

MR. SEIGENTHALER: I think that in a sense it was. That was in 1961? I think particularly after November 1963 his approach to life, as well as politics, substantially changed. I think Bill and I will agree that he went into what Arthur Schlesinger has characterized as a "black period." I think there were several illustrations of it after the President's death and he had a hard time coming through that period.

Another anecdote: it relates, I think, directly to his own development on civil rights. He went up to New York to lecture a group of black intellectuals on the civil rights movement. James Baldwin, Lola Hansbury, Ken Clark and Lena Horne were there. There was a meeting in an apartment in New York. He went in and Burke Marshall went up with him and he went in to tell them how they should get involved in the civil rights movement in the South. He let them know what the administration was doing and how the administration was waging this fight for their people and challenged them to get involved, too. "Those of us who have wealth, influence and education, which I'm sure is pretty much the same thing, you all need to be involved." He said there was a young student there who had been active in the civil rights movement who said he wouldn't fight for his country: "I've seen what government can do to crush the spirit and lives of people in the South. I'm ashamed of my country and I won't fight." Bob reacted very badly and said to this young man, "I don't want to listen to that. If you don't have any love and devotion to your country, I don't want to hear it." And Baldwin, Clark and Hansbury ripped into him and said, "Listen, don't tell us about blacks in the South, let us tell you about blacks in the North." And they did. It was brutal. It was a terrible three-hour meeting. He came back to the office the next day and realized that they had turned on him. The whole year I was there I couldn't recall a worse day. He continued the relationship with those people who had been in that meeting, reestablished ties with them, and I think by 1968 certainly had them all supportive of him. But at one point, I think that was his style, to say, "We who have should dedicate ourselves." And most often he was effective with it. Most often he not only got away with it but managed to do very well. But sometimes he misread the audience and suffered from that.

QUESTION: The movies all show his playing on his brother's feelings with some of the same evoking of conscience.

MR. SEIGENTHALER: That's right, but I would hasten to add that it was not an act with him. It was not a contrived device. It was a passion of his.

AMBASSADOR BATTLE: I think he was the least contrived person I've ever met. I think that was one of his early problems. If he was going up the mountain, he was going straight up that mountain. But I find that he did mellow. I think he did learn that a lot of issues can be achieved without a frontal attack, as it were, but Bob was never one to duck and I don't think he had a dishonest thought in his head. I mean he did what he thought was right.

MR. SEIGENTHALER: That's right. You know he started at his home, Hickory Hill, this series of seminars. I think that was self-education as much as anything else. Many people thought he never brought anything away from one of those exchanges. But I think he never walked away from a single one of them without rethinking his own position.

I think the President had a very firm fix on himself. Maybe as early as 1958 campaign for reelection but certainly by the time he was in the White House. I think he understood as well as a President can his own definition of how he wanted to govern.

I think Robert Kennedy was much more visceral in his approach to government than cerebral. Jack Kennedy was much more cerebral. I think Robert Kennedy grew and matured. I certainly think he mellowed after the President's death. I agree with Bill on that. But, I also say that his reaction to problem solving was consistent. His attack on labor management and racketeering, his attack on the civil rights wrongs, and his attack on the war in Vietnam—each was a pretty consistent response that ran throughout his career. The method of response was more sophisticated as he matured. But he had that driving passion to confront what he saw as wrong. I begged him not to run for President in 1968. I said, "It is a waste of time, it's hopeless. You're not going to unseat a sitting President." I was wrong, of course. I said, "You are still so young. You can support candidates all over this country for the next four years and be the dominant figure in the Democratic party. Let Gene McCarthy and Hubert Humphrey decide who is going to fight Richard Nixon. It really doesn't make any sense for you to run." But he knew that he had something to say that went beyond where Gene McCarthy was. I think there was just a driving passion to get into that and to deal with it in a different way than McCarthy was dealing with it. And so he rejected my advice on that. I spent two days on a plane trip out to California trying to convince him that he was wrong about it and when we left he said, "Well, John, the only thing I've got to lose is my father's money." And I knew that I had lost, that he would run in 1968. I left the newspaper for a period to help him. I'm glad I did.

That was another thing about him. I think he had a biting sense of humor. He was the butt of his own humor more often than making someone else the butt of it. But that is one of the aspects of his personality that quite often is missed.

QUESTION: Was there any sense drawn by the attorney general and the President that there was a considerable body of opinion and support for a smooth transition on civil rights in some sections of the South such as in the business community, the academic community and other institutions that were ahead of everybody? Was there any awareness of that?

MR. SEIGENTHALER: No. I think there was a superficial awareness of it. There was, during the course of the campaign, contact with people like Mrs. Tilly, Skelly Wright, and others who had worked with the Southern Regional Council and other groups. But he was most of all a politician. His brother and he were most of all politicians. Their contact was with politicians. The first major southern politician to endorse Jack Kennedy was John Patterson, the racist governor of Alabama.

Most of the contact and conversation that went on was conversation with politicians, politicians who didn't want to be told, who wanted the President and attorney general to listen. There was a superficial awareness that there was intellectual support for progress in the field of civil rights. There was an understanding that the Southern Regional Council, for example, was around. Ralph McGill was there. Bill Baggs was there. But, there was not a sense that this was a way to bring about positive change. If you could have predicted the inevitability of Martin Luther King's success, it would have been politically practical to chart a different course. But if you assume that the confrontations are going to grow out of court decisions, not out of street demonstrations, you think you can buy a great deal more time. I think they thought they could buy a great deal more time than turned out to be the case. In the absence of being forced to do otherwise, they didn't seek help where they well might have been able to get it.

In town after town, once confrontations occurred, there was only one way to start the dialogue going, and that was to go to the very white leadership you are talking about who had some credibility on both sides, both among blacks leaders and white segregationist politicians.

In the final analysis in city after city it was those people who ultimately brought about the change on the local level. But the Kennedys' view of the South was dominated by these southern politicians, all of whom were powerful and many were powerful in the Congress. Kennedy dealt on a daily basis with James Eastland who was chairman of the Judiciary Committee. And Bill Battle mentioned Judge Smith in the House. When Judge Smith put pending legislation in his pocket and went to the farm, the administration was hamstrung for weeks. Those politicians so dominated the life of Congress and so dominated the political life in the various states that it was difficult to see that the crises ahead were going to be so substantial that they would overwhelm the politicians too.

QUESTION: Couldn't they see any alternatives?

MR. SEIGENTHALER: Not much, if you think the answer is to deal with the political establishment, and if your view of the way to change the system is to change the political establishment. What Bob Kennedy was saying to King that day was, "you register these people to vote and Jim Eastland will change his mind because he'll have to—or there will be somebody replacing him." And that is a one-liner that is not as simplistic as it really sounds. What he was saying to King was, "Look, we can change this thing working together and the best way to do it is not worry about segregated bathrooms and riding in the back of buses and sitting down at lunch counters. Just change the political process. You'll change the politicians—or you'll change their minds. They will have no alternative once you get black registration where it should be."

His address initially was to deal with the political system. He never really understood why that didn't make sense to Martin Luther King. He didn't understand the moral imperative that forced King into small cities. Macomb comes to mind as a place where there was deep trouble. There were hundreds of Macombs. Macomb, Mississippi was one place where we went. In the final analysis we were almost pleading with King not to go in there because the potential for violence to those in the movement was so great.

But looking back on it, in retrospect, in hindsight, if you had understood at at the outset that first the courts and then the political system are not the total answer, then alternatives would have been much easier to recognize. The need to find them would have been paramount to solve the crises. It is fair to say that, compared with most politicians we can remember, they were more intellectual in their approach to problems. But they still were, more than anything else, political leaders who looked to the political process as the first resolution, the first answer.

QUESTION: One comment. I couldn't agree more about the way they were shaped by the movement and not the other way around. A young colleague of mine named Carl Brauer wrote a book about Kennedy and the second reconstruction and argued the other way. I always thought that was wrong. But I'm really struck by the fact that they had the awareness that you described during the campaign of 1960 and that the conversation with King was such a revelation. When Greensboro had taken place in February, it was clear to so many of us that the momentum was going to be in the hands of the students, the young people. And they were passing King by. Lots of us realized already that King had lost control, that the young students, while they idolized him and took their moral cues from him, were going to go into the streets. We had sit-ins in restaurant after restaurant during the spring of 1960. SNICK was organized. Hadn't that made an impact on him? Or did they think it was passing thing?

MR. SEIGENTHALER: They knew the movement was there and they knew that King was there but I think he felt reasonably certain that either King or other black leaders would seek to bring about change in a different way. Part of it was a hope that it would happen that difficult way.

You have to remove yourself to a time when the federal law enforcement establishment exercised power in only a few very narrow areas. And the FBI was not anxious to move. The FBI was lethargic. Kidnapping, bank robbery and auto theft were about the three areas where the federal government thought it had any power at all. And then, except for kidnapping, only when interstate commerce was involved. I mean the federal government looked upon its law enforcement establishment as basically impotent in terms of dealing with "local problems." Hoover liked it that way. And so if you are Hoover you look at Greensboro and you think it's going to be a problem but it is going to be somebody else's problem. If there is some way to get it into court and we are ordered to do something and the court tells us we must act, then obviously we can act and we will find ways to do that.

Burke Marshall started very early trying to find ways to intervene in a number of those suits. He tried to get the courts involved as early as possible. Then you could get some federal investigation ordered. Hoover could not ignore an order. Once you began to establish that sort of legal beachhead, once you make it clear that the courts were involved, and once a court said to the FBI "investigate this, it may be in violation of the civil rights," then you are not dealing with the FBI as a law enforcement agency that essentially does not want to move. When a court gives you an order to act, you are saying in Greensboro, is there a civil rights violation? Or in Macomb—which is the first place Burke moved to get an investigation of police brutality saying—is there a violation? What then would happen is Hoover would say, "I'm going to go down there and my agent on the scene has been working with these local fellows to solve bank robberies and car thefts and they are not going to want to put those local police, who are in the Klan, in jail. They are not going to ask them about what they've been doing at night and whether they've got sheets in the closets and whether they are burning crosses on lawns." It is not an exaggeration to say that the Klan infiltration of the southern local police establishment, at that time, was substantial. It was overwhelming. In some cases even if you are able to get the federal courts involved in a civil rights question raised in 1961, the possibility of getting a meaningful investigation by the FBI was often minimal. At the outset they were psychologically above it, emotionally above it, and thought it was outside their ken, really, to change local attitudes. The FBI thought they were largely impotent to move.

As Robert Kennedy said during the Freedom Rides to a writer named Peter Moss, "Emotionally, I am totally in sympathy with them." In retrospect that looks so cold and almost heartless. But what he was really saying is that the Klan's got an army out there. They bombed the bus and burned it and beat people up last Sunday and I don't even have the power to go in there and find out who those people are who did it. That's a local law enforcement problem. Today you'd have the Justice Department in there in thirty minutes. There would be agents combing the area. You would have investigations going and a grand jury by the end of the month. You have to take yourself back to a time when that was unheard of, unthought of. It is hard to believe, but it is true that the concept of states rights in law enforcement, in a lot of areas, still had not been destroyed. In the civil rights area this was true as late as 1961. The position sounds sort of silly, but the idea of a federal law officer superceding the right of a state or local officer was heresy. Unless you go back to that period and remember that that's the way it was, it is really impossible to understand why we seemed so impotent in dealing with these problems.

QUESTION: Convince me again that J. Edgar Hoover was not extraordinarily antagonistic or benevolent toward that?

MR. SEIGENTHALER: I'm not sure I really want to convince you of it, but unless you've seen the characterizations in these docu-dramas where he stands around and says to an agent, "Hey, boy, this man Kennedy is dealing with homosexuals. Love your mother, boy." I never saw J. Edgar Hoover like that. Every time I saw him he was very business-like, very concerned about how far he could go, what he could do and what he couldn't do. I thought there were some days—one, for sure—when they should have kept him in a cage. But most days I thought he was cogent, reasonable and rational. He clearly understood that there were things that he had to do and things that he couldn't do. And things he didn't want to do.

I would just move ahead to the Nixon administration and point out that there was one day when they presented him with the so-called Houston Plan which was literally designed to give the White House the power to burn the constitution. And J. Edgar Hoover was the lone voice in that administration who said, "No, you can't do this. This clearly violates federal law and the constitution." Part of it was imperial. It was a territorial imperative. He wanted to keep them off his turf but, beyond that, he apparently made an eloquent plea on behalf of constitutional rights and oiled his law enforcement to get it down.

I will acknowledge that he used the power of office to intimidate, harass and even blackmail Presidents and congressmen and United States senators. I think he did that very selectively. There is no doubt that he kept dossiers on a number of people. I was one of them. I think he used them very selectively. And up until the time of the civil rights movement I think he ran an exceptional agency. When he was confronted with a challenge that required a major change, he began to fight back and then he began to abuse his power grossly and routinely. You can't look at cointelpro and say that the architect of that was not a malevolent figure. But I don't think he was sexually psychotic or perverted. Those are the characterizations that you get, that he had a sick fixation over sex and his mother and Clyde Tolsen. I don't believe any of that.

In the last days when I was in the administration we did, on certain days, sit around the attorney general's office, which had ceilings about twice as high as this one, and we would be talking about something the FBI was failing to do and the attorney general would say, "Are you there, Edgar?" I don't think he was and I don't think anybody in the room thought he was but by that time we were laughing about it. Looking back, it isn't very funny.

Very early in that administration I was the recipient of some information by former agents who said they had been forced to cut his grass, paint his house, pick him up at all sorts of hours. They had evidence that he was taking free hotel bills at the Waldorf Astoria, piddling stuff. I put it all together in a folder and took it to the attorney general and he looked at it and said, "The next time we go to the White House bring it with you, I want to give it to the President." I did that. A few days later Ken O'Donnell called me on the telephone and said, "Do you believe any of this stuff?" I said they sounded perfectly rational. He said, "Well, if you put it all together what have you got?" I said not very much. He said, "Well, that's what the President thinks, too."

Within a week we got a memo that indicated Hoover knew that we had gathered the information and passed it on and then there came a flood over a period of three months of twenty-five thousand letters. This was all very inhouse, very quiet but there were twenty or twenty-five thousand letters in support of J. Edgar Hoover as director of the FBI: "We know the Kennedy administration is trying to get rid of him and doesn't like him." He had the most phenomenal network of agents and I'm sure that a memorandum went out to the field officers saying, "Those of you who support the director please let the President know. There are forces at work trying to undermine him." They really responded. Then we would see letters that appeared in Letters to the Editor columns in papers across the country saying Kennedy is trying to get rid of J. Edgar Hoover, please write, don't let him, call your congressman. We would get congressmen calling. So I'm not suggesting that he was a figure that deserved canonization. There were aspects of his personality that were reprehensible and that I was not fond of. Neither was the attorney general. But I do think that some of the characterizations, in order to find a villain, go far beyond the facts of history in making you want to hate him as a sexually perverted personality. So that's why I say that I think the revisionist historians, in the same way I think they have overemphasized President Kennedy's private romantic encounters, have overdramatized the characterization of Hoover until he is not a recognizeable figure.

I really think that in the final analysis I don't know what is going to happen to American history if this docu-drama revisionism continues. It worries me an awful lot.

NARRATOR: We are grateful that there are some newspaper men who were better professors than people who get paid for doing it, and we also hope that this kind of a contribution can be the Miller Center's little move in the direction of a better kind of revisionism. We certainly thank you.

III.
KENNEDY AND THE ECONOMY

THE KENNEDY PRESIDENCY: THE ECONOMIC DIMENSION

Secretary C. Douglas Dillon

NARRATOR: On a previous occasion, Douglas Dillon spoke in this same room about another concern, constitutional reform, an area which he has continued to pursue. It's a pleasure to welcome him again as the former secretary of the treasury in the Kennedy administration. He had served as undersecretary of state for economic affairs and under secretary of state in the Eisenhower administration. Following an educational background at Groton and Harvard, he came to occupy major leadership positions in the business and financial world. He served with the United States Navy in World War II, receiving several awards and rising from ensign to lieutenant commander. He maintains continuing interests in the arts, especially the Metropolitan Museum of Art which he headed for fourteen years; he has been chairman of such important boards as those of the Rockefeller Foundation, the Brookings Institution and the Board of Overseers of Harvard University. His leadership at

Dillon, Read & Company, Inc. is well known to many in the business field.

I recall from a study group experience in New York some years ago a high tribute being paid to Mr. Dillon. A mixed group of academic and public affairs people took a poll of what public figure had made the best use of the intellectuals on his or her staff in government. Mr. Dillon won that poll two to one in votes around the table. He has held ambassadorial positions; he has been recognized throughout the world for his leadership in business, finance and education. He is an Associate of the Miller Center. It is a great pleasure to welcome him as a speaker in our series on Portraits of American Presidents. Mr. Dillon is here to discuss the presidency of John F. Kennedy.

MR. DILLON: Thank you. I was told that it would be a good idea if I started off by saying a few words about economic policy in the Kennedy administration and then left the bulk of the time to answer questions which is really what I prefer. I did put my thoughts down to clarify them and not to ramble on too long. So if you don't mind I will use this paper to begin with.

My first glimpse of the possible outlines of a Kennedy administration economic policy came in late October of 1960 when the full text of a speech on economic policy by Senator Kennedy was published in the press. This speech was to have been delivered in Philadelphia, I say "was to," as I very much doubt if Kennedy ever actually delivered such a speech. It was extremely detailed and did not seem suitable for a campaign audience a week or two before election day. Be that as it may, the speech was released to the press as Kennedy's, to publicize the economic policies he intended to follow if elected. I read it carefully and, as a former New York investment banker, could find nothing in it to fault; it was conservative in its general approach and most impressive in its grasp of detail. It surprised me as I had not thought of Senator Kennedy as having this sort of interest or expertise. I later learned that he had relied heavily on the advice of Professor Paul Samuelson of MIT in preparing this speech, which apparently was designed to offset Republican attacks on him as a typical Democratic spendthrift.

When Senator Kennedy first asked me to consider joining his Cabinet as secretary of the treasury, I referred to this speech and asked him if it still represented his thinking. He said, "Yes," and mentioned Professor Samuelson's role in preparing the text. When he approached me Senator Kennedy said that he was extremely concerned about the weakness of the dollar and the substantial weekly losses of gold from the Treasury's stock. At that time, in late November of 1960, we were losing gold at the rate of several hundred million dollars a week as foreign central banks turned their dollars in and demanded gold in return. This loss of gold had started earlier in the fall when, due to a slipup at the Bank of England, the price of gold rose suddenly one day from its pegged value of thirty-five dollars an ounce to something over forty dollars an ounce.

During the campaign the Republicans had mounted strong attacks on the Democrats in general and on Senator Kennedy in particular as being financially irresponsible. So, after Senator Kennedy's election, foreign countries began to convert their dollars to gold as a measure of protection against the unknown. I, in common with other financially oriented businessmen and bankers, felt this was a most serious and dangerous situation.

During my first meeting with Senator Kennedy, he assured me that he was determined to pursue sound financial policies and to restore international confidence in the dollar. He told me that, as a first step, he wished to name someone as secretary of the treasury who had the confidence of the international financial community. He hoped that this action would slow down or halt the gold outflow until he had an opportunity by his actions to show that his administration would follow sound financial policies. He also said he had not been able to identify any Democratic candidate for the Treasury post who would have this effect on the financial community. Therefore he hoped that I would consider accepting the job if he could overcome the resistance in the Democratic party that would naturally arise when word got out that he was thinking of a Republican such as me. Senator Kennedy told me that in his opinion only the appointment of a Republican with a sound financial background would have the shock effect necessary to stem what he felt was a looming financial crisis.

I told Senator Kennedy that I was taken aback by his suggestion, as I had been a lifelong Republican and had given strong financial support to Vice-President Nixon's campaign. However, in the light of the serious problems with the dollar, I would have to think carefully about his proposal. He then told me that, if I should become secretary of the treasury, it would be on a strictly nonpartisan basis with no political speeches or other political activity to be expected of me. He also said that he would look to me as his chief financial adviser and would expect to follow my recommendations. After this meeting two weeks or more passed without further contact, and I made a trip to Europe to sign the agreement setting up the OECD. On my return Senator Kennedy called me and said that he wished to move ahead promptly with the announcement of my appointment and asked me to come to his house.

After calling on President Eisenhower and informing him of what was in the wind, I went to Senator Kennedy's house and we had a final meeting. At this meeting he introduced me to his brother Robert whom he was about to name as attorney general and whom I had never met. Robert Kennedy was with us for most of this meeting. The President-elect said that he wished to reconfirm his earlier statement that he would look to me as his chief financial adviser. He then said that to mollify opinion in his party he would like to substantially upgrade the role of the Council of Economic Advisers and to appoint a recognized liberal Democrat as its chairman. His idea was for the council to have a much more public role than it had had in the past. He hoped that I would have no objection to this arrangement and he wanted to give me his word that in the event of disagreements between the Council of Economic Advisors and the Treasury, he would in the end always side with the Treasury. The only exception would be in case differences developed of such a magnitude as to require a change in the office of secretary of the treasury. Should that ever eventuate, which he did not expect, he asked me to give him assurances that I would depart from office quietly and not make the sort of public fuss that occurred when President Eisenhower's first secretary of labor resigned.

I told Senator Kennedy that I would gladly give him such an assurance and that on the basis of his statements regarding the primacy of the Treasury in financial matters, I had no objection to the enlarged role for the Council of Economic Advisers and indeed could see many advantages in such a setup. I then said that if Professor Samuelson were to be his choice, I was sure, on the basis of the October speech, that there would be no problem. Senator Kennedy told me that Professor Samuelson had turned down an offer to take the position and had recommended a Professor Walter Heller of the University of Minnesota. I told the President-elect that anyone that he and Professor Samuelson wanted would be fine with me. At this point we all went down to the front steps of his house where he introduced me and Robert Kennedy to the press as the next treasury secretary and the next attorney general.

During the ensuing years of his presidency, Kennedy scrupulously lived up to his bargain. There were few disagreements between the CEA and the Treasury that required presidential decisions. But whenever they arose President Kennedy, if forced to a decision, always fell back on a phrase like the following: "Well, the secretary of the treasury is my chief financial adviser so I will just have to go along with him."

This also applied to differences with other departments in financial matters. I particularly recall one instance with the State Department when George Ball felt that we could get a better financial arrangement with the Germans in a fashion that we in the Treasury opposed. Secretary Ball insisted on a meeting with the President which took place in the Cabinet Room. After much argument back and forth President Kennedy finally ended the meeting using the very phraseology I've just described.

The essence of President Kennedy's domestic policy was that he combined a liberal outlook in social matters with a relatively conservative financial policy. He told me during our first meeting that history showed that many forward-looking liberal regimes had been wrecked on the rocks of unsound financial policy. He said that he was determined that this would not happen to his administration.

There were two major financial problems facing the Kennedy administration as it came into office. The first and chief problem was how to stimulate the economy so as to recover from the economic slowdown or recession that had become apparent during the summer and fall of 1960. The second problem was to improve our balance of payments so as to maintain the strength of the dollar. Fortunately we found ourselves in a good position to stimulate the economy. The Eisenhower administration, with its policy of financial restraint, had succeeded in putting an end to inflation. Prices were rising no more than one or two percent a year. It was agreed early that primary reliance would be placed on stimulation through tax reduction rather than through greatly increased spending. Some spending increases seemed desirable, and they were proposed in an early modification of the budget for fiscal 1962 that had been submitted by President Eisenhower. But this spending increase was relatively minor.

On tax reduction, the Treasury strongly favored giving priority to business taxes in the hope and expectation that this would kill two birds with one stone. It would stimulate capital spending and thus help the economy while at the same time it would help our balance of payments by modernizing U.S. industry and thus making it more competitive in world markets. Since it did not appear politically wise to take on too many things at the same time, the first Kennedy tax bill dealt with business taxes, leaving individual rates to be dealt with later. Its centerpiece was the investment credit, a form of subsidy for business investment that was working well in Europe but did not exist in the United States. This was coupled with a drastic simplification and easing of the rules for depreciating plants and equipment.

The first Kennedy tax bill also contained a long list of relatively modest loophole closings, most of which were accepted by the Congress. After this bill was approved in mid-1962 we moved to a drastic cut in individual rates, recommending an average reduction of about thirty percent. This was sent to Congress by President Kennedy in early 1963; unfortunately he did not live to see its final enactment in early 1964. The results of these two tax bills were very favorable. The economy moved forward close to full employment; revenue grew rapidly and recovered the entire loss from the rate reductions; and inflation was held in check, remaining at the one to two percent level.

The performance of the U.S. economy during these Kennedy years and in President Johnson's first year was the best in the postwar era, thanks to his policies and to the groundwork laid by President Eisenhower in stopping inflation. President Kennedy fully understood that as the economy reached a level approaching full employment it would be necessary to have balanced budgets or preferably modest surpluses to avoid inflation. It is one of the major tragedies of his assassination that this policy was not fully understood or followed by his successors.

During the Kennedy administration the United States shifted from a passive to an activist role in international monetary affairs. The Treasury took the lead in many new initiatives largely developed by Robert Roosa, the under secretary for monetary affairs, who is a great expert, indeed a world expert, in this area. However, despite all our efforts the best we could do was to achieve a standoff. The dollar did not weaken and the loss of gold was minimized. But this result was only achieved by a series of different initiatives that barely preserved the status quo. Lower interest rates in the United States compared to much higher levels in then prosperous Europe served as a magnet to attract borrowers and cause dollars to flow abroad. Interestingly enough this was the exact converse of the situation that exists today when the dollar is supported by an inflow of foreign funds to take advantage of the current high United States interest rates.

To sum up, the Kennedy economic policy was to stimulate the economy at a time when it was operating well below capacity and inflation had been successfully contained. This stimulation was applied through substantial tax reduction, both individual and business, with little reliance on spending increases. Priority was given to business tax reductions so as to help United States business maintain its competitive position versus the newly modernized factories of Europe and Japan. While there were some modest increases in spending over the amounts proposed in the final Eisenhower budget, there was no major expansion of spending during the Kennedy years. The results achieved were extraordinarily favorable. This was due to President Kennedy's willingness to take a long view. He got the best advice he could and then stuck with it, resisting all political temptation to curry favor by spending money on the pet programs of special interest groups. I often heard him say, "If this policy is right it will pay off in the long run; that is what interests me, not the ephemeral day-to-day popularity that is readily available by simply giving in to any and all demands for special spending programs." He was at all times conscious of the dangers of overstimulation and resurging inflation which he was determined to avoid.

It was tragic both for him and the country that he was not given the opportunity to try and manage an economy which was reaching full employment. I for one am confident that the result would have been just as successful as was his effort to get the economy up to speed without igniting inflation.

QUESTION: You didn't get the credit as ambassador that I am going to give you because I watched you get NATO started. It is probably one of the most unique combinations of nations ever put together. Mr. Ambassador, did you ever believe it would get put together and what do you think has kept it together?

MR. DILLON: Well, that was actually started a few years before I went to Paris, although it kept expanding during my time. It was put together because of fear of the Soviets and that is what held it together in the earlier years. That is still there although the situation is somewhat more difficult today because there are differences in economic policies between the allies that didn't exist earlier when Europe was flat. Also the Soviet threat has changed. It no longer is solely or primarily on Western Europe but the threat is all over the world wherever they can find an easy place to push. That is something that is often not so clearly apparent to our European NATO allies. So there are certain strains that develop when they take either different views or like to put aside the problems that occur in other parts of the world and say it's our problem.

QUESTION: Mr. Ambassador, do you have an opinion as to whether or not we should stay in UNESCO or get out?

MR. DILLON: I'm no expert on that but from what I know about it I think we should certainly get out unless they make very substantial changes. I don't think these are in the cards until or unless we do get out. And I think that if we do get out and they don't make those changes, there will be some other countries that are fairly important who will follow our example. Then I think there will be changes made the same way as they were made in the International Labor Organizations (ILO). Certainly UNESCO has done a lot of good things and does do a lot of good things. If they could get the politicization that has taken place there out and have a little more sense in their budgets, I think the most useful thing we could do is go back in. I think we will.

QUESTION: I am interested in the Johnson administration. What changes did you see in economic policy during that period in which you were there?

MR. DILLON: I didn't see very many during the period that I was there, but they were incipient and they began immediately after I left. Of course, though, the budget for fiscal 1965 was submitted in January of 1964 and had been largely prepared under President Kennedy and so was similar to the type of thing I've been talking about. An interesting indication is that the tax bill had been held up in the Senate because Senator Harry Byrd, Sr., who was the chairman of the Finance Committee, had said that he wouldn't report it out until he saw what the budget was. He didn't want the budget to be too much, and he wanted it held under one hundred billion dollars. I told that to President Kennedy and President Kennedy said, "Well, if that's what it takes, that's what it will be." I think the year before it had been ninety-eight or something like that.

President Kennedy hadn't told that to anyone; he just told it to me and it was our understanding. President Johnson started out, making great publicity that the budget figures submitted by the various departments were very high, a hundred and six or a hundred and seven billion dollars, and he was going to wrestle with them and cut them down. And after about three or four weeks, he said he had gotten these people to cut them down to one hundred and three billion but that wasn't enough and he was going to struggle some more. He finally sent a budget of ninety-eight and a half or ninety-eight and three-quarters billion dollars which was quite similar to what Kennedy had promised me he would do. But Johnson had taken great credit for this; he said that it wouldn't have happened except for himself. When I went up to tell Harry Byrd what the budget was going to be and that we now wanted our bill to be reported out Senator Byrd said, "Yes, O.K., but you don't know Lyndon the way I do. He is going to be the greatest spender the United States has ever seen." In a way with the Great Society and hostilities in Vietnam requiring increased defense funds, that's what happened, and that changed the policies rather dramatically. President Johnson refused to increase taxes to balance the budget at the time we had reached full employment. As a result inflation got started and we have suffered from it ever since. And that was a major difference from the Kennedy policies, but it didn't happen during the first year that I was there.

My relations with President Johnson, were very different. I had very close relations with President Kennedy and saw him frequently and could see him at any time without notice. That was not true under President Johnson although it was not too difficult to get him on the telephone. He would always answer a telephone call, but, if you wanted to see him, you had to have an appointment and wait and so forth. So I saw very little of him. He more or less told me I could handle the Treasury and he wasn't very interested in it during that first year as he was running for election. So I was pretty well left alone.

QUESTION: Mr. Ambassador, do you think it's possible that we can next year coordinate fiscal and monetary policies to reduce the horrendous debt we have? What would you recommend doing?

MR. DILLON: Well, I think there have been a lot of recommendations. A group, which I'm a part of, has made a recommendation, and I think there is a general consensus of what has to be done. I certainly hope that after the election, no matter who is elected, something on this order will be done. A substantial cut in these big deficits can be achieved through three major things: 1) some reduction in defense spending from the levels President Reagan has recently espoused; 2) some substantial savings in the non-means tested programs such as social security, Medicare, and pensions, and things of that nature, largely by capping them in some fashion so that the cost-of-living increases are more reasonable and don't follow exactly with the index; and 3) by an increase in taxes which I believe should be largely consumption-oriented taxes not just an increase in income tax rates. I think with that, if you could put something like that on top of the down payment of one hundred and fifty billion dollars over three years currently under consideration, you could get the job done. If you could put one hundred and twenty-five billion a year in reduced expenditures and increased revenues on top of that or something like that amount then you would save enough on interest from a lower deficit so that you'd have a total cut in the deficit of maybe as much as one hundred and fifty billion a year, then we'd be in the ball game. We'd be down to deficits of no more than fifty billion dollars or so, and those we could live with.

QUESTION: I would like to know whether you would think it would be useful to separate again the capital, administrative and trust fund budgets so that people would understand better what is going on.

MR. DILLON: It would be very complicated. If it could be done it might be very useful. But it's very hard to draw the line as to what's capital and what is operating, particularly when you get into the defense field which is so big. Is a new tank capital or is it operating? If you need a new tank for your operations and people think it is capital and so it doesn't matter, that wouldn't be very useful.

QUESTION: Last week Mr. Griffin Bell sat where you are sitting and predicted that eventually the government is going bankrupt. Would you make that harsh prediction?

MR. DILLON: No, I'm always optimistic. I don't know Attorney General Bell but I've always been optimistic and even though the situation looks very serious, I would only agree with him if we don't do anything about it. But at the last minute we usually do something, and it seems to me the country has reached the state now where it is politically not only possible but desirable to do something. The voters are interested in this and seem to realize that inflation and big deficits are connected and want to get rid of them. So I have a feeling that something will happen next year. I hope I'm not wrong.

QUESTION: You spoke about President Kennedy taking a long view despite the pressures from political groups. How would you encourage this since it is so necessary?

MR. DILLON: This is a thing that has to be in the individual. I think it's very hard to encourage that. That was, of course, a great difference between him and President Johnson, who always kept very close to what the polls said and always had them in his pocket. He liked to follow the polls and didn't want to get out front too much. When someone would say, "Well, that's what you should do but it's not politically possible," I heard Kennedy reply more than once, "No, but this is the right thing to do and it's going to work. Let's do it. If it works people will like what the final result is even if it takes two or three years and they will reward me." Obviously, this approach might not work during the year before the election when he would have been running for reelection. I think it might have been a little too much to have expected quite that same approach from Kennedy during that year. But certainly in the first two years of his presidency, that's the view he had and which he often expressed.

QUESTION: We hear a lot of discussion with great concern about the conflict between the secretary of state and the national security adviser. Is the possible conflict between the economic adviser and the secretary of treasury a built-in problem for the President as a structural matter?

MR. DILLON: Well, it's something any President can handle. It just depends what he wants. Of course when I was in the State Department the role of national security adviser was much less, and President Eisenhower looked to the State Department for his advice. In the Kennedy administration, that was not quite the case with the Council of Economic Advisers. The council was there—a bunch of brilliant economists—and they had all sorts of ideas and some of them were good and some we didn't think were so good. What Kennedy had said to me was not said publicly. He said it to me and I never mentioned it publicly. But that is the way he worked. I think we are far enough into history now to tell the facts. There were only a few differences—I wouldn't call them major. I think in the first year the council would rather that we had tackled individual tax reductions sooner than business tax reductions, because they felt it was more stimulative. If you gave a lot of money to the consumer right away the economy would jump up quicker. And we at Treasury felt, largely for balance of payments reasons, that it was very important to do it the other way around. Well, the President decided to do it our way.

There were a number of cases like that that he decided. For instance the council was always more sensitive to interest rates. If we wanted to sell longer term bonds and pay four and one-half or six percent or whatever rather than three percent for short-term money or whatever the rates were—I've forgotten the exact ones but they were in those areas—the council thought that made a big difference; we didn't. The President went along with us in things like that but we never had any major differences. I think it is clear that, if a President wants to have things run easily, it is desirable for him, either publicly or privately and usually more or less privately, to make clear who his chief advisers are instead of having six of them, all different ones, competing. Then nobody knows. Some Presidents may feel this is a way to get the best advice. Maybe it is but personally I don't think that is the way to run the government. That doesn't mean that a President can't get all the outside advice he wants.

On the economy, President Kennedy looked to all sorts of people and talked with them, but then, when they gave him ideas, he would get hold of me and say, "What about this?" I usually knew that it was something he hadn't thought about himself because often his questions were quite complex. I would think about the question and give him the Treasury view on it and that would be the end of the matter.

There was one particular fellow with whom we had a rather amusing relationship. He was at that time our ambassador to India and he was also a well-known economist, Mr. John Kenneth Galbraith. He had quite a different idea of how to stimulate the economy. He was all for major spending increases and no decreases in taxes. So he would tell President Kennedy that, and we would argue about it a bit, but then the President went along with us. But Galbraith used to come back from India every so often and every time he would talk with the President about something he thought we were doing wrong. The President would either send me a memo or call up and ask something. Finally, about the third time this happened, when the President called me and asked me something that sounded Galbraithian, I said, "Fine, Mr. President, I'll look into it and tell you what I think about it but I just wonder if Ken Galbraith is in town?" The President started laughing and said, "He's right here. Do you want to talk to him?"

QUESTION: Mr. Secretary, the harmonious relationship which I deduce existed between the financial troika at your time as secretary of the treasury with Federal Reserve and the Council of Economic Advisers seems in recent years to have developed into more of a public debating society rather than a collegial philosophical approach to the problems in the country. Would you comment, castigate, or reprimand any one of the three now? Mr. Volcker, Mr. Regan, or the Council of Economic Advisers?

MR. DILLON: My own feelings are that they seem to have relatively different economic approaches. I know Paul Volcker. We first recruited him when I was secretary of the treasury to come to the Treasury in a junior capacity. I believe that Volcker's approach and that of Martin Feldstein of the council is correct and Secretary Regan is overoptimistic in some of his ideas and not realistic financially. To the extent that the rows are of that nature I would believe the right is more on the side of Feldstein/Volcker and not on that of Don Regan.

QUESTION: Does this suggest any adjustment from an organizational standpoint?

MR. DILLON: Well, apparently President Reagan does not work quite the way President Kennedy did. There are several sources of policy in the economic field and there are numerous sources of policy in the foreign field and that seems to be the way he wants to work. I don't think it is as efficient but whoever is the President has to work the way he wants to and that's apparently the way President Reagan wants to work and so that's what we have to live with.

QUESTION: Mr. Secretary, how strongly do you feel pro or con toward a proposed constitutional amendment for a balanced budget?

MR. DILLON: It's sort of like King Canute. If you have such an amendment that is strict it won't work. If you have one that is realistic it will have to have so many loopholes in it that I don't think it would really accomplish very much. So I'm not very keen on this particular exercise. I think it is much more important to get the country and the Congress to realize that it's important to keep a reasonable balance. I would be in favor, maybe, of some legislation that would require the Congress by a special majority of sixty percent or something like that to vote for amounts that were over some limit. But certainly when you have a recession and taxes go down, it's not the time to force a balanced budget. As we learned to our sorrow in the early thirties, cutting expenditures to keep up with decreasing receipts just doesn't work.

You have to have a deficit at such a time to hold yourself together. Conversely, when everything gets going well you should have a surplus and you shouldn't spend that. So a balanced budget amendment wouldn't prevent you from spending all the money when you were on the up side which you shouldn't do either. So I don't think it's really very practical although it sounds like a simplistic answer to a very complex problem.

QUESTION: Were you sorry to see the gold standard dropped after all your efforts during the Kennedy administration?

MR. DILLON: No, I wouldn't say sorry because I was only an observer by then. But, earlier, all of us felt that with a flexible exchange standard we would have many more problems with trade than actually proved to be the case although there have been some. But we, and I guess everybody else in the financial community at that time, underestimated the flexibility of the international financial system. We underestimated our ability, with superior communications and all the recent technical developments, to hedge money ahead so that corporations can operate successfully all over the world with constantly shifting exchange rates which is what they've been able to do. That was something we didn't foresee, the extent to which that would be possible. I do think that too much variation in exchange rates can sometimes cause problems. The dollar being somewhat overvalued now is bringing a very difficult situation with our balance of payments once again. I don't know what the net result of that is going to be, but it could be that, if we slow down and there isn't such a great demand for money and our interest rates go down, you could see a very rapid fall in the value of the dollar. Rapid movements one way or another I don't think are very good. I think we've just got to keep on learning, and I hope that ways will be found, as time goes on, to cooperate better internationally. Gradually they have done it in Europe with this snake that they have between the different European currencies, where they keep their exchange rates relatively stable; they can trade well between themselves but they can change when they want to. Maybe something like that will eventually be used on a worldwide scale. It might be the best result.

NARRATOR: Did you have any trouble with the White House as such and the White House staff?

MR. DILLON: No, never, partly because of my relationship with President Kennedy. As I said I could go see him any time I wanted to if it was of importance or I thought it was something that he was interested in. He had a system where all I had to do was to walk over to the White House and go into his secretary's room, Evelyn Lincoln's office, which was between his office and the Cabinet Room. She had a hole in the door into his office and she would look through that hole. When she saw there was someone in there she would say there is someone in there and I would just wait. And the second that someone went out the other door there would be a buzz and she would open the door and say, "Mr. President, Secretary Dillon has something," and he would say, "Come in," so I'd go in and get my business done and get out quickly because you can't waste a President's time.

On minor things I found the White House staff, as it was then set up, very useful because there were all sorts of different times when you might have minor differences with the Department of Commerce or the Agriculture Department or whatever. When it was those sort of things, either I or one of my under secretaries used to talk either with Ted Sorensen or Mike Feldman. We always found them very useful and very helpful. There was nobody there like they have now. No domestic council, which has to approve everything and which acts through numerous committees.

President Kennedy didn't believe in that. He worked with the secretary of state, the secretary of defense, the secretary of the treasury and of course the attorney general very closely. The rest of his Cabinet, at least in the first three years, were more peripheral to his interests, and he didn't see so much of them. They didn't have the same sort of relationship and some of them didn't like it. A number of them resigned: Ribicoff in Health, Education and Welfare and Postmaster General Day. I don't think he had ever seen the President on a working basis. That's the way Kennedy operated.

NARRATOR: We had another omnibus question: When did you meet the President? How did you get involved in the whole effort? What were your first impressions of the President as leader? Did they change during the period of the administration? What kind of balance sheet would you draw up of strengths and weaknesses?

MR. DILLON: I knew him, of course, because he was in the Senate. He was on the Foreign Relations Committee and, as such, when I appeared for the State Department he'd be there occasionally although he was not a very regular attendant at meetings. He was thinking, at that time, of running for the presidency so he was around the country more.

Also I met him in a rather unusual fashion. My daughter knew him from the south of France where she lived and had a house in the summer. In 1958, she was coming over to visit us, and we wanted to have a little dinner for her and didn't know how to get younger people. The only people I knew then were much older than we were because I was one of the youngest fellows in the Eisenhower administration. My daughter suggested, "Why don't you get a hold of the Kennedys and they might help," so my wife got hold of them and they organized a dinner for us to give at our house. They both came and that's the one time he was in our house, before I joined his administration.

I did have one substantive session with Kennedy in 1960. I had developed in the State Department a program to try to improve our relations with Latin America and there was a meeting to be held in Bogota in late August of 1960, maybe it was early September. I had developed a program of aid to Latin America. The Brazilians were talking about something called "Operation Pan America." We thought we would embrace that and help finance it and be on the side of justice and fairness in Latin America rather than being always against them. I got that idea sold in the administration and President Eisenhower approved it. But to have it mean anything we had to get some money authorized by the Congress or maybe even appropriated. So we sent legislation up right after the Democratic convention. Kennedy was the nominee, and he had already made clear that one thing on which he was going to campaign was the need to do much more with Latin America. He had developed quite a program for this.

Here we were coming up and stealing some of his thunder. So I went up and met with him alone in the Capitol where he had a special office at that time, right near the Senate Chamber—he was the nominee—and I spoke to him about this, and he was very good. It was disappointing to him. He realized this was important and right for the country, so we made an agreement that he would allow this bill to pass—no bill could pass at that time without his approval as the candidate—he would allow this to pass authorizing the money on the understanding that, if he was elected, he would then be able to come back for the appropriation when he could make any change he wanted. This is what he did, launching the Alliance for Progress and making it considerably bigger than what we had planned. But he was very generous when I went to see him, politically generous, and he said, "O.K., if this is what you think is right, I agree although I wish you had left it to me. But since there is this conference and the United States has to do something, O.K., you can do it," and they passed the law, and we went down to Bogota and had quite a successful conference. So that was my one meeting with Kennedy before his election. Now that's the background, the rest was in what I said.

What I think you should do is take a look at or get out of the files of the *New York Times* that economic speech that he gave which was very detailed and very good and that impressed me. So when I started to work with him everything could only be better from what he had said. It worked very well.

If you want to know what his strengths and weaknesses were I think his only weakness, his chief weakness and he had one, was inexperience. But he was a quick learner. There was the Bay of Pigs and there were some things of that nature. He had some rows with Congress but he learned very rapidly, and he never made the same mistake twice. I think he would have been one of our most successful Presidents if he had been able to serve his full eight years. It was tragic that he wasn't. He had some trouble in the early days with Congress, I think, largely because of his youth, and the fact he had only been in the Congress a very brief time. Suddenly this young fellow who had been there for one term turned out to be their President, and they were going to show him that he might be that, but he still had to come up and deal with them as the overlords of the legislature. But I think that would have all worn off and it was on the way out. I think he would have been a very great President. He was a great President, but by his accomplishments, he would have been more readily recognized than he has been in more recent years. But I think that as time goes on what he accomplished will be better recognized than it has been recently.

NARRATOR: Would you want to say one last word on his administrative ability? Several people have talked about that.

MR. DILLON: Well, I thought it was good because of the way he treated me. He did the same thing with the Defense Department. You might say he neglected other departments but he let them run themselves, he believed in letting his Cabinet run things.

There is one thing worth mentioning which was a change from Eisenhower. President Kennedy came in strongly influenced by Professor Neustadt and the idea that the presidency should be a very strong office. He had the erroneous concept that President Eisenhower had not been strong, which wasn't the fact as I think is being gradually recognized now. But Kennedy believed Eisenhower wasn't strong and that he had to be much stronger and make all major decisions. So one of the ways he did that was to put out an edict very early on that any actions that were of any significance and were favorable would have to be announced by the White House. So we would get telephone calls in the beginning from Pierre Salinger saying, "What announcements have you got for us to make this week?" and so forth. If it was something good, the White House would announce it; if they thought it was boring or no good they would say you and the Treasury can go ahead and announce it. That made it appear as if more was coming out of the White House than actually was in the sense of the making of policy. But with respect to the State

Department, I just don't know. Kennedy felt toward the end that he had spent too much time on the details of foreign policy.

NARRATOR: Recently we heard two of Kennedy's strongest admirers, Theodore Sorensen and Arthur Schlesinger, Jr. They said that in retrospect he may have been too activist and interventionist in foreign policy, not only the Bay of Pigs but maybe he had a little bit of an inclination to intervene in Latin America, intervene in North Africa and so forth. You were in the middle of it and we've learned today—some of us for the first time—the history of your leadership in the Alliance for Progress from this early episode you mentioned. But whether it's Latin America or wherever it was, do you think we were too eager to intervene?

MR. DILLON: No, I don't. I take issue with that. I do think that that's what I call inexperience. The Bay of Pigs I laid to inexperience rather than being too interventionist. This was a plan that had been set up earlier during the Eisenhower administration without any commitment to carry it out, but it was there on the table so it could be carried out. This I think was one of the main mistakes that President Kennedy made.

Following some of the advice of Professor Neustadt, he abolished effectively the National Security Council as it had worked under President Eisenhower. That destroyed the various channels of communication on a somewhat lower level between the State Department, the Defense Department, the CIA, the military services, and Treasury, if you will, and substituted for it a much more personal and more informal arrangement. Those arrangements finally got pretty well in place and worked all right but, at the time of the Bay of Pigs only a couple of months after his inauguration, they were not working as yet. President Kennedy authorized the Bay of Pigs to go ahead without fully knowing what was involved. And that couldn't have happened if he hadn't changed the National Security Council. He did not realize because no one ever told him that part of the plan was that, if the original air strikes were not successful, it would be necessary to have naval air intervention from American carriers. The carriers were there ready to act. That was always part of the plan. I know, because I was in charge of the preparations for the Bay of Pigs in the final months of the Eisenhower administration. When they came to Kennedy and said, "Now is the time for this," he was very surprised and very upset and said, "No," and that was the end of the operation. He then took full responsibility himself which was a very brave and proper thing to do. I don't think he was too generally interventionist. I think that is more hindsight in the aftermath of what happened in Vietnam. I think he was quite pragmatic and quite balanced, and I don't think he would do either too much or too little. I don't fault him on that at all.

NARRATOR: I'm sure all the rest of you feel as I do; we would like this to go on for a couple more hours. Perhaps some day it can. We do hope that Secretary Dillon will come back. There are so many areas in which he has been active that we do cherish his thoughts and his views on these matters. Thank you very much.

JOHN F. KENNEDY AND THE ECONOMY*

Walter W. Heller

NARRATOR: Walter Heller is one of the nation's most respected economists. He served as chairman of the Council of Economic Advisers under Presidents Kennedy and Johnson and has continued to advise government officials of subsequent administrations. He is a distinguished professor of economics at the University of Minnesota.

1. The Selection of the Chairman

QUESTION: Would you like to comment briefly on how you came to be appointed Chairman of the Council?

MR. HELLER: I've been told by people that I went down to Washington—somebody wrote something on this—knowing that I was going to be asked to be chairman of the Council, but I had no idea. Well, excuse me, that's not quite right. For all I knew, I was going down there for a consultation about positions. Sarge Shriver, Kennedy's brother-in-law and chief recruiter, called me. He came into the DuPont Plaza to meet me and he got a call the

*Reprinted by permission of Westview Press from *The President and the Council of Economic Advisors: Interviews with CEA Chairmen*, edited by Erwin C. Hargrove and Samuel A. Morley. Forthcoming from Westview Press, Boulder, Colorado.

moment he got there. I heard him say, "Yeah, yeah, I know we need a woman. Yes, yes, I know we need a black." So as I met him for the first time, I said, "I have my burnt cork and a wig and I'm ready to go." But I really didn't know. Somebody from a Chicago paper had called me and said, "Do you know that you're going to be offered the chairmanship of the Council?" My reaction was, "C'mon, you have to be kidding." My assumption had always been that if Paul Samuelson . . . wanted to be Chairman of the Council, he could have been. He is and always has been one of my heroes. But I think the role he played as outside adviser may have been an even more effective one than he would have played as Chairman, just in terms of the range of his interests and his desire or lack of it on the administrative side.

QUESTION: Do you think it was his recommendation to Kennedy on your behalf that led to your appointment?

MR. HELLER: It was one of them, I'm sure. It was Samuelson, it was Galbraith, it was Orville Freeman, and it was Hubert Humphrey—a combination, I guess, of economic and political backing. But it was, as I say, a surprise to me. I did not know that that was the job he was going to offer me. . . . Hubert Humphrey recalled that he talked with me about the Council and that I said that I would not take a position on the Council as a member, but that I would be very much interested in the chairmanship. It's a conversation that I shouldn't have thought I would have forgotten, but apparently there is a strong belief in the Humphrey camp that that's the way it came about. I don't think it's terribly important. All I can tell you is that I recall vividly I ran into the Dean of our Graduate School on the plane on the way back to Minnesota and told him of the surprising offer I'd just had and added, "I don't know whether I'm going to do it or not." He said, "You're going to stew, and you're going to weigh all the pros and cons and then you're going to say yes." He was right, of course. I just cite that as an indication that I was not at all privy to the fact that I was going to be offered the chairmanship of the Council.

2. The President and Economic Policy

QUESTION: Let me ask you now to talk about the two Presidents you worked with. Perhaps you could either compare them or deal with them individually as we go down this list of questions. What were their casts of mind, their modes of thought, how did they think about economic questions, about the Council?

MR. HELLER: How did the two Presidents think about economic questions? How did they link their values and ideology to economic questions? How did they think politically about economic questions? I think I would describe both Kennedy and Johnson as quite eye-minded, that is, they both liked to read. We did do 300 and some odd memos for Kennedy during his Presidency, and Kermit Gordon often said, "You should just publish those memos sometime." Kennedy was capable of digesting rather lengthy and fairly penetrating memos, and it was Ken Galbraith who tipped me off on that early in the game. Ken had some very good pieces of advice and some bad ones. One was not to assault Kennedy with the whole Council, but rather to hold the reins tightly in my own hands. But I had decided from the very first to have a kind of coordinate Council. I knew that I couldn't keep or attract people like Tobin and Gordon and, as staff members, Okun and Solow and Arrow, unless they shared in the decision-making and policy-making process. We had it so organized that I quite frequently had Kermit Gordon or Jim Tobin carry things all the way up to the President without my being there. Now that was, perhaps, the exception rather than the rule, but it happened often enough, and it tells you something about Kennedy. Once he had confidence in a person, he didn't care about protocol. What he was interested in, was getting to the essence, getting the facts, getting the analysis, and he really did have a steel-trap mind. We were often amazed at his capacity for understanding a particular set of relationships in economics; I think he probed more deeply than Johnson ever did and had the ability to grasp it. I guess our favorite example—certainly Jim Tobin's and mine—was the session we had on the balance of payments not so very long before the assassination. We sat in the Cabinet room and he tripped up Bob Roosa, of all people, on a couple of questions relating to the balance of payments. He said to Roosa, "But I thought you told me a month ago or so that it was the other way around?"

QUESTION: Is it true that by the time of his death, he knew the balance of payments as well as anybody at the Treasury?

MR. HELLER: Well, I don't think you should condemn the Treasury. I don't want to carry this too far, because there were still things that he didn't understand as well as we thought he did. One way to illustrate this is to zero in on my first meeting with Kennedy in Minneapolis in October of 1960. Since Kennedy was running about an hour and a half late on his schedule I concluded that I wouldn't have a chance to meet him. I had already gone back to my car and was going to go home. I thought, "You know, that's kind of stupid. I really ought to meet the candidate." So I went back, and by good luck, Hubert spied me, grabbed me by the elbow and ran me right past the

Irish mafia—O'Donnell and O'Brien, O'Dungan and O'Sorensen—and marched me right into the presence. There was Kennedy, standing between the rooms of the Presidential suite with his shirt half off—not what I would regard as a propitious time for an economics discussion. I really did think that he would just dismiss me and say, "Send in your ideas through Archie Cox or Ted Sorensen." But the way Hubert introduced me, he couldn't just dismiss me. He said, "Jack, I want you to meet the finest economist west of the Mississippi." Well, we made it by just six blocks, but if we had met in St. Paul, Hubert would have said something equally dramatic. Kennedy, who, as I say, was way behind on his schedule, stopped right then and there and the entire room fell dead, dead silent. He said, "Well, now, if you're such a good economist, tell me, can we really achieve the 5% rate of growth that we promised in the Democratic platform?" I said I thought it would be extremely difficult; that, when you are talking about growth rates, you are talking about the basic growth in the economy's potential and that involved investment in human beings and plants and equipment. But if you are talking short-run expansion, the main barrier is on the demand and not the supply side. It was going to be very hard to make 5%. My answers there aren't important. What are important are his questions. He went on to say: "Seymour Harris tells me that we can't grow all that fast with these high interest rates. But then I'm told that Germany has been growing very fast with a 5% interest rate. How about that?" Well, I discussed that. He had 5's on the mind, and his first and third questions, in particular, are significant. He said, "You know, Paul Samuelson tells me that I can turn a $500 billion economy around with about a $5 billion tax cut. How is that possible?" "Well," I said, "of course, you are only working on the gap. First of all, you know, there's a $50 or $60 million gap and there's the multiplier"—imagine discussing the multiplier with a man who's standing there half-dressed. He went through about five questions. I wrote the discussion up (in a memo of October 4, 1960) and sent it to the people who were closer to him—Samuelson, Galbraith and Harris—because I wanted them to get some feel for the trend of his thinking. But the questions were well put. He was so good at asking the questions that I neglected to emphasize the fact that he didn't know the answers. Of course, if he had, he wouldn't have needed an economic adviser.

There are two sequels to the story: about three weeks or four weeks before the assassination he turned to me once and said, "Walter, how well have we done on economic growth—how fast have we grown since I've been President? How fast has the economy grown?" And I said, "Well, Mr. President, we have actually expanded at a rate of 5% a year, but you have to distinguish between what part of that was growth in the economy and what part was closing the gap." He stopped me right there; he said, "Walter, in politics we don't make such fine distinctions." As far as he was concerned, he had his 5% growth rate, but it wasn't the growth of economic potential, obviously; it was the expansion of the economy.

The other sequel was that all the way through to the time when John P. Lewis was vetted as a member of the Council, he still asked that question about how you can turn a $500 billion economy, then a $600 billion economy, around with a $10 billion tax cut. I say that because we mustn't really fool ourselves, as we sometimes do. One ought to remember that a President has to think about one or two things other than the economy; in between times some of the things that he has grasped at one point slip away from him, and he needs to have them explained to him all over again. There can be instant understanding, but there is not necessarily retention.

QUESTION: Are you saying that President Kennedy really thought more substantively about economic questions than he did politically, or was there always a political dimension as well?

MR. HELLER: There was always a political dimension. You remember that quote that I used in *New Dimensions* in which I noted that when we met at the Carlisle in New York on January 6, 1961, he said to me something like; "Professor, I want you to use the White House as a pulpit for economic education, but always remind them that the recession started in the Eisenhower administration." Now this is so typical of him; he'd say that with a wry smile or a wink.

He really did not want to use that word "recession." When I went down to father Joe's place in Palm Beach for the announcement of my appointment (December 23, 1960), we were just going out on the veranda when Kennedy asked, "What are you going to tell them?" I said, "I am going to tell them that there have been seven months of recession, three years of slack, and five years of slow growth." He said, "Recession—do you have to use that word?" "Well, Senator," I replied, "I have to tell you that it is a recession. *Business Week* calls it a recession, the *Wall Street Journal* calls it a recession, why shouldn't you call it a recession?" He said, "Well, I'm very much concerned about the psychological impact of that." I persisted, "But that bridge has been crossed; you're really beyond that." And he said, "Well, I don't like it. However"—that was always a little signal with him; when he said, "However," you knew you were in—"go ahead and call it a recession." So I did. We spent further time persuading him that confidence came first from recognizing the facts and showing that you had a program to deal with the facts—not suppressing the facts, not glossing over them. He was basically very responsive to that kind of argument. He was, in general, just a total pleasure to work with. He caught on fast.

Hardly a session with him went by where there wasn't some humor introduced into the picture, where he wouldn't be laughing a little bit at himself. Ego—they say every President must have a towering ego, but I did not see that in Kennedy. For example, in the famous or notorious speech of August 13 or 14, 1962, when he said that we wouldn't have a quickie tax cut—but we would have a sizable net tax cut in 1963, he used some terrible, dull charts that we in the Council of Economic Advisers, of all people, had gotten together for him. He was talking in his office to the country at large on a TV program. I was sitting there in the Oval Office with him, and at the end you always feel inclined to say something nice, and I said, "Mr. President, that was just a great speech." He said, "No it wasn't. It was dull." He knew it. And that was right. It was a pretty dry, pedantic speech. Now, it's true that he could get angry—indeed furious, on occasion if the *office* of the Presidency was slighted. I saw him just a moment after the Business Council refused to stand up for him when he went into the East Room after the Steel Crisis. When he came back into the room—I was waiting to see him about something—he said, "You know, those bastards sat on their hands and didn't get up when the President of the United States walked into the room." Now you could interpret that, if it were LBJ, as ego; not in Kennedy's case. It was the Presidency—and I feel quite firm in this judgment—that was being insulted, not John F. Kennedy. Well, those are some general feelings.

One had this marvelous sense all the way through that he was getting it, that you didn't have to draw him detailed pictures. Of course, he thought instrumentally about economic questions: How would the economic advice that we were giving him and the economic measures that we were recommending serve as instruments for his broader ends? Like all modern Presidents, he recognized that a laggard economy could thwart him on a lot of his other objectives. That was the biggest thing we had going for us, once he understood that the Council's recommendations could improve what happened in the economy, could get the economy moving again. Ted Sorensen said to me, "You know, you were going back to Minnesota at the end of three and a half years. Kennedy would not have let you go, because he said yours was the one part of the program that one could really point to and say that it had gotten the country moving again; the economy was moving again and was helping to make possible all the other things he hoped to do in his second term." So, he recognized economics as a terribly important instrument and we felt he was very disciplined. We had lots of evidence that he read our memoranda because he would say something in a press briefing, or in a discussion with a foreign economic dignitary, or just in a meeting with us that he couldn't have gotten anywhere else but from our memo. Working in the Kennedy Administration—with rare exceptions—was sheer joy. You always had the feeling that the most competent ideas would win out.

QUESTION: Before we leave the question of how presidents think about economic questions, perhaps you could offer a comparison or contrast with LBJ.

MR. HELLER: Yes, I should like to. Let me just add one other thing about writing memos to the two Presidents. With Kennedy, one really could write out a narrative account—one could have a ten-page memo and not feel that his interest would flag. One device we used with Kennedy, but not with LBJ, was some humor or quip or something in quotes; I used to try to put at least one into every memo, because I sent them not only to Kennedy, but to Dungan, Sorensen and O'Donnell, to Pierre Salinger, the Vice-President and Arthur Schlesinger. I was trying to weave a "web of interest" around Kennedy, and I wanted them to read those things. An important part of our eventual open access to the White House was that all of these people essentially got on board.

In Kennedy, however, you also had a President who was willing to penetrate and find out what lay underneath some of the recommendations. Let me give you an example of how we introduced economic analysis and theory into the President's thinking. After the first uptick in the economy in June 1961, Bill Martin said, "Mr. President, you've got to look out now for inflation." We said, "Mr. President, we don't have to worry about inflation. There's no chance of having inflation in this slack economy." And in those days, long before "stagflation" and "momentum inflation," there really wasn't. He would ask, "Why not?" Then we would give him the simple, Keynesian arithmetic of the gap, which we had developed at that time and after which came Okun's law. At the same time, we got in a plug for doing something about cost-push inflation on grounds that the only real threat to price stability at those low levels of operation might come from business and labor groups with excess market power. In a very simple way, we were giving him little lessons in economic theory, economic performance, how these things work.

Putting things, goals, in quantitative terms was a terribly important part of this undertaking. In his Buxton lecture, Jim Tobin brought out the importance of quantitative goals—the role that those played in getting the President committed to an expansionary economic policy. All during the Eisenhower administration, they talked about full employment but never defined it. We got Kennedy to accept 4% as our full employment goal. We were condemned by some as being heartless for having such a high unemployment goal—using unemployment to beat inflation. We were condemned by others for being so dumb as to think that you could ever get down to 4% unemployment with all that structural employment around. We were vindicated on the latter: we were down to 4.4% unemployment in mid-1965 just before escalation in Vietnam with no sign of inflation. That was one goal. He could understand something like that. Or the notion of the gap as I mentioned, he had some trouble with that and had to be reminded of the logic. After all, that was teaching him some of the structure of economic thinking.

Let me give you another example of Kennedy's interest in contemplating issues. Very shortly before the assassination, I was going up to testify before the Senate Finance Committee on the tax bill. I prepared testimony and tossed it in with the President's (JFK's) reading matter. Because it was raining and he was out at Camp David (or was it Atoka?), he read the whole thing from A to Z and called me. We talked for some 25 minutes about the testimony. He understood the progression. "Walter," he said, "first we're going to get your tax cut and then we're going to get my expenditure programs." He understood that he had to get the tax cut to stimulate the economy, that the revenues from a prosperous economy would later enable him to get the programs that he wanted. He had come to understand that expenditure programs would have to wait until his second term.

With Johnson you had to be much more staccato in your style. Bill Moyers said to me, "Walter, you can't just load everything into a wheelbarrow and bring it over here. The President wants to have it in bang-bang-bang fashion." Then Johnson told me, "Now I don't like long memos; those Treasury memos put me to sleep. I don't like these long, drawn-out affairs. I want them so that there are generals and majors and sergeants and privates." So I developed a staccato style with the indented bullets and the indented dashes. One day, after he'd been President for maybe three months, he took one of my memos and held it up in a Cabinet meeting and said, "This is Walter's memo and this is the way I want you all to write your memos." I thought, "What a good way to lose friends and alienate people." Johnson reminded me of someone whose name may be totally unfamiliar to you: Randolph Paul. When I worked in the Treasury in the 1940's, Randolph Paul was the General Counsel and was in charge of tax legislation and tax reform, one of my lifelong interests. But Randolph Paul made it a point to learn just enough about a subject to enable him to draw from it the essential things that he needed to make a decision and then leave the details to others. I always marvelled that he was able to come out right so often without more depth penetration. It was more fun to work with Kennedy on economic matters because of that depth penetration, but I'm not sure he needed to go so deeply into some of these things for him to make valid decisions on economics. Johnson was quick; he was surprising in what he absorbed. It was always amazing what he would bring out in these head-to-head sessions with small business or big business or labor or university presidents. What he suddenly had at his fingertips was incredible. I don't think the country ever understood that. LBJ, however, wanted his memos in staccato form and did not want lengthy pieces. He insisted on our three-times-a-week economic news notes, so he always had something in his pocket to haul out when he had a meeting with somebody or a press conference or an interview. Like Randolph Paul, LBJ learned enough about the central issues and relations and facts to make intelligent decisions on economics, but he wasn't interested in going beyond that. In that sense he wasn't as much fun. But he listened. The inputs of the Council, if you had to put weights on them, actually weighed more heavily with him relative to those from the Treasury than they did with Kennedy. He relied on us even more than Kennedy did, and LBJ and I had first-rate personal relations. In that sense, he was a pleasure to work with.

QUESTION: Was that because of the different values of the two men?

MR. HELLER: Good question. Kennedy was a pragmatist. Kennedy's Yale speech revealed his feeling that we were getting to the point where most of the questions of economics were technical. That Yale speech was remarkable. All kinds of people claim credit for it—if you ask Galbraith, he wrote it; if you ask Schlesinger, he wrote it; if you ask Sorensen, he wrote it. If you ever asked me . . . The truth of the matter is that it was crafted the way so many of these things were. First, Ted Sorensen asked us for 20 shibboleths or myths in economics that needed to be destroyed or exposed and then he drafted it or it was redrafted. On the plane to Yale, Kennedy, with the *Wall Street Journal* on one side—I didn't see this—and with the *London Economist* on the other, rewrote parts of the speech. So I always say Kennedy wrote it. In it he said that we had reached the point where a lot of the great philosophical debates had been resolved; now we had to learn to push away these shibboleths blocking policy, such as worries about deficits, public debt, and rigid budget balance, and attack the problems themselves. You can see why that would be a major economic policy departure for a president.

Now, what about his basic values? I think his reaction to the poverty problem tells you as much about how those values evolved as anything else. He obviously was deeply concerned, far more deeply than President Eisenhower had been, with the plight of the unemployed, with wasted resources. At the same time, he was somewhat politically bound by the balanced budget concept and the criticism by Nixon. He'd say time and again, "Nixon will slaughter us if we go the expenditure route.'' At the beginning, therefore, we had to have a balanced budget or seem to.

Even before the inauguration, he said, ''You (meaning the Council of Economic Advisers) have to get me an anti-recession message within ten days.'' With the speech scheduled for February 2, that was an incredible order, but, of course, we were delighted. We didn't have a new staff really put together yet, but we had enough to start with. My office was the command post for that and we worked until three, four, five o'clock each morning. We had an anti-recession message put together very quickly. As you recall, tax cuts were ruled out because of the sacrifice doctrine. He had told me in the house in Georgetown, ''I know you're for a tax cut; I know Paul Samuelson's for a tax cut. I can't come in on a platform of sacrifice and the very first thing hand out tax cuts to people. That just won't wash.'' So we had to work out an anti-recession program without a tax cut.

We also had to fight the anti-recession battle, as I mentioned before within the bounds of a balanced budget. As economists, we were shocked when we were told that in one of our first White House meetings. I think the distinction you have to make is that Kennedy knew it didn't make any sense to balance the budget. Later in 1961, my notes tell me that at a briefing breakfast before one of his press conferences, Kennedy said he wished he had Eisenhower's ability to run big deficits without damaging his image as a budget-balancer, ''He could get away with it; I can't.'' He knew—again it's terribly important to separate shadow from substance—as far as appearances were concerned that he had to have a balanced budget; as far as economic substance was concerned, he fully understood that you do not have to balance the budget when the economy is slack. With the Council's help, the commitment to do so was watered down to read in the State of the Union message: ''Within that framework, that is of the Eisenhower spending and revenue estimates, barring the development of urgent national defense needs or a worsening of the economy, it is my current intention to advocate a program of expenditures which, including revenues from a stimulation of the economy, will not of and by themselves unbalance the earlier Budget!'' Now, that was a work of art. We counted seven escape hatches. And that, again, was one of the pleasures of working with the Kennedy group.

I want to put in a footnote. At the first, we economists were very suspect in the administration, because it was largely peopled with lawyers. One of the great banes of the existence of this republic is the fact that, with all due respect, lawyers had such a hold on the Congress—the House, the Senate—and the White House, as of that time. Those lawyers didn't really, honestly believe—Ted Sorensen, I'd say, first among them—that economists could think straight, and present logical, sequential arguments. It took a while to capture Ted Sorensen, and it's always terribly important to capture the man who is closest to the President, and that meant Sorensen, and then Moyers, and then Califano. There, by the way, you had real coordination of policy: all three of them, utterly superb in my opinion in pulling things together for the President and bringing them to the President, not prejudicially, not angled the way they wanted them, but honestly bringing the President, when we didn't do it directly, the pros and cons, the give and take.

QUESTION: Do you think the President needs a generalist?

MR. HELLER: Oh, absolutely. I had hoped that Carter would make more use of Stu Eizenstat this way, because Stu is first rate. He knows how to get the essence of the issues and how to present them. Once we won Sorensen's respect and once he saw that what we would do for the President in economic matters would improve not only economic policy but the President's chances of achieving his objectives, there was no further problem and he had independent confidence in all three of us—in Tobin and Gordon and myself—and that had a great deal to do with our access to the President.

QUESTION: Let's go back to the point you were making about Johnson and the Treasury and the Fed and the difference in values between the two men.

MR. HELLER: I think Kennedy's values evolved a great deal during the time he was President. He first became very conscious of the poverty program quite early in the game in connection with Appalachia and went out there, looked at things, and was deeply concerned. Then around Christmas of 1962, he read the poverty articles in the *New Yorker*. . .

QUESTION: Those were Dwight MacDonald's articles, right?

MR. HELLER: Yes. It was Dwight MacDonald's articles that helped get him started.

QUESTION: He just picked those up by chance?

MR. HELLER: Yes. Then he asked to see some other things that had been written. I brought him Keyserling's and Harrington's books one day (and never got them back). He asked to see these things and he read them and he was obviously deeply affected. When he gave his first three-network interview where Sandy Vanocur and two of the other top people interviewed him, he did bring in this whole question of poverty and how concerned he was about it. Then Kenny O'Donnell told me one day in March of 1963 that I shouldn't worry about the tax cut, it would pass, I should worry about other things. I began to worry and got Bob Lampman to worry about the fact that while the tax cut could open up opportunities, there were lots of people mired in poverty who couldn't possibly take advantage of them and that therefore we had to have a separate poverty program. So first of all I had Bob put together the things he had done—the best work on the subject in the United States—namely measuring what had happened to poverty, what the sources of poverty were, what groups were impacted, why people were mired in poverty. We gave Kennedy this factual account about in March of 1963. Then something triggered my political interest in it: in June it was said that some Republican group—I've forgotten which Republican policy committee—was going to zero in on the poverty problem. At that point I wrote my basic memo to Kennedy saying in effect, "You really should have in your 1964 program an attack—[I didn't call it a war on poverty, but an attack]—on poverty, and here are the kind of things that it might include. Unless you tell us not to, we're going to go ahead and work on them." We worked on them through the summer and—this, I think, is well known—the very last thing I talked to him about—three days before the assassination—was the poverty program, and he said, "It's going to be part of my program." We didn't know how big it was to be. I think that does address itself to the values question. . .

QUESTION: Some people say that Johnson was more effective in translating economic ideas and shaping issues with Congress than was Kennedy.

MR. HELLER: He went about it differently. They had very different instruments of persuasion. Kennedy's conviction was really a dedication to the democratic process. He really, honestly felt that you had to persuade the public or at least the major movers and shakers, policy-makers, men and women of affairs; they had to understand. He felt that he was building this base of understanding in his first term and that he was going to capitalize on it in the second. Johnson's idea was quite different. Johnson's idea was to bring the key policy-makers, the key power centers, into the room and strike a bargain with them. For example, he finally got aid to education through by saying in effect, "Now, you can't have all you want. You Catholics will get this, you NEA will get that, and you up there in Congress will get this. Now, are we going to have this program or aren't we? If you'll stick together on the general dimensions of the agreement that we have around here, we'll get it through." As the *London Economist* once put it, it was the end of ideology. The idea was to get your objectives straight, then get to the key power centers out of the public eye, and strike a bargain that would ease the path of the legislation through Congress. That's the way he got the aid to education through. With regard to the tax cut, he always kept telling me—I didn't know how much of this was flattery and how much was truth—but he kept telling me, "Walter, I'm going to go for this tax cut, because you're for it and because you say it's going to help the economy and it's not going to create inflation and it's going to balance the budget. But you know, if it doesn't do that . . . "—he had some very expressive suggestions as to what my fate would be. His idea was that the success of the measure would itself be the education device. Kennedy was quite different. He felt the people had to be persuaded that this was the right way to go and then you could move.

QUESTION: So, Kennedy wanted the Council out front, a public role, whereas Johnson didn't want you up front for fear you would queer the deal.

MR. HELLER: I think that's a fair way to put it, in part. But I don't want to imply that Johnson curbed our public role all that much or that he tried to politicize the Council—he didn't. Once a position was firmed up, he was glad to have the Council explaining it. And Kennedy didn't want us terribly far out front, just a little bit. He didn't want us so far out, and he didn't want different people in the administration popping off the way they did in the Carter administration! The idea was to work out those differences in a rational manner, in a sense behind closed doors, get all the actors into the play, but once the agreement was reached, then everybody—this was Kennedy, now—would go out and be on the same basic wavelength. He would say, "Walter, you can go out ahead of me. You can test some of these ideas." I have described that as "riding point." Riding point is a very honorary position, a very exposed one—I got hit over the head a number of times for that. But it was a different way of proceeding. Johnson held tight—in fact, tighter than I liked—and you really had to stay on Johnson's wavelength. He had as his end goal the party line. Kennedy was never so afraid. He might go out this way and test a little bit more about wage-price guideposts or about monetary policy. But you knew about where the curbs were, that you couldn't go beyond a certain point. I think it's fair to say that the Kennedy administration gave the feeling of a coordinated policy.

Now, the two Presidents also had different ways of handling "outriders". Whenever Kennedy wanted to see Paul Samuelson, he would call me and say, "I'd like to talk with Paul. Can you find out when it's convenient for Paul to come in?" I don't mean to say that there was never a case where the gap between Hyannis Port and Cambridge was bridged without my knowing it, but Kennedy had a sense of propriety about organizational relations. LBJ, in contrast, had Bill Moyers call me at the end of December 1965 to say,

"The President wants you down at the ranch tonight." This was around noon. I'm in Minneapolis. I said, "Well, there's no transportation to the ranch." He replied, "Oh, yes, there is. He's diverted a jet there and Colonel So and So and Major So and So are piloting it. You be out at Wold-Chamberlain Field at such and such a time and they'll take you down there." Then Bill said, "And no one else is to know about this." I asked, "Bill, are you saying that he doesn't want Gardner Ackley to know?" "Yes, for the time being." That is no way to operate. So on this occasion (with a bit of a lag) and on others when LBJ asked me to spend a day or two at the White House, I'd make sure that Gardner knew what was going on in advance.

Now let's continue with values. LBJ had a deep, deep gut feeling for the underdogs, the blacks, the Mexican-Americans, the poor, the unemployed. The language he would use would absolutely curl your hair. He might talk about "nigras" and what not in private—whether for shock value or simply being true to his native tongue, I just don't know—yet he did more for civil rights and the blacks than anybody other than, say, Hubert Humphrey. Now Kennedy had made a good start. LBJ deeply felt the fate of the Hispanic Americans; he was so proud of the fact that the first place he ever taught was in that little town down there in Texas, where they could hardly speak English, and of his civil rights record and his appointment of blacks in the administration. When we were at the ranch six days before his death, he told us that his civil rights advances were his proudest accomplishment. He could be as crude and as earthy as you please and still, from his NYA days and from his beginnings, he really had a deep, genuine commitment to the cause of the underdog.

QUESTION: Did LBJ's interest in some of these issues and approaches change as he got more and more preoccupied with Vietnam?

MR. HELLER: Remember, he thought he was doing the right thing in Vietnam. He constantly claimed that if he knew how to get out of it he would, but he didn't know how. This would preoccupy him, but don't forget that at the same time he was launching his Great Society program. He felt that he could do both, but if he raised taxes to finance Vietnam maybe it would impinge on his Great Society programs. So it's very hard to generalize on that—very hard to generalize.

QUESTION: Could you describe CEA recruitment and staffing patterns?

MR. HELLER: I did not find that a big burden. We were always recruiting—this was the essence of what I called the use of "in and outers." I have always thought of that as a great asset. Sure, you want a few people—especially the statistical types—who are there right along and who represent continuity. Of the staff Steve Saulnier left behind, David Lusher was, in spite of some difficulties, the most valuable member. There were a couple of others. I saw what the Republicans did in 1953 when they came into the Treasury. They made the most egregious errors by just cleaning out the whole stable. They threw out superb people simply because they had been in the Truman administration. What they did was pretty brutal. In spite of the fact that CEA professionals don't have Civil Service protection, I was bound and determined to give them all the time they needed to find another job. So I called them in one by one and said to Dave Lusher and a couple of others, "If you'd like to stay, you're welcome to." Dave, of course, stayed. One of the other two did and one of them didn't. To the others I said, "I think it would be better if you would look for another job, but you can have as long as you want to find that job." Most moved quickly, but one staff member took two years.

We had very little trouble recruiting people because of the basic attraction of the Kennedy administration. Kennedy's charisma plus the general quality of the Council we had, made the recruitment problem a lot easier than it might have seemed. We tried to draw in a very wide range of people as either special consultants or general consultants. So recruiting wasn't a very big problem. It did take new appointees several months before they really got rolling. We tried to get them for a minimum of 15 months, and that worked pretty well.

Dillon was the major counterweight to the Council, and we were the major counterweight to Treasury. Kennedy made that apparent when he brought me down to Washington to the house in Georgetown. He said, "I have Doug Dillon in the other room." This is when he popped the question with this kind of emphasis: "I want him to be my Secretary of the Treasury and my right bower, and I want you to be my Chairman of the Council and my left bower." It was clear that he perceived the desirability of some balance.

The Treasury is a terribly important part of this complex because, of course, the Treasury and the Budget Bureau had lots of line functions—everything in government budgeting had to go through the Budget Bureau, everything financial had to go through the Treasury. Things would go on that at times we wouldn't hear about right away, or on which the Treasury would have a different point of view. Dillon had an enormous amount of clout, both inside and outside the government, and there was, of course, continuous contention. No one should blink at that. On the surface we always operated very compatibly—Dillon was a gentleman; I hope I was.

IV. KENNEDY AND THE DEPARTMENTS

A CABINET PERSPECTIVE

Secretary Orville Freeman

NARRATOR: I'd like to welcome you to a Forum on the Kennedy presidency. Orville Freeman is one of the four Cabinet members who served throughout both the Kennedy and Johnson administrations from 1961 to 1969. His achievements are well known. If this were the time and place, one could recount how close those achievements came to opening up another chapter in history. Those of you who read the accounts of the selection by John F. Kennedy of his vice president know that Governor Freeman was the top contender up to the point where a decision was made to choose a person with more political influence in the southern states. So history passes us in the night and carries a leader along a course no one can ever quite foresee.

Orville Freeman was born in Minneapolis. He was a graduate with an A.B., magna cum laude, and LL.B from the University of Minnesota. He was chairman of the Minneapolis Civil Service Commission and secretary and then chairman of the Democratic Farm Labor Party in Minnesota, a party which produced that remarkable group of political leaders—Hubert Humphrey, Walter Mondale, Eugene McCarthy, Arthur Naftalin and, not least, Orville Freeman. He was governor of the state of Minnesota from 1955–1961 and as noted secretary of agriculture in the Kennedy/Johnson Administrations from 1961–1969. Then he became chairman and chief executive officer of Business International Corporation. He is a member of various corporate boards, particularly boards and commissions in the international arena. For example, he is a member of the executive committee of the Japan-U.S. Business Advisory Council, chairman of the India-U.S. Business Advisory Council, chairman of the U.S.-Nigeria Joint Agricultural Consultative Committee, and chairman of the Board of Governors of the United Nations Association. He had a distinguished combat record in World War II, reaching the rank of major in the United States Marine Corps.

After this recitation of striking achievements, he has only one black mark. Rather than having been an associate of the Miller Center, he is a member of the Advisory Committee of the Hubert Humphrey Institute at the University of Minnesota. But, of course, given his political history nothing could be more appropriate. It is a great pleasure to welcome Secretary Orville Freeman.

MR. FREEMAN: Thank you very, very much for that very kind, thoughtful, and generous introduction. I thought for a moment that you might introduce me the way Ambassador Sol Linowitz was presented once. He claims that a master of ceremonies introduced him by saying, "I'm sure that most of you here know our distinguished speaker by reputation, and many of you have heard him. I'm sure those of you who haven't heard him are looking forward to what he's going to say."

I'm honored and flattered to be invited to speak on the office of the presidency. The study of the presidency is obviously of great importance. If our country is to remain the leader of the free world and if we seek to expand human freedom and well-being and take advantage of the opportunities of modern technology and knowledge to reach around a world that has become highly interdependent, the office of the presidency is the focal point. The leadership and direction must come from that center. So, it becomes of preeminent importance to learn from the successes and shortfalls of the office.

But the office of the President, in my judgment, is not really an institution. I would describe it with the word "instrument" rather than institution. It is peculiarly shaped by a man who holds it. You may recall, it is the only office or department in Washington that has a total and complete turnover, outside of the logistical and maintenance staff. The Andrew Jackson spoils system still operates in the White House. Thus the office of the President is distinctively patterned and shaped by the man and his way of doing business.

An analysis of the presidency must therefore be flexible, sensitive to the variations and changes that take place with each office holder. Different styles, different commitments, different personalities and different ways of operating provide a comparative basis on which to build a solid evaluation of the institution or, as I would say, instrument.

I, of course, had only firsthand experience with two Presidents, almost three years with Kennedy and five years with Johnson, but I can think of no two Presidents who were more different in their means of operating in the presidency. They had quite distinctive styles. In order to draw comparisons, I would like to do something that is probably unique. I would like to use the recollections and words of twenty years ago. During my tenure as secretary of agriculture, I kept a diary. I now have nine notebooks about ten inches thick. I have never read them. But, when I was invited to come here, I went back, took them out, and over the last few days browsed through them. What I propose to do today is to read some excerpts from that diary dictated during the transition.

November 23, 1963, 5:15 p.m. What a day. I just snuck out of my big office and into this little office to dictate the frightful events of the past two days. President Kennedy is dead. He was assassinated yesterday in Dallas, Texas. The Cabinet was on the plane, had left Honolulu when the word came en route to Tokyo. We turned and came back to Washington arriving at 1:00 am. Jane and I sat and talked until almost morning and with only a few hours sleep I came into the office this morning. Then we went to the White House where we assembled in the Cabinet Room. Mike was with us. We then walked over under the portico by the Rose Gardens, through the doorway by the swimming pool, down the hall in the White House on the east side, up the steps and into the Rose Room where we waited with congressional leaders and then filed into the East Room. Jane said to me, "What an imprint on this place, since we first came, from the Kennedys." The casket was elevated on a kind of podium. Around it there were some kneeling racks for people who wished to kneel and pray. There was one big spray of flowers, otherwise all was very plain and dignified. The casket was closed.

The spirit of the man permeated everywhere. We went to the West entrance where I always go, and Jane and Mike followed me, up the steps by Ted Sorensen's office, by Kenny O'Donnell's office into the Cabinet Room where most of the Cabinet officials were already assembled. It was almost like the end of the trail; it will never be the same. I walked into Mrs. Lincoln's office, being rapidly changed over, and into the President's office where they were moving out his things. The desk, always cluttered with pictures and pieces of ivory and all kinds of gadgets, so much so that I often marveled how he could possibly work on it, was now clean.... The partition in front of the ancient desk was partially slid back. The ships that he loved and kept around the room were piled in one corner. The room had already been painted. When we came back from viewing the casket it was almost totally bare. I said to Jane, "It'll never be the same," and she said, "True, but we must go forward."

November 21, 1963, 9:00 am. One hour out of Honolulu I noted my Cabinet colleagues going forward into a compartment where Dean Rusk and Douglas Dillon were seated. Then Bob Manning, the press man from the State Department came for me. He was somber but I didn't think too much about it because I figured that they were going to have a staff conference. He took my breakfast tray and I squeezed Jane and opened the door. There was a mood of great seriousness. The thought flashed into my mind that maybe something had happened in Japan so we can't go. Then someone said, "The President has been shot in Dallas. They don't know if he is dead or not. Governor Connally was also shot." There were conflicting cables and I looked at them. One said he was dead, quoting a Secret Service man. Another said he was seriously wounded and that he was receiving a blood transfusion. So far they were not positively confirmed. We could make no direct contact. So Dean Rusk said we should turn back and we all agreed that we should, and we did, without waiting for definite confirmation.

Then the messages began to come in and we discussed what to do. First, Rusk was going back to Hawaii to pick up a special ship and go to Dallas. I asked him why, and he really didn't have a very good answer except some comment about the secretary of state participating at the swearing in and also concern as to who had their finger on the nuclear button. I asked Rusk, and he said there was a letter from JFK to LBJ in the event of a temporary period of disability. So Rusk was going to Dallas. They were desparately trying to make telephone connections and Rusk did reach Ball on the telephone, and Ball's information was no more than ours. It was not clear whether the injury was fatal or only serious.

We sat around not knowing what to do or say, and then word came that we should all return to Washington, and Rusk asked the obvious question, "Who said so? Who is there in Washington?" Nobody seemed to know who sent that word.

Then we got word that Connally was in the operating room, that the President was alive and getting blood transfusions and in an emergency room. There was a ray of hope. I pointed out grimly that I was walking proof that a man could get hit in the head and still live, and told them where the bullet went through me. And so we waited.

The final confirmation came. Dean Rusk said over the plane intercom, "Ladies and gentlemen, this is the secretary of state. I deeply regret to inform you the President is dead. May God help our country." I think those were his words. There was dead silence. Some sobbing and tears. . . . A strained atmosphere. Jane took my hand, the bad one, and squeezed it so hard that it hurt and she said, "Poor Jackie." Then she said to me, "I'm so glad you were not named vice president in Los Angeles. I'm too selfish." I must say that the thought had been in my mind, too. How different it might have been, but who knows, as the hand of fate writes the picture.

Jane and I visited en route on the plane, and she expressed her affection for this great man now gone. She put it well when she said that under Kennedy there was a growing sense of progress and purpose and direction in the country. We were making progress and the national economy was moving ahead. In the international field we were making progress as well. . . . What a crime that he must be gone. He would have won that election in 1964. . . . He had had a wonderful reception in Dallas. We could have gone forward with the program to abolish poverty, to spread freedom. With an election mandate behind him and the years of experience and the energy and ability and the affection he could have moved it, but somehow God saw otherwise.

As I've said earlier, Jane and I sat up for a long time and talked. She said what a remarkable crowd John F. Kennedy had brought to Washington and that they must not leave now; there is still too much to be done. She was right. I must admit the thought had gone through my mind a few times that I don't know how it would be to work for Lyndon Johnson. I do like him but I've used the expression about him that I wouldn't like to work too close to him because "he'd suck your guts out." I meant it not unkindly, but that he was a demanding strong person that gave you the feeling that he is putting his tentacles around you and that you are subject to his will on your almost every move. I think that's almost what he did with the Congress and we'll see what he does with the Cabinet. But Jane is right and it needs to be carried on, and this is what I told Ted Sorensen today when I went to see him, and he said, "ten years of my life." As Dick Goodwin said, this was his life, his family, his every waking thought and action. So it was. What a crushing blow.

Jane said she had confidence in both Lady Bird and LBJ's sincere deep humanitarianism. Someone said that some months ago, John Connally, governor of Texas, had told Lyndon that he was going too far in the civil rights matter both actually and politically but that Lyndon had stood his ground, and so he has. What will happen now?

Bob McNamara reported to me that the decision was final that the burial would take place in Arlington and that they had found a magnificent site between the Lee House and the Lincoln Memorial. Apparently the land in question was under control of the military who hardly knew they had it and he immediately exercised his power to acquire it. "It will be almost a shrine," he said with tears in his eyes. He also said that it could never be quite the same again with John F. Kennedy gone—that among other things he had reached the hearts of people around the world with a quality and a style and a sophistication which epitomized the age and the times in a way Lyndon Johnson couldn't approximate. However, he concurred with me that we were fortunate to have a strong man like Lyndon in the driver's seat.

The evening of the burial we were at Hubert Humphrey's home with a number of people. While we mixed around at Humphrey's we watched the dreadful television sequence that went on over the two assassinations, President Kennedy's and then the subsequent shooting of the man who shot the President. The rest of the world must think we are going insane here with these kinds of events.

So much for my diary. I hope I didn't belabor you too long with the memories. But I think my recollections of the transition period serve as an introduction to the contrasts between Kennedy and Johnson. What were the differences in style and commitments that shaped the institution or as I have said, "instrument" of the presidency under these very different men?

First, I think it's fairly clear that the Johnson method of exercising power from the presidential office was an all encompassing one. He reached into everything. Amazingly, he seemed to know everything that was going on. It's been said he knew what was under every log in Washington because he put most of it there. It really was amazing but it was also disconcerting because the White House was not very well organized. No one could speak out other than Johnson himself.

In contrast, I would describe the Kennedy White House as almost a public administration picture book operation. It was extremely well organized; policies were reviewed and set. The presidential assistants in the White House were professionals; they had been with Kennedy a long time; and so could speak for him. When you are carrying out an overall policy and you needed some guidance, most of the time you could go to Kenny O'Donnell or to Larry O'Brien or to Ted Sorenson or to Mike Feldman or to Lee White, or to McGeorge Bundy and get guidance. If they said this could be done, you could almost be positive that they reflected accurately the President's desires.

That kind of delegation, in my judgement, is the way to run the White House effectively, i.e., with a relatively small staff of very able people who have close working relationship with the President. Such Presidential assistants could work closely with Cabinet officers thereby facilitating agreement when jurisdictions overlapped. They had enough prestige and stature so that Cabinet officers would usually follow their lead, making it unnecessary to carry a lot of questions to the President. President Kennedy delegated effectively. Not that Kennedy didn't follow what was going on; he was informed and he was tough and determined. He could be ruthless. In the campaign of 1960, the "Irish Mafia" came to be quite famous and were charged with steamroller ruthlessness, rolling over anything that got in their way. I could tell you some interesting stories about that from the convention of 1960 when I was privileged to nominate Jack Kennedy and as Humphrey's campaign chairman in the primary contests in Wisconsin and West Virginia that year. But we don't have time for that.

QUESTION: Do you feel that the Kennedy people treated President Johnson badly after President Kennedy was killed? And also after Johnson won the election on his own, do you feel that he changed his attitude toward the press and the staff and that he just didn't cater to them the way he had prior to that time?

MR. FREEMAN: I don't think Kennedy's people treated him badly. It was just a hard fit. I almost resigned myself a few times. To bridge working with two such different people was very difficult. LBJ did ask the Kennedy people to continue. He wanted them to stay on. He never forced any of them out, to my knowledge, but he gradually brought in people who were his long time associates. To do so is in the nature of that office; the need for unquestioning loyalty and commitment is compelling. The commitment of those closest to Kennedy was strong and emotional, so they just gradually moved out. There was no real antagonism except between Johnson and Bobby Kennedy.

QUESTION: That did exist, didn't it?

MR. FREEMAN: It did very strongly. At the first Cabinet meeting LBJ called, it was really hard. We were sitting in our assigned places. The President sat almost directly across from me. To see anybody but Jack Kennedy in that chair that morning was just heart-wringing. Bobby delayed coming in and then he walked around the Cabinet table behind the President's chair to his place as attorney general. His countenance was cold and scornful. He sat down, all eyes on him. He said absolutely nothing. These two men were very much at odds. Bobby had vigorously opposed the selection of Vice-President Johnson in Los Angeles which LBJ never forgot.

QUESTION: Did either Jack Kennedy or Lyndon Johnson have a specific agricultural policy that they directed you to pursue as secretary of agriculture?

MR. FREEMAN: No. Neither really had a clear policy. Neither of them knew very much about agriculture. And in that I was kind of fortunate because I pretty much designed the programs. John Kennedy initially had espoused Clinton Anderson's General Farm Bureau policy which was no government involvement in agriculture whatsoever, as epitomized in the Ezra Taft Benson program in the Eisenhower years. That's just fine if you have a strong demand and a reasonable supply to balance, if the weather stays steady and a host of other outside uncontrollable forces don't intervene. But the situation of grain carry-over made him realize that this no government intervention philosophy wasn't always going to work.

The forecast that I faced when I first walked into the office of the secretary of agriculture in December, 1960 was that by August, 1961 we'd have 600 million bushels of grain and no place to put it. There was no storage space; even the moth ball fleet was full. I had nightmares. What was I to do, dump it in the ocean? The only recourse was to somehow not produce the grain supply projected. There wasn't another way. So Jack Kennedy knew something had to be done by the government. He said one time that I was a good secretary of agriculture but I cost too damn much.

Now Johnson was a rancher. He knew a good deal about cattle and a lot about rural America especially southwest Texas. But as for the economics of agriculture—supply and demand balance, reserves, trade, farm prices, the overall picture—he knew relatively little. So I was pretty much able to design and carry forward the farm program. The problem was to keep both Presidents involved and supportive as our programs developed. The basic answer to your question is neither of them had any great interest or knowledge. For the most part, I was able to operate without much interference from the White House. But we worked very hard to keep the President and the White House staff informed.

QUESTION: Mr. Secretary, you stated that the office of the President is an instrument rather than an institution. Now having served under two Presidents with such widely differing characteristics and subjected to distinctive personal as well as political pressures, would you make any changes in the job definition for the President in the Constitution?

MR. FREEMAN: I don't think so. I used the word "instrument" to make a point: The office of the President is not something that can be institutionalized in a way that will be followed by one President when he succeeds another. Rather, the office will be peculiarly reflective of the man who is in that office. And the flexibility to permit that is in the Constitution. The broad definition in the Constitution has made it possible for a wide variety of types of leaders to operate within the context of the needs of their times. I would not tamper with it.

QUESTION: Would you mind telling us what your efforts were to sell grain to Russia?

MR. FREEMAN: Yes, that is a fascinating story. Late one afternoon, I had a call from Minnesota from a very close personal friend of mine who was in the grain business. He'd been up in Canada, gotten word that the Russians were interested in buying grain in the U.S. So I began quietly checking around and found that to be the case. At the following Cabinet meeting, I brought the subject up. It was one of the few times when a policy question really got the Cabinet's attention. Neither President used the Cabinet very well as an instrument to define policy. I think that shortfall was a weakness on the part of both Presidents as it is in most private corporations. The chairmen of most private corporations fail to get their Boards of Directors involved in policy making; the Boards listen to management reports covering a lot of details that add up to management business rather than Board matters.

In this case the question was: Do we dare sell grain to Russia? What's the politics of it? The so called "Irish Mafia" around the President—the O'-Donnells, the O'Briens, etc.—wanted no part of selling grain to the USSR. They thought that to do so would be politically disastrous. Senator Humphrey and myself and a few others thought otherwise. We thought that it was acceptable to sell the Soviets anything they can't shoot back at you. But not every one agreed. The result was a tough political decision to make.

Jack Kennedy was very nervous about it. In order to get the labor movement quieted down, particularly the maritime workers who were militant anti-communists, he made a little deal on the side with them that grain we sold to Russia would go on American bottoms (ships). That little political side deal turned out to be damn expensive because the Russians weren't prepared to buy wheat with that extra cost tacked on. It no longer made much sense for them to buy American wheat. So we jockeyed around for quite an extended period of time and nothing happened. But basically the decision had been made that we would go forward when the Russians were prepared to buy it under our terms.

And then the head of Continental Grain got an idea. He got the idea that maybe the Russians would take hard Durham wheat. Durham at the time was in very long supply. As a result, a strong subsidy for export was available which could offset the additional cost of shipping on American bottoms. So Continental put the first deal together and we sold a substantial volume of Durham to the USSR. Once the first sale had been made, it went on from there. But politics almost jammed it up.

QUESTION: You pointed out that neither President had a great deal of knowledge or interest in domestic agricultural policy or technical details. But obviously there are a lot of international political implications for our agricultural policy concerning surpluses. Over the last couple of decades have you seen a general evolution of a conceptual framework or has it been ad hoc in trying to reach some accord on in the use of surplus as an instrument for foreign policy?

MR. FREEMAN: There have been great changes. In the last dozen years we've almost doubled our grain production and ninety percent of that production has gone into export. As a result, we have become dependent on world markets to a degree that was not the case during my tenure as secretary of agriculture. At this moment with the world recession and a turn down in the level of exports and in the level of grain moving in world trade we are hit hard. Yet looking to the demand side, we must not forget that there is an increase in world population of seventy million people a year. That's a lot of mouths to feed.

I believe that our problem in the future will be not one of surplus but rather light supply and even shortage. We're going to have a problem to produce enough. This is so because when developing countries return to a decent growth rate of five percent plus, their consumption of grain will increase dramatically. As incomes rise, people want more protein, animal protein. And animal protein is enormously expensive in terms of grain consumed. If you project production and consumption of grain on a basis of world economic growth of five percent a year, the developing countries with massive population will face exploding demand. If that happens, and I believe it will, the world will face a serious supply problem to produce enough grain to meet the demand. Even now with carry-over, something like a sixty-five day reserve is far from excessive on a global basis.

Wait until we see what the current drought does! It's too early to say, but it may cause a very sharp cutback in feed grain production. Weather plays tricks. When I became secretary of agriculture in 1951, there was a one-hundred and five day world carry-over. Now it's sixty-five days and there are a billion more people in the world. Much turns on contingencies that can't be forecast—weather changes, recession, expansion, world politics, economic stability, economic growth. But it is clear that economically, our country and our agriculture is much more dependent on the outside world than was the case twenty-five years ago.

When I left the office of secretary we thought we had done very well increasing agriculture exports to eight billion dollars in 1968. In 1981, the U.S. exported forty-five billion dollars worth of agricultural commodities. American agriculture is extraordinary. It is really a world miracle; two and a half percent of the people in this country feed us better and cheaper than anybody in the world and we still export forty billion dollars worth of food around the world.

QUESTION: What about food price supports?

MR. FREEMAN: Well, the housewife is always going to complain about food prices and the farmer is always going to complain about product prices and neither one is ever going to be completely happy. My philosophy is that you need to have a continuing program with a minimum price support base. When I was secretary, we changed from a high-price support program to a floor price. Then the world market determined prices. That's still the case. But some countries intervene rather than permit market forces to prevail. That's another problem.

When weather and other uncontrollable uncertainties impact supply and demand in a major way, there must be some kind of government assistance plan to protect inefficient producers. You can't turn this volatile instrument loose and expect the market to accomplish adjustment under extreme conditions. I've argued for many years that industrial economics and agricultural economics are two different animals. Personally, I'm committed to free market principles in my own business and worldwide. The less government involvement in the main, the better. And the same is true in connection with planning; there is nobody smart enough to carry out real centralized planning. The Russians have proved that. The more the market operates, the better the results even if some suffer in the adjustment process.

But agriculture is different because people have to have food to eat or they starve; you are dealing with completely uncontrollable forces, and planning is more problematic. It's a lot more difficult to run a one-thousand man operation on one hundred thousand acres of ground than it is to have ten thousand men in a factory on one acre of ground. But economists, even the agricultural economists, seldom make this distinction between agriculture and industry. The other point is that a farm program is not a welfare program. You get down to this business of payments to idle land. It is charged that payments are too big to large farmers. What's the purpose of payments? It's to manage production. Who has production? The efficient operator may have six hundred acres, he may have two thousand acres. So if you are going to ask him to take his land out of production you are going to have to pay him that amount in order to do so. Now the fact that that amount may be very small for someone who has 100 acres or less and lives at poverty level is not strictly pertinent. The farm program isn't designed to alleviate poverty. There are or should be poverty programs designed for that purpose. But people think of poverty and land reduction programs as the same. They are not the same. A farm program to manage production isn't a welfare program. A farm program is an economic program to make it possible for agriculture to continue to operate efficiently.

QUESTION: As I understand your policies during those eight years, there were some innovations that have set some precedents. Do you feel that during that period and maybe subsequently the agricultural policies of the United States were essentially developing without a real presidential directive and leadership? Was it totally ad hoc or do you feel you set some policies and precedents that have had some continuing impact?

MR. FREEMAN: The question is whether the programs in place were used or not used in the period in question. The answer is yes, but new ones were also designed and passed into law. It took time and hard work but it was done. Both presidents gave support but didn't get deeply involved. In the early 1970s, the world market strengthened. The Russians moved to a protein food policy, real animal proteins. We were having a Business International Roundtable in Moscow when Prime Minister Kosygin said the Russians planned to cut the differential on protein in their diet with the U.S. (which was fifty percent) in half in the coming five year plan. That meant twenty-five million more tons of grain consumption. They entered the U.S. market and bought twenty-five million tons of grain. Then the U.S. had a couple of crop shortfalls. Supplies got tight. There was good economic progress around the world and markets exploded. Earl Butz was secretary of agriculture during that bonanza period for agriculture. "The market works," he proclaimed. "Everything is fine. What's all this nonsense of needing farm programs?" So Earl Butz went around making speeches and telling stories. Everything was rosy.

Then once again the situation turned completely around. Worldwide recession hit markets, bumper crop costs had climbed rapidly and farm income plunged to an all time low. For a long time the current administration refused to act, to use the programs available. It seems to me they should have seen what was coming. They could have moved quite some time ago. They could have used the instruments available to move land out of production and keep a reasonable supply balance. But they didn't do it. Very late, under great pressure, they came up with the PIK program. It's going to cost twenty-one billion dollars, the most we've ever spent in history on a commodity program. The previous high was between four and five billion dollars. It's just an apostasy and of course now with an unprecedented drought a real shortfall in feed grains threatens.

One significant event has been to establish by law during the Carter presidency a grain reserve. It's called the Farmer's Grain Reserve. The farmers don't like reserves. They'd rather have too little than too much because then the prices are better. But following the shortfall of grain in the early 1970s with the production shortfall and the Russians coming in and buying heavily, Congress became conscious of the fact that a shortage could be dangerous. Secretary Bob Bergland pushed through Congress legislation authorizing a reserve grain carry-over.

QUESTION: I really want to say that I think President Kennedy is the only President that ever recalled all of our fifty agricultural attaches stationed in the fifty countries. They were called back for the President to meet with them and get their opinions on world affairs.

MR. FREEMAN: Another story about Jack Kennedy comes to mind that shows the differences between him and Lyndon Johnson. In 1962, we were having serious problems on the dairy front; carry-over had climbed very high and with it expenditures. It was an economic and political problem. I decided to bring all the dairymen to Washington, D.C. and put on a big hoopteedo! I got the President to agree to come to speak to them. I told him, "What I want you to do is this. I'm going to put a glass of milk on that podium shelf and when you finish your speech I want you to take that glass of milk and drink a toast to the dairymen of our country." He said, "Orville, I can't do that." Jack Kennedy never acted in an ostentatious manner. I never saw him put on a silly hat or clown around like many politicians. So he said, "I can't do that," and I said, "Come on now. It's just a little politics and you need a little corn. Drink that milk!" He said, "I can't do that." Anyway, I put the glass of milk on the podium shelf. He gave his speech and when he came to the end of it, all of a sudden he picked up the glass, raised it high, drank, almost shouted, "I salute you!" and nearly ran off the podium. But he did drink the milk. Lyndon Johnson, on the other hand would have toasted the dairy farmers with both gusto and pleasure.

QUESTION: Being an historian, I am always interested to what extent Presidents have a sense of their relationship to the American political tradition or the history of the presidency particularly. I want to say, "sense of history" but that's rather philosophical and too large. I would prefer to think about it in terms of a sense of American history and particularly a sense of the history of the presidency. Obviously, FDR had that; I think Truman had it to a certain extent. I think Kennedy perhaps also had it though I suppose that's only problematic so far. I was curious to have your reaction to that.

MR. FREEMAN: Well, first I think Kennedy did have it. I don't know how you define an historian but I think it has something to do with the sense of the sweep of history. One of the most outstanding qualities of Kennedy was his capacity to stand apart from himself, to look at himself as one in a certain period of history and to relate to the times accordingly. He did not take himself too seriously. Not that he wouldn't get emotional and angry and determined but he had great self-control and a level of detachment that was just extraordinary.

A quick story. At the time of the Cuban missile crisis, the President sent the Cabinet out making public appearances all over the country to demonstrate that everything was under control. Suddenly, we were called to return to review the action proposed by the working committee and make the final decision on what to do. The Cabinet was standing outside the Cabinet Room waiting in the Rose Garden for the President who was running a little behind schedule.

All of a sudden he came through the French doors of the Cabinet Room with some African head of state; I don't remember which one. He took that foreign leader around and introduced him to every single one of us. You would think it was the Ides of March. He was just that relaxed and cool. There was no sense of tension or weariness. Instead, he exuded complete self-control.

He walked down the way, put the chief of state in a limousine, stood there and waved him off and then came back. We followed him into the Cabinet Room and when the final decision was made to meet the Cuban missile crisis, not a hair ruffled on Jack Kennedy's head. That kind of detachment was possible I think because he had a sense of acting in history. I don't suggest he was a history scholar per se but he had a feel for the sweep of history.

As a matter of fact, until he ran in the presidential primaries he knew England better than he knew the U.S. In a very real sense, he got educated about his own country in the 1960 presidential primaries. There is a case to be made that the American primary system forces an education on presidential aspirants. By the time they get through running around this huge heterogenous country, shaking hands from morning to night, speaking ten times a day, exposed to vilification and abuse and criticism, loved and pushed and pawed again and again, they come to know the country and the people. Pretty hard process but I am convinced that it is a useful and even necessary test.

NARRATOR: Mr. Secretary, thank you very much for sharing your observations on the presidency with us. We hope we can welcome you many, many times again to the Miller Center.

V.
KENNEDY AND THE PRESS

IMAGE AND REALITY
Charles Roberts

NARRATOR: We are pleased to welcome you to a Forum on the Kennedy presidency. Today we have someone who is almost coming back home. He's a West Virginian. That's as close as you can get, I guess. He did his undergraduate work in journalism at the University of Minnesota and was editor of the *Daily* there. He was a friend of Hubert Humphrey, who came back to the university at about the time that Charles Roberts was in attendance. He worked for a number of newspapers over a ten-year period, then for *Newsweek* for twenty-two years. Fifteen of those years he spent as White House correspondent covering the Eisenhower presidency, the Kennedy presidency, and the Johnson years. He retired from active journalism last year but continues to write and to be called on in various ways.

When we asked the question for an earlier publication—who could write the most authoritative account of John F. Kennedy's relations with the press—everyone of whom we inquired immediately said, ''Chuck Roberts.'' He was on the first press bus under the assassin's window in the fateful shooting of John F. Kennedy in Dallas. He was present at the swearing in of Lyndon Johnson aboard Air Force One in Dallas. He and Merriman Smith were the two reporters who returned to Washington on Air Force One after the assassination with the Johnson and Kennedy parties.

He has earned a number of awards including a Newspaper Page One Guild Award for an investigative reporting piece of writing that he did in the *Chicago Daily News* exposing the connection between a harness racing syndicate and a group of state legislators in the 1950s. A Long Island paper did a similar expose the next year and got a Pulitzer Prize, but magazine reporters can't win Pulitzers. His byline was widely known and respected during his year at *Newsweek* and we are especially pleased that he could be with us to talk about the Kennedy presidency.

MR. ROBERTS: I suppose you've heard this a hundred times but I'm struck with how appropriate it is to be talking about Presidents and Presidents and the press in the heart of Jefferson and Madison country, the homeland of the two Presidents who perhaps did the most to secure the rights of the press, and in turn became critics of the press, which is typical. I want to reciprocate for that gracious introduction by saying that I have followed your studies with great interest and I think you've made an enormous contribution to our understanding of the presidency.

I may not make a contribution to our fund of knowledge about the presidency but I can give you a perspective on President Kennedy. A reasonable man could argue that the press made Kennedy and destroyed Johnson.

Kennedy himself, quoting an old *New York Times* ad which plugged their classified ads, once remarked that he got his job through the *New York Times*. And certainly the friendliness of that paper when he was a relatively obscure senator, plus the debates, which were a media event, helped elevate him from a back seat in the Senate into the White House.

If some of what I say about President Kennedy sounds familiar to some of you it may be because I'm excerpting my remarks on him from a long piece that I did for *Ten Presidents and the Press,* a fine publication edited by Ken Thompson.

Although it happened only a generation ago, few of us remember now what a stir was created by the first presidential news conference to be televised live from Washington. It happened on January 25, 1981, just five days after Jack Kennedy took the oath of office. A record crowd of 418 reporters were there, bathed in TV lights, for a dinner-hour, prime-time show. That was 106 more reporters than had ever covered a presidential news conference, and an audience of 60 million people watched in living rooms and bar rooms across the country as this new young President dramatically announced before eleven TV cameras that the Soviet Union had released two American airmen that they had captured. There was a possible break in the cold war. And then he fielded very gracefully questions from reporters for about forty minutes, which was about ten minutes longer than his aging predecessor had allowed his press conferences to run. His performance was almost flawless and from my assigned seat in that State Department auditorium (which was also an innovation), I sensed from the moment the President walked on stage that the presidential press conference would never be the same again. It had not only become show business, confirming the dire predictions of the recalcitrant writing reporters who didn't want it that way, but it had also, as my magazine noted in its next issue, opened a new era in political communication.

News magazines sometimes are guilty of hyperbole when they are trying to describe something in a way that the newspapers missed. But that conference I think was momentous and historic, at least in the history of Presidents and the press. His decision to go live changed the presidential press conference more than any other single innovation in the eighty-year history of scheduled meetings between the President and the press. And in an administration that was later accused of managing the news and taking reprisals against correspondents who refused to be cheerleaders, that innovative news conference was the most successful of Kennedy's approaches to the media. So let's examine it first and then look at some of his other relations with the press.

You could argue that going live with the press conference was just an adaptation to the electronic age. But if you look back at the way the press conference existed before Kennedy crossed the New Frontier you see a different picture.

President Eisenhower's press secretary, Jim Hagerty, had permitted radio taping of Ike's press conference since 1953 and filming of those press conferences since 1955. In each case they were recorded for broadcast at a later hour, usually long after prime time. Sometimes they aired just before the national anthem, they got so dull. And Hagerty reserved the right to edit those films—a totally different thing from a live news conference.

Throughout the fifties, a decade of tense relations with Moscow, the compelling argument against going on the air while actually jousting with reporters was the belief that one slip of the tongue could cause an international incident. Kennedy's top foreign policy advisers, McGeorge Bundy and Dean Rusk, were among those who were firmly opposed to a live press conference telecast. But Kennedy, just a month before his first news conference, while he was still President-elect, made the decision to take the risk. He realized that if he slipped he could fire off a correction or a clarification of his error by the same lightning-fast medium that first aired his blunder.

Pierre Salinger informed us of Kennedy's decision to go live at a briefing in Palm Beach, Florida just a few days after Kennedy had entertained us at a Christmas party at old Ambassador Joe's oceanfront home. Despite a prevailing mood then of *bonhomie*, most of us print reporters, comprising the vast majority of the press corps then, objected vociferously to the idea of making a TV spectacle out of a news conference.

Most of us had been in Washington much longer than Salinger if not Kennedy, and thought we had a better feel of how a press conference ought to be run. Many argued that the new format would destroy the give and take or what Truman called the "rough and tumble" of the press conference and that it would make actors out of honest newsmen. Both of those prophecies came true. But Salinger reminded us that it was not our press conference but the President's and he rejected all efforts to preserve the status quo.

Those live cameras at that first news conference transformed what Teddy Roosevelt called the "bully pulpit" of the presidency into a podium far more powerful than anything envisioned by Teddy Roosevelt. They gave the President the upper hand forevermore in his verbal bouts with the press. They also enabled Kennedy's successors via satellites that were launched later to address not only this country but the chancellories of the world, instantly and without any ambassadors as middlemen. So it was really a huge transformation in the news conference.

Most important, politically, the live cameras handed the President a platform from which he could speak over the heads of reporters and editors, the anchormen and the commentators, what Kennedy commonly referred to as the "hostile press." He could go over their heads and speak directly to the voters.

I remember Ted Sorensen, who was against Kennedy going live on TV, later told me, "We couldn't survive without TV." It became a powerful weapon in the President's hands. Kennedy liked his own invention so much that he held twenty news conferences that first year—and that contrasts with just six that President Reagan held in his first year. There is no doubt that the American people also liked the live televised news conference. In June of 1962 Young and Rubicam researchers found that ninety-five percent of the people they surveyed who watched the press conferences considered them a worthwhile experience. And, surprisingly, some respondents, who were not pro-Kennedy, who thought he was not doing a good job, took a favorable view of the news conferences.

Franklin D. Roosevelt, as you know, had made a similar breakthrough with his fireside chats on radio. But the live TV news conference is a far more effective vehicle because in good times or bad that spontaneous, unrehearsed give-and-take encounter with reporters will command greater attention. Of course if a President with less charisma than Kennedy had first gone live on TV it is possible that the TV conference would not have become the part of the presidency that it is now. And I think it is a custom that all Presidents are now obliged to respect.

Kennedy's quick wit and facile tongue made press conference watchers out of millions of people who had never read, and never will read, transcripts of presidential news conferences. Five administrations later, it is almost inconceivable that a future President, no matter how inept on camera, would risk the wrath of the media and the voters by refusing to face the press and the public simultaneously on the "box."

Rereading the transcripts of Kennedy's conferences after twenty years, one is reminded of the old saying that everyone laughs at a rich man's jokes. Some of his fast rejoinders that rocked the room with laughter in those days, even when they were designed to evade embarrassing questions, are not funny when you read them today.

But it was a growing infrequency of press conferences, rather than a lack of humor in them, that brought about the first criticism of Kennedy's press relations. That was in the fall of 1961 when, after he had weathered the Bay of Pigs and the Berlin Wall crisis, the President almost went into hiding and didn't hold a press conference from August 30 until October 11. This, of course, did not conform to his campaign promise that he would hold a press conference, or at least see the press, once a week.

By November of that year he had fallen behind Ike, who ironically had been criticized by the Democrats for eight years for the infrequency of his news conferences. I was noting in a memorandum to my editors in New York that "many reporters feel he is now less responsive to questions than President Eisenhower was. . . . The transcripts of his conferences are full of evasive filibusters."

Kennedy was asked a question that may have anticipated the Miller Center's study of the press conference. The question was, "Mr. President, have you given any thought to some of the proposals advanced from time to time for improving the presidential press conference, such as having the press conference devoted all to one subject, or having written questions at a certain point?" Kennedy replied, "Well, I have heard of that, and I have seen criticism of the proposal. The difficulty is, as Robert Frost said, about not taking down a fence until you find out why it was put up. I think all the proposals made to improve it will really not improve it. I think we do have the problem of moving very quickly from subject to subject, and therefore I am sure many of you feel that we are not going into any depth. So I would try to recognize perhaps the correspondent on an issue two or three times in a row, and we could perhaps meet that problem. Otherwise, it seems to me it serves its purpose, which is to have the President in the bull's-eye, and I suppose that is in some way revealing."

The irony of that is that he spoke about being in the bull's-eye just two months before Dallas, where he was killed by a rifleman with a telescopic gunsight.

Now, let's look at his press relations other than the news conference. Although the news conference is the most visible, it's not by any means the end-all and be-all of presidential press relations. Kennedy cultivated the media in many other ways, many of them innovative. He broke new ground in some of his dealings with the journalists who chronicled the New Frontier: first, by the matter of allowing reporters far greater access to members of his White House staff than had been granted by any previous administration; second, with TV specials including in-depth interviews with network correspondents; and third, a tour of the White House with his wife Jackie. These things may seem routine now but they were brand-new then. Also there were similar exclusives, similar to the TV interviews, for print media, including many magazine picture spreads and stories on "A Day in the Life of a President."

I did one of those very trite stories. Nearly everybody else did. They gave tremendous exposure to the President. Then he had his White House luncheons for editors and publishers from the hinterlands. There were more "perks" for journalists including invitations to lunches, state dinners and social functions.

The access to White House staff was, for reporters certainly, the most important of those innovations. Under Ike, literally, you couldn't see any White House staff, with the exception of Sherman Adams, without first clearing it with Jim Hagerty. Under Kennedy, suddenly it was possible to see his top advisers in their offices or at lunch. This was a great break for correspondents who didn't want to live only on handouts and news distributed at Pierre Salinger's daily briefings.

The TV specials were also a stunning success from the President's point of view. At the first interview with network correspondents he got nothing but softball questions from the TV correspondents, who were apparently in awe of having the President on the air live with them almost one-on-one. They almost entirely forgot the adversary relationship that is supposed to exist between journalists and the President. And then Walter Cronkite and Chet Huntley practically turned their news shows over to him, each in turn when their networks went from the fifteen minute format to the half-hour format for their evening news shows. And finally, ABC was even allowed to tape a close-up of the President in his command post during his battle with Governor George Wallace over the integration of the University of Alabama. These were all breakthroughs.

The luncheons for editors and publishers generated many editorials that reflected a greater understanding of the President's problems. Once the publishers—who for the most part were not nearly as friendly to the President as their correspondents were—heard him talking close up about his problems they were more understanding. But one of them, you may remember, backfired. At a lunch for Texas publishers, Ted Dealey, publisher of the *Dallas Morning News*, stood up and read a 500-word statement calling for "a man on horseback to lead this nation." And he also said, "Many Texans in the Southwest think that you are riding Caroline's tricycle, instead of being a man on horseback." Kennedy had to call in some of his friends in the press to put out that fire, to refute Dealey's argument that he was a weak President.

As a result, in the end Dealey was criticized more in the press for his intemperance than Kennedy was. Kennedy had more close friends in the working press than any President in memory and he did not hesitate to use them in defense of the New Frontier. These friendships proved mutually beneficial to both the President and the reporter when Kennedy wanted to put out an inside story with assurance that it was in friendly hands.

For example, Charley Bartlett and Stewart Alsop wrote for the *Saturday Evening Post* an all-but-authorized, behind-the-scenes account of how the Bay of Pigs crisis was handled. Of course, that had been the first blunder of JFK's administration. Their piece made him look a lot better than he did in the contemporary newspaper accounts.

Then Ben Bradlee and I, with access to FBI files that had been conveniently made available to us, collaborated on a *Newsweek* piece that I think effectively put down what we called the "John's other wife" story. That was the widely circulated rumor that Kennedy had been married to a thrice-married Newport socialite before he got married to Jackie. Having *Newsweek* refute that rumor, which was gaining national circulation, was much more effective than putting out a White House statement doing the same thing.

They were smart. All of us were able to write more authoritatively than ever before because of this unmatched access to officials.

The first strains in this very friendly relationship with the President and White House staff began to appear when we realized that Kennedy was not only the friendliest but the most thin-skinned of Presidents. Kennedy and his staff were quick to compliment and reward a "good" story, that is, one favorable to his administration. But they were extremely intolerant of anything critical. And what was worse, reporters who did critical stories found that their sources of information were drying up. Their invitations to lunch were vanishing and suddenly their calls weren't being returned. Kenny O'Donnell really summed it up. He said, "You are either for us or against us." That was the Irish Mafia view of the White House press.

Merriman Smith, who was then dean of the White House correspondents, marvelled at how the White House could spot little critical stories. He said, "Put it in a paper of 3,000 circulation, 2,000 miles away and they'll see it. They must have a thousand little gnomes reading papers for them."

Another characteristic of JFK's thin skin was that the story had to be *all* favorable. You could do a piece that might say several nice things about Kennedy, or at least present them in a favorable light, but then if you had a negative paragraph back on page 83 with the truss ads they would spot that and say, "Wait a minute, what's your basis for challenging us?"

I think the public first became aware of this supersensitivity when it came out that the White House had canceled its subscription to the *New York Herald Tribune*. It was staunchly Republican, but it was doing a good job of covering the White House. One story that particularly irked them was the *Trib's* coverage of a lavish entertainment for the president of Pakistan, down at Mount Vernon. The emphasis of that story was on its cost rather than on what a grand party it was. So that put the *Tribune* reporter in the doghouse.

It was after that that Kennedy said at a news conference that he was "reading more now but enjoying it less." Then *Look* Magazine did a survey about three months later and in a spread entitled *Kennedy vs. the Press* reported quite a remarkable turnaround. *Look* found that twenty-five or thirty Washington correspondents had been reprimanded by members of the Kennedy family or White House staff, or had been questioned by the FBI or Pentagon security officers. Several complained that the White House had put a freeze on them for stories that did not pass the White House's test of friendliness.

No reporter that I know faulted Kennedy for managing the news while he and Khrushchev were eyeball to eyeball at the brink of a nuclear war on that question of Russian missiles in Cuba. But when that embargo on all information concerning negotiations with Moscow continued long after Khruschev had agreed to remove the missiles, the press perceived, as the *New York Times* put it, that it was "being used more than informed."

Arthur Krock, a one-time mentor of Kennedy, instrumental in getting his first book *Why England Slept,* published, wrote at about this time, "A news management policy not only exists at the White House, but in the form of direct and deliberate action has been enforced more cynically and boldly than by any previous administration in a period when the U.S. was not at war."

The bullet that killed Kennedy made him a hero, posthumously, to all but the most dyed-in-the-wool Kennedy haters. His martyrdom assured him, at least temporarily, a better niche in history than he might have earned if he had served out that first term and perhaps a second term.

Now historians are taking a harder look at that brief tenure. They are finding, in many cases, that his rhetoric was better than his record. They are also finding some character defects: That celebrated war record and his sole authorship of two books are now questioned. It is well documented that he didn't tell the truth about his state of health, and that he taped phone conversations with unwitting White House callers, including reporters. And of course there is the evidence that he was a compulsive philanderer.

These latter-day disclosures raise some troubling questions for journalists. If Kennedy's shortcomings were known or suspected, as many were by the way, why weren't they reported more effectively? Was Krock right when he charged that Kennedy managed the news by what he called "selective personal patronage" and "social flattery" of correspondents and commentators? Were we the victims rather than the beneficiaries of those briefings and contacts with JFK that left us, again quoting Krock, "in a state of protracted enchantment evoked by the President's charm and the aura of his office"?

I think that all reporters who covered Kennedy would acknowledge that these questions are valid, but in the next breath argue that to pose them now, particularly the problem of Kennedy's peccadillos, is to ask them out of context. In the pre-Watergate days of Camelot, most reporters at the White House, I believe, thought that what a President did in his spare time after 6 p.m. was his own business—unless it interfered with the performance of his duties. Some, I might add, lived by the Biblical injunction: Let him who is without sin cast the first stone.

As for Krock's charge, there is no denying that Kennedy flattered and charmed the press. What is debatable is the extent to which we were rendered uncritical. The fact that reams were written about Kennedy's attempt to manage the news is certainly evidence in mitigation of the charge. If we were captivated, we at least protested while the seduction was in progress.

But most of us now reaffirm what we knew then, that an arms-length relationship, such as that we had under Eisenhower, is better for both the journalist and his readers. Whether that should be an adversary relationship is a tough question—and that's for another day.

The irony of what is happening now is that as estimates of Kennedy's presidency go down, his marks for skillful handling of the press must be revised upward. If his presidency is to be branded as mediocre and if his administration got a much better press than it deserved, then he must be acknowledged as the greatest manipulator of the media since FDR and an even greater communicator than Ronald Reagan. One thing is certain. Whatever his motive, as the first President to admit the public via television to his news conference, his distinction is secure. He did open a new era of political communication.

QUESTION: Did *Newsweek* try and manage any of the stories that you wrote and were you personally seduced by the candidate?

MR. ROBERTS: I think I can honestly say that I was never seduced. I had some misgivings about the piece we did on "John's other wife." Certainly we served his purposes in taking this file from the FBI—which incidentally never said flat out that Kennedy had never been married, nor did the White House ever say that. The story was that he had been married to this girl, and, with his connections with the church, after they decided it was no go, they simply had an annulment, with the cooperation of Rome. That is not the kind of thing I like to get into every day—where you are doing the President's work for him. That's the only near-seduction I would admit to, or that I can recall.

QUESTION: Did *Newsweek* try and manage any of the stories? Were you told to write only favorable pieces?

MR. ROBERTS: Absolutely not. Of course, I had a bureau chief who had been his neighbor and good friend, a fellow Harvard man by the name of Ben Bradlee. Ben was running the *Newsweek* bureau then and I was assistant bureau chief and White House correspondent. Ben was very friendly to Kennedy and often at our Wednesday story conference, by a telephone with our editors in New York, he would float story suggestions about what a great job Kennedy was doing on one project or another, let's say the Alliance for Progress, which turned out to be mostly rhetoric, and I would find that by the end of the week I couldn't deliver as good a story as Ben had promised. We used to kid about that. But if you go back and look at *Newsweek* over those years I don't think we were sycophantic or Kennedy worshippers by any means.

QUESTION: I will tell you why I am asking the question. Did he capture you in the primaries, too? I'm interested in medicine, and the statement that Janet Travell and Bobby (Kennedy) issued on his (JFK's) disease was absolute literary screening, partly right and partly wrong.

MR. ROBERTS: He did have Addison's disease.

QUESTION: No question about it. Everybody knew it. But you didn't follow it up. The press completely accepted Bobby and Travell's statement, that he "had mild Addison's disease, but he truly didn't have it because he didn't have tuberculosis." We can't find any evidence that any press man followed that up. But it's all out there in print.

MR. ROBERTS: To my knowledge it didn't appear in any reliable printed medium until it appeared in the *New England Journal of Medicine,* and his name wasn't used.

QUESTION: No, it was in the *Times*. It appeared in certain annals of surgery. But that was a year later, and the patient was described as a thirty-nine year old senator from Massachusetts. You know the incident I'm talking about. The press never did follow it up.

MR. ROBERTS: Oh, yes. I know it very well. Janet Travell and one other medical doctor signed in on that.

QUESTION: Who knew nothing about Addison's disease.

MR. ROBERTS: Well, I don't think Janet Travell did. Her specialty was the relief of pain. But to get back to your point about the press not following the story up, we didn't have the knowledge we have now. I think a lot of these things are judged in hindsight. Put yourself in the position of a reporter in 1960. He's handed a report. He has reason to suspect all charges made by politicians in a campaign, such as that made by India Edwards. Then he receives in refutation of that charge a statement by two medical doctors. He takes their word that he (Kennedy) has a mild case, but totally manageable and not life-threatening. It didn't occur to me to go and find some other doctor in Boston to refute that medical report.

QUESTION: When Humphrey got sick, you went to every doctor in Washington and every doctor in New York and every doctor in Minneapolis.

MR. ROBERTS: I didn't. Victor Cohen of the *Washington Post* did. He did a great job.

QUESTION: There has been a change hasn't there?

MR. ROBERTS: Yes. We know now that we were bamboozled in some cases. Of course, Watergate was the watershed in terms of reporters never accepting as gospel everything that comes from the White House. Now they question everything. But in 1960 we were aware that Kennedy was being treated with corticosteroids because about every fourth or fifth day we would see him with a balloon face.

QUESTION: Have you gone back to the Cuban missile crisis? He was the fattest that day.

MR. ROBERTS: There were many times when he had a moon face. I inquired about it and was told this was a reaction to the corticosteroid shots he was getting. But again, I had no knowledge and no way of checking up without leaving my beat and making a project out of it. If you are covering that beat, the so-called nerve center of the free world, you can't go off and spend the time it takes to do the sort of investigative reporting that you are talking about.

QUESTION: I just want to question further about the alleged marriage of Jack Kennedy. I had two students on the White House staff then. One was part of the Irish Mafia in Princeton. The second came to the White House via George Ball and his law firm to Clark Clifford and then to advising the President. He did some of the research on balancing the budget and some of the checking out of the alleged marriage. The version he gave to me was that he thought Kennedy had a clear-cut case, that he had never married before.

The second thing that I was told concerned Ted Kennedy and the time he was running in the primary for U.S. Senate, when he announced his candidacy. The President was very concerned about the fact that Ted had cheated on an exam and how best to handle that. My friend's advice to him was to plant a question at a White House press conference, so that it would come out early. They decided to get it out very early. Then the President was asked the question, to which he said Ted had cheated, yes, he had done the wrong thing, but he had suffered, paid the penalty, and was running now for senator. And it did cool the thing because it came out very early in the campaign.

MR. ROBERTS: Well, certainly planted questions have existed for many years. They go back at least to the days of Eisenhower. Thinking about planted questions reminds me of an incident. Maybe this is a confession. At the urging of Kenny O'Donnell, a part of the Irish Mafia, I once asked Kennedy a question. He gave me a very curt, noncommittal answer, and said in effect, "I don't know anything about that and I'm not prepared to talk about it." I later decided that O'Donnell's motive was that he was trying to move the President off of dead center and toward a position that he favored.

Maybe I'm trying to say they're not all bad. I didn't think so then or I wouldn't have asked that question. Maybe with hindsight they are all bad—because it certainly comes under the heading of being a part of and participating in news management.

QUESTION: On reflection how happy are you with the televised news conference as a source of news?

MR. ROBERTS: I think as a source of news its value is almost nil. It's a show, a show that the President doesn't have unless he has something to say that he thinks will help his cause. He usually has several things on which he wants to discourse and do a sales job.

Of course, sometimes there is a disclosure of some news that has not been revealed before. But the questioning is so rigid, so formal that there is very little give and take. It is a way of the President putting out the news so that it does him a lot of good. As a way of the press getting at the news, I don't place a very high value on it.

QUESTION: So what was the contribution then of Kennedy's introducing the televised news conference?

MR. ROBERTS: What I said is that it changed the format forevermore and it gave the President this powerful weapon that he hadn't had before. I didn't say I think it's a great thing. I just said it was a momentous thing in terms of the presidency and the press, a breakthrough in the history of that relationship.

QUESTION: You mentioned the President using the press as a weapon. I can recall President Kennedy's news conferences, which we looked forward to with a great deal of anticipation and a great deal of joy in some cases. But then the reverse of this, what's really disturbed me, was the treatment that President Carter received in the last weeks of his presidency by Sam Donaldson and Lisa Myers. I think they helped to destroy him. What is your reaction to that? They were brutal.

MR. ROBERTS: I don't know that I would quarrel with that judgment. I don't want to go into names of colleagues but I think a lot of pepople do get carried away with their own importance and try to engage in a kind of one-on-one spitting match with the President knowing that it's going to get them a lot of notoriety. The question is—is it an honest effort to probe and get an answer to a question? One example of abuse that I remember was Dan Rather in a Nixon press conference getting out of line, going beyond what an honest questioner of the press usually does in his exchange with the President.

NARRATOR: Maybe the thing to say about a journalist is that if today's presentation is any index, we do know what a good journalist thinks about a problem. Chuck, you've been straightforward and open on what you think on some issues where it's so easy to let passion and feeling rule and you've given us one of the clearest presentations we've had. Thank you.

VI. KENNEDY AND FOREIGN POLICY

REFLECTIONS ON FOREIGN POLICY

Secretary Dean Rusk

EDITOR'S NOTE: The essay which follows is part of a longer presentation by Secretary Rusk on "The President and the Secretary of State." It is included here because of the light it throws on the Kennedy administration and the relationship between President Kennedy and his secretary of state. It contains valuable insights on problems of executive-legislative relations, summit diplomacy, consultation with allies and differing philosophers within the Kennedy presidency.

When we think of a president, we think of a moving target. Let me just go back through my own memory and list some names that I can remember. As I do so, please reflect for a moment on the extraordinary differences among the people I will name: Woodrow Wilson, Warren Harding, Calvin Coolidge, Herbert Hoover, Franklin Roosevelt, Harry Truman, Dwight Eisenhower,

John F. Kennedy, Lyndon Johnson, Richard Nixon, Gerald Ford, Jimmy Carter. What extraordinary diversity among those people! About the only thing they had in common was that they were white, male, American citizens over thirty-five years of age, and each became President of the United States. Generalizations about the President are pretty tricky. Franklin Roosevelt was not the President that Calvin Coolidge was. John F. Kennedy was not the President that Lyndon Johnson was—I'm not putting that in any particular order. We are talking about birds on the wing.

Then, circumstances play a major role, as with the Great Depression in Franklin Roosevelt's years. I was sitting with President Kennedy when he called in about thirty congressional leaders late one Monday afternoon to tell them about the Cuban Missile Crisis, what he proposed to do about it, and what he was going to say in two hours' time in a television speech to the nation. No senator or congressman present raised any question whatever about the President's authority to bring us to the brink of a possible nuclear war. At that moment, the prevailing feeling around the table was expressed to me by two or three of them on the way out: "Thank God, I'm not the President of the United States!" So, circumstance has a lot to do with the office and how it operates.

John F. Kennedy did not feel that he had a mandate in the election of 1960. He was elected by a few tens of thousands of votes—he used to say the votes of Cook County, Illinois. So he was very cautious about selecting the items on which he was prepared to do battle, particularly with the Congress. He was much more cautious than many people think, given his other attributes, whereas Lyndon Johnson, with his massive vote in 1964, put through the Congress a formidable legislative program because the circumstances of his office were different.

The law, as well as circumstances, determines a President's policies. Today is a working day in the Department of State. Some three thousand cables will go out of that department to our posts and to other governments all over the world. A considerable number of those cables will be based, not upon personal direction from the President and the secretary of state, but on law. A much larger percentage of those cables will have their content determined by law rather than by something called policy guidance emanating out of the White House or the seventh floor of the State Department. So, the law is very important. And, if there are times when a President asks you to do something which is contrary to the law, then he's got a problem and you've got a problem.

President Kennedy once asked me to spend some money on a particular matter. My lawyers and I concluded that there was no appropriation which would provide funds for any such purpose. It would be unlawful for us to spend for that purpose. So, I called the Attorney General, whose name was Bobby Kennedy. I didn't get much help from him because all he said was, "Well, if you go to prison your salary will continue while you are in prison." I reported back to the President that I simply could not make the expenditure because we had no appropriation to cover it and he did not pursue the matter. That issue can arise on more important matters.

Dean Acheson once remarked that in the relationship between the President and the secretary of state it was of the greatest importance that both of them understand at all times which one is President. Sometimes that can be forgotten. Mr. James Byrnes, for example, forgot that about Harry Truman and Harry Truman was the wrong President to be forgetful about. Sometimes the secretary of state will have an independent political base: William Jennings Bryan, Cordell Hull, James Byrnes. That doesn't always work out very well because of the underlying and fundamental constitutional relationship.

Nevertheless, I think it's well for cabinet officers to have a measure of independence in their relations with the President, at least enough to cause the President to have to think about what the cabinet officers say to them. How do we achieve that? The Dutch have an interesting way of doing it. I haven't checked lately to see whether it is still in effect, but in the Netherlands when someone joins the cabinet, from that moment on they are guaranteed a full year's pay when they leave the cabinet. This is sometimes referred to as the "go to hell fund." It seems to give a little measure of independence to the cabinet officer under those circumstances. I think in our system the key thing would be that a President know that a secretary of state is not trying to hang on to the job, but that he is ready to go at a moment's notice. I tried to make it very clear to both President Kennedy and President Johnson that I would be happy to take my departure at any time that they wanted me to do so; and that, I think, is the way the relationship ought to be.

Of course a President and secretary of state should officially be very close. Should that extend to their personal relationships, to something called genuine personal friendship? Well, one has to be a little careful about that. George Marshall felt very strongly that personal relations should never be allowed to intrude into public policy matters. You should never approve or disapprove a recommendation because Bill or Joe made it. He went to some pains to keep himself at arms length, for example, with Franklin Roosevelt. On one occasion at least, when Franklin Roosevelt called him "George," he said, "It's General Marshall, Mr. President." Secretary Marshall always called us by our last names, never by our first names. He very rarely complimented anyone who was still working under him, although he could be very generous when that relationship no longer existed. I suspect he had in his mind that he might at any time as a matter of public duty have to fire somebody. He didn't want personal relationships standing in the way.

I was very close to President Kennedy, for example, but I never played touch football; I never got pushed into Ethel's swimming pool. I laughed at Bobby Kennedy when he tried to get me to go on a fifty mile cabinet hike. I reminded him that when I was a captain of infantry, if I had taken my company on a fifty mile hike without proper conditioning, I would have been court-martialed. So, I was never a part of the Kennedy social circle, although the relationship officially was very close indeed.

There must be instant and ready access to the President on the part of the secretary of state. The President is free to seek and get advice from anyone in the wide world, from his chauffeur if he wants to, from senators, congressmen, people in the media, political leaders in the precincts, around the countryside. But he must always be available to and hear the views of the secretary of state. I personally think it would be intolerable if a cabinet officer had to get the permission of a White House staff person to see the President. In my own case I had access to President Kennedy and President Johnson at any time, and that, sometimes, included three o'clock in the morning. The world is round and at any given time only a third of the world is asleep and the other two-thirds are likely to be up to some mischief somewhere; you have to be able to be in touch with the President in the middle of the night.

I personally believe that if there is going to be an effective relationship between the President and the secretary of state there must be a high degree of confidentiality in their communication with each other. I believe the President is entitled to have no blue sky showing between him and his secretary of state on foreign policy questions. As President Kennedy once put it, domestic questions can only lose elections but foreign policy questions can kill us all. The question of confidentiality is of considerable importance. When I first became secretary of state I found, holding over from previous practice, that when I talked to the President over the phone there was somebody in the outer office who would listen in and jot down a very short memo on the conversation and circulate it to anybody in the Department who was supposed to be involved in the question. That went on for some time before I discovered that it was even happening; I stopped the practice and used a phone in my own office to talk with the President that could not be cut in on by anybody in the outer office. I never wrote memos of conversation between myself and President Kennedy or President Johnson. I didn't come home at night and write diaries about the day. I thought if the Presidents wanted their own record—and they usually had note-takers at their meetings—that was up to them. I had a certain aversion to the practice of some that I've seen in the past (for example, Mr. Forrestal) who seemed to be building up their own record over and against the President.

Similarly, we'd have meetings, National Security Council and cabinet meetings, with as many people as this, sitting around the room. Everybody wants to be there; it's prestige, it's fun, it's exciting to sit in on a National Security Council meeting or cabinet meeting. Arthur Schlesinger wrote in his *A Thousand Days* that in those meetings I used to sit like an old Buddha without saying anything. He was quite accurate in that, because when people like Arthur Schlesinger were in the room I kept my mouth shut. My arrangement would be that I would meet with the President either before or after such a meeting, often with Bob McNamara, just the three of us; and we'd talk over what had come up or what was coming up before any final decision was made. You'll find, when someday you get access to the notes on the famous Tuesday luncheon sessions with President Johnson, that the conversation was very candid, the disputes were very sharp, and there was full and free discussion. We knew that the people sitting around that table weren't going off and talking to the *Washington Post* and the *New York Times*. I'm quite sure that being in the public glare inhibits the frankness and candor of discussion.

QUESTION: From your *Foreign Affairs* article I got the impression that you didn't want the President to ever go to a summit meeting and then right away President Kennedy went to Vienna. I assume you tried to talk him out of it.

SECRETARY RUSK: I think every secretary of state is going to be very dubious about negotiations at the summit, partly because there is not time at the summit for the kind of detailed, careful, precise discussion and formulation that good negotiations usually require. If there's not time at the summit then the American President is at a disadvantage because, when he goes off to one of these meetings, expectations are built up that he's going to come back with a success; so he's under pressure to produce a result. The other side may not be under such pressure. Then there is the problem as to when you bring the court of last resort into session. It could well have been disastrous if Chairman Khrushchev and President Kennedy had met face to face during the Cuban Missile Crisis. The trouble is that Presidents don't agree with secretaries of state on this. There's something about the chemistry of being President that causes many of them to think that if they just sit down with somebody they can straighten everything out. So we will have summit meetings. Now let's exclude good will meetings; there's no problem there. I'm talking about negotiations at the summit.

President Carter went to Camp David with President Sadat and Prime Minister Begin. He had run out of other options. Other procedures didn't seem to be very promising and the situation in the Middle East was becoming more and more dangerous. But, more importantly, he was willing to invest *time*. He spent over ten days up there with them in what President Sadat, with a smile, called "house arrest." This was an exception that proves what was said in my article about some of the dangers of summitry.

I, personally, was not enthusiastic about the Vienna summit in June, 1961, and I think the results were negative. I don't happen to agree with Mr. Kennan and one or two others who thought that President Kennedy ought to have responded to Mr. Khrushchev's long, ideological opening with a long, ideological reply. Instead, President Kennedy said, "Mr. Chairman you're not going to make a communist out of me and I'm not going to make a capitalist out of you, so why don't we talk about some of our real problems."

I think we ought to be very careful about attempted negotiations at the summit. They tend to lead, at best, to agreements in principle. George Marshall used to tell us never to agree in principle because all that means is you haven't agreed yet; you need to get the fine print spelled out before you know whether you have a meeting of the minds. The Vladivostok agreement between President Ford and Mr. Brezhnev on the twenty-four hundred ceiling for missile launchers took years to put arms and legs on that sort of agreement in principle. I'm still dubious about negotiations at the summit.

QUESTION: You have emphasized at some length the importance of the secretary of state, and the administration generally, supporting a policy decision once it is made. It seems to me that no policy is absolutely perfect. Most of them, even the best, will begin to run into trouble. In the course of time you begin to pick up a certain amount of public criticism; there are always pressures for modification and change. I'm wondering how you feel about the role that say, Dean Acheson, John Foster Dulles, you, or Henry Kissinger played in this important task of, not defending policy, but seeking the modifications that seem to be demanded by changing times.

SECRETARY RUSK: I think that within the structure of the executive branch one should always feel free to propose and recommend a change in policy, provided it takes that form. But it is out of bounds, in my opinion, to go off and leak information to the news media for the purpose of undermining the policy or simply to refuse to obey instructions with respect to the implementation of policy. One should always be free to recommend changing the policy. Sometimes changes in policy can occur without going all the way to the President. Many policy decisions are made every day in the Department of State without going to the secretary or the President; the secretary makes a lot of changes without going to the President. So that's fair and free, and colleagues should be free to do it.

There's one very intriguing question to me, however, that's worth some thinking about in terms of a study of the Presidency. Each person more or less thinks of himself as playing his particular role. The business of being limited to one's own role can be a very good way to serve a President badly. For example, in connection with the disaster of the Bay of Pigs, I had been a colonel of infantry, and chief of war plans for the CBI theater during World War II. As a colonel of infantry, I knew that this brigade didn't have the chance of a "snowball in hell." But I wasn't a colonel of infantry; I was sitting there in a very special cubicle. I failed President Kennedy by not insisting that he ask a question that he did not ask. He should have turned to our Joint Chiefs of Staff and said to them: "Now gentlemen, I may want to do this with U.S. forces, so you tell me what you would need in terms of U.S. forces if I ask you to do it yourself rather than with this Cuban Brigade. I want that by noon tomorrow." By the time the Joint Chiefs had come in with their sustained and prolonged bombing, their several divisions, a massive fleet, and their big air force, it would have been obvious to the President that that little brigade didn't have any chance at all. But we were playing our roles too closely in the opening stages of a new administration. One thing that I think I learned was that a cabinet officer should not limit himself just to his own role. He should feel free to move beyond it and talk things over with the President across the board.

QUESTION: My question has to do with the role of the legal advisor of the State Department at a level of more than merely telling you you can't do this, because law is not simply a bundle of restraints. As someone said during the Cuban Missile Crisis, "It helps a hell of a lot to have law on your side." In your experience as secretary of state did you often call on the legal advisor, not merely to tell you what you couldn't do but to suggest how law could operate effectively in support of a policy? For example, you mentioned three thousand cables and all of that . . .

SECRETARY RUSK: . . . and a considerable number of those would require clearance by the legal advisor's office because matters of law are involved. However, the legal advisor during the sixties was always there in the morning meetings. Even when we had smaller morning meetings in advance of the larger morning meetings, with these six or seven people, the legal advisor would be there in that smaller group. I myself have been criticized by people like Dean Acheson, George Kennan and Hans Morgenthau for giving too much weight to law. When I came to Georgia Law School, I put on my first exam two quotations. One was from Dean Acheson: "The survival of nations is not a matter of law," and one from myself: "In a nuclear world, the survival of nations may depend upon law." I let my students sweat those two statements out.

What I tried to do with Abraham Chayes and with his successor, Leonard Meeker, was to give them *carte blanche* to intrude themselves into any question in the Department without being invited. I remember calling them "the conscience of the Department." This will vary greatly with Presidents and secretaries of state and the temper of the times. But I think law is a very important factor, not for sentimental reasons but for very hard-headed realistic reasons.

QUESTION: You've said that one of the glories of our system is that ultimately it produces a consensus. What happened to the consensus in the 1960's? Then, I think, we didn't produce one.

SECRETARY RUSK: There was strong support for Vietnam through 1966 around the country. Almost literally every day we would have on our desk a twenty-four hour summation of evidence of public opinion. This would include resolutions of national organizations, important editorials and speeches, and excerpts from the *Congressional Record,* all sorts of things. But the American people are impatient about war, thank heaven, and the change came not because of what was happening on college campuses or in the streets; it came when people at the grassroots, like my cousins in Cherokee County, Georgia, came to the conclusion in 1968 that if the government could not give them some idea as to when the war was going to be over, we might as well chuck it. We became aware of that change at the grassroots during the first half of 1968, and I, myself, assumed that whoever took office as President in January 1969, would have to bring that war to a conclusion very rapidly. But it's quite right that the consensus disintegrated in the last two years of the sixties.

QUESTION: I would like, if I may, to go back to this question about meeting foreign heads of government. I want to talk about the value to the United States of the President meeting with allied heads of government, especially as the relative importance of allies is increasing in the world. I know from my own experience in the British Foreign Office how much every British Prime Minister has valued a personal relationship with the American President. I'm not talking about negotiation carefully prepared, but about the personal relationship.

Recently a very eminent man in the French Foreign Office said to me that one of the things that distinguished de Gaulle is that he was the only head of government in France that this senior official could remember who didn't want to establish that kind of personal relationship with an American President as the head of our alliance. Now the secretary of state has a great responsibility to be sure that this finds a place in the President's timetable, in the President's mind. I wonder if you would like to say something about that?

SECRETARY RUSK: Well, the general practice is that, once a year, the State Department will recommend to the President a program for such meetings in the course of the coming year. Usually there are many more applicants than one can find room for, but usually one does find room for visits between ourselves and our key allies. Britain was always on the list if the British Prime Minister so wished. Even that gets complicated. There's great pulling and hauling among countries to get on the list; and for many countries—this is not true of Britain—they have the view that somehow if they come to Washington on an official visit they will go back with a big bag of goodies. And when you tell them that that's not the purpose of such a visit, that it won't happen, they say, "Oh well, we won't ask for anything." Then the visit is laid on and they say, "I can't go back empty handed." So these things are a little more complicated than they appear at first.

But I think we have a problem in the alliance. For instance, in the first paragraph of a recent lead article in the *Economist* not long ago, the writer said in effect that the movement of Russian troops into Afghanistan was the fault of Mr. Carter and the United States, as though somehow the United States, the American people, are mercenaries sitting over here available to go and tidy up things in various parts of the world if they go wrong while Europe enjoys business as usual and the comforts of life. I'm concerned that there are no British, French, Italian, Japanese, or German ships in the Indian Ocean these days. It would mean a lot to the American people if some of those other flags were flying there. But that's beside the point. Still, these personal relationships can be very important where the leaders are after the same purposes.

President de Gaulle is a very special case. Talking to de Gaulle was like climbing a mountain on your knees and opening a little door at the top to listen to the oracle. There was never any exchange. When I was in Paris I would go in and make a courtesy call on him. He'd ask me to be seated, then he'd say, "well, Mr. Secretary I'm listening." He would never raise any question on his own initiative. He never got over the fact that you (the British) and we refused to accept his proposal for a tripartite committee to govern the free world. Eisenhower rejected it, Kennedy rejected it, and he never forgave us for it. It's ironic that the tactics he used to achieve his purpose of restoring the position of France had exactly the opposite effect. In NATO we got to the point where we just went ahead with our business without regard to France.

QUESTION: Should the role of the alliance be increasing in importance? The allies have considerably improved their condition economically. What role should the alliance play? I saw in a German paper a criticism that when Carter retreated to Camp David, no foreign leaders were consulted and no allies were brought in on the series of consultations he had. What is the role of the NATO alliance?

SECRETARY RUSK: Well, one has to take account of the fact that when an alliance succeeds—and no member of NATO has been attacked since the alliance was formed—public interest in it and support for it tend to diminish.

This matter of consultation is a very curious one. The way to consult is to consult. But should the President of the United States be the one that always has to take the initiative? If somebody could check the records of NATO to see how often questions have come up on the initiative of the United States for consideration in NATO compared to how often this has been done at the initiative of any other member of NATO, you'd be shocked at the result.

The same thing happens with Congress. They talk about consulting. Do you know that in eight years not more than six times did any senator pick up the phone, call me and say, "Look, next time you're down this way, drop by; I'd like to talk to you about something," or, "Let me drop by your office on the way home; I want to talk to you about something." Let's give them full credit for being considerate of the time of the secretary of state. But they sit there expecting to be convinced, and very little initiative is taken from the Capitol Hill side of it to consult, except through formal hearings.

Even in the meetings of the Senate Foreign Relations Committee, Chairman Fulbright and I spent a good deal of time trying to get a quorum. Very often I'd go down there and they would start with two senators present, and in the course of the morning maybe three or four senators would come in to check their names on the list and stay for a few minutes and then go out. I wasn't there to do a "Flip Wilson show." I didn't expect to be the most entertaining fellow in the world. But when we had television, they all turned up, half of them with makeup on, all ready for the show. We have got to work harder on this process of consultation between the executive and legislative branches. But the most difficult thing will be to get senatorial and congressional time.

By the way, there is something that has happened for years that I think the public doesn't know much about. In the mid-sixties we started having a meeting at 9:00 on Wednesday mornings in the House of Representatives to which every member of the House of Representatives was invited. At each meeting there would be a senior officer of the State Department to talk about some important sector of foreign policy. They'd spend at least an hour there taking questions and comments from any member of the House who wanted to comment. The attendance would vary from maybe sixty to three hundred depending upon who was coming and what the subject was. But any member of the House of Representatives who attended those meetings regularly would go away at the end of the year with a far broader and deeper understanding of what's going on in the world than any member of Parliament would through question time in the House of Commons. In my time as secretary we never had an embarrassing leak out of those meetings. It was taken for granted that these would be private meetings and it was a great instrument for exchanging views back and forth.

Every committee of the Congress now becomes involved in foreign policy. I'd like to see the Senate Foreign Relations Committee and the House Foreign Affairs Committee given overriding responsibility for looking at foreign policy as a whole and free to call in bills pending in any other committee for the purpose of putting in their own reports on how the proposed action fits into foreign policy as a whole.

There is another thing that makes a difference here and affects the President and the secretary of state in their relations with Congress. In the early sixties we could talk to four senators: Russell of Georgia, Humphrey of Minnesota, Dirkson of Illinois, Kerr of Oklahoma; and go over on the House side and talk to Speaker Sam Rayburn, and we knew what the Congress would do and would not do. They could tell us, partly because they could tell the Congress. LBJ used to refer to these people as the "whales" of the Congress. I can make a pretty strong case against the whale system, but what do you say for five hundred thirty-five minnows swimming around in a bucket? There is no one today, no reasonably small group of people, who can speak for the Congress in the absence of a formal vote. And this complicates our system to an extraordinary degree.

QUESTION: Your word about the importance of a close relationship between the President and secretary prompts me to wonder what your view is of the office of the national security advisor. One hears a good deal these days about how troublesome the present secretary finds the national security advisor. Mr. Rogers certainly found his advisor troublesome. Those of us living at a distance from Washington often get the impression that today we have in point of fact two secretaries of state. Is there anything in the logic of the conduct of White House business that makes it necessary now for a president to have, not only a secretary, but this additional figure who presides over the National Security Council and who seems indeed to be a second secretary?

SECRETARY RUSK: Again I'm biased, but I wasn't aware of any problem during the sixties with Mr. McGeorge Bundy and then Mr. Walt Rostow in that job. I think they had about a dozen officers on their staff. If McGeorge Bundy made a recommendation to President Kennedy on foreign policy, he would make it to me at the same time. We had complete confidence that no one was going to go around cutting somebody's throat. But during the early years of the Nixon administration the NSC staff went up to around a hundred, about a hundred officers over there, a little State Department across the road, away from the troops, away from the flow of responsibility and the flow of information. The number now is back to about fifty, but that's still too many in my judgment.

When you get people on those assignments they become promoters of their own pad, protectors of their own situation, and the possibility for tensions will be present. Mr. Brzezinski had his own press secretary. That's ridiculous. It's hard enough keeping the White House press secretary and the State Department press secretary on the same wave length to have still another person in there. It just doesn't make any sense. So I think this is something Presidents have to watch very carefully.

QUESTION: I wonder if you see an efficient and effective relationship between the secretary of state and the President, and an efficient and effective national policy? Does the one in any way imply the other?

SECRETARY RUSK: During the Eisenhower period, they prepared a pretty thick manual for President Eisenhower on U.S. national security policy. When President Kennedy took office some of the planners, including some of my friends, decided that they had to bring it up to date and to convert it to a Kennedy policy; and they worked on it prodigiously. But when they got through with it neither President Kennedy nor I would approve it as a matter of official policy because we couldn't tell what we were approving. If you talk about policies too generally, it doesn't give you any guidance as to what you have to do tomorrow morning at 9:00. By approving general statements, you may trick yourself into thinking you have a policy when you don't.

So I'm a little skeptical about the attempts to reduce policies for a world community of 160 nations and a throbbing, boisterous American people of 220 million into a few general statements. If people want to generalize about the way policy is hammered out over a period of time by what one does in a given situation, that's all right; I don't object to that. But some of these generalizations simply aren't guidelines of policy.

QUESTION: I was referring actually to a close relationship between the secretary of state and the President. If that is an effective working relationship, does that necessarily imply an effective decision-making procedure?

SECRETARY RUSK: It suggests a better decision-making procedure than there would be if there were not a close relationship between the two. But, the President and secretary, plus a few other colleagues, can make mistakes, the disaster of the Bay of Pigs, for example. So a close working relationship doesn't guarantee that wise decisions will be made.

KENNEDY AND THE NUCLEAR QUESTION

McGeorge Bundy

NARRATOR: We would like to welcome McGeorge Bundy, special assistant to President Kennedy for national security affairs. Someone in a crowd of this kind said, "This gathering and response testifies either to the popularity of the speaker or the inclement weather." You can draw your own conclusions about the choice.

McGeorge Bundy was born in Boston and educated at Yale. He did research and writing at the Council on Foreign Relations. He published a book that we all go back to coauthored with Secretary Stimson and called *On Active Service*. He joined the faculty at Harvard first as a lecturer and then went up the ladder as an associate and then full professor. He was dean of the faculty in arts and sciences, a position beyond which most Harvard people aspire to nothing else in this world. But Mr. Bundy went on to become Mr. Kennedy's special assistant. He served in that capacity from 1961 to 1966. He became president of the Ford Foundation and held that position until 1979. At the ripe old age of sixty he decided that someone else should bear the burdens of philanthropic activity in New York and became a distinguished professor of history at New York University where he continues research on the history of the nuclear crisis. There would have been an enormous gap in our portrait of John F. Kennedy if we had been unable to visit with McGeorge Bundy this morning, particularly with respect to Kennedy, foreign policy and the nuclear issue.

MR. BUNDY: Thank you, Ken, for what you said and the element of truth in it I won't attempt to essay. I've gotten to the stage where I find that critical examination of complimentary introductions is a great mistake.

The problem I want to talk about is the problem of John F. Kennedy and nuclear questions. When we get to discussion if you want to go to other questions for any reason, I certainly don't object and will do my best. But it does happen that this is the one subject that I feel relatively well prepared on because I am working on a study of presidential decisions about nuclear weapons problems and I have spent the summer revisiting the Cuban missile crisis and surprised myself by finding a lot of things I had taken for granted that I had to look at again.

I think one can begin by the simple assertion that for President Kennedy, as I think for his predecessor and in a different way for most of his successors, there wasn't any doubt that the problem of not having nuclear war was at the head of the agenda, not in the sense that it was the thing that took the most time but that it was the single most important thing to make sure of on his watch. Already by 1960 it had been clear for years that with the advent of survivable shared thermonuclear forces, you could not do better in this field than Churchill's famous "balance of terror." Eisenhower's papers and indeed his press conferences are full of his own conviction on the point, and Kennedy shared it. And he also understood and never let out of his mind the fact that this question in its most urgent form was entangled in the overall relationship between the U.S. and the U.S.S.R.

Kennedy had a great concern about proliferation and worried in a more or less private, nonoperational way—in particular about what would happen when the Chinese got the bomb. As you will recall, the relationship between the Soviet Union and the United States was cordial by comparison with that between the United States and the China of Mao in the late fifties and early sixties. But there wasn't much to be done about that. The broader question of nonproliferation appeared primarily in a context I'll come to a little later, the context of the right way of treating friendly countries with nuclear aspirations of their own.

It is curious that the particular issue on which he campaigned and which he had to confront when he came in was the missile gap. The missile gap is really not a Kennedy problem so much as it is a Kennedy inheritance. It was natural for an opposing candidate to pick up on the apparently authoritative warnings of so many panels and commissions in the later Eisenhower years and in my view, it is still a very interesting failure of exposition on the part of General Eisenhower that the missile gap lasted as long as it did. Nobody gave more attention to the problem of surprise attack and the problem of adequate modernization of forces than Eisenhower. His basic weapons decisions were timely and prudent. There never was a missile gap. He knew it, but he didn't find a way of saying it persuasively—in part because of an excessive respect for the requirements of security as they were then perceived.

But in any event, that was where Kennedy arrived and it wasn't two months before he had to decide how to deal with the evidence available inside the new administration that there wasn't any gap. That was not executed with the finesse that he would have liked because it was not easy to spell out why one suddenly changed one's view. Indeed it wasn't until the fall of 1961, in a very carefully orchestrated speech by Roswell Gilpatric, that the real situation was set forth.

There wasn't any missile gap. There was instead a serious problem, from the beginning, of deciding on force sizing for the future.

There were really three forces at work: One was the careful analytical process of the Pentagon under McNamara and the band from Rand, which did lead to essentially prudent choices of weapons, based consciously and clearly on the criteria of survivability and versatility—survivability being by far the most important in my view and I think in theirs. Second was the instinctive sense that you didn't have to have too much, which was strong in the White House staff and present in the President's mind. Third, there was the political requirement, missile gap or no missile gap, that the program presented be seen as sufficient in the Congress. It's instructive that JFK felt that he used up his political capital for moderation in successfully supporting the decision not to proceed with the B70 bomber, a bomber which would have been, I think by fairly general retrospective agreement, the largest waste up to that point in nuclear procurement.

The battles that we had were moderated and decided by the President, who was, as I say, of two minds on this matter. On one side was the argument that a Wiesner and a Kaysen would make for the White House staff—that so and so many submarines were really enough and so and so many Minutemen were plenty. The countervailing argument which was always phrased in terms of "I hear your argument but this is the least I can go to the Hill with;" it usually came from McNamara. That argument continued right through the Kennedy administration and, as it happened, we were having the semifinal round on the upcoming budget, on the 22nd of November. It was in McNamara's conference room that I heard the news from Dallas, and we were having the same argument: on one side, we're planning too many of this or that, and on the other, this is what we need politically.

In a way, by comparison with our contemporary debates over such enormous questions as Star Wars or ground based strategic survivabilities, these battles were small. They were at the margin of a basic decision which can be criticized from both directions and has been. General LeMay ran for vice-president on his own megatonnage gap in 1968, and scholars like Desmond Ball take the view that Kennedy was excessive in his procurement. The difference between what Ball thinks right and what JFK actually did is on the order of hundreds of warheads, not on the order of thousands, like our current differences.

On balance, I would defend as reasonable, sensible, and well managed the way in which the Kennedy administration took the raw material created by the Eisenhower administration's initiatives and shaped it into the survivable triad. (We didn't ever use that word. I don't even know when that word came into practice and if anybody does know it would give me great help to tell me.) The triad consisted of the three forces which were already in training—well into development in the case of the Minuteman and in production in the case of the others. The B52 force, the submarine force—Polaris at the time—and the Minuteman force made up the three-legged survivable force and it is essentially what we have still, of course with all sorts of modernization. The enormous complication of MIRV and the new vulnerabilities that come from accuracies and all the other new problems we face now were simply not in sight in the years of the Kennedy presidency.

A third early exposure to the nuclear problem and one that I still find puzzling to look back on was our effort to produce a serious civil defense program. There were both political and rational motivations for that. Nelson Rockefeller was red-hot for civil defense and Nelson Rockefeller was the possible rival for 1964 that JFK took the most seriously.

But there was also a rational argument. There is a finite chance that this terrible thing will happen. If it does, a reasonable and prudent program, a shelter program in those days, would save millions of lives. Kennedy was very careful to separate his advocacy of civil defense from any notion that it somehow strengthened the deterrent, because he didn't find that argument persuasive. But what that effort showed us, and fairly quickly, was that there is no way of having a large-scale and effective civil defense program in the United States without arousing a level of public alarm that would be damaging in all sorts of ways. We eased away from it. Kennedy, if he could have done it alone, with no political repercussions, if he could have made effective fall-out shelters appear in major urban centers overnight, would have done it. But there wasn't any way of doing that, and he presently recognized the political difficulties of the problem and let the program fade away to the shadows where it has been ever since.

Occasionally new civil defense language gets written in the White House. My friend Sam Huntington believed that he had made a major contribution in the Carter administration by reviving the rational case for civil defense and so he did, in terms of paper directives. But I don't see any big new program, and neither do you.

Civil defense for this country is an intractable problem, and his recognition of that reinforced Kennedy's deep conviction that the only really sensible thing you could do about nuclear war was not have it. He understood that point right from the beginning. There was a practice, developed in the Eisenhower administration of an annual mock nuclear war, a paper war done by people who were in charge of something called the "net assessment." And they would run the war and see how our warheads did against their warheads and how many million casualties this produced. There is plenty of evidence in the Eisenhower papers that Ike found those exercises sobering, but he believed in that kind of briefing and went through it regularly.

There was one in the Kennedy administration. Dean Rusk tells the story of coming out of that meeting with the President walking across from the Cabinet room to the Oval Office to discuss something else. As they walked the President said to him, "And we call ourselves the human race." There was no second exercise of this sort in the Kennedy years. One was enough to show JFK that the results were inescapably unacceptable, if I may indulge in his own kind of understatement.

The next place we meet the nuclear problem in the Kennedy administration is in the Soviet reactivation of the crisis over Berlin which had been an on-and-off affair in the last two years of the Eisenhower administration. Khruschev had explicitly said that he couldn't do much business with Eisenhower after the U2 episode of 1960. He said that he would wait for whoever was going to be President to reopen the matter of the threat to peace he claimed to find both in the existing situation in Berlin and in the absence of a peace treaty with East Germany. He reopened the matter with energy in the spring of 1961 and particularly in Vienna in June. We had of course seen the Berlin crisis coming. We had known that we would have to have a position on Berlin. The very strong sentiment which the President came to share—which wasn't, I think, from him downward so much as from the incoming crowd upward—was that we should deal with the Berlin crisis diplomatically by framing a policy which hung onto the essentials but was more flexible on things that didn't directly effect access, or the status of the city, or the rights of the Allies. But we also thought we must be prepared to strengthen deterrence primarily by strengthening conventional capabilities, thereby producing a situation in which it would be much more credible to our friends in Moscow that interference with access would produce responses which could be sustained and which would create a credible connection between any Soviet act of force in Berlin and the possible engagement of the strategic nuclear forces of the United States. It wasn't that those strategic forces needed to be stronger; it was that other forces needed to be stronger to make that connection more credible. For shorthand, I will call it the Acheson approach because the former secretary of state, who was asked to run a Berlin task force in those early months, was certainly the most eloquent and energetic advocate of this basic position, which Kennedy accepted.

That is an example of a shift which operates in a number of ways during the Kennedy administration, toward conventional as distinct from nuclear capabilities. Neither Kennedy nor anyone close to him believed that once you had done what you needed to do about nuclear weapons they could then be considered as usable as conventional weapons. The rejection of that idea completed a transition which is one of the most interesting events of the Eisenhower administration, which in its first year explicitly committed itself to the notion that nuclear weapons could and should be considered as conventional weapons. This doctrine was actually written into NSC directives at the end of 1953, although it was one in which Eisenhower didn't truly believe. He did not act on it in the way he handled his crises, but it remained the formal doctrine. A strong feeling which Eisenhower did have was that what you had to do was simply to stand firm in Berlin, and that the risk that any conflict would become general was already sufficient for deterrence. That is a position which was never proved wrong, but Kennedy's was different.

My own present guess is that both policies were sufficient. In the Berlin case, as we now look back on it, what is clear is that Khrushchev hoped to create a sufficient sense of danger so that others would make concessions. Only a madman, he argued, would make war over something so small and relatively marginal as the status of West Berlin and why shouldn't it be a free city and why shouldn't there be a treaty. Dean Rusk has another wonderful story on this point. In 1963 when he went to sign the Test Ban Treaty, Khrushchev took him off for a walk and said, "You know, I've never understood why you people were so stubborn about Berlin," which by then was way on the back burner, "because you know, Eisenhower didn't want a war over Berlin, De Gaulle didn't want a war over Berlin and MacMillan certainly didn't want a war over Berlin. Why was it only the Americans?" "Well," Dean responded, "You know, Mr. Chairman, there is a streak of madness in Americans."

One will never know what would have happened if there had been a test but what we do know is that Khrushchev never made the test. In the end it was not certainly the conventional strength on the spot, but simply the finite but real risk of escalation. Even if had not been a nuclear war, there was the risk of an aftermath in terms of massive rearmament, the Korea-type effect of a move. But the move never came. Kennedy was never comfortable about Berlin. He felt that a further test was more likely than not right up to the time when the real test developed elsewhere, in the Soviet introduction of nuclear missiles into Cuba. That is clearly the climactic event in matters of nuclear danger of the Kennedy years, perhaps the climactic event of the nuclear period of history so far and it is the one I would like to spend a little more time on.

The missile crisis raises all kinds of fascinating questions and not all of them by any means are nuclear, but the nuclear questions are at the center. It was caused by an act relating to nuclear weapons. Khrushchev made a decision sometime in the spring—his memoirs tell us in May—and the crucial moment in those memoirs as he describes it is when he is alone in Bulgaria. A simple moral: don't ever let a head of state be alone in Bulgaria on a state visit; a state visit to Bulgaria probably couldn't fully occupy a very lively mind. He found himself brooding, as he had for years and sometimes in public as in his visit to the United States, over the asymmetry of the degree of threat and the locations of the threat posed in the nuclear age. He said to Walter Reuther in 1959, "How would you feel if we put missiles in Mexico and Canada? You have put them all around our borders." Reuther rather incautiously said, "Go ahead and try."

In 1962, as his memoirs tell us, he reached the conclusion that there is a double ground for this adventure. The one he puts first is that he needs to defend Cuba, a new outpost of socialism. And the second, and the one that he seems to me to express with more feeling in the memoirs, is that he wanted to redress the balance of power; it was time for the Americans to understand what it was like to have these kinds of weapons and that the introduction of the weapons that he had, medium-range and intermediate-range missiles that were already deployed in Europe but have since become familiar to all of us as the SS4's and SS5's, would do that job. You can argue, and people have, that we had driven him in this direction by our very explicit explanation that the only missile gap that existed was a missile gap in reverse. In any event I don't think there can be much argument that he did indeed introduce the missiles primarily for their strategic balancing value. He was putting them in for *nuclear* reasons, not to use but to remedy a perceived feeling of inferiority.

Khrushchev had been a great practitioner of atomic diplomacy, though not a successful one. He did truly believe that talking about what his missiles could do to the small countries of Western Europe like Germany, France, and the United Kingdom was effective, and he went on doing it. Then when the true balance was exposed he put them into Cuba.

There is a very interesting failure of understanding here. We, the administration, led by the President but including all of us in the levels where we had regular and direct access, expected no such thing—with one exception. The professional intelligence officers expected no such thing.

When we issued a warning in September we did it because of the requirements of domestic politics, not because we seriously believed that the Soviets would do anything as crazy from our standpoint as placement of Soviet nuclear weapons in Cuba. Only one man, foresaw it, worried about it and that not in May when it might have been most helpful to our Bulgarian thinker but only in August after rumors began to spread: John McCone.

I think that this is instructive. John McCone shared with Khrushchev a great belief in the political utility of nuclear weapons. He had been the head of the Air Force and the head of the Atomic Energy Commission—two assignments that tended to make a man stand tall in his belief in nuclear strength. He did sincerely and deeply believe that there was reason to attend closely to nuclear balances, to worry about the other man's deployments and possible deployments, and generally to conduct one's self as if a marginal change in the nuclear arms race was a highly important matter. That was his mind-set. He was therefore very well equipped to understand Khrushchev. The rest of us in a way were not. I think that from the President down, the Kennedy administration didn't really think that about nuclear weapons. JFK did believe that it was politically fundamental to be able to say that we had attended to any possible missile gap and further to be able to assert that we had guarded the flame of nuclear strategic superiority. It was this requirement that we be able to make this claim—for the self-confidence and reassurance of our own people and our allies—that moved us, rather than any belief that any such advantage would translate into a usable political diplomatic card. In that we were very different from Nikita Khrushchev. I think that is one reason why we didn't guess that it might be coming and so did not give timely warning. We gave warning at a time when it would have been very hard, as Graham Allison (among others) points out in his book *Essence of Decision,* for Khrushchev to turn off an enterprise already far in train. It never occurred to us in April or May of 1962 to give a warning when it might have changed the Soviet mind ahead of time.

So it is a nuclear crisis. It is also a crisis of nuclear misunderstanding and particularly of an enormous nuclear misunderstanding on Khrushchev's part. But what Khrushchev miscalculated was not our attitude toward the strategic balance as such. That was not what mattered most, at all. After all we never reacted in any fashion of this kind in later years when Soviets engaged in a strategic buildup of enormous proportions on their own territory. It never occurred to us to say that this was unacceptable or to enforce a reversal of Soviet policy when we discovered that they were making nuclear weapons or hydrogen bombs or at any point afterwards in their massive buildup of weapons in the Soviet Union. It was nuclear missiles *in Cuba* that were neuralgic.

What I think we are dealing with here is not a strategic question but an enormous and deeply felt and nearly unanimous national reaction. In the context of the warnings by Senator Keating that this was happening, it became perfectly clear to the American political leadership and particularly to the President himself that such a move would be intolerable and that we had better say so, and JFK did say so in September. Thus, at one and the same time, we came late to our warning, but when we made it, absolutely firmly defined a position from which we could not have moved when the crisis broke if we had wanted to, as none of us really did.

Having said that "the gravest issues" would arise, and having made it perfectly clear that what we were talking about was nuclear weapons, the one thing that was instantly clear to the President when I gave him the bad news on October 16 was that he must act. But how? He was confronted with an enormous decision.

I won't take you through the processes of decision or the intense interaction of military movement and diplomatic communication that followed until the crisis was resolved on the twenty-eighth of October. I'd rather focus sharply on the nuclear aspect. The management of the crisis was not primarily nuclear. The management of the crisis required a selection among conventional weapons, of constraint or of active force, the development of a diplomatic and political position which could be set forth in a presidential speech, a process of diplomacy engaging allies, primarily by the Organization of American States, for the purpose of giving a legal and political base to the quarantine, communications with other allies, and a very intense series of exchanges with Khrushchev, leading presently to a satisfactory resolution. That resolution has three main elements: the withdrawal of the missiles (the weapons you consider offensive are a very interesting way of describing it), an assurance against an invasion of Cuba, and a very secret assurance that our missiles in Turkey would also come out.

What I want to ask now is a harder question, one that Kennedy did ask himself a lot. We know there is a nuclear cause here in Khrushchev's sense of the need to fix a bad imbalance. But what can we say about the result? In what way is that nuclear in its nature?

Well, it is and it isn't. The resolving element of force in action and in early prospects and the resolving pressure of what was in effect an ultimatum on October are not nuclear. They are primarily naval, and secondarily the clear prospect of the use of air power and of the Army against Cuba, thus a prospect of unacceptable defeat in Cuba piled upon the effectiveness of the blockade and reinforced by the President's very clear-cut limitation of time. John Scali, on Friday, passes a message that there are only two days left for a decision, and on Saturday Bobby Kennedy tells Dobrynin that we need a clear answer the next day. The movements of forces are all visible. Khrushchev's speech of December 12th is to be taken at face value when he says that he recognized that time was running out, and that he really had to resolve the crisis.

So in that sense it is not a nuclear resolution but there is another sense in which it is. The urgency that led to this de facto ultimatum was an urgency about nuclear danger. In its more superficial form it was, are these missiles going to get to be operational? I myself think, looking back on it, that this concern drove the government and the President to a greater insistence on a rapid resolution than was truly necessary. It was certainly important in the first week to consider whether we needed to act before those weapons became operational. But in the second week of diplomacy and of quarantine we right along assumed that some of them could be operational. It is now still uncertain whether Soviet warheads ever got to Cuba. I have recently talked to two of the people who were directly involved in the intelligence at the time and they differ on the point. Nobody ever saw nuclear warheads as such but people did see or thought they saw in Cuba the same vehicles that were assigned uniquely to the conveyance of nuclear weapons in the Soviet Union. Some say they were there to be ready for an air delivery and some say they wouldn't have been there unless the warheads also were there, but nobody knows. But for a President with a true sense of nuclear change a probability of one in ten that warheads are there is enough for him to have to assume that they are there. He's not going to be comforted because no one has actually seen and counted warheads. If the systems are operational, their capacity to launch nuclear warheads has to be assumed. That was where we already were in the second week of the crisis, and we could have endured that situation for another while because the likelihood that Khrushchev would actually fire the nuclear weapons by choice was as near zero as it could get; it had been effectively foreclosed by the warnings in the President's speech of October 22.

But that is not quite the way we were thinking. We were not worried about what we would consciously decide to do; we were not going to fire nuclear warheads on purpose. We didn't suppose that Khrushchev wanted to do that either. What we were concerned about was the more than sufficient probability that if this matter continued, someone would shoot in such a way that someone else would shoot back. As the President put it at the height of the crisis, "it is not the first step or the second step that concerns me. It's the fourth or fifth and the fact that there will be nobody left to take the sixth."

I think in retrospect that we overstated that risk. But so, I think, did Khrushchev.

A very interesting illustration of our dilemma comes on the morning of Saturday, the 27th when Khrushchev sends the second message in which, instead of offering a straight trade of the missiles for a no invasion pledge and an end of the quarantine, he introduces the missiles in Turkey. Looking back, I think that this is probably a quite characteristic Soviet effort to change the bidding. If your first bid looks as if it might work and your man says in reporting back this is quite promising, then your natural instinct is to see if there is a little more give. Soviet negotiators do that routinely all the time. But we didn't see it that way that morning. What is much more important is that Lewellyn Thompson didn't see it that way. Thompson had established himself in those weeks as a man who had accurately foreseen very important things—that there would not be a Soviet reaction in Berlin, for example. And his advice as to what was meant by everything that had happened up to that point had been sound, but he didn't know what to make of the Turkish missile proposal. And I think this was not because his judgment was deranged but because the possibility that it meant something deeply disquieting had to be only one in ten to be more than enough.

If the second letter meant that Khrushchev was no longer in command, or if it meant that someone else was pushing him around, then indeed one had very grave questions as to what might happen next. What I would emphasize here is that a small worry is a sufficient worry, because we aren't talking here only about a possible increase in a level of force of the traditional and conventional sort. We are talking about what happens if things get to a point where, for fear of what the other man will do, your commander begins to say to you, I need orders. We know from Curtis LeMay's memoirs what we knew also by regular encounters with him—that in his view if push ever came to shove the ultimate requirement on the President of the United States was to give the command to preempt and send the whole SAC attack force on its way.

I don't quantify that possibility. I think it would be a mistake to try. I never knew how to quantify it at the time but that sense of events conceivably getting out of control—what Kennedy saw as the ultimate danger the President must guard against, what Khrushchev later described as the smell of burning in the air—is an extremely important resolving force in the last twenty-four hours of the crisis.

There is lots more to be said about that and I've talked a great deal longer than I intended to, I will now simply remind you very briefly that we went on from the sunny morning of the 28th to the difficulties of the Nassau meeting and the puzzlement of what kind of relationship we would have with the United Kingdom and with France. We never did solve the problem of relations with France on nuclear matters. The pain and distance which that created lasted for a long time. I've referred too briefly to the problem of nonproliferation. We had no well-developed nonproliferation policy. I could linger endlessly over the travails of the multilateral force which was never Kennedy's idea and which he eventually put quietly into the back room—from which it was wheeled out to a receptive Lyndon Johnson by its true believers after he was gone.

I'd like to take a long time over the test ban. That has great lessons in it, a lesson of the need for presidential leadership if you want anything to happen and the lesson of limitations, too. I think most of us looking back, I know Wiesner and Seaborg the head of the AEC who has done an excellent book, regret that we missed the comprehensive believe that it was a very serious miss. I agree with them. We missed for two reasons: first, the enormous difficulty of getting adequate confidence in verification (where we had a misunderstanding with Khrushchev that was avoidable if we had managed it better), and second the very strong convictions of the nuclear weapons makers that the national safety required a continued right to test. So we settled for the atmospheric test ban and counted ourselves lucky and successful to get that much.

One can say that when Kennedy made up his mind that he wanted and would accept an atmospheric test ban, he also made up his mind to enforce restraint, to settle for a single set of atmospheric tests although the Soviets had had two—this is exactly the kind of thing that it takes the executive force to decide.

Kennedy never addressed in any final way the very grave problem of "enough is enough." He never abandoned the belief that superiority was a requirement of political leadership in the United States. It's not an accident that the last speech in his public papers, an undelivered speech designed for use in Dallas, Texas on November 22, 1963, is a speech in which he planned to remind the Texas audience that he had come to Waco in 1960 to tell the people of Texas that he proposed to make America number one again, "Not number one if, not number one but, but number one period." He was back in Texas to tell them that he had done it, and the speech then goes on to talk about numbers of Polaris launch, numbers of Minuteman constructed, numbers of B52s deployed and all the rest.

Kennedy was a man of great intrinsic wisdom about nuclear weapons, but not yet ready, anymore than his predecessor who understood the matter as he did, to take the lead in bringing it across to the country that a sufficient level of survivable nuclear strength had long since been reached by the United States and also by the Soviet Union, in the net assessment he had seen. At these levels the notion of superiority, as a later statesman said, was open to the question, what in the name of God does it mean? The two Presidents who could have taught that lesson best, at different points in their careers were Eisenhower and Kennedy. I think it has to be marked against them: in Eisenhower's case it was a failure; in Kennedy's case I would claim an incomplete.

NARRATOR: Someone once said about presentations that some make us clever for the day and others wise forever and some of the things we've heard are in this latter category. We do have at least one National Academy scientist in our midst and we have others who in the government have dealt with these matters in the scientific area in their official positions. The rest of us are observers and ready to learn. Who would like to ask the first question?

QUESTION: First, to what degree was the Soviet perception of the early Kennedy policy a factor in their miscalculations in the Cuban missile crisis? I have in mind here Arthur Schlesinger's comment which has always troubled me in *A Thousand Days* that the one thing one learned in the administration from the Bay of Pigs was how to deal with the missile crisis in October a year following more effectively. My concern would be had the Bay of Pigs not been bungled you might possibly not have encountered the missile crisis the following October. So I wonder to what degree the Bay of Pigs, the Vienna meeting, and other actions of Mr. Kennedy might have led Khrushchev to misjudge the sort of man he was dealing with.

At the other end of the crisis, what "guarantees," "understanding" came from it and what is the present status of those?

MR. BUNDY: Those are both excellent questions and as you know they have both been much rehearsed by later students.

I think the Bay of Pigs would have to suggest to anybody that the new management was pretty dumb. That is a separate subject and it is certainly possible that Khrushchev read it as a failure of resolution, leading him to believe that Cuba was the place where Kennedy might flinch. I've always thought that the notion that Kennedy seemed weak at Vienna is a bum rap, but again it is possible that Khrushchev misread him (Shevchenko says he did.) In American comment, that judgment comes most from Kennedy's own gloomy view of the meeting, and the way he backgrounded James Reston instantly after the meeting and the way James reported that. But Chip Bohlen never thought—and he was the expert hearing those conversations—that Khrushchev got the impression that Kennedy was weak. The transcript doesn't suggest weakness, nor did the parts of the conversation that I heard, which didn't include all of them because Kennedy was a great believer in getting rid of all the small-fry and getting off alone. In any case, I don't think that was the basic problem. I really think it was Khrushchev's frustration. I think there is great strength in this motive, which didn't seem to most of us at the time to be compelling. A few understood it; Rostow was telling everybody in the summer of 1962 that Khrushchev was frustrated, frustrated over Berlin primarily but secondarily over various other adventures, and that was likely to lash out somewhere. But not being particularly nuclear-minded, Walt never suggested that it would be missiles in Cuba.

I think that it was frustration and the picture that Khrushchev gives of walking around in a mental agony in Bulgaria, while it may be a bit too colorful, like many of his descriptions, seems fairly near the truth. They thought that they could get them in and then present us with them. And then indeed we might have been abashed. I don't know why they thought they could manage that. That is an extremely interesting question and there are also very interesting questions about why they didn't put in the SAM's early enough to interfere with the U2's and so forth.

QUESTION: As for the end of the crisis, would you state your problem again. What about the assurances?

MR. BUNDY: They are all on the record except for the one about the Turkish missiles. They are all unilateral. There is no signed document, nothing that both sides have put their hands to. I think they are at once clear and less than a contract. They fundamentally have to do with removal of the Soviet nuclear presence and on our side with an undertaking not to invade Cuba, which is something Kennedy didn't want to do anyway. That is about all there is—that and an unilateral private assurance that the Turkish missiles would come out—we had wanted them out for a year and a half.

The U.N. verification never happened. That had been in Khrushchev's October 26th letter and in the demarche, as I recollect it. But we did count the missiles going out. They put them on the decks and left them up there to be counted although some people kept saying they're being moved to caves. There is a continuing political hassle as to whether we really got what we set out to get but I think the record is clear that we did. Kissinger later complained about the absence of written agreements, but he himself could not get a written agreement when he came to cope with the problem of a possible submarine base; these things don't work that way.

It is not possible to be precise at the edges of such an understanding as is illustrated by the case of the IL-28's. I explained carefully to a national audience on October 14 that I knew of no evidence and I thought there was no likelihood of Soviet missiles in Cuba and that everything they had sent so far was consistent with what they had done with other countries. Of course one basic reason for thinking they wouldn't put nuclear weapons in Cuba is that they had never done it before. It is the very natural reaction of intelligence estimating.

When I said that, I knew IL-28's were on their way in. We had seen the crates, and I was justifying my comment, in my own mind, because they had indeed sent IL-28's to Egypt. So they are simply doing what they do with their friends—that was our position on October 14. But once the missiles got in there, the IL-28's became weapons that we considered offensive, and after October 28 it took another three weeks to get them out, in talks between McCloy and Kuznetsov, up in New York.

So that's all the assurances were. They have been operationally sufficient. There is still debate as to whether we should have gone further. Within our own councils Dean Acheson said he thought we should have turned the screw one more rivet. I don't know how many colleges take *Esquire* and keep it on the shelves, but Acheson's review of Kennedy's book is one of the important documents on the missile crisis and it appeared in that unlikely journal.

Recently young Rodman, writing in *Commentary,* seems to think we should really have continued the crisis. Of course the President decided very clearly in his own mind in the first week that the only serious and sufficient object was to get the missiles out and that was what he would focus on and that was all he would focus on. That is the way it turned out.

I don't know. It is an interesting speculation whether in the late 1980s we are now in a sufficiently unified national mold with respect to nuclear weapons in the Western Hemisphere so that we would go back to the brink—however near the brink we were or were not—over some intensification of Soviet submarine capabilities. The President of the United States said that this didn't keep him awake just this year. I think he was right to say that. Because what else are you going to do about it? If you can't fix it, laugh it off. It is a pretty good way to deal with many nuclear deployments, in my opinion.

QUESTION: I wonder if in the intervening, twenty years you find yourself any more sympathetic with secretary Acheson's position?

MR. BUNDY: Well, I tried to strengthen his basic case myself. I was the strawboss of the air strike option between Friday noon and Saturday noon. But my champion went off to his farm. He said, "Look, this is no place for a former secretary of state, working in an exercise of this sort when he has already had innings with the President and when the President and his most trusted advisers are pretty clearly settled on something else." And he went away.

That had the effect (as is suggested by Allison) of making the particular air strike which the President had to judge on Saturday and Sunday a lot more massive than Acheson had intended, because it was the Air Force's air strike and not Dean Acheson's.

I do think it is a great exaggeration to say, as Bobby does in his book, these were all wonderful, wise and thoughtful men and if six of them had had their way the world have blown up. I think that is baloney. I think the world would not have blown up but I think that the course of international relations would have been much more harsh if we had solved the problem by the air strike method.

QUESTION: Is the U.S.'s current situation in the world under control?

MR. BUNDY: Well, I think that on some matters there is nobody in charge, to be very blunt about it. I think there is a strategic procurement program going on in the United States that has no mind in charge of it. On the other side that has been true for quite awhile and I think the puzzle is very severe. When I say "no mind" I don't mean that there aren't people with a rational view of what they need the weapons for and a case to defend it. But I think that there are too many of them in our case. We have branches of the Air Force with competing programs; we have Navy programs; we have Cruise missile programs in great variety; we have aircraft programs; we have ballistic missile programs of different ranges and varieties nobody has put together an argument that is available for anyone to read as to why all of these things are necessary. It is simply asserted that they are.

The Soviets have done the same thing. There is a race going on, for the comfort of numerical advantages, in a situation in which it remains as true as it was twenty-five years ago that any actual use of these weapons is totally unpredictable in its consequences. The secretary of defense, Casper Weinberger, who is not a fool, was asked at one point in the last year or two, "What do you think will happen, Mr. Secretary, if anybody ever uses these weapons?" He said, "I haven't any idea and nobody else does either." And that is right. But if that is right then how can you make rational preparations for some form of protracted nuclear war? You can't, and yet that's what defense directives say we should be doing.

QUESTION: The thing that is puzzling is we had Vice Admiral Masterson a year ago who was secretary to the Joint Chiefs of Staff who spoke to us approximately an hour concerning the prolonged nuclear exchanges that were being discussed and prepared for, apparently, by the Joint Chiefs of Staff as an operational plan.

MR. BUNDY: They had been told to do that. They are military men.

QUESTION: Isn't this a piece of what you would call double insanity?

MR. BUNDY: I think it is a piece of double think, that we honestly know there mustn't be a nuclear war but when you think about it as a trained military man, you want to win. You change "win" to "prevail" because win sounds foolish. "Prevail" is foolish, too. One of the things JFK did was to knock "prevail" out of the vocabulary. It was in the basic national security policy paper that we inherited and he didn't want to say that. He didn't believe it.

QUESTION: What is then the way out?

MR. BUNDY: The way out is to recognize that you can't fight it. All that you can have is a sustainable, survivable deterrent force. We already have that. There is a limit psychologically to how far you can let the other guy have more than you have. Many people think that limit was reached in the early seventies when the Soviets built the SS18's and the SS19's and we did not match them, and that became the window of vulnerability. The underlying concern of the Committee on the Present Danger was not because they really thought those weapons would be used but that they thought the threat of their use would be effectively coercive. It hasn't turned out that way. We've just come through the years that Paul Nitze used to describe as the years of maximum vulnerability. Nothing happened. I think what we have to do is to recognize that both sides long since have vastly more survivable force than they need. There are things that have to be tended to. Communications are not all that survivable. That is a very serious matter. Technological change does threaten the survivability of once very secure forces like the Minuteman. But the solution that has been advanced, of remedying that problem by putting a more attractive target in the same silo, doesn't make sense. It makes sense only if you are planning to go first with those weapons at some point.

So I think we have made a lot of bad choices in the last few years, but I think the underlying point is that the base of public understanding has never been laid. As I say, it was not laid by the two Presidents who were in the best position, in terms of prestige and understanding, to lay it, a long time ago. These weapons really aren't good for anything except preventing their use by others and for that a relatively modest supply, given the way they look when you think of yourself on the receiving end, does the job.

QUESTION: Did Kennedy ever discuss what he could and couldn't do on the nuclear crisis in the same language he did China? He said he simply couldn't in the first term do anything about China.

MR. BUNDY: You know I'm not so sure he was all that clear that he could do anything about China in the second term. China was not a subject that he approached with great enthusiasm. This was typical Kennedy—what are you going to do? You are not going to liberate Chiang Kai-Shek. What are you going to do? Well, we'll ask Averell. We've got to send an ambassador over there who can cool Chiang off. We're not going to have the CIA man, Chiang's best friend, run things anymore, and we brought Ray Cline home and he was enormously valuable in other ways. Let's get an ambassador who can handle this notion that it is time to go and liberate the mainland. So they picked Alan Kirk who had been my boss in World War II and had commanded the Normandy landings for the American task force. His assignment was to have regular conversations with Chiang about the difficulties of an amphibious invasion of the mainland.

QUESTION: I really wanted to offer a little footnote to the research which you are conducting. Shortly after Lyndon Johnson became President, Fidel Castro—at that time I was Ambassador to Cuba—made a speech to the students of the university about the importance of physical courage. He said that if we wanted an example, it was courageous of the Soviet government to put the missiles in Cuba. It was an act of cowardice to take them away. And since the government never had any proof that any missiles were there because we had not been able actually to observe these—

MR. BUNDY: You weren't flying U2's yourself?

QUESTION: No. But we did have people driving about the countryside noting the types of vehicles. So the next time I found myself alone with Fidel, I said to him, "That was very interesting about Khrushchev being cowardly to take away the missiles. Do you think that if he kept the missiles there Kennedy would not have done anything about it?" He said, "Well, do you doubt that?" I didn't say anything. He said, "What are you thinking?" and I said, "Well, I'm thinking that I wouldn't count on Lyndon Johnson, the new President, to do nothing because that seemed the obvious thing to say. I had no other use for this statement except that it did seem wise to offer that point. But what I am saying is, whether true or not, it was Fidel's line by then that there had been missiles which were taken out. That was what he said in public. It is what he said to me. That doesn't prove that he was necessarily telling the truth.

MR. BUNDY: Missiles, certainly. Whether there were warheads is what we never knew.

QUESTION: Missiles there were. And the implication of all this, though, was the warheads as well.

MR. BUNDY: I agree. And Fidel is not the only one who has said different things at different times but he is one of the more important ones. In later years he has remarked that he understands the matter better than he did when he was young.

QUESTION: I wasn't talking about the judgment so much as the fact.

QUESTION: You've mentioned the proliferation a bit in passing but I wonder how you assess that it complicates the main considerations of the two nuclear powers.

QUESTION: Do you think the nonproliferation treaty has really helped that situation?

MR. BUNDY: Some. I don't think treaties govern that kind of national decision. If you'll look at who has visibly and believably gone nuclear they are not people who would have been constrained by a treaty. Roughly in the order of development, the United States, the U.S.S.R., the British, the French, the Chinese, the Indians, and the Israelis all have in their view important reasons. The one reason they have in common is that in every one of these capitals there is a very deep-seated conviction that the residents are in the center of the universe.

QUESTION: I get the feeling that right now the two superpowers are like the big husky football teams. Neither has a quarterback and they are playing a kind of touch football. I gather part of the problem was when Eisenhower did take personal blame for the U2 thing and I know one person made a comment that he thought several centuries of diplomacy had gone down the drain. We're groping here with our own presidential crisis at the moment. I don't know whether you see any hope for our national situation, the world situation right now.

MR. BUNDY: I made some sharp remarks about the management of the strategic nuclear competition on both sides but I think there is a lot of prudence in high places in both countries still. I think there is curious aspect to this nuclear competition. The zest with which it is pursued is totally disconnected really with any belief at the top of either government that one has got something usable. There hasn't been an effective nuclear threat by anyone to anyone for at least a decade now. And I don't think that is an accident.

QUESTION: Do you consider the current positioning of the Cruise missiles and the Pershing 2 to be a positive factor for stabilization?

MR. BUNDY: I've always thought that that whole episode was unnecessary because, going back to my earlier proposition, it starts from a belief that somehow because you have an emerging ratification of equality at the strategic level and so inequality at less than strategic levels becomes very important. It isn't said quite that sharply in Helmut Schmidt's famous speech of 1977 but that is the implication and it gets built up over the next year or two and turns into the 1979 agreement of NATO, the double track policy.

I think the thing to do with the SS20's was to say okay, they're spending billions and billions of rubles. The threat to the West has not changed one bit. They already have thousands of warheads that can be fired at Western Europe if they choose to fire them that way. This is a modernization which is excessive and it's a nuisance, but we are self-confident. That's the right way to deal with that problem. And I think it is a great mistake for Americans to blame Helmut Schmidt. Schmidt did make those remarks. They were put into that speech by his "defense adviser." He would have done better to reread his own book, *Defense and Deterrence,* which is one of the most important and constructive volumes analyzing the nuclear danger that there is. It comes out for no first use incidentally, so this also is not a new idea.

The real requirement on American leadership is not to get into deployments which are defended only because they are regarded as politically necessary. If it is not militarily necessary, it is not politically necessary. This one was not militarily necessary. It is not militarily effective. We have the authority of Paul Nitze, in Strobe Talbot's new book, for the correct proposition that neither the Cruise missiles nor the Pershing 2s is a particularly good weapons system considered in military terms.

So it would have been better if it had never happened. Now once the decision was made, the situation changes. Because it does become a political matter whether Russian pressure is going to be seen to have turned us around. That is quite a different point. What I think is the primary lesson in terms of my underlying theme is that the Soviet pressure didn't work. In fact it back-fired. What any Western European leader needs is a good denunciation from Andrei Gromyko just in time for the next election.

QUESTION: This week we learned that President Reagan kept his negotiations with Mr. Gromyko rather confidential, away from the Defense Department with the exception of Mr. Weinberger. Doesn't that cause trouble and difficulties for the State Department and the President?

MR. BUNDY: I think if Weinberger can't speak for the Department of Defense the President had better get another secretary.

QUESTION: Doesn't that raise some constitutional question?

MR. BUNDY: I think it is quite sufficient to talk to the secretary of defense to consult the Defense Department. It certainly would have been in Kennedy's time. Don't you think?

QUESTION: I think so, yes.

MR. BUNDY: Why? What is constitutional about a requirement to talk to the assistant secretary of defense?

QUESTION: No, but in the sense he has to do these things secretly?

MR. BUNDY: What's wrong with that? I think if you can't have secret negotiations you are going to have terrible trouble.

QUESTION: I agree with you on that but the fact that he has to exclude the military. . . .

MR. BUNDY: He didn't exclude the military. The secretary of defense who doesn't know how to speak for the military is not a proper secretary of defense.

The Joint Chiefs don't have to be consulted before every meeting with Gromyko. They surely weren't before we met with Gromyko on the 18th of October, 1962 and wouldn't have expected to be. The real constitutional error is to assert that claim.

QUESTION: Well, I'm not saying that they should be consulted. I'm saying it poses a problem.

MR. BUNDY: No. I think not. It poses a problem to insist that they should be.

NARRATOR: We are very pleased we have had this opportunity this morning. It has been educational and instructive for us all. We've gotten a little bit closer to an understanding of a terribly important presidency. But the added dividend is that we've explored the single most fundamental issue facing the nation which is the nuclear problem. Thank you very much.

VII. KENNEDY AND VIETNAM: TWO VIEWS

KENNEDY, NATO AND SOUTHEAST ASIA

Ambassador Frederick E. Nolting

NARRATOR: By your record-breaking presence at the Miller Center, Ambassador Nolting, you have proven what I thought would be the case—there is little need for any introduction this morning. As a matter of fact, Frederick Nolting probably ought to introduce the Miller Center to you since he was so largely responsible for its beginnings, early history, furnishings, foundations, and all the other things that got us started.

Aside from a very distinguished military career, in which he rose from lieutenant junior grade to lieutenant commander in World War II, Ambassador Nolting's career may be divided into four parts: diplomat, banker, scholar, and educator. That of diplomat is the most central to our concerns here this morning. He spent eighteen years in the Department of State, leaving with the permanent rank of minister. During that time he was concerned primarily with European and Far Eastern affairs. One of his functions was officer in charge of dealing with Swiss Benelux affairs. So if any of you have any Swiss bank accounts, today is the time to raise any questions you may have. He was alternate permanent representative to the North Atlantic Council. He became our deputy representative to NATO. He was concerned with the office of political affairs at NATO. He dealt also, in the fifties, with Mutual Security Affairs as a special assistant to the Secretary of State for Mutual Security Affairs. He was a member of the United States Delegation to the Sixth General Assembly. He served as coordinator of Far Eastern foreign assistance, and one could go on indefinitely. But in those eighteen years he gained the respect of a great many people, some of whom are present today.

It took him less time to reform, improve, and strengthen the private sector and the economy. I counted sixteen years but I may have missed a few years. He began with an investment firm, I think, in Richmond. He served there prior to World War II for five years. He then came back, after his distinguished career in the State Department and served as vice-president in the European office of Morgan Guaranty in Paris and subsequently, assistant to the chairman of Morgan Guaranty in New York.

His major area of responsibility was in the Far East during a very critical and much discussed period in our history: the Vietnam War. His preparation for that centered primarily on his service in the government in both Far Eastern and European affairs. He served as ambassador to Vietnam from 1961 to 1963.

His role as educator began as a graduate student at the University of Virginia. He received not one but two Master's degrees, one from Virginia and one from Harvard. He also received the Ph.D. from Virginia. He returned to the University of Virginia after his service in the private sector to become the first director of the Miller Center. It is appropriate that we now turn in our consideration of the Kennedy presidency to Ambassador Nolting. He will not only talk about the Vietnam period, but also about his other areas of responsibility at NATO, Mutual Security, and national defense, as they relate to the European area. It is a great privilege to have you with us.

AMBASSADOR NOLTING: Ken, you have a fabulous memory as well as a very generous nature. I can't begin this talk without paying tribute to Ken Thompson's work here at the Miller Center. I know because I tried it for awhile. He has really made a national institution out of a small beginning, and I can't think of a greater contribution to the University of Virginia, and to the enlightened governance of our country, than what you have done at the Miller Center.

NARRATOR: Thank you. I had solid foundations on which to build.

AMBASSADOR NOLTING: My views of the Kennedy administration and its accomplishments in foreign policy do not coincide altogether with some of the previous speakers at these Forums. I was struck by a few things Arthur Schlesinger said. He spoke of the New Frontier's "addiction to activism" as "its besetting sin." I do not disagree so much with that, but I think it needs a great deal of qualification. He made no direct reference to Vietnam or to Southeast Asia. He did talk about the "fantasy of counterinsurgency." I simply raise a question about that, recalling the situation confronting the United States at that time. Khrushchev and the Russian government had made it clear that their attack on the free world would come through wars of "national liberation," as Khrushchev termed them, not through a major confrontation with the West. We were afraid of that. Counterinsurgency was one of the options which was available and useful in the defense of the free world, if wisely used, as the British did in Malaya.

These are a few more observations: Dean Rusk, in his contribution, makes no mention of Southeast Asia in the early sixties. He makes no mention of Vietnam until he speaks of the drying up of grass roots support for the war effort in 1966. He makes no mention whatsoever of the United States' role in the sixties, particularly in 1963, in the overthrow of the government of South Vietnam. Something ought to be on the record about that—not just a gap in the history of this period.

Ted Sorensen, a close friend of President Kennedy, did make one reference to Vietnam saying: "We didn't give enough attention to Southeast Asia and Vietnam in particular." Well, that's the understatement of the year. There was every effort made to try to bring the State Department, in particular, and the White House into the Vietnam issue early on. It started before my day and it continued until President Kennedy's death. By that time, we were so deeply involved in bailing out the military junta that the U.S. had helped put into power that President Johnson thought there was no way out, except through the use of a great number of American combat forces. Sorensen also said that the Laotian settlement of 1962 was a great diplomatic triumph. Well, if that was a triumph of diplomacy, I don't know the meaning of the word. Averell Harriman was the negotiator. He told me that he was under instructions from President Kennedy to get a settlement of the Laotian question at any cost. In the early days of the Kennedy administration, President Kennedy went on television and said we were going to take a stand in Laos. Those of you who know the inaccessibility of Laos can understand how horrified the Joint Chiefs of Staff were to hear that the President had decided to make a stand in Laos. There wasn't any way to get in there except by air, and that didn't make much sense. So the President backed off of that idea and decided Vietnam was the place to make the stand. But then, as if in order to open up the flank of Vietnam, he ordered the Laotian settlement. This treaty definitely weakened, both physically and from the point of view of morale, the chances of the successful defense of South Vietnam.

One other remark about Sorensen: He thought the Cuban missile crisis was a very great American success. I agree with that, in part. It was handled better than anything I know of in the tragically short administration of President Kennedy. It was successful in avoiding nuclear war. Nevertheless, the fact that the United States was successful in getting the Russians to back away from the installation of missiles in Cuba was only to come back to where we were before the Bay of Pigs. It is not, it seems to me, proportionate to talk in terms of a big success without mentioning the previous big disaster.

I am trying to fill in some gaps in this oral history. However, one must keep in mind that my view is only one of many. I think one always finds that there is a difference between the viewpoint of those in the field abroad and those who serve in the inner circles in Washington. Certainly I was not one of the inner circle people in Kennedy's administration.

This leads me to what I'd like to say first about Kennedy and our European allies in NATO. I was in NATO for several months during the Kennedy administration and for about five years under the Eisenhower administration. The difference between those two administrations with respect to our European allies was very great. I have no doubt in my mind that the NATO system of this great North Atlantic alliance functioned much better under Eisenhower than it did under Kennedy. There are several reasons for this. General Eisenhower was known and respected. He was tried and true from the point of view of the NATO countries. His record as supreme commander helped, as well as his willingness to consult and consider—in terms of U.S. policy—the views of our NATO allies. President Kennedy was not inclined in that way from the perspective of the NATO countries. Our European allies were attracted by his freshness, his dynamism, his personal attraction, and his oratory. But they felt that he was untried; he was less willing to consult; he was less reliable as an ally from the European perspective. For example, some of our allies were alarmed by his earlier speeches in the Senate in which he went all out for self-determination of European colonies, particularly those in Africa. While the idea of self-determination was generally acceptable to most of the colonial powers in NATO, they didn't want it to happen overnight. They had to have some preparation time.

Another point I would like to make is that the NATO allies did not feel that Secretary Rusk was as close to or had as much influence with Kennedy as John Foster Dulles had with Eisenhower or Dean Acheson had with Truman. They felt a certain reserve and distance there. Perhaps that was overcome in later years but this was, I think, the prevailing perspective from NATO in the first year of the Kennedy administration. There was no consultation in NATO whatsoever under the Kennedy administration on the Southeast Asian problem. While the French had set a not very good precedent on this, the United States had argued for years—and I was on the Political Consultation Committee—the benefits to be derived from constant consultation on political problems, however thorny they might be. To have our government, because we had a hot potato, refuse to talk about it, was not good diplomacy or statesmanship.

As we all know, no President ever has a clean slate to write on, not even George Washington, and certainly no modern President. Therefore, one has to think about continuity and distribute responsibilities, praise, and criticism in accordance with the flow of history and the dynamics of the process of ruling any country. Just as Kennedy inherited from Eisenhower the makings of the disaster of the Bay of Pigs, so Johnson inherited from Kennedy the makings of the disaster of Vietnam. It is very difficult, however, to say where these things could have been halted or where they could have been changed.

My thesis is that the great error of the Kennedy administration was its misunderstanding of the issues involved in Vietnam in the sixties, and its reaction to those issues. More speciflically, the error was in its refusal to understand that the elected constitutional government of Vietnam was the best available. If we were to help South Vietnam survive at all, the only available vehicle which could sustain and carry forward the country was the government that had been in power eight years (after two elections) and which had run into a great deal of Communist-inspired trouble. Now, this change of U.S. position came about, from my point of view, rather suddenly. In 1961 and 1962, our efforts to help South Vietnam through its duly elected government were for the most part successful. The testimony on that comes not only from Washington but other capitals, including especially France. This may surprise you, because France had a chip on its shoulder about Americans taking over its responsibilities in helping South Vietnam. But Couve de Murville, for example, told me on two occasions that the American effort in 1961 and 1962 in South Vietnam was succeeding from the point of view of the French interests still there, and they were considerable. The Michelin Rubber Company, the major banks, and the major shipping companies were all saying, "Keep it up; the country is beginning to get pacified; it is beginning to work."

When we first arrived with our families we could hardly go out of Saigon without an escort, and then you took a chance on getting ambushed. By 1962 we could drive to many provinces without escort and without much danger. You'd have threats of assassinations and bombings and so forth, but our children went to school there and we lived a normal life. This was just one indication of the gradual pacification brought about by the Diem government with our help and advice.

It is true that the Kennedy administration had stepped up the amount of aid from the Eisenhower level of about $150 million a year to, until 1963, about $350 million a year. I remember that figure well because every morning going to the office I'd say, "My God, what am I going to do with this million dollars today to make it worth it to the American people?" And I certainly don't claim that we succeeded every day or even every other day. But on the whole it was getting better. Even Ho Chi Minh testified that 1962 was Diem's year. He gave this to Wilfred Burchett, an Australian correspondent of Communist leanings, who spent most of his time either in Hanoi or with the Communist Viet Cong in South Vietnam. His testimony, I thought, was significant. He said not only that 1962 was Diem's year but, after the overthrow of Diem's government in 1963, he quoted one of the Communist leaders as saying they could not imagine that the United States would be so stupid as to preside over the overthrow of the only government that had any standing and status in South Vietnam. Why did we do this?

The Buddhist crisis is generally regarded as the releasing cause. There was, however, more to it than that. This comes back directly to the Kennedy administration. It was the impatience of the gung-ho boys; it was the 1964 election coming up; it was the desire of President Kennedy to make up for the bullying he got from Khrushchev in Vienna in the first meeting; it was the Berlin Wall which was a slap in the face and which we didn't do much about—except for Kennedy's famous speech, "Ich bin ein Berliner." That didn't take one stone out of the Berlin Wall; it was perhaps encouraging to the West Berliners but, to my mind, it wasn't any great diplomatic stroke. On Vietnam in 1963 the influences upon Kennedy were divided. The State Department, my own department, took the lead in advocating such great pressures upon President Diem as to make it impossible for him to govern. This pressure was reciprocal in the sense that the more pressure there was from Washington, the more the Buddhist agitators put pressure on our press, and through our press on Washington, to get rid of the Diem government.

Another thing that was absolutely clear, which we reported countless times, was that the number one objective of the Viet Cong was the overthrow of the Diem government. That was the identical objective of the radical wing of the Buddhist movement. This radical wing did not represent the Buddhist population by any means. It was a new organization founded only the year before. There never had been a hierarchical organization of Buddhists in Vietnam. Each bonze had his own village to look after and his own marriages and burials to perform, but he wasn't responsible to the next guy on the totem pole. There wasn't any overall Buddhist organization. So, this was a new thing which was formed for a political purpose and it achieved that political purpose. While I have no proof of this except circumstantial evidence, I firmly believe that it was infiltrated and controlled by the Viet Cong through Hanoi. I think the misunderstandings of our government with respect to that fact was one of the biggest contributing factors to our change of policy.

In the 1950's, almost every year somebody would come up with a story about NATO in "disarray." Compared to the Kennedy administration in 1963 on the issue of Southeast Asia, NATO's disarray was nothing. You could sit around the NATO council table and settle issues with the representatives of fifteen nations much more readily and reasonably than you could with the representatives of the various departments and agencies in Washington in 1963. This was so much so that President Kennedy himself at one meeting in 1963 said, "My government has gone completely to pieces. Who is right? Who has the information? What shall I do?" Unfortunately, Averell Harriman took the bit in his teeth and ran off with the show.

He wasn't any older then than I am now and I don't see how anybody could have been so vindictive, authoritarian and bullying as he was of everybody, including the President of the United States. His hatred of the Diem regime became greater and greater. It originated with President Diem's reluctance to sign the Laotian agreement which Harriman had negotiated. There was a personal friction between them on that. I had the job of persuading Diem to sign because there was very little else he could do. Harriman was out there in 1962 and threatened to cut off all American aid if he didn't. Now, this involved not only Vietnamese objections to the treaty, which had no safeguards, but the Thais objected to it just as strongly as the Vietnamese did. But this started a personal distrust that certainly made it much more difficult to get any reasonable exchange of views in the National Security Council meetings that followed in the fall of 1963. It was very, very difficult.

Another factor was that President Kennedy had appointed Henry Cabot Lodge as the new ambassador to Saigon. Lodge and Harriman had, I think, agreed beforehand that the only thing to do was to encourage the dissident generals to revolt, to take over. Lodge was pulling from the Saigon end for this while Harriman was pushing from the Washington end. Some of the rest of us were trying to stand in the way to hold the fort, so to speak, but to no avail. Again, politics came into it very strongly for the reason that there were two very distinguished pillars of both parties—Lodge, whom I thought of as a piece of Republican asbestos to keep the heat off of Kennedy, and Harriman, who still had a lot of the political force of the Roosevelt heritage.

Now the young President was caught in a dilemma; there was no question about it. There were several things he could have done, but the worst alternative was what he opted to do. Even worse than the practical consequences of the coup were the moral effects. I will not go into the sequence of events here because I believe it is now clear that after the revolution things went from bad to worse, regardless of the number of troops that we put in and regardless of the fact that the cost went up dramatically: Fifty-seven thousand American lives, eight years of dissension in our country, huge increases in public debt, and the inflation which afflicted us throughout the seventies. The actions of the Kennedy administration set the stage for all this.

There is just one more point I would like to make. You have developed, Ken, in your books a theme which appeals to me a very great deal: the role of morality and ethical dealings in foreign policy. Even worse than the practical results in Vietnam were the moral consequences. Diem's was a government to whom our President had personally promised non-interference in its internal affairs. Just before I left Saigon in August 1963, President Diem asked me whether this change of ambassadors meant any change in U.S. policy. I said, "No, I'm assured, Mr. President, that it doesn't," and he said, "Well, would you just check that for me?" I sent a special telegram to what was called the highest levels and got one back from "the highest levels"—that's supposed to be the President, although you never know for sure—saying, "No change in policy and you can tell him that straight out." So, I took the telegram and translated it for him. While it was in my hand he said, "Mr. Ambassador, I believe you, but I'm afraid your information is incorrect." He was quite right, because by the time I got back to Washington this thing was out of hand and there was nothing we could devise to stop it. I want to say that the denials that were made after the coup in November, that our government had nothing to do with it, were too much for me to take. I don't think that anybody ought to try to cover up something of that sort when it is, in the first place, immoral and deceitful, and in the second place impossible.

QUESTION: I can't remember whether the domino theory antedated Mr. Kennedy's presidency or not, but it certainly was in its ascendancy during his term and later, as Vietnam became more difficult. It has always intrigued me that there hasn't been a fair analysis of the working of that theory in the twenty-twenty gaze of hindsight. Indonesia, for example, is a country that had all the marks, under Sukarno, of heading into the Communist camp. It did not happen, however, even though they had a great massacre which, perhaps, contributed to its prevention. With your perspective, I'd like for you to comment on the domino theory. Was it viable in the beginning? Did it have any continued aspects which are defensible today?

AMBASSADOR NOLTING: Yes, I think so, Leigh. If it's taken literally, as one domino falling right after another, one knocking the other one over, that, of course, is not what was meant. The cumulative effect of Communist victories are very great. Kampuchea (Cambodia) is certainly one example now in that area. So is Laos. Of course, it didn't go as far as Malaya. That was stopped by the British before they got out. But I think there is a certain momentum that builds up. In the case of Vietnam, it has been argued that through enormous sacrifices that effect was held up, to a certain extent, for eight years and that that gave other countries a chance to strengthen their resistance. To what extent that is true, I'm not sure, but I do think, in general, the domino theory, while an over simplification, has a certain basis in fact.

QUESTION: Mr. Ambassador, had the Kennedy administration retained support for the Diem regime, and had the administration, the secretary of defense, and the Joint Chiefs decided to take decisive action and support within the first two or three years of the buildup of the Communist effort, before North Vietnam really came into it, could we have succeeded in keeping South Vietnam a free country?

AMBASSADOR NOLTING: Do you mean after the revolution or before?

QUESTION: If they had retained support for President Diem's regime and the military had made a decisive decision.

AMBASSADOR NOLTING: My opinion is that the answer is yes. With our continued support of the legitimate government, which was gaining ground on Ho Chi Minh, I think that with continued American support, there was a chance of coming out with a fairly stable solution—a divided Vietnam, somewhat in the pattern of Korea or Germany, which is certainly not a very satisfactory solution, but one we have had to settle for in several cases. The chances of that happening, followed by gradually getting the two halves of Vietnam together through trade and other means, would have been good—and that without American combat forces.

I might make one other remark which is *apropos* of the domino theory. I think one of the conceptual errors of the Kennedy administration early on was to think about the three states of Indochina—the old French Indochina—as separate entities. They are racially separate, but they had been grouped together a long time under the French empire. As a strategic area, the Communists always thought about it as one area. It didn't make any difference to them which side of the Laotian or Cambodian border they were on. They thought about it as one area including North Vietnam, South Vietnam, Laos, and Cambodia. Because we weren't sufficiently educated on that part of the world, myself included, we looked at the countries separately; we thought they could be defended separately. That was a big conceptual error on the part of the United States.

QUESTION: Ambassador Nolting, may I say something? I was in the Joint Staff at that time writing papers in this particular area. There were two teams of us writing papers in this area and for one thing, we weren't allowed to do anything to try to win the war. That was a rule set down. And, for another, when we would try to look at it as a whole area it would be split up for us when it went across the river. There were two ways to stop things at that point. Both involved moving the war supplies out of China, down into South Vietnam through Laos, and through North Vietnam itself. And the Chief's staff proposed to close off the port, Haiphong, Hanoi, and to close the valley coming down from China which was very narrow and could have been closed with one explosion. This was in the early sixties during the secret war in Laos, the top secret war in Laos. Excuse me, we couldn't even say there was war.

AMBASSADOR NOLTING: Very interesting.

QUESTION: They called it Co Chin China historically and they changed it to Indochina under the French and we lost the threads of the strategic implication of that early on. We had a mental block about Indochina being part of the empire of France. I can remember when it was a single, strategic entity, Co Chin China.

QUESTION: I just wanted to say how much I endorse what Ambassador Nolting has said. I suppose professional diplomacy moves different minds in the same direction. This is so very much how I see it. I just wanted to put that on record. And I also wanted to make two other endorsing remarks. One is about the attitude of the European allies toward the Kennedy administration. I think there was in Europe, admiration and affection for Kennedy as a bright young person—something new. There is no doubt, I think, that the European governments were more unhappy with the Kennedy administration than with any other administration since the war. We only had two years of Kennedy, but certainly those two years produced a deep malaise and unhappiness in European governments. I think there is no doubt about that.

The second thing I wanted to say was about Cuba. I was the British ambassador in Cuba during those years. I think there is no doubt that the Russians—this I owe really to Fidel among other people—always had two options. If they could get away with having missiles in Cuba, well and good. That would have compensated for the river of money they were pouring into Cuba because Cuba, on the whole, has not been such a success for the Russians. And if they didn't, they could always retire. I think when one is talking about U.S. policy towards Cuba, I don't know that getting Russians to accept their plan B instead of their plan A was such victory. For the Bay of Pigs operation was a setback all over Central America. In other words, I agree with Ambassador Nolting's judgment that, although the negotiation was brilliantly handled by the Kennedy brothers, it didn't really get the U.S. back to square one.

AMBASSADOR NOLTING: There is also the fact that, as a part of the secret deal, NATO's southern flank was badly affected by our agreement to withdraw our missiles from Turkey. Ever since there has been this weakness in the southern flank of NATO.

QUESTION: And Turkey protects the Middle East; it protects Israel.

AMBASSADOR NOLTING: This was part of the deal that was not made public—the removal of the missiles from Turkey. I'm not sure that we came further than half-way back on the deal. I'm glad to hear your testimony as British ambassador in Cuba that you feel that too.

QUESTION: Yes, I do, a lot.

NARRATOR: You wouldn't want to say whether it was also the policy of your government, at the time of the coup, to be as critical of what was being done as Ambassador Nolting is.

QUESTION: Well, this was the high-water mark of nonconsultation with your allies, the Vietnam opposition. I remember Prime Minister Harold Wilson laying down instructions which were sent to British ambassadors in various places saying: "This is Harold Wilson. Our attitude is no public criticism of our American allies whatever they do." To send out the word publicly like that clearly meant that we were unhappy. Kennedy, however, gave little attention to this.

It does seem to me that the ignorance of your policy outside France, about Vietnam, is appalling. I also think that most of the time the European allies didn't really know what they were talking about. They had quite good ambassadors on the spot, but I don't think the government or the press or the Parliament of a country like Britain, or a country like Germany, really knew what was going on in Vietnam. Therefore, I'm not sure that our judgments are really all that valid.

AMBASSADOR NOLTING: With the exception of the Bob Thompson mission—the British mission under Sir Robert Thompson. That was successful counterinsurgency, the very thing that was criticized by some of the speakers here.

QUESTION: Yes, and the very thing that's criticized in Central America.

QUESTION: I'm going to come back to nonconsultation. I was intrigued by your remark that the Kennedy administration did not consult with the European allies about the involvement in Southeast Asia. I wondered if perhaps that might be attributed, in part, to American sensitivity about getting involved.

AMBASSADOR NOLTING: Yes, but I don't think our allies in NATO would have viewed it that way. To my mind, it was just because we had a very difficult problem that we didn't want to talk about, just as the French didn't want to talk about Algeria (although that was a different thing because Algeria was a province of France). But Vietnam was something that we wanted to do on the side, do it ourselves, and didn't want anybody else to tell us how, I suppose. At least, that was Washington's view at the time.

QUESTION: And outside the NATO treaty area you had a say?

AMBASSADOR NOLTING: Yes indeed. That's an important point.

One point I keep coming back to in my mind is that the general interpretation of America's getting a thumb in the wringer in Vietnam, then our hand, then our arm, is not true. I don't think it was true under Eisenhower and I don't think it was true under Kennedy up until his last tragic months. I think that the U.S. support of the coup was a political decision of crucial importance. It was opposed by the CIA. I should make this very clear because anytime anything like that happens everybody says, "Oh, the dirty CIA did it." The CIA was then under John McCone and Pat Carter and they were absolutely opposed. All the "tea leaves" (intelligence reports) in each of the NSC meetings said, "No, don't do it, you'll get into a worse fix. Don't support the military junta. They are no good." That was my view also. That was, ironically enough, President Johnson's view.

I remember after one of the meetings Johnson, who was then vice-president, said: "Keep it up, you fellows arguing against this change, this foolish move, keep it up." I remember saying after one of those remarks, "Mr. Vice-President, you carry an awful lot of weight and you can see that we are beleaguered here and we could use some help." Vice-President Johnson said, "President Kennedy has invited me to attend these NSC meetings on the condition that I do not express an opinion."

QUESTION: Mr. Ambassador, both Mr. Ambassadors, you put a finger on something I want to make a point of. Each of these presidencies come into a continuation, not in isolation. They don't get a clean slate. You talked about plan A and plan B of the Russians. Well they've got plan A and plan B any place that they want to move: Ethiopia, Somalia, Laos, Cambodia. So, I'd like you to take it one step further in your conversation. In Malaysia you did something about it. How would you apply that case to the present and future?

AMBASSADOR NOLTING: Frank, I don't think that you can draw specific analogies or parallels between the South Vietnam case and the case in Central America or anywhere else. I think you should, and our government does of course, have plans and alternative plans for almost every eventuality. When to put them into action and when not to is really the crucial question I think that you raised. My instinct is one of extreme caution in moving in to take, or to manipulate, power in other governments. But that doesn't rule out doing it when you have to. It is a question of judgment. In the case of Vietnam I think the judgment was very bad. I think it is generally bad when we try to move in on internal situations. I don't think this is a very good analogy, but perhaps the Middle East would be a whole lot better if we hadn't interfered with the Shah.

QUESTION: And would you say Southeast Asia would be a whole lot better if President Marcos is not overthrown with American aid?

AMBASSADOR NOLTING: With American aid, yes. If the Filipinos overthrow him, that's not our responsibility. We don't get involved in the same sense that we got involved in the overthrow in Vietnam.

QUESTION: Or the Shah.

AMBASSADOR NOLTING: I'm not so well-informed about the Shah and I don't think it's an exact analogy by any means. But it seems to me that, more times than not, when we move in on something of that sort, we do it wrong.

QUESTION: Mr. Ambassador, I want to ask a a follow-up to Professor Claude's question. In early 1963 I was in Vietnam as a member of a group coming from the Pentagon. There was talk to this group that they were about to launch a national liberation campaign, everything looked good, there was going to be an effective victory on the side of South Vietnam. And, of course, events proceeded on and you have alluded to some of the mistakes as you saw them. I have since read the comment that the reason we ultimately lost in South Vietnam was because the North Vietnamese were more willing to die for their cause than the South Vietnamese were for their cause. The reason for this was that the South Vietnamese saw us as being the government of South Vietnam. Furthermore, the Asia for the Asians' aspect of Ho Chi Minh's cause was such that, in effect, we were precluded from ever being able to achieve success because it was too much our government, too much our control of the affairs in South Vietnam. I wonder if you would comment on that.

AMBASSADOR NOLTING: Well, I think we were always under that handicap from the year 1954 on, but nowhere near as much as after taking the responsibility for a new revolutionary government. President Diem's greatest fear—or vulnerability—was being called an American puppet, from which the Viet Cong would profit. That's one of the reasons we had such a hard time with the press. They wanted the Americans to claim everything good that happened as an American victory, while we tried to hide it under a bushel saying, "No, this is a Vietnamese government action," whether it was the building of a new school, the opening of a hospital, the land reform, the increase to three rice crops a year in the delta through hybrid seed, or the increase in education. We tried not to make it seem an American achievement, which was very hard for our press to take. They thought this was a concession to the Vietnamese government that we shouldn't be making. They wanted us to be nationalistic—not helpers but bosses.

I don't think the North Vietnamese were any braver. They had a cause that was more clear-cut, in a sense, because of foreign aid to the south. Of course, Russian and Chinese aid in large quantities to the Viet Cong was not made public. I think this advantage was vastly increased by the coup. In fact, the political base of South Vietnamese nationalism was removed and destroyed with the overthrow of the Diem government in 1963. This was the major reason why the military governments which succeeded it were so unsuccessful.

QUESTION: When McGeorge Bundy spoke here he described Mr. Harriman as quite a strong force in the Washington group. What would have been the relationship? Would Bundy have been a junior partner, you might say, or some such relationship, with Harriman performing a sort of ministerial role? Rusk was probably not nearly on top of this thing or McNamara. I'm trying to think of the group that was pushing for the overthrow of President Diem.

AMBASSADOR NOLTING: Mike Forrestal, who was young in those days, was brought into the White House staff under Bundy and President Kennedy said, "You keep an eye on Averell Harriman. You are my eyes and ears on Averell Harriman." It was like trying to tie up a stallion with a piece of string—he couldn't do it. Furthermore, instead of Forrestal keeping an eye on Harriman, he became Harriman's man. He was one of those who was pushing in the White House for a change, an overthrow.

McGeorge Bundy was equivocal on the subject, in my opinion. Our friend Dean Rusk was also. George Ball was in Harriman's camp and so was the assistant secretary for Far Eastern Affairs, Roger Hilsman. The majority of the military, the Joint Chiefs of Staff, certainly the CIA, Maxwell Taylor and I, and a few others were very much opposed. It would be interesting, if you get Bob McNamara down here, to quiz him a little bit on this.

QUESTION: I would like to go back, in a sense, to Leigh Middleditch's original question and ask what we have learned, Mr. Ambassador, if anything, about the possibilities of negotiating settlements. As you know, much of the literature now speaks of missed opportunities for negotiating settlements in Vietnam. I really have two points here, the latter of which you may not wish to put on the record. The first is, were there any pursuable conditions under which a negotiated settlement that would serve our interests could have been accomplished? And secondly, did Governor Harriman really think that would work in Laos, or was this seen as a domestic political ploy?

AMBASSADOR NOLTING: Let me take your last question first because it was chronologically first, in a way. I think Governor Harriman did, really and truly, think that the Russians were going to police the Laotian treaty—he used the word to me—and make the others tow the line. That meant the U.S.S.R. would make the North Vietnamese take out the forty thousand troops who were in Laos, making the Ho Chi Minh trail into what Joe Alsop later called "the Harriman Memorial Highway"; that they would let the Souvanna Pouma government into the territories controlled by the Pathet Lao, the Communist Laotians; that they would make a real effort to have this tiny country taken out of the area of conflict, thereby blocking off a good part of the Ho Chi Minh trail and the supply routes from North Vietnam and China. I think Harriman really believed this. I think it was naive. He told me he had a "fingertips feeling," which I couldn't dispute successfully because he had been to Russia as ambassador. I said that my fingertips told me just the reverse.

On the other question about the chance for a negotiated settlement, I think there were several opportunities. One of them which came up—this came recently into play in the State Department history—was whether or not Nhu's reported talks with the Vietcong and representatives from Hanoi could have led to a negotiated settlement. Well, that was reported after I had been recalled. I never believed that Nhu was selling out his brother or his government. But I do think that, in desperation, he was probably trying to work out a negotiation that would have let South Vietnam continue to be independent, possibly with certain concessions to the North. I think that was one opportunity. Early on there were many, but that's the most recent.

NARRATOR: Before wishing you all a Merry Christmas I would remind you that in the session just before Christmas we've followed the practice of having a speaker from the Miller Center family. Fritz Nolting remains part of that family. We are pleased he could be with us this morning for his important presentation. Thank you very much.

KENNEDY AND VIETNAM

William P. Bundy

NARRATOR: I would like to welcome you to a Forum with Mr. William Bundy. Few people are as well qualified to discuss issues in public affairs with eighteen years of public service in five administrations from Truman to Nixon. His path in life was determined by the fact that, in contrast to his Boston-born brother, he was born in Washington. Harvard's loss was the nation's gain.

He received his bachelor's degree from Yale in 1939. He served in the Army of the United States rising from private to major commanding a small signal corps unit which in collaboration with the British broke high-level German ciphers in the Ultra operation and made a major contribution to allied success. He graduated from Harvard Law School in 1947 and practiced law in Washington from 1947 to 1951. He entered the government in 1951 joining the Office of National Estimates in the Central Intelligence Agency with several years as the CIA Deputy on the Planning Board of the National Security Council. In 1960 he was on leave from the CIA as staff director of the bipartisan Commission on National Goals, editing its report, *Goals for Americans* and writing a supporting chapter on population and economic assistance. In January 1961 he joined the Kennedy administration as deputy assistant secretary of defense for international security affairs. He was promoted to assistant secretary in ISA in November 1963, and then moved in March 1964 to the State Department to become assistant secretary for East Asian and Pacific affairs continuing to 1969 in that capacity. From 1969 to 1972, he was at MIT as a visiting professor and research assistant and part-time columnist for *Newsweek*. From the fall of 1972 until June 1984 he served as editor of the respected journal, *Foreign Affairs*, publishing important articles such as a long account of the year 1983 and a valedictory article "The Last Dozen Years: What Might We Learn?" in the summer 1984 issue.

It is a great privilege to have him with us. He is a good friend of Ambassador Nolting who made an earlier presentation on Vietnam. We asked ourselves who was the most even-handed spokesman for a different point of view from Ambassador Nolting and everyone responded "Bill Bundy." Nolting and Bundy have deep mutual respect for one another whatever differences there may be. So it's a great privilege to have Bill Bundy speaking to us this morning.

MR. BUNDY: Thank you very much, Ken. I would only make one minor amendment to your introduction and that would be that in the collaboration with the British the role of the Americans must not be exaggerated and certainly not the role of our little unit. It was a fifty-fifty operation as somebody put it, "one rabbit, one horse."

Let me first, as it were, state my viewpoint. I was in the Pentagon during the period 1961-64, and was deputy assistant secretary in ISA throughout the Kennedy administration. In fact my nomination to be assistant secretary in ISA was approved by the Senate almost at the moment that President Kennedy was assassinated.

My relationship with President Kennedy was never a close personal one. Although we had been classmates in a little elementary school in Brookline, Massachusetts at the ages of nine and ten, and played on the same football team, I was not close to him thereafter and never felt myself a member of his inner circle during his presidency.

In my Pentagon job, and later in the Department of State, I was heavily involved in Southeast Asian matters; indeed I had followed the situation, and U.S. policy, there quite closely during the 1950s, though my work with the Board of National Estimates at CIA and as the CIA staff man with the Planning Board of the National Security Council. From 1961 to 1964 I was largely responsible, under Secretary McNamara, for the administration of the military assistance program; this thrust me into policy on Vietnam and Southeast Asia, and as Secretary McNamara himself got heavily into the subject I became in effect his civilian action officer.

My job was, of course, in Washington. I had never been stationed in Southeast Asia, although I had visited Vietnam in 1956 and again in 1958, and made at least two more trips during the Kennedy years, culminating in a ten-day visit in September 1963. Up to that important visit I had not been particularly engaged in the political side of the Vietnam situation. Indeed, one of the characteristics of policymaking in the Kennedy administration concerning Southeast Asia, and especially Vietnam, was that there came fairly early to be a division of labor, the State Department dealing with the political side and the Pentagon with the operational and military-related side—with very few general meetings or broad discussions between the two except at times of major decision or crisis.

Thus my responsibilities and exposure were different from those of Ambassador Nolting, my personal friend since 1940 and a man I deeply admire. I was your guest, Fritz, on my earlier trips to Saigon, and I recall at least one call on President Diem in which I accompanied you. But in that hectic and crucial summer of 1963, the so-called Buddhist crisis, I was not deeply involved until mid-September, and indeed was on leave from mid-August, when Ambassador Nolting left Saigon, until mid-September—so that I do not believe, Fritz, that you and I were ever in the same room or in the same discussions during that period.

So much for my vantage point at the time. Now, as to my present views on President Kennedy and Vietnam—and Laos, which is inseparable from any standpoint—I have had the benefit, for my remarks today, of reviewing this brown document before me which is part of the manuscript of an incomplete history memoir on policy in Vietnam and Laos. This volume covers the period from January 1961 to President Kennedy's assassination, and there are two other volumes taking the story up the late fall of 1965, with some notes on later periods. It is a manuscript I wrote when I was a scholar in residence at the Massachusetts Institute of Technology from 1969 until March of 1972, when I moved to New York to prepare for taking over that fall as Editor of *Foreign Affairs*.

Thus I have worked on the Vietnam story as a historian—or if you will as a participant historian—seeking to make use of my graduate training in history under William L. Langer of Harvard. At any rate, I tried to make the manuscript as professional as I knew how, and when I was writing it did have access to my personal files as well as to the Pentagon Papers, although for security and clearance reasons I could not cite specific materials at the time. However, with so much material now having come into the public domain, I cannot believe there is any remaining security problem of significance, and have discussed with Ken Thompson the possibility that I might make a copy available for your library, in some appropriate fashion. My presentation today draws heavily on that manuscript, which reflects my best recollection, analysis, and judgment of the course of events and of the key decisions and the reasons for them. Although I have not worked seriously on the manuscript since 1972, I find that it holds up reasonably well and needs only occasional references to later disclosures or issues.

Let me start on Southeast Asia in the Kennedy period where the Kennedy administration itself started, which was with Laos. It was there that conflict was at or near a boil when Kennedy took over from Eisenhower. I do not mean, of course, to discuss the Eisenhower period in detail, but it is necessary to understand where things stood as we of the new administration went down to our offices in those snow-laden days of the transition and started in.

Certainly our plates were full. We had the ongoing crisis over Berlin, trouble in the Congo, the festering situation in Cuba (on which the new administration had only just learned of the major covert action plan that had been in train for nearly a year), Laos, and—definitely fifth in apparent urgency and priority—Vietnam.

Laos was right at the top. In his final briefing by President Eisenhower just before the Inauguration, Kennedy had been given an outline of the situation and Eisenhower had concluded that Laos was truly a vital interest, the place to make a stand, and "you've got to hold there, with allies if possible, alone if necessary." (These are the precise words as recalled to me earlier this week by Dean Rusk in a recorded interview. The substance of the meeting, I now find, is also in President Nixon's new book, *No More Vietnams*.)

That was Eisenhower's parting advice—and the way the whole government was moving at that point. So President Kennedy had to make, over the next two months, a very major decision concerning Laos, whether that was a place to stand—or whether there was some alternative course of action that, if not good or promising, was at least less bad. That kind of choice is very often the case with decisions that Presidents have to make.

We got advice from many quarters, including our principal European allies, Britain and France. Both had followed Laos closely as the situation there had become more critical over the previous two years, and especially in the closing months of 1960, and both had developed doubts and misgivings about the course that U.S. policy had taken. Things had never gone smoothly in Laos under the 1954 Geneva Accords there, which had tried to lay down a coalition framework involving the Communist Pathet Lao, the right wing, and in the center the so-called neutralist group led by Prince Souvanna Phouma. At different times the Communist side had breached the accords, and so had the right wing. And in early 1960 the Eisenhower Administration threw its strong support behind the right-wing leader, a gentleman named General Phoumi Nosavan, who took over with a lot of help and advice from the CIA on the spot and eventually with small-scale U.S. military teams working with his forces. (I myself was never involved with the covert side of the CIA. At a slightly earlier time when Laos was boiling, in the spring and summer of 1959, I had followed what was happening very closely as briefing officer for Secretary of State Herter at the prolonged Geneva conference over Berlin—but during 1960 I had been on leave from the CIA with the Eisenhower Commission on National Goals.)

So one crucial element of judgment in those early Kennedy days was whether Phoumi was really a strong and effective leader capable of successful military action and running a workable government. As events unfolded in those first weeks, and as we got the opinions of others, it seemed more and more clear that, far from being a real "strong man" in any sense of those words, Phoumi Nosavan was—to use a term later coined for Chancellor Erhard of the Federal Republic of Germany—a "rubber lion" (*gummi loewe*). Nothing in his later career, I might add, shook my belief that this was a right judgment.

And a second crucial element was whether the Lao themselves were, in general, effective fighters especially if they were to be up against forces heavily laced with North Vietnamese. And here I vividly recall the judgment expressed by our Ambassador in Laos, Winthrop Brown, at a head-to-head meeting with the Chairman of the Joint Chiefs of Staff, General Lyman Lemnitzer, and his special assistant, General C.H. Bonesteel. Brown was an experienced judge of men and events, tough-minded and objective—who had served with (and in many ways resembled) Ellsworth Bunker, and who went on to outstanding success as Ambassador in Korea and later Deputy Assistant Secretary for East Asia. He also had a way of speaking very softly, so that one had to lean over to hear him. On this occasion he said, over and over, quite simply: "General, I have seen the Lao and have had the reports of my attaches. These people will not fight." And he went on about their form of Buddhism and other factors behind this conclusion—which again I think history has vindicated as to the main Lao people (as distinct from the hill tribes, notably the Meo or Hmong, who did fight extraordinarily well).

At any rate, both judgments had, I am sure, a lot of impact on President Kennedy, adding up to the conclusion that it was just not going to work to join forces with the Phoumi group and try to help them gain control of the main parts of the country. Laos was in all possible ways, strategically and in many other ways, not a good place to take a stand.

Moreover, as a series of unsuccessful small military actions in February 1961 solidified the feeling that a Laos campaign alongside Phoumi was a poor bet, the President came to see an alternative course, on the advice primarily of Averell Harriman. He had joined the administration from the outset as Ambassador at Large, and in the course of a long world trip in February came to know Prince Souvanna Phouma, then outside Laos after having been pushed to one side about 1958 and then driven out entirely by Phoumi. Contrary to earlier U.S. judgments that Souvanna was weak, Harriman judged him to be both wise and potentially tough, if the U.S. itself really supported a neutralist-led government (as it had not done in the latter 1950s).

I won't go through all the events of March, April and May of 1961—which did include a dramatic TV speech by President Kennedy, designed as I now see it to create enough of an impression of U.S. readiness to resort to force to give spine to the negotiating option that was emerging. Very promptly after that President Kennedy met personally with Prime Minister Macmillan, who basically agreed with the negotiating approach and was prepared to assume the British role as co-chairmen (with the Soviets) of a Geneva Conference whose foremost aim would be a return to a coalition government and a neutralized Laos. With essential provisions on these points would go renewed bans against the presence of foreign troops in Laos and against foreign political interference—although, in light of the experience since 1954, most of us did not have too many illusions that such bans would be fully observed especially in respect to use of the Ho Chi Minh trail.

So this objective emerged, and was reinforced when President Kennedy met with Khrushchev in the famous Vienna meeting in late May. Laos turned out to be the only subject on which there was agreement between the two. Khrushchev seemed to be saying, "Yes, I can buy that one. We really don't need a confrontation over Laos"—this while making the most threatening noises over Berlin.

So a new Laos conference got under way in May and June, reflecting the Kennedy administration's first concentration in Southeast Asia there and not in Vietnam. And on Laos, consulation with the British and French was and remained very close—although Southeast Asia was not discussed in the wider setting of the NATO Council with which Ambassador Nolting was so familiar. As I had seen in my work on Laos at the 1959 Geneva Conference on Berlin, the British and French had never been happy with our forcing the issue in Laos itself. They had never approved the U.S. support for Phoumi and they were much happier, and made it clear they were much happier, with the policy of moving in the negotiating direction and supporting Souvanna Phouma.

So this was the basic policy that evolved in March, April and May. Concurrently, of course, there came the debacle of the Bay of Pigs, which was a major setback, especially in psychological terms, and certainly led to the view that the Soviet Union and its leaders were judging U.S. resolve to be at a very low level. And it was against that background that President Kennedy first turned his attention seriously to Vietnam. Obviously, he had focussed on the selection of Fritz Nolting as Ambassador (rejecting at least one suggestion that Colonel Edward Lansdale be sent). And in those first months he had approved certain limited increases in aid programs for South Vietnam. But it was not until after the Bay of Pigs that the administration went, so to speak, into high gear over Vietnam itself.

I will come back to that shortly. Let us first trace what flowed from the basic decision over Laos, and try to judge whether the Laos decision was a wise one, primarily from the standpoint of its impact on the area as a whole.

The Laos negotiations proceeded unevenly through 1961, with essential provisions for external neutrality in place by the end of the year, but no agreement on an internal coalition. Early in 1962 there were some rather sharp exchanges with Phoumi—who was of course going to be downgraded under the new arrangement—and there were difficult negotiations with the Thai, whose Prime Minister Sarit Thannarat, was a backer (and I believe also a distant cousin) of Phoumi. Thus, in the spring of 1962, in the face of threatening Communist actions in Laos, a limited contingent of U.S. forces was sent to Thailand for several months, to reassure the Thai and to show U.S. resolve generally, that we were standing ready to act if the other side breached the accords as they were finally hammered out and signed in late spring 1962.

The upshot was a new set of Geneva agreements on Laos, the 1962 agreements. This was negotiated by Averell Harriman, with William H. Sullivan as his principal assistant, and in his recent memoir, *Obbliqato,* Sullivan tells some interesting and colorful stories about the negotiations. The agreements, of course, provided for a renewed neutral status for Laos, and the ban on foreign troops should have affected the Ho Chi Minh Trail. I think Averell Harriman did believe that there would be at least some diminution in the use of Laos territory for that transit purpose, and the hope certainly was that Laos could be put to one side and its role in the Vietnam war reduced as much as possible.

In the event, North Vietnam—as all historians make clear—did not really conform to any of the provisions that were not of benefit to it. In particular it did not take its forces out—whereas the U.S. went through punctiliously with that withdrawal agreement—and it did not diminish its use of the trail. In other words, it was clear right from the beginning that they were not truly playing the game. In due course, in the spring of 1963, the Communist members of the new coalition government withdrew, and from then on there were recurrent frictions—although nothing really serious during the period of the Kennedy administration. Thus, right from the signing of the new agreements until the end of the Kennedy administration, there was a recurring question of whether you simply dropped the agreements or denounced them and retaliated, and this raised the same basic policy question that the original choice had raised, namely, was this the right place to stand? Progressively it seemed impossible to do more than protest strongly, pillory the North Vietnamese—and to some extent divide them from the Soviet Union, whose role in North Vietnam and in respect to North Vietnamese actions in Laos (which had been very strong previous to mid-1961) was in fact very much reduced. So there was a major issue there, and I simply describe what seem to me sound reasons for not attempting to react in the only way that would have been really effective, namely the introduction of U.S. forces into Laos.

In sum, there is no question that the Laos agreements did not help the conduct of the war in Vietnam itself. But by that time, late 1962 and early 1963, we were (or seemed to be) in a much stronger position in Vietnam, and it simply did not seem worth it to open up a second front. Again, this would have been in the most difficult possible terrain, with complicated logistics and many other difficulties. On the other hand, Souvanna Phouma did fulfill the expectations that lay behind the policy, demonstrating considerable capacity and ability to govern. As it became clear that the North Vietnamese and their puppet Pathet Lao were continuing their presence in Laos and occasionally causing conflict, there evolved a system of additional advisers and U.S. support for the government, while still trying to preserve the concept of a neutralized Laos. This position—and our deferring always to the desires of Souvannah Phouma himself to maintain at least the facade of neutrality—contributed to the lack of official acknowledgement (and I am choosing my words carefully) of supporting actions that led progressively to more extensive action (mostly after the end of the Kennedy administration) in Laos, in the end in most of Laos, so that eventually there was a considerable war going on there. In due course this was christened "the secret war" and how it operated is not really relevant to the Kennedy period, although in effect its nature derived from the framework created under President Kennedy.

And here I would pause to note that that war was really no more "secret" than our session here today. It was known to every senator who came within a hundred miles of Laos, or even just to Bangkok, or within fifty yards of the meetings of the Senate Foreign Relations Committee. So there was a lot of hypocrisy about this at a later point—the press knew what was going on, visiting Senators knew it—and altogether there has been a lot of nonsense about the true nature of the "secret war." In essence, its nature derived from the honest and full support of the United States for the concept of neutralization in Laos, which was the aim and end of Souvannah Phouma throughout, so that he was the one who insisted that the U.S. role not be acknowledged publicly.

That, then, is the way the Laos situation evolved during the Kennedy period, and to some extent afterwards. The 1962 accords were certainly not a working agreement in any full sense. But we did believe it to be important that they had created a model for a possible future neutral status of Laos, and that it was important to continue to keep that possibility before us.

And here I might add that the policy of seeking a neutralized status of Laos was never considered to extend to the quite different situation in South Vietnam—although we did envisage that at some future point South Vietnam might be strong enough to stand on its own, and that at that point the question of a neutral formal status could have been considered. But at no time during President Kennedy's tenure did it appear remotely realistic to suppose that you could apply the Laos formula to South Vietnam. This explains—and I think fully justifies—the strongly negative reactions of the Kennedy administration to various suggestions for a "neutralist" approach to South Vietnam. The most notable of these was the formal proposal by General De Gaulle in August 1963, in a speech that I thought was not very well intended in terms of helping the United States. And the idea did crop up recurrently, but was always treated very negatively throughout the Kennedy period—and indeed after.

Now let me turn more fully to policy on South Vietnam itself. The result of the careful review in early May 1961 was a considerable step-up of our military training personnel in South Vietnam, so that for the first time we were clearly in excess of the numerical limits imposed under the 1954 Geneva accords. The U.S., of course, had not signed those accords, although it did make a statement that it would do nothing to interfere with or disrupt them. As we saw it, we now faced a situation where Hanoi was breaching the most fundamental aspect of the accords—against armed external interference—and thus it seemed justified to go over the numerical limits, initially by a small amount. This point was well understood and argued, and I think the justification for this relatively modest reciprocal breach of the accords was totally convincing. There was certainly a right to respond to the much greater violations in which North Vietnam was visibly engaged by that time—and, as history shows, had been engaged in since roughly the spring of 1959.

Another policy action at this point was to dramatize the American firmness in Vietnam by the highly publicized visit by Vice-President Lyndon Johnson. This was a remarkable occasion in which he looked hard at the situation and in one statement compared Diem to Winston Churchill. But in his private report to the President—now on the historical record—Johnson was equally clear that the faith of Diem and the South Vietnamese in U.S. resolve was shaky, and he used the figure of speech that if this were a banking situation he would say that the banker had said that you were all right for now, but that this was the last extra notch he would give you. At any rate, the Johnson visit was intended as a clear and strong demonstration of U.S. support for South Vietnam. And I would add that the firmness of this position, at this particular time, undoubtedly owed something to the sense that American credibility had been shaken by the Bay of Pigs, and in Asian quarters to some extent by the decision to go the negotiating route in Laos.

Then, through the summer of 1961, developments on the ground were uneven, but things seemed to turn sour in September and early October, so that the very great concern then felt in Washington led to the sending out of a mission headed by Maxwell Taylor, who was at that time President Kennedy's military adviser, and Walt Rostow, who was deputy to McGeorge Bundy, the National Security adviser. The Taylor/Rostow mission went out to Vietnam and stayed a considerable time, coming back with a disturbing picture of the situation and a recommendation for the sending of substantial American troops under the heading of a flood-relief program. There had in fact been serious floods in the Delta at just that time, although as it turned out these receded rather rapidly during November.

This led to a very hectic decisionmaking period in which in the end there were very clear internal statements of the importance of Vietnam and of Southeast Asia generally, within the government. The actual decision was made, however, not to accept the recommendation for sending organized U.S. force units, but rather to limit the additional effort to the sending of very substantial additional advisory personnel, together with helicopters, propeller-driven aircraft, and many other supply items and facilities. The American advisory presence started with a few thousand and increased by the end of the Kennedy administration, I believe, to about sixteen thousand.

That decision, made in mid-November and executed progressively over the next two months in its first phases, was made known privately to many members of Congress, but was not highly publicized. Part of the thinking that lay behind that rather quiet treatment—at a time when Berlin and the Congo were both very much more to the fore than South Vietnam in any case—was that the additional American input even more clearly violated the terms of the 1954 Geneva accords, although the justification for doing so still seemed totally convincing from any legal or moral standpoint. It was for that reason in part that it was thought not necessarily wise to make a big public announcement of it, which would undoubtedly have stirred up a lot of controversy.

As things developed, Secretary McNamara became in effect the executive officer for the Kennedy administration in the carrying out of this policy and in the making of successive action decisions, beginning at a Honolulu conference in December of 1961 and continuing through a series of such conferences extending particularly to one in July 1962—at all of which I believe Ambassador Nolting was present.

Whether the November 1961 decision to go this gradual route was a wise one is of course open to question. It is the first of many decisions that can be put under the broad heading of "gradualism" and it raises the inevitable question whether it might not have been much more effective to move "hard and fast" at that point by introducing organized U.S. forces on some significant scale. As I have noted, that option was brought before the President during the late 1961 review, and he rejected it. I do not know his exact reasons, but I would point out—and this is basic to the whole discussion of the subject of decisions on Vietnam in the Kennedy presidency, at least up to August and September of 1963—that there were in the late 1961 period several other issues that seemed much more pressing, or important, or both. Thus, the decision on whether to take a much stronger and harder line on Vietnam had to be taken in the light of other commitments and possible needs. In particular, in the late 1961 period the Berlin crisis was still a critical and very high priority problem.

There can be little doubt that it would have taken an extraordinary effort to galvanize the American people at that time in support of the introduction of organized American forces into Vietnam—although hindsight analysis may well suggest that this could have been the time to start using the hard and fast approach. As it happened, I myself wrote an internal memorandum suggesting that this might be a better approach, but I hasten to add that I did not push this, and will take no credit for it.

In any case, the November 1961 decision set the pattern for the rest of the Kennedy administration, which was to make that policy work, introducing advisory personnel, eventually in very substantial numbers, and in a situation where on occasion American air advisers were undoubtedly sitting in the front seat of the aircraft in combat situations. In other words, there was —and was known by the press to be—a small degree of actual participation in the conflict by U.S. troops. And this inevitably meant the beginning of U.S. casualties—I have forgotten the numbers, but they were small at this stage, something like 190 in the course of the Kennedy administration. The American advisers were in harm's way. And I might add that the initial group of advisers was a remarkable crew, almost all regulars, and with some very special individuals—I particularly recall Brigadier General Charles Timmes, and there were many others with that special quality of being able to deal with the Vietnamese.

The policy was then tested through the year 1962, and by that time—I think in late 1961—a major feature of it was supplied by Sir Robert Thompson, the British expert on counterguerrilla and counterinsurgency operations who had been a key figure in the successful British campaign to clear up Malaya earlier. He came to Vietnam as an adviser, and worked closely with the U.S. mission and with the South Vietnamese, and it was his recommendation to embark on a strategic hamlet program that became the centerpiece in the effort to deal in the countryside with the security problem. At the same time a strong effort was being made to improve the South Vietnamese forces—which had been trained in the 1950s too much in a conventional mode—and to get them so that they could conduct effective operations against guerrilla action.

The year 1962 did indeed become a very successful year for this program, and my manuscript uses the same quotation that Fritz Nolting mentioned in his presentation, namely that Ho Chi Minh himself said that "1962 was Diem's year." The progress was not by any means uniform, and President Kennedy's own year-end assessment, at a press conference in December 1962, was measured and careful. He expressed the judgment that we were clearly better off than we had been, but did not carry it further than that.

Then we went into the year 1963 with the policy very clear and apparently working reasonably well and understood at all levels. All sorts of new features had been introduced, and in general the effort was to do everything possible within the limits of the policy, leaving out the introduction of combat forces. One example of this was a much more extensive communication system and much improved mobility. At the same time, I think in retrospect that we perhaps did not do enough to get U.S. personnel out to all corners of the country, so that we remained rather too dependent on the assessments of the South Vietnamese government itself. We did have our own assets, but they were limited, and this was a problem, so that there were members of the press, notably David Halberstam, who began even during 1962 to report that things were not as favorable as was being claimed. And in particular, there was one action in early 1963, at a place called Ap Bac, in which the South Vietnamese forces were rather badly mauled in a small local action.

But by May of 1963 the predominant judgment of the people on the ground was upbeat, particularly on the part of General Paul Harkins, who had been appointed in early 1962 to head a new military assistance command structure in Vietnam as a result of the November 1961 decisions. Harkins definitely felt that progress was being made, although I also remember, in the early months of 1963, a distinctly more gloomy assessment, by an Australian named Colonel Serong, who came to a meeting of the Counter Insurgency Group (CIG)—which monitored the war in Washington—and was very bearish about the strategic hamlets program, contending that it was being extended too fast and too far, and with too much political motivation, especially on the part of Diem's brother, Ngo Dinh Nhu.

In other words, the reporting was mixed as it reached the President, but the predominant view by May of 1963 was very optimistic, and this was particularly reflected at a meeting held in Honolulu on May 6, 1963. Indeed the reporting was sufficiently upbeat at that point for the President to accept Secretary McNamara's recommendation that we should now start planning, or set up a plan, for the progressive withdrawal of the American advisers, trying to get them out by the end of 1965 or before if that were possible.

There are occasional dates on which history seems to take dramatic turns. And this was the case here, for it was only two days after that Honolulu meeting that there came the first of the serious Buddhist disturbances in the city of Hue. And there then emerged the Buddhist movement as a significant and largely disruptive force. I have seen what Ambassador Nolting has said about this in his presentation, and I respect his judgment. Undoubtedly the Viet Cong, and the Communists generally, did make an effort to infiltrate the Buddhist movement, but the prevailing judgment in Washington was that the Buddhist uprising had fairly deep roots and was not simply a radical fringe or simply Communist-inspired—whatever quiet Viet Cong support it may have had. As we saw it in Washington, support from the North Vietnamese or the Viet Cong was simply not sufficient to describe the situation. The Buddhists did seem to us to have a very serious and significant sense of grievance—not because there had been anything that could properly be described as religious "persecution" but because the cast of the government was heavily dominated by Diem and his brothers, with a very strong Catholic representation generally—so that the Buddhists could well have had the feeling that they were treated to some extent as second-class citizens. Ngo Dinh Diem, as you may remember, was one of several brothers, and in particular his brother Ngo Dinh Nhu acted very much as his close second-in-command, and was engaged heavily in propaganda and other special activities in all directions. Then there was also a third member of the family, Ngo Dinh Can, who was in charge of Central Vietnam, while still a fourth brother, Ngo Dinh Thuc, was the Archbishop in Hue and had very great influence and power there.

So this visibly Catholic cast of the top government existed. It was of course well known and went back many years—it was Senator Mike Mansfield among others who had assisted in finding Diem in 1954 (at a Catholic institution in New Jersey) and putting him forward as a man who might be able to lead the new South Vietnam. Catholics were a minority in South Vietnam, but a rather cohesive one, and the impression among many elements of the population was that they held a disproportionate number of the commanding positions.

Moreover, by this time, the Diem regime—which had been so effective in the years after 1954 and perhaps roughly until the end of the decade—had become somewhat more ingrown and narrow. Certainly the voting at the second of the two general elections of this period had not been even approximately fair and did not reflect the very substantial opposition that appeared to exist on the political plane alone, and quite apart from the Viet Cong.

Moreover, there were many charges of corruption by officials in the regime, and a general sense that it was not as strong as it had earlier been.

This corruption and deterioration of the Diem regime was a serious and basic thing as perceived in Washington, and seemed to have a good deal to do with the Buddhist movement and its activities. Then, in the month of June 1963, the situation got worse—and I remember vividly that this was the first time that from my post in the Pentagon, primarily concerned with operating and military-related matters, I became significantly aware of this. As I have noted earlier, there did tend to be a division of labor, with the political side being handled entirely through the State Department and the operating side through the Pentagon. But by the summer of 1963 the political side had come to the fore. This was the time when Buddhist monks (bonzes) were pouring gasoline on themselves and burning themselves in the squares in Saigon. Diem made certain compromises and concessions, but they did not stick, and it was a bad month. And I would say, not totally parenthetically, that the treatment of Ambassador Nolting at this stage was from any standpoint a serious error—primarily in the State Department, but to some degree necessarily involving the President. Ambassador Nolting had gone on a month of leave, and I have never understood why an ambassador on leave should not have been summoned back or at least categorically and fully informed of what was going on in Vietnam. That seemed to me an inexcusable way to treat an American ambassador.

By that time it had already been agreed that Ambassador Nolting would be leaving in the early fall of 1963 after a strenuous two-plus years, and by that time also the selection had been made of Henry Cabot Lodge as his successor. The choice of Lodge was of course a very striking one. He was a man who had been a Republican, a very strong Republican, all his political career. He was the man who had actually lost his Senate seat to John Kennedy in 1952, and in 1960 he had been the vice-presidential candidate for the Republican party.

I do not know directly why Lodge was picked, but I assume that it was partly because it would help to prevent Vietnam becoming a partisan issue in the 1964 elections. It happens that Henry Cabot Lodge died only yesterday. And I hope I may take the liberty of quoting what I myself wrote about his qualities in the manuscript that I have been using as the basis of this presentation:

> According to those who were consulted in the process of selection, the President's choice reflected primarily his confidence in Lodge's integrity, patriotism, and basic loyalty to any administration he might serve. Apparently, the hint that Lodge might be available had arisen from the fact that in 1962 he had worked on Vietnam while at the Pentagon on active

duty as a reserve officer, and then in 1963 had requested duty in Vietnam itself.

Thus, whatever he thought of Lodge as an opponent, the President and the major people in Congress had high respect for him as a man who was devoted to his country. With such stature and capability, he was sure to be very much the man in charge in Saigon. And, as I have noted, the enlisting of such a prominent Republican could have been seen as an immense political help at a time when Vietnam might become an issue in 1964 and later. The situation compared a little bit to the appointment of Henry L. Stimson as Secretary of War, by Franklin D. Roosevelt in June of 1940. Certainly, and this is worthy of note, the choice was a signal of the administration's commitment and also of its opposition to any plan to withdraw and let South Vietnam go. Lodge felt strongly that the U.S. must support South Vietnam to the end, and had been a supporter of American policy there since 1954.

I mention this point in part because there have been several public references, notably in a magazine article by Kenneth O'Donnell, a very close assistant to President Kennedy, and also from Senator Mike Mansfield, that at some point in conversations in the May 1963 period President Kennedy gave these two the impression that he was thinking in terms of getting out of Vietnam after the 1964 election. As I have noted, we were indeed engaged at that point in producing plans to progressively reduce our advisory presence, and the question arises whether the President was truly implying an unconditional intent to withdraw.

My own comment on this starts with noting that the subsequent revelations by O'Donnell and Mansfield came at the height of anti-Vietnam sentiment and go alongside other literature on the Kennedy family suggesting that President Kennedy would have acted very differently from what was done later. But I think this line of thought is open to grave doubt. Was President Kennedy affirming an intention to withdraw under any and all circumstances? I do not believe that, not at all. I believe the President was simply reflecting what I have already described, the optimism of that period and the assumption that the progress we then perceived would continue, and that therefore it would make it possible to withdraw the American forces—but consistently with, and indeed in the interest of, having South Vietnam stand firmly on its own feet. In other words I believe that the suggestion that Kennedy really thought we should withdraw *come what might* is simply not historically the correct assessment of his views. And I would fortify that conclusion by referring particularly to what he said in early September 1963 about the danger that China would become dominant in the area, his belief in the domino theory and other fundamental points that had always lain behind American policy in Vietnam.

Then you go into the summer of 1963. By that time there is no question that Averell Harriman, who at this stage was the Undersecretary of State for Political Affairs, and Roger Hilsman, who had become Assistant Secretary for what was then called Far Eastern Affairs, were persuaded that the United States could not go on supporting Diem as they perceived him. Particularly, they felt that we could not stomach the pretty unsavory activities of Ngo Dinh Nhu and his wife, Madame Nhu, and that the deterioration was rapidly reaching the point where it might be necessary to consider supporting some change of government. (I would add that while Ambassador Lodge may have come to share this view to some extent before he arrived on the scene in mid-August, I find it hard to believe that he and Averell Harriman, not particularly kindred spirits, would have formed any solid view, let alone any agreement, before he went out.)

The existence of this view, particularly by two very prominent members of the State Department, is of course a necessary part of the story in itself. But in addition, the situation during the summer was greatly complicated by the fact that they made no secret of their views. I recall that I myself was present on one social occasion when Hilsman expressed himself rather vehemently in criticism of Nhu, and in some extent in criticism of the policy of sticking with Diem. Thus, almost inevitably, the press picked it up and began to report that this was the view of the key people in the State Department. (I would note that I have no recollection that Ambassador Lodge himself was involved in this kind of loose talk, and I repeat my judgment that he may have been inclined to be skeptical about Diem but to doubt that by that time he had in any sense made up his mind.) In any case, this loose talk was in itself a great and cardinal mistake, which was not the President's but which in my judgment he should have very promptly and sharply slapped down. Because once this kind of talk got into the American press, it became much more difficult for the people on the ground, and for the administration generally, to work with Diem to try to improve the situation in a quiet way—against a backdrop of published reports that people in the administration already had it in for Diem.

And it was against that backdrop that Ambassador Nolting returned to his post in mid-July to finish up his tour, with instructions to convey certain clear suggestions to Diem and lay a foundation for what he and others undoubtedly hoped would be some improvement in the political situation. At the same time, he was instructed to reiterate the basic U.S. commitment to Diem. I certainly was moved by the account in Ambassador Nolting's presentation here, that when he did this Diem replied, "That's simply incorrect." That was a reflection of some very unfortunate practices in Washington, certainly great indiscretion and, one could almost say, very bad discipline at that time.

Then, in the middle of August, Ambassador Nolting came home, and Cabot Lodge arrived on the scene. Almost at once—within two days as I recall—he was met by what can only be considered an extremely provocative action on the part of Ngo Dinh Nhu, in the form of an intensive raid on the Xa Loi pagoda in Saigon, conducted not by the army itself, but by a special security force that was particularly under Nhu's control. The pagoda raid raised the temperature in Washington to the boiling point, as I later put it together. (I should note again that this was a period when I personally was on leave and then had a military assistance mission in Greece, so that I was not directly involved.)

The result was a famous cable of August 24, 1963. Undoubtedly that cable was very sloppily handled, particularly in that it was cleared with most key people, including the President himself, over the phone, so that there must have been a good deal of double talk as to its real nature and timing. It was occasioned by an inquiry that came to Lodge (through a covert contact) from a group of senior military people in South Vietnam, asking the U.S. view on a possible change of government. The cable authorized Lodge to give them an encouraging reply, in effect a green light for approval.

Thus it is appropriate to call that cable "the green light cable." Naturally Lodge acted at once and had his representative talk to the senior military people. However, it rather quickly developed that they did not have any clear plan or cohesion, and were not very impressive generally. So, within a week the specific enterprise was cooled off, at least as Washington saw it, and the "green light" turned at least to orange. But of course a signal had been given, and the senior military undoubtedly now had the possibility of a coup very much to the forefront of their minds.

The next three weeks was a very complicated period, which included the sending of one military officer (General Victor Krulak) and one State Department officer (Joseph Mendenhall) who fanned out into the countryside and into political circles respectively, and brought back (perhaps not surprisingly) sharply conflicting reports. And there were some very intense policy discussions which have been fully documented in various collections of the relevant papers and records.

And here I get personal. About September 15, I returned from my European trip and was visited at my home, on a Sunday, almost at once by Michael Forrestal, who was on the National Security Adviser's staff at the White House and was indeed (as Ambassador Nolting has said in his presentation) very close to Governor Harriman—both personally and professionally. Mike Forrestal went right to the point and told me bluntly: "Look, the government is at sixes and sevens over this Vietnam issue. There has never been a time when it was so divided, whether we stick by Diem or go with the military or whether we try to hang on and get reforms. And the President is determined to resolve the question soon with as good advice as he can get. You personally have not been involved emotionally or in any other way in this and you have got to get into the play.''

So I went to my office on Monday to find that the President had directed McNamara and General Taylor to head up a group to go to Vietnam. McNamara in turn asked me to be executive officer of the group, bringing together people who were not firmly committed on one side or the other in this controversy—which by then had been the cause of some bitter and unpleasant exchanges between key figures (as Ambassador Nolting's presentation accurately reflects). In digging out my old datebook to verify the date of my return from Europe, I have now come on two entries that reflect the effort to understand the arguments on both sides, before the McNamara/Taylor party left for Saigon, on Sunday September 22. On the day before, my datebook shows that I had lunch with Ambassador Nolting (obviously to understand fully the arguments for sticking with Diem) and then met at three that afternoon with Roger Hilsman, the strongest advocate of removing Diem unless he would make drastic changes. The mandate of the McNamara/Taylor mission, as conveyed to me, was to go out and take a hard look at the whole policy of supporting Diem and as well at the military situation, how the war was going.

And I have never had reason to doubt that that was a precise and accurate statement of what the President intended as the mission of the McNamara/Taylor group. Later on there were those who said that it was really designed to be a coverup for what had already been decided. I do not believe that. It was not the way this or any other President works, and I do not believe that is the way Robert McNamara would have behaved in any circumstances. And I vividly recall that McNamara, on the flight out to Vietnam, emphasized to the members of the group—who included William Colby from CIA, William Sullivan from State, Forrestal himself and one or two others—that we were to attack the problem keeping our minds as balanced as we knew how to make them, and that the report would definitely include the opportunity for individual members to dissent if they did not agree with any language in it. So that was the state of mind in which the group arrived in Saigon.

And for the next ten days it was the longest and far and away the most thoroughgoing such visitation from Washington—I came over the years to have grave reservations about most such visitations, feeling that they were a burden for Ambassadors and was never sure that they provided enough to compensate. But this one I thought was deadly serious and important. There were those of us assigned particularly to look at the political issues, talking to everyone available, and there were those who went with McNamara on a series of exhausting field trips to assess the situation on the ground.

Basically, the McNamara/Taylor group concluded that the military situation was showing progress—they were prepared to accept the judgment of those on the ground that it was in slightly better shape. In hindsight, that may well have been a seriously wrong judgment, but it was at any rate the general thrust of what was conveyed on the military side.

The political side was my own principal concern, although I also went on a couple of field trips. There we got somewhat contrary advice. The mission itself was not totally unanimous in having grave reservations about Diem and Nhu and feeling we ought to think about abandoning them—although this was the view of Lodge and most of his senior subordinates. This included his deputy, William Truehart, a man who up to the spring of 1963—as Ambassador Nolting's deputy—had been strongly in support of the policy of standing firm with Diem. In the view urged by Lodge, Trueheart and several others, the whole structure would have to be reformed, and one possibility that was considered was whether it was possible to get rid of Nhu and keep Diem. If that seemed impractical, and it did progressively seem impractical to the group to separate the brothers, then the conclusion was that we could not go on as we were.

But that was clearly not the view of the CIA station chief, John Richardson, nor of General Harkins, and it was not the view of some embassy officials at the lower level. So there was a division in the advice we got from official quarters.

What then represented the most decisive influence on the eventual conclusions of the McNamara/Taylor group? Here I want to include something—for the first time on any oral record so far as I know, although it is in my manuscript. This is a report on the testimony given very privately in Saigon to McNamara by two individuals. One of them was a European scholar and writer who had followed Vietnam intensely for years and had written books on it. This European had been a strong supporter of Diem over the years, but this time he volunteered to McNamara his judgment that Diem simply could not persist, that he had become so narrow, so out of touch, and so under Nhu's influence that he could not go on. By that time, in early September, there had been a crackdown on students at the University of Saigon, and this was part of his evidence. It was this man's considered view that if Diem would not change his ways, an alternative regime would be less vulnerable in terms of simply carrying on with the war and holding the country together. So that was one important judgment.

And a second judgment, perhaps even more influential and again volunteered, came to McNamara after secret hints and in a secret meeting, by one of the very senior officials in the Diem regime itself, the deputy head of the defense department and a man on whom the U.S. mission had always strongly relied and whom they regarded as perhaps the single most able and solid official in the regime. He told McNamara that he and other officials had been so affected by recent developments—including in many cases the arrest of their children during the student disturbances at the University of Saigon—that they simply could not go on. Diem had lost his touch and could not hang on—at least as he was operating.

So those two pieces of testimony were a very great—and I would think perhaps decisive—influence on the political conclusions that were finally embodied in the McNamara/Taylor report that we drafted in Saigon and then on the plane coming back to Washington. One is always influenced by judgments that are, if you will "counter-intuitive"—that is, where a person who has taken one position in the past, in this case to stand firm, now comes and says exactly the opposite. I do not know at what point these two particular sources—or others in the official family who held the same view—had reached their conclusions, and this may well not have been until September, in the wake of the pagoda raids and the student disturbances. But that was the conclusion that was conveyed to McNamara in the last week of September 1963 and that went into the judgments that were in the McNamara/Taylor report, on which I did a great deal of the drafting.

The report led to White House statements that drew headlines by announcing that we were continuing with a program to reduce the advisers with a view of getting them out by the end of 1965. But it was much more important, as things turned out, that the report recommended several actions that were immediately taken, to suspend negotiations on certain ongoing aid programs and in particular to suspend support for the special forces under Nhu. These actions were designed to put pressure on Diem in the direction of major reforms, and Ambassador Lodge was to play it cool and wait for Diem to come to him for specific suggestions. In effect, the plan was to distance the U.S. mission and government from Diem, in a clear signal of disapproval of the repressions.

And the internal recommendation of the report, adopted by the President but not made public, was that the United States should not encourage a coup against Diem, but that if coup planning should again emerge, the United States should indicate that it would not be opposed to considered action.

Particularly in the light of the events at the end of August —when the "green light" had been given—the fact that the report did not ringingly endorse Diem and that it did lead directly to certain actions limiting the immediate aid programs—this was bound to create a climate that was at least not unfavorable to a coup, although it was not then supposed that this could happen soon.

In the event, a signal from the senior military group was given as early as October 5, in a conversation with the CIA man who was Lodge's authorized contact with the group (Colonel Lucian Conein). When the group asked what the attitude of the U.S. would be toward a coup, Conein was then authorized to state that the U.S. would support a successor government if it was effective and if it was prepared to continue with the war and the effort to preserve a non-Communist South Vietnam. Those of us on the political side of the McNamara/Taylor party had not expected renewed coup planning to emerge this quickly, but this was the signal that was now conveyed. And there were a series of other contacts through the month of October, in which among other things the potential leaders of the coup were told in the strongest possible fashion that the United States wished to avoid assassination or killing of Diem and his top people if it were humanly possible. Indeed, toward the end of October there was particular concern that a coup attempt might lead to an indecisive military conflict within Saigon itself, which seemed the worst possible development.

In essence, then, the administration did take the position that it would accept a coup and acquiesce in it—although it had not been actively encouraging such a coup, at least since the standing down of the initial approaches in late August. But the coup leaders specifically refused to indicate when they might act, and so there was no duplicity on the U.S. side on the actual day of the coup, November 1. In fact, Lodge had scheduled a serious meeting with Diem at just that time to try to press him again to take reform steps, and one can at least speculate that if Diem had undertaken to do so the U.S. attitude might have changed.

In any case, the coup went forward on November 1, shortly after the U.S. Pacific Commander, Admiral Felt, had paid a formal call on President Diem. No American was informed until the coup actually got under way, and Lodge then promptly got in touch with Diem offering to assist in getting him out of the country safely. But Diem declined this offer and he and his brother Nhu fled to the suburb of Cholon, where they were picked up late that night or early the following morning and killed on their way to some other destination.

This killing was a great shock to President Kennedy personally, and to all of us who had been involved in the sequence of events. The exchanges with the coup group had specifically urged every effort to avoid just this, although of course there was inevitably the chance that this would happen and that risk was accepted. But I think it is fair to say that every reasonable effort was made to avoid that outcome.

The main question of course concerns the basic decision to go this route—

in effect to recognize, and to some extent help create, a situation where a military coup was entirely possible, and then to acquiesce in it and not to discourage it when it was actually known to be in train. What I have tried to give you is the reasoning that lay behind that basic decision by the President. A crucial part of that reasoning, as I saw it, was that to stick with Diem—unless he were willing to reform—was to stick with a losing horse who would in due course collapse and create a much more chaotic situation than might arise if this senior military group, who appeared competent and balanced, could take over earlier.

There was of course a moral factor as well, in that it was unattractive to support a leader who was conducting violent attacks on his own students, on the Buddhists, and others—which was the reason why Congress itself at this stage itself took action to hold up certain aid programs—and there was undoubtedly a small degree of pressure on what one might call liberal moral grounds. But the basis of the judgment as I saw it, and as I always believed, was actually that it simply would not work to go on supporting Diem, that he was a poor bet even on the most cold-blooded basils. That was the judgment reached in late September and early October and on the basis of the advice that I have at least outlined here.

And I might note that along the way, there really was no significant discussion of the option of withdrawal. And I continue to believe that what President Kennedy said in the early September inaugural newscast broadcasts, on two networks, about his belief in the domino theory and his belief that we simply had to hang on, was a true reflection of his state of mind and that he was not, at least up to his death, minded to take a withdrawal option seriously.

What I think was not adequately discussed during the making of this crucial decision, and what emerged very rapidly, was that to involve the United States this deeply in the politics of Vietnam had certain inevitable effects—not only to create the risk of further coups in the future, but also to deepen the American commitment generally. It may be that we did not give enough thought to this point—it certainly became very clear later, and is a basic part of what any U.S. administration, or indeed any nation, must consider when it makes this kind of decision.

There is, as we have already noted, a moral dimension to the issue that is of great importance. What should a country do when it is supporting, or in the position of being a major supporter of, a ruler whose practices have become not merely a little repugnant and harsh, but apparently creating a situation that could erupt into civil war or drastic disturbance? What is the moral thing to do in those circumstances?

At the time, these issues were not discussed at great length, but they were very much on everybody's mind. For the plain fact was that the United States was perceived as being the major supporter and sustainer of the Diem regime, so that it was inevitably tarred with responsibility even for its internal behavior. To go on as we were had in itself a moral negative.

The problem is, of course, a generic one. The same thing has been true in many other situations where the United States was the principal supporter of a particular regime that showed signs of going sour. It was true with respect to Rhee in Korea and later with respect to Park, it was true with respect to Somoza in Nicaragua, and it is true today—although perhaps to a lesser degree than in the other cases—of Marcos in the Philippines.

In such cases there is, as I say, a moral negative to the continuing support of a ruler going sour. But there is also a moral negative to any effort to intervene in the internal affairs of another country. And there are also, of course, important practical calculations to be made—which may indeed be the best basis for a final decision. The case of Somoza illustrates the problem. Might he have reformed if greater U.S. pressure had been put on him? Was our support continued way past a useful point, to the point where the opposition in the end turned out to be communist-controlled? Concerns of this sort reverberate through many of these situations and the decisions are always difficult: in the case of Vietnam, when we were actually conducting a war alongside a government in trouble, the circumstances were perhaps the most difficult possible.

I do not know what the answer should be in such cases, except that I am confident that one cannot be flatfooted in either direction. What I am principally trying to do is to say that the issue was thought through rather seriously in the Kennedy administration. What was not thought about as much as it should have been, I think in hindsight, was the danger of this coup leading to what became a revolving door character of leadership in the government of South Vietnam in the following two years at least. Although the military group that was conducting the coup seemed to be the best that could have been found, we did clearly have an excessive degree of confidence in its ability to handle the government affairs and we also very much underrated the disruptive effects of a change of government on administrative capacity right down the line. I think, in hindsight, our initial belief that the coup might have been clearly to the good put too much weight on what was certainly an apparent outpouring of popular feeling in support of it in the early part of November, and on the fact that the coup group included at least one senior patriotic hero, General Duong Van Minh, colloquially known as Big Minh.

Well, that was the last major decision of the Kennedy administration. In the three weeks between the coup and his assassination it became clear that the underlying situation was in fact very much worse than had been estimated by the McNamara/Taylor group as recently as late September. And at another meeting, just before the assassination, this was brought out, so that, had Kennedy lived, he would have had to come face to face with this deterioration and how to respond to it. As it was he never had a chance to come to grips with the new situation, and it is, in my judgment, wholly speculative to try to judge how he would have dealt with the decisions that confronted President Johnson from late 1963 right through to early and mid-1965, or thereafter.

Looking at the whole story of the handling of Vietnam in the Kennedy administration, I think one has to say that it was a failure. But, like each of the Presidents who wrestled with the problem, he had to deal with situations that had arisen under his predecessors, and there can be no saying how he might have dealt with the situation at the time he himself left office. Five American Presidents—Truman, Eisenhower, Kennedy, Johnson, and Nixon—had responsibility for the conduct of policy in Vietnam at crucial phases in the story. Each of these must be judged in terms of the situation as it came to him and in recognition of the fact that his handling was not the whole story.

As for Kennedy, one can certainly judge that he did the best he knew how, although he probably would have shared the view of myself and many later historians that he gave inadequate personal attention to Vietnam, except at the two critical periods of decision in late 1961 and in the fall of 1963. But one must always remember how many other difficult problems he was wrestling with, in a very troubled period with an exceptional number of foreign policy crises. And the decisions on Vietnam, in particular, were always choices of evils, in which he was between the proverbial rock and the hard place, and certainly were about as painful as they could be.

But, in any case, I have tried to give you a picture of how these decisions were taken—especially the three major decisions of his administration: Laos, the advisory program, and Diem. I hope this presentation at least explains them so that they can be better understood.

NARRATOR: Who will ask the first question?

QUESTION: I seem to sense that you gave encouragement and support to General Minh and the coup group, but it seemed that you were saying, "Yes, yes, go ahead" without a clear idea of what he was after or an attempt to control and influence him and the others in the group. Looking at what happened with the Shah and Khomeini, and what happened with Somoza, is this perhaps an ongoing problem with our government—that we might encourage actions without really looking at what the results are going to be or attempting to control events?

MR. BUNDY: Certainly the problem in Vietnam had a lot in common with the problem of Somoza in Nicaragua—although I would not have said that it was comparable to the problem of the Shah, in that we did not, in Iran, encourage any opposition group, including Khomeini, prior to the fall of the Shah. In the case of Vietnam we did know, or thought we knew, quite a lot about the members of the group. They were senior officers for the most part, with General Big Minh as the most visible one and the one who seemed likely to become the titular head of the new government. But the others were also respected officers who had apparently performed well. And alongside them there were senior civilians who were prepared to participate in the government, notably a former vice-president and a distinguished mayor of Saigon. All in all the group appeared to be as promising an alternative leadership as we could find in Vietnam, and while we thought that the military initially would be taking the lead and would have most of the senior positions, we did think that there would be a strong civilian voice.

It was, of course, true to say that this was a government installed outside or even in contravention of the constitution. But this factor, while important, did not seem decisive, particularly in that the second of the elections under Diem had hardly been a model of freedom or democracy.

In any case, the key question, as I have already indicated, was whether the group could govern effectively, reaching out to all elements in the population and handling the war itself competently. For those tasks we did think they had promise. But, in hindsight, it is obvious that we overrated their cohesion and their capacity both, and in January 1964 they were in fact overthrown by a single general, General Khanh, in the second of the many sudden changes of government that took place in the ensuing years.

QUESTION: The situation in Vietnam was immensely complex, with an issue throughout whether the North Vietnamese, under Ho, were basically communists or whether they were not honest and sincere nationalists. In your discussion you tend to draw, or assume, a conclusion that upset many people at the time—that is, when you talk about the situation and how they fought the Americans, you do not seem to clearly recognize that there was a nationalist revolution in process in North Vietnam. You pass over them very quickly as Communists. The point I want to make is that at that time, when discussion of intervention in Vietnam was considered, how much discussion was there of having to sit down and think about the people involved in Vietnam and their popular support?

MR. BUNDY: We always thought—and I think this was the President's perception, certainly my perception and the perception of all those in the policy circle—that the North Vietnamese were indeed nationalists, and for that matter the Viet Cong and the South Vietnamese as well. But the fact that Ho and his colleagues were also Communists was very important, and we needed to decide which came first.

What we could not doubt was that they were aggressively and implacably determined to achieve control of all Indochina, in the name of the Lao Dong, or the Indochina Communist party. This had been the main objective of that party since its founding, and there was never the slightest doubt that that was what they were after. While the motivation was indeed nationalist in large part, it was the Communist side that gave it this extra edge and contributed to the use of violence and in effect aggression from the North.

Now one of the other questions concerns the Soviet and Chinese roles. In fact, the perceptions of these roles shifted rather dramatically in the time-frame of the Kennedy administration. During the first roughly two years, the Soviet factor was paramount, and there is good evidence that Kennedy's decisions in the fall of 1961 were related in his mind to the necessity to stand firm in Berlin—where the ongoing crisis was of much higher priority at that time—and that this was a factor in his decision then and perhaps also in the spring of 1961. Moreover, in the decision to go the negotiating route in Laos, the Soviets were again regarded as the key to the situation—a judgment that may have been exaggerated or erroneous in hindsight. As it turned out, whatever their intentions may have been about keeping the Laos accords, they seemed totally unable to control the North Vietnamese in their wholesale breaches of those accords.

As for the Sino-Soviet split, that had become quite obvious in late 1960 and even more so in the party congress and in other exchanges in the fall of 1961. But both were still supporting Hanoi, which was in a position to play them off against each other.

Over time, the China factor came to seem much greater than it had in 1961 and early 1962—partly because at that earlier time China was having a terrible agricultural crisis and considerable economic difficulties. Then, after the Sino-Indian war in the fall of 1962, the perception, not just in government but in wide observer and expert circles throughout the world, was that there had been a rather dramatic increase in what might be called the expansionist tendencies of China. It was undoubtedly this perception that President Kennedy had in mind when he said in September 1963, in one of the inaugural newscasts, in response to the question whether he believed in the domino theory, he replied: "Yes, I do. China is so big and looms so large that it simply cannot be regarded anything but seriously." (This is a paraphrase.)

Now that view did not mean that China was regarded as the central moving force of what was going on in Vietnam or in Indochina as a whole—since we judged all along that the basic objectives were those of North Vietnam in that area. But the Chinese were taking an aggressive and thrusting line in their policy practically throughout Asia in this period, and thus, given their enormous size and perceived weight in Southeast Asia, it seemed to us overwhelmingly likely that if North Vietnam succeeded within the Indochina area, it would immensely increase the possibilities for China extending its influence or hegemony in other parts of the area.

Now that is a very rough sketch of the conception of the opposing forces as it existed by the end of the Kennedy administration. As for the nature of the struggle within Vietnam itself, it was of course true that Vietnam had been divided, in 1954, only on a temporary or provisional basis—at least according to the letter of the 1954 accords. But what had happened in the 1950s was that that division had hardened, very much as the similar division hardened in Korea in the period prior to 1950, so that it had become one of the several situations of divided countries in the world. And as Secretary Rusk was fond of saying, when the argument was made that these were all Vietnamese, he would reply that we would hardly regard an incursion of East Germans into West Germany as simply a fight between Germans. South Vietnam at least by 1960 had become recognized as a national entity, with diplomatic recognition from many quarters, so that an attack on it, essentially what North Vietnam was doing, was entitled to be regarded as aggression.

QUESTION: To what extent were Congressional leaders involved in the development of the policy to support the change from Diem in South Vietnam?

MR. BUNDY: That I do not know in detail, partly because of my role as I have described it, which did not involve dealing with the Congress on matters that were primarily political. But it is true that by late September there had been very sharp criticism of the Diem regime on the Hill, and I assume there may well have been conversations between the White House or the State Department and the people there. I particularly recall a very strong speech by Senator George McGovern at the time saying that we simply had to get rid of Diem or he could not go on supporting what we were doing—with the implication that if Diem did leave, he would support the war.

But I do not know of any evidence that the President called in the leaders of different parties and opinions within Congress or consulted carefully on the subject.

NOLTING: Mr. Chairman, I would first like to thank our friend, Bill Bundy, for his very frank and informative talk. He has squarely addressed the issue which has been on my mind for many years—namely, the change in U.S.

policy in 1963, leading to the overthrow of the Diem government and, in my view, to our country's subsequent deep involvement in war.

I have to say that there are fundamental disagreements between us on this issue. Mr. Bundy seems to defend the Kennedy administration's decision to support a military *coup d'etat.* I think, on the contrary, that decision was a disastrous blunder. It is generally admitted that the coup would not have occurred without U.S. encouragement of the dissident generals. I think, also, that it was immoral to go behind the back of President Diem and connive in his overthrow. We should, at the very least, have given this ally of nine years a fair chance to survive, even if the Kennedy administration decided, for whatever reasons, that it could not continue its aid to his government.

You mention several factors influencing the change of American policy. One was the view of Ambassador Lodge. Ambassador Lodge arrived in Saigon on August 22, 1963. He had been there only two days when the first "Green Light" telegram was sent to him from Washington. He acted upon it promptly. I wonder how two days can be considered as adequate experience, especially in a situation so complex. Of course, there was much backing and filling on both sides before the coup actually took place. But I think the die was cast in late August. You also mentioned the testimony of a European scholar and a member of Diem's government as very influential upon the McNamara/Taylor mission in September 1963. One wonders sometimes why we have a trained intelligence service and a trained Foreign Service.

Finally, I come to my question. In the light of events over the last twenty-two years, do you believe that the actions of the Kennedy administration regarding Vietnam in the fall of 1963 were in the national interest of our country or were they mistaken and incorrect?

MR. BUNDY: I still question the use of the word "incorrect" in describing the decision concerning Diem, because you are comparing a known outcome with an unknown one. That is, it is certainly true that the outcome was bad. But it is not to me by any means clear that it could not have been at least as bad, or perhaps even worse, if Diem had gone on alienating important elements in the population and in the groups that were necessary to assist in government, and if you had then had a chaotic situation of deterioration and replacement by some group or other. What we shall never know is whether Diem might conceivably have undertaken serious reforms—but the best we could judge at the time, having applied a good deal of advice and given him a lot of time, was that he could not. And I say that as one who had watched Diem perform, particularly in 1954–55, with great effectiveness and courage. In fact I had admired very much how he had handled himself in that critical period and then for several years thereafter. Moreover I had met him at least twice and been impressed by him—in the company of Ambassador Nolting on at least one occasion as I recall. And what we were essentially concluding was that his regime had lost touch and lost capacity and cohesion, in a way that happened not infrequently in Asian situations, both in history and during the contemporary period. In a very real way he was losing what the Chinese call "the mandate of heaven"—that is, his hold on his people. So it is not at all clear to me what would have happened if he had gone on as he was, or whether the outcome might not have been at least as bad. And I have tried to make clear that the McNamara/Taylor group did have the testimony of these two special witnesses, including particularly the senior man who had been perhaps the most valuable man in the Diem regime, that he simply could not go on the way it was, especially with what had been done to the students, including his son.

As for taking the advice of the man on the ground, it is of course true that Ambassador Nolting, the ambassador who had been there for two and a half years and just left, vigorously opposed the decision to weaken our support for Diem and in effect acquiesce in a coup. But it is also true that Ambassador Lodge strongly urged the policy that was followed. Thus I do not think it is fair to say that we were acting against the advice of the men on the ground, in that the ambassador who had taken over, Ambassador Lodge, felt very strongly that we should move, perhaps even more strongly than was done. And while the mission was divided, it was true—as I've already pointed out—that the deputy, William Truehart, had come to feel in agreement with Ambassador Lodge's position, and that there were many others who felt the same way.

And, as to Ambassador Lodge himself, by late September he had been on the ground for six weeks, he had seen the student riots, he had seen the political developments of all sorts, and his judgment was entitled to a lot of weight. Moreover, he had had communications with the coup group, including the exchanges in the week that followed the so-called "green light" cable of August 24, and he had seen that the green light was at least to a considerable extent turned off, and that key people in Washington were clearly not persuaded that a coup was wise.

So he had been weighing the problem for several weeks—indeed throughout the summer— and given it a lot of thought, as well as a lot of discussion with his subordinates, most of whom in the Embassy had come to feel change was imperative. And I do think you have to give him, and all the others concerned, credit for an honest attempt to assess, and advise in terms of the U.S. national interest. In sum, I just do not think that not listening to the man on the ground is a fair issue to raise.

NARRATOR: We are terribly grateful to Bill Bundy for stopping off en route back to Princeton from Athens, Georgia where he talked about many of these things with Dean Rusk. He has made a lasting contribution to our understanding of Vietnam.

VIII. KENNEDY AND DEFENSE

KENNEDY, DEFENSE AND ARMS CONTROL

General William Young Smith

NARRATOR: We are very pleased to welcome you to a Forum on the presidency with reference to arms policies, strategic questions and arms control with General William Y. Smith. I am going to need a little more help than usual in the vital statistics.

The first part of the story is easy. General Smith was born in Arkansas. He was graduated in 1948 from the U.S. Military Academy at West Point and entered the Air Force; he had a very distinguished career as a fighter pilot in the United States, Europe, and in combat missions in Korea. He was wounded in action. He returned to the United States and taught at his own institution, the United States Military Academy. He received the Master's degree in Public Administration and the Ph.D. in Political Economy and

Government at Harvard University. After work in Air Force planning, he was named Air Force staff assistant to General Maxwell Taylor, in the Kennedy White House and subsequently assistant to General Taylor, when he was chairman of the Joint Chiefs of Staff. He served in a dual capacity, assisting McGeorge Bundy as a member of the National Security Council staff.

Thereafter, he held a whole series of staff and command positions in the United States Air Force in Europe; he was military assistant to two secretaries, Harold Brown and Secretary Seamans. He was commander of the Oklahoma City Air Logistics Center. He was director of Doctrine, Concepts and Objectives of Headquarters, U.S. Air Force. He was director of Policy Plans in National Security Affairs in the office of the assistant secretary of defense for International Security Affairs. Then in 1979 he became Chief of Staff of SHAPE (Supreme Headquarters Allied Powers, Europe). In 1981 he became Deputy Commander and Chief of the United States European Command. In 1983 he retired from the U.S. military.

Most recently he has been a fellow at the Woodrow Wilson International Center for Scholars of the Smithsonian in Washington writing a book on strategy, arms, and arms control. He visited the Miller Center during an earlier period and we are delighted that we finally caught up with him again. We are very grateful as a nation that he has held the vital and crucial positions that he has in the United States Air Force and the United States Military. It is a pleasure to have you with us.

GENERAL SMITH: Thank you very much. The introduction was kind but I'm sure you heard more about me than you want to know.

I understand that you have been focusing on the presidency of John Fitzgerald Kennedy. I want to talk to you about arms control and I want to focus on John Fitzgerald Kennedy, but I think we can understand his role in arms control better if we look at him in the context of other Presidents who have dealt with arms control matters. And so I want to tell you a few stories about some other Presidents, most of which you will know, perhaps a few you don't know. I will conclude with some observations about how Kennedy compared with the others.

Now I think I'm safe in saying at the outset that every President since World War I has had to deal with arms control or disarmament while he was President. The first one I want to talk about is Warren G. Harding. He was President when the Washington Naval Treaty was signed in 1922. That was a treaty that set a ratio on the tonnage of capital ships that the British, the United States and Japan could have—the famous five-five-three ratio that we all remember. What that meant was that the United States could have five hundred thousand tons of battle ships, the British five hundred thousand tons, and the Japanese three hundred thousand tons.

A conference convened in Washington in November of 1921. At that conference the United States, Great Britain, Japan, France, Italy, China, Belgium, the Netherlands, and Portugal attended. Now if you are like I am, you say, "Well, I can understand some of those governments being there, but I can't understand those little countries attending." I mean those countries that aren't big naval powers—China, Belgium, and The Netherlands. The reason they were included is because Far East matters were discussed, and those countries, particularly The Netherlands, Portugal, and Belgium, had interests in the Far East at that time. So they attended this conference and participated in the discussions on the size of the ships.

Now what was President Harding's role in all this? When President Harding took office in 1921, pressure was building for some kind of disarmament in the United States. Revulsion against World War I was beginning to appear in the American society. This plea and this clamor for disarmament was fostered by people like Senator Borah of Idaho, who kept repeating, "We've got to do something in disarmament." Most people thought that the League of Nations would handle disarmament. Once the United States decided it wasn't joining the League some people in the United States said, "Well, if we're not going to get disarmament that way we better get it some other way." In fact there had been on the books since the 1916 Naval Act a congressional mandate that directed the President of the United States to convene a conference on disarmament not later than the end of World War I. Once World War I ended and the League of Nations was talked about, people said, "O.K., we'll wait." But it was this 1916 proposal that came back into play in 1921.

In 1920 candidate Warren G. Harding was running for President. During that campaign he was accused of being a weak leader and uninspiring. His speeches lacked appeal and seemed to convey no vision and no precision about what he intended to do in the way of policy once elected. Of course, the new President wanted to show that he was a leader who could get things done. And he saw in this disarmament conference a way to do that. He could exert his leadership, achieve results, and show people that he could do something important. So he endorsed the naval conference in 1921. He may not have been able to avoid it even had he wanted to, but the point here is he did endorse it. And he played a direct role in the formulation of the U.S. position.

The position taken by the United States at that conference was that every nation should stop where it was in the building of battle ships. Understandably, the naval leaders of all the countries didn't want to do that. They said, "No, if we are going to limit arms it should be on the basis of what the national needs are. The United States should not limit its arms below what we think we need for defense of the United States and its overseas interests.'' That was discussed for several months in and around the government, but the policy formulators couldn't reach any agreed conclusion. They finally decided to stop where we were. There is some argument for saying that Harding is responsible for that decision. He is reported at one point to have said, ''I won't tell you anything else, but naval construction has got to stop.'' But if you read Secretary of State Hughes' memoirs, you will find that he takes credit for it. President Kennedy once said, ''A good idea has a thousand fathers; a bad idea doesn't have any—it's an orphan.''

Anyway, President Harding had a role in making that decision, and during the negotiations he played an important role. He was very careful to select as members of the commission to advise the secretary of state during those negotiations a broad spectrum of people. He included two key senators, one from Massachusetts, I think, the other from Missouri. He had military leaders like Tasker Bliss from the Army and Elihu Root, the statesman. He had good people; so he knew that if he could get a good treaty, he was assured of Senate support.

Also, Hughes used to report to him every day at the end of negotiations so that the President was kept well informed. The result was they negotiated the treaty in a short period of time, between November and early February, and it was ratified by the Senate at the end of March. In fact the Senate had that treaty but fifty hours and then they ratified it. In all fairness, they'd had a little argument about the China part earlier. But so far as this part was concerned, they ratified it in only fifty hours. No hearings; it was all done on the Senate floor. You can read it in the *Congressional Record*. The vote was seventy-four to one in favor of that treaty.

At President Kennedy's initial press conference when he became President in 1961, the first announcement he made was that he had commissioned a special group of advisers to prepare for him a new position and a new draft treaty on a comprehensive nuclear test ban. It is significant that at his first press conference, the first statement he made was on arms control. Now in fact President Kennedy had been for a comprehensive test ban since 1956. He was one of those who supported Adlai Stevenson, the Democratic candidate, who favored a test ban. Kennedy in 1956 came out openly for Stevenson's proposed test ban. In 1960 during his campaign he said that he would honor the moratorium on atmospheric testing. In 1958 the United States under President Eisenhower had agreed to a moratorium on atmospheric testing with the Soviet Union. Candidate Kennedy said that he would honor that moratorium, and he would not test underground until all reasonable opportunities on that issue had been exhausted.

In addition, Kennedy as President had a deep fear of nuclear war. He believed that nuclear testing made it easier for people to use nuclear weapons. He had a particular fear of nuclear war—fear for the consequences for mankind. He believed that more efforts ought to be made to get a nuclear test ban. He believed that had President Eisenhower tried harder in 1960 they could have gotten a comprehensive test ban.

President Kennedy said, "I'm going to try to get a test ban," and he had his newly commissioned group come up with a new treaty. He tried it out on the Soviets and the Soviets were very uncooperative. In fact, they backtracked from what they had said before. In September of 1961, after the President had been in office hardly nine months, the Soviets broke the moratorium on atmospheric testing. They conducted a series of atmospheric nuclear tests and the United States was forced to begin atmospheric testing some months later. But the President didn't give up. In August of 1962 the United States introduced a new treaty that called for either a comprehensive nuclear test ban or a partial test ban covering only the atmosphere, underwater and space. The Soviets still didn't respond.

After the 1962 Cuban missile crisis, the President wanted to do things to encourage good relationships with the Soviets. The President put the test ban at the top of his agenda the following December when negotiations with the Soviets began anew. He tried again to get the Soviets interested but they didn't respond. In June, 1963, the President made a speech at the American University in Washington in which he said, "We've got to open doors to peace. There's got to be more harmony in the world. We've got to understand the Soviets better. Everything they do is not wrong; everything we do is not right." It was a very understanding and statesman-like speech. Whether that had any direct effect or not on the Soviets we don't know. We do know that a month later in East Berlin, Khrushchev said, "I won't negotiate a comprehensive test ban that requires international inspection but I will negotiate a limited nuclear test ban where compliance is checked by national means." Within a period of about two weeks Ambassador Harriman was in Moscow with a team. In August a treaty was initialed in Moscow, hearings soon followed in the Senate, and the treaty was ratified later that fall.

Now President Kennedy's personal commitment to arms control was evident throughout those negotiations, particularly in Moscow. From Moscow, Harriman had to report to the President once a day on what had happened. The President consulted with his advisers and sent word back to Moscow about what to do. So the President was in effect involved intimately in negotiations.

He also kept the Senate leaders apprised of what was going on so that when the treaty was initialed they wouldn't be caught off base. Now all this had to be done in great secrecy but he kept a few people informed so that they wouldn't be caught off balance.

President Kennedy did one other thing. He made sure as he went along that he had the support of the Joint Chiefs of Staff. He had the Joint Chiefs participate in the development of the U.S. position. The Joint Chiefs weren't always happy with it, but they never felt strongly enough about it to get up and walk out of the meeting. My recollection is—and I was working for General Taylor at the time—that the President didn't consult with the Joint Chiefs directly during the time of the negotiations in Moscow. He did consult with them immediately after those negotiations to be sure he still had their support. In doing that he reminded them of the Bay of Pigs in 1961 and the miscommunication between the President and the Joint Chiefs during the Bay of Pigs. After that the President said, "I expect you people as Joint Chiefs not to look at things only in military terms but to look at them in the broader perspective of national policy." The Joint Chiefs in their support for the test ban treaty said that although they saw in that treaty technical, military disadvantages, those disadvantages were far outweighed by the broader political ramifications in terms of improving relations between East and West.

Next there were hearings in the Senate. Those hearings weren't all friendly. Senator Hickenlooper, for one, couldn't understand why the Chiefs supported it. In fact, Hickenlooper asked General LeMay, Chief of Staff of the Air Force, "What do you mean making these decisions on broad international questions? You are military experts. Why don't you confine yourself to military things?" General LeMay, who was much more broad-minded than a lot of people think, said, "Look, we've been around a long time. We've dealt with these matters. All of this is not new to us. We're capable of making judgments in a broader perspective and that's what we did." I was talking with General Taylor on these matters the other day, and he commented that getting General LeMay to support that treaty was something he was proud of. Once General LeMay made up his mind, he stayed with it. The treaty was ratified 80 to 19.

I'd like to mention briefly a few other Presidents. In 1976 Jimmy Carter campaigned on reducing military budgets and getting an arms control agreement with the Soviets. I believe that his fear of things nuclear and of nuclear war was as great, if not greater, than President Kennedy's. I do know from personal experience—I was then assistant to the chairman of the Joint Chiefs of Staff—that one of the first things President Carter discussed with the Joint Chiefs was getting a comprehensive test ban. He wanted badly to get some arms control agreement with the Soviet Union. His first proposal on this was in SALT, the Strategic Arms Limitation Talks, and he called for deep cuts in strategic nuclear weapons. That was too much for the Soviets. They said, "We are not going to talk about that." So the rest of the time was spent talking about strategic arms limitations in the context of the proposals that had been made earlier by President Nixon and President Ford.

Over all those years in negotiating SALT, President Carter kept on top of the problem, both in terms of talking to the Senate and in terms of talking to the military. He had Secretary Vance and the chief negotiator, Paul Warnke, talk to the Senate so that everyone was kept well informed about the progress of those negotiations. In June of 1979 President Carter met with Brezhnev in Vienna and they initialed a SALT II Treaty. He came back to the United States to get ratification. The atmosphere at that time was good, and there was talk that perhaps the next thing to do was to get agreement on a comprehensive nuclear test ban. By that time there was a threshold test ban treaty which also had been initialed by the nations but not ratified by the United States Senate. As you know, the SALT II Treaty was never ratified by the United States Senate.

The Senate did conduct hearings beginning in the late summer of 1979. It became apparent that ratification was going to be a problem. There was nothing new about that because the Senate has always had difficulty trying to get that two-thirds vote. The only exception I know is the one I mentioned in 1922.

But the President and his people sincerely believed they would succeed, because, among other things, they had the support of the Joint Chiefs of Staff. The Joint Chiefs of Staff testified on the SALT II Treaty and said they supported it. They had some questions about it, as you would expect, but they supported the treaty as a modest but useful step. They were among the first people that the Senate called; so their support was on the record early. The Carter administration felt that with the support of the Joint Chiefs of Staff they should be able to get approval for the treaty. They saw it essentially in terms of the Panama Canal Treaty, which just barely got through the Senate. But the picture changed when the Soviet Union invaded Afghanistan. President Carter was upset because Brezhnev evidently had told him that they weren't going to invade. President Carter had what he thought was a good relationship with Brezhnev, and suddenly Brezhnev lied to him. So he decided that he would not try to get ratification of the treaty under those conditions and asked the Senate not to vote on it. So the SALT II Treaty is still before the Senate but has not been acted on.

I'm going to talk briefly about President Reagan. It is interesting to note that he has favored adhering to the SALT II Treaty provisions even though neither side has ratified the treaty. He says we ought to keep adhering to those terms until we get something better. It seems that arms control more and more is becoming important in his administration. I think that neither side was in a position to get any agreement during those first four years. And now for a lot of reasons there is pressure on both sides to do something. It's too early to write a final judgment on what arms control is going to do under the Reagan administration.

Now let me compare President Kennedy with others in terms of arms control. All Presidents have been interested in arms control for political reasons if for no other. It is hard to be against arms control and run for office. Everyone has to be for arms control for political reasons. President Kennedy was certainly that way. If you read about President Kennedy you find that up until about 1960 his interest in arms control was primarily political. He didn't really think much was going to happen, but it was a good thing politically to be for arms control. I think after his election he became personally interested in arms control and committed to it. While very much committed to it, he was also prepared to use it again for political purposes. In 1963 President Kennedy made a western trip. At that time he naturally was already thinking about his campaign in running for the presidency again, and he was not at all sure how he was going to do in 1964. He was looking for an issue. When he went out to Utah and started talking about the limited test ban, his people said, "That had a much greater appeal than we thought it would, and that's conservative Utah. If that issue has that much appeal there, you can imagine what it has anywhere else." So President Kennedy apparently was preparing to use arms control as a major issue in his campaign in 1964 for two reasons. One, he fully believed in it; and second, he thought it could serve him politically.

Not all the Presidents have been personally committed, however. Some have looked at it primarily for political reasons. But all Presidents after a certain period of time have a sense of history, and they want to know how the history books will look at them. From that perspective you are going to be for arms control. I don't think we've had a President in recent memory that had a better sense of history than President Kennedy. *Profiles in Courage*, if nothing else, shows that sense of history. Because President Kennedy had a sense of history, he was for arms control.

Some Presidents have had a real dread of things nuclear and have wanted to take every step feasible to reduce nuclear weapons. The two that come to mind are President Kennedy and President Carter. One time President Kennedy was talking to Kenney O'Donnell about testing. Kennedy said, "I'm worried about the children." He added, "Look, I'm not talking about my own children. I'm talking about the children of the world. What are we doing to this atmosphere if we continue testing? What is going to happen to the children of the world?" Therefore, he was very much against nuclear testing.

Other Presidents have seen arms control as a way to reduce military expenditures. But President Kennedy didn't look at arms control in that context. He wasn't trying to reduce defense expenditures. During his tenure he said,

"We are going to increase defense expenditures," and he did. He was looking at arms control purely in terms of trying to get some sort of agreement with the Soviets.

Some people, including President Harding, went for arms control because they wanted to demonstrate leadership. It was a tool to demonstrate leadership. I think that also was probably true of President Kennedy at certain times but his motives and interests went far beyond just trying to demonstrate his leadership. Again it was a personal commitment.

Let me just make one final point in conclusion. Michael Howard, a noted British historian, has written that in the West successful military policies depend on two things, deterrence and reassurance. Deterrence means deterrence against the possibility of attack by an enemy, particularly in this case the Soviet Union and its allies. He said that government leaders also have to reassure their publics that the chances of war are slight and that the leaders are doing everything to reduuce them even further. If they can't do that, the people will not support the defense policies of their government. Arms control serves the purpose of reassuring the people that the government is trying to reduce the threat of war. Therefore, it seems clear to me that not only have Presidents in the past been interested in arms control, but Presidents in the future, in order to maintain that reassurance, are going to be even more interested in arms control. As historians study that, I'm sure they will look back at how John Fitzgerald Kennedy dealt with those issues. Thank you very much.

NARRATOR: How did you happen to get into this part of the Kennedy administration? Who were some of the players? What was General Taylor's role in this whole issue? Who were some of the other players? How did this matter of the relationship between the White House and the NSC on one hand and the State Department and Defense Department play out? Anything you can tell us about that would greatly help our oral history effort.

GENERAL SMITH: General Taylor wrote the *Uncertain Trumpet* which talked about reducing reliance on nuclear weapons and increasing conventional forces. So President Kennedy was predisposed to some of the ideas of General Taylor. Then at the time of the Bay of Pigs he called upon General Taylor to conduct an investigation of the Bay of Pigs and the involvement of the CIA, the State Department, and the Joint Chiefs of Staff. At that time General Taylor was selected to become military representative of the President. General Taylor held that position from the summer of 1961 until the first of October 1962. During that time he established good relationships with McGeorge Bundy. The person who dealt with defense matters primarily in the White House at that time was Carl Kaysen with whom we used to work closely on defense matters. There was a good relationship established and even when General Taylor went to the Pentagon, one of us, first an army colonel for nine months and then I for a little over a year, served on the NSC staff as well as an assistant to General Taylor. Therefore, we had good contact with the people on all these issues, and we could talk with them informally about some of the pitfalls.

In the Department of Defense at that time the person who was primarily responsible for arms control was Paul Nitze, who was the assistant secretary of defense for International Security Affairs. He had working for him a captain, a naval captain, named Zumwalt. I happened to be General Taylor's man on arms control, so I dealt with all these issues. At the office of secretary of defense level, we had good communications. I could tell them, "Look, if you try that you are in deep, dark trouble. If you try another alternative we may be able to sell it." We kept working trying to find things that did not jeopardize our security and that the military could accept. With the White House I could talk to Kaysen the same way.

With the State Department our relations then were less close at my level. I mentioned that the Joint Chiefs got involved. There was a committee set up which included the secretary of state, the director of the Arms Control and Disarmament Agency, and some members of the NSC staff. The chairman of the Joint Chiefs later was also made a member of that group. They used to meet when proposals got to a certain stage of development and discuss them. Those of us at staff level of course worked in developing those papers. There was constant communication therefore; but until Harriman went to Moscow in July of 1963, few thought any arms control agreement was anywhere near. No one thought that the Soviets would take them seriously.

The military in our government are advisers. It has always been interesting to me how that line is drawn. If you are working on something that a particular administration likes and you are cooperative, then you have a full range of expression. But if it is something about which you say, "That's not going to work," then you are told, "The role of the military is to advise. You are limited only to military things."

NARRATOR: There really wasn't in those days a lot of friction between the NSC, the adviser, the State Department, and the Defense Department? There was more cooperation and less public relations by either side?

GENERAL SMITH: Yes, I think there was more harmony because the Kennedy administration was more of one mind about what they wanted to do. There was some tension between the military and the people who really wanted arms control, particularly on a comprehensive test ban, because the military believe you've got to have some inspection; it's got to be a satisfactory inspection. The Joint Chiefs had been, in principle, for a comprehensive test ban, but only under some international inspection that would guarantee the other side lived up to the provisions of the treaty. During the Kennedy administration there was a question of how many on-site inspections were needed and how to monitor Soviet nuclear activity. There were arguments raging about that. To say all was harmonious is a mistake. If the Kennedy administration had tried to go for a comprehensive test ban, I doubt they would have gotten it. But in terms of a limited test ban treaty they were able to get that because the technical means were considered to be adequate to judge what the Soviets were doing in terms of testing in the atmosphere. If we knew what they were doing and chose not to do anything about it, then that's our own fault.

But the Chiefs were worried. General Taylor in 1963 said they were worried about a euphoria where people would say, "Now that we've got arms control we don't need arms any more." I tried in 1979 to have the Joint Chiefs use that same word, "euphoria," but even though they didn't know that General Taylor used it in 1963 the drafters of the paper still didn't like it. They used another term which said essentially the same thing, conveying fear of a feeling of overconfidence. The Carter administration was strongly of one mind. You have two points of view in the current administration on arms control, and both points of view find expression. One thing has been true of government ever since I've known anything about it. If you can't get your way in government, you talk to someone out of government who will help you. Yes, there always is a lot of discussion and a lot of hard feelings. Nothing in government is easy, but once the President decides what he is going to do, then everyone either lines up or gets out. Most of the time they line up.

QUESTION: I wonder if you would care to comment on the strategy of the Defense Department under Secretary Weinberger as it fits into the overall issue of arms control.

GENERAL SMITH: Secretary of Defense Weinberger firmly believes that more money ought to be spent on defense. Everything else is subordinate to that. You may have read in an article recently that he went to the President with a budget greater than the Joint Chiefs of Staff recommended. The Joint Chiefs are reported to have said, "This year is going to be a bad year. Why don't we give a little bit?" This was before all this talk about the budget freeze came in. We'll do better preserving what we have if we give a little bit." Weinberger in effect said, "Not me. I'm going to go for the whole thing.'' He is firmly committed to more money for defense and everything else is subordinate to that, arms control included. As he looks at the record of arms control a case could be made that not much has been gained. He thinks it deludes people and gives them a false sense of safety rather than achieving results. Although he has been for some arms control agreements, he has not been in the forefront.

People don't always get what they want. He is going to be under a lot of pressure. I think that with the changed mood in the Congress, there has got to be some serious negotiating. I think he is astute enough to know he is going to have to bend a little. To get what he wants, he is going to have to let other people get something that they want. Therefore, maybe not in words but in deeds, he is going to be more accommodating. And of course Secretary of State Shultz is now trying to assert himself in arms control. After all, that is a primary role for the State Department.

QUESTION: I think perhaps that Weinberger is using the same tactics of bargaining that the President is famous for having developed—just sticking firmly by what he says and not giving in until the very last possible moment.

GENERAL SMITH: That's right. You know who else does that? The Soviets. You see it right now. They say, ''We're not going to talk again.'' Then they change their mind. In negotiations right to the last minute they say, ''We're not going to get an agreement.'' Then they come in and say, ''O.K. we agree.'' We ask, ''What happened?'' They say, ''Don't ask us what happened, we just now agree.'' It is a good tactic because my experience has been that on arms control we spend more time negotiating with ourselves than we do negotiating with the Soviets.

QUESTION: Do you think it is important for a President to play both sides of the coin—to have a strong hawkish rhetoric and while also playing the more compromising President? If that's true, do you think that Kennedy failed in that?

GENERAL SMITH: In terms of being strident, I think that changes with the times and can change even during the tenure of a President. When President Kennedy came in office there was the missile gap, there was the Sputnik, and Khrushchev was saying, ''We're going to surpass you by 1980.'' Kennedy was saying, ''Don't tread on me.'' It was important for him to say that at that time to reassure the American people and the world in terms of American strength. Later things began to change and you get a better perspective about the United States versus the Soviet power, particularly after the Cuban missile crisis, which demonstrated clearly to everyone that the Soviets were not about to take us on for a number of reasons including the fact that at that time we were superior in terms of nuclear forces. He could then be much more accommodating. You know it is much easier to be accommodating when you are stronger than if you think you are weak.

QUESTION: I suppose one of our biggest problems is we don't trust what the Soviets tell us; therefore verification is a most important thing with this. With our satellite intelligence how much more verification do we need? How would it take place? If we had on-site verification we would only see, I guess, what they would show us.

GENERAL SMITH: To answer that question, there is no such thing as perfect verification. But to answer the first part of your question, what one can see from outside the Soviet Union is not enough. Unfortunately it is not enough. Often we Americans have the feeling that if we can see something we understand it, but that's not true. As you get these more complicated agreements it is going to require at least looking at some storage facilities, maybe some production facilities. It's true the Soviets will only show us what they want us to see, unless we draw up the rules of the game so that we have the right to look at a certain number of facilities a certain number of times a year if we have evidence prompting our inquiry. Verification is very difficult because the rules have to be drawn up so precisely. Since no one can foresee every circumstance that is going to emerge, it's very difficult to get adequate verification procedures. Characteristics controlled by the treaty, you must leave the channels clear so that we can receive the data by our radios and therefore we can by national, technical means see that you are abiding by the treaty. That's the only way we can check the characteristics of how many warheads and related items. The Soviet Union responded that they believed we were getting too much information. So they encoded some of the channels of communication. As a result, the United States gets just a lot of jabbering on some channels. It doesn't give us anything meaningful. The United States considered this a violation of the treaty. That argument began even before the treaty was initialed. The Soviets were not giving us data we thought necessary to verify by national technical means.

QUESTION: Is it possible for a quick evaluation of Mr. Nixon's contributions to arms control?

GENERAL SMITH: Yes. President Nixon was seriously interested in arms control and got the SALT I agreement and the ABM Treaty which turned out to be very useful. President Nixon was good in these matters. I was going to say he was a tough negotiator but people have found some fault with the SALT I agreement, because in any agreement like that you are going to take risks. He was willing to take risks to get reductions on nuclear arms. And if you look at his record it stands up very well in arms control with the other Presidents.

Now in terms of his personal commitment, I know less about that than I do some of the others because I haven't studied it in depth. But if you look at the transition that took place between the mid-sixties to the mid-seventies in terms of our thinking about strategic matters, President Nixon had a lot to do with having us accept the concept of parity and essential equivalence rather than trying to maintain superiority. If some other people had done that they probably wouldn't have gotten away with it. But when he came in office he said, "We need sufficiency, we don't need superiority." He saw the developments ahead and tried to get a policy that was compatible with them, and he did a commendable job.

NARRATOR: I'm sure I speak for you in thanking General Smith. He has not only looked at one but several Presidents. He has not only spoken for himself but in a sense for several other key people whose views we've sought on the Kennedy presidency. This is his second time at the Miller Center and we trust there will be less time between the second and third visits than between the first and second. We are most grateful.

IX.
KENNEDY AS LEADER: HISTORY'S JUDGMENT

KENNEDY: RETROSPECT AND PROSPECT

Theodore C. Sorensen

NARRATOR: Ted Sorensen literally needs no introduction. We all remember with nostalgia the role he played in the Kennedy White House, his great book on Kennedy following the presidency, and now his most recent book, *A Different Kind of Presidency,* with its provocative and challenging proposals for breaking the political deadlock and assuring the future of the presidency. Normally one extends the dialogue in introducing our guests but in this case there is no need unless the person who was most helpful in urging Ted Sorensen to visit us, Ambassador Bill Battle, cares to say one word about how Ted Sorensen was viewed from Australia when he was ambassador.

MR. BATTLE: Well, as Sir Robert Menzies said when they asked him over here how he viewed our integration problems: "From a very great distance." But there is no doubt that Ted was probably one of the closest persons to Jack Kennedy during the campaign and the administration. Certainly any of you who have read his books and the other books know that his is the objective true picture of what went on. It's just a great pleasure to have him.

MR. SORENSEN: I will begin by recalling a visitor to my office from Great Britain in the fall of 1963 who told me that he thought the Cuban missile crisis and John F. Kennedy's peaceful, successful resolution of that crisis would prove to be like the Greek stand against the Persians at Salamis in 400 B.C., that is, that it would not only be a great turning point in history but the start of a golden age. A month later John F. Kennedy was dead, fifteen months later we had combat troops in Vietnam (which was advice he had always rejected); and in the years that followed we had more assassinations, riots in the ghettos and on our college campuses, and high crimes and misdemeanors in the highest places of government. It was clearly not a golden age.

At first glance the answer to the question, "Is anything left?" is a somewhat pessimistic answer. John F. Kennedy said in his inaugural that the torch had been passed to a new generation, presumably with the expectation that that trend would continue. Yet, if John F. Kennedy were alive today he wouldn't be as old as the President we have in the White House now.

In foreign affairs, Kennedy's proudest accomplishments were those that followed the Cuban missile crisis. The limited nuclear test ban treaty, he said, was the first step on "a journey of a thousand miles," quoting an old Chinese saying. Unfortunately, no steps have been taken since, and the two superpowers are not even in communication today about further steps. Kennedy and Khrushchev, after the anguish of the missile crisis, agreed on a hotline between the White House and the Kremlin, but today there are no communications of any kind—other than a rather bitter vituperation—flowing between the two capitals.

Kennedy talked more than once—particularly during that long western swing that he made in 1963, but even before the Cuban missile crisis as well—about what he called the unthinkability as well as the unwinability of a nuclear war. But in recent years our allies in Europe have become alarmed by loose talk from Washington about how we would go about a tactical nuclear exchange and how, if we evacuated enough cities and distributed enough shovels, we might be able to win such a war.

One of John F. Kennedy's principle objectives in accelerating the exploration of space, focusing as he did on a manned lunar landing to give the U.S. some thrust and bargaining power, was to prevent the militarization of outer space. He did not want to see space occupied by a hostile power. During the year 1963 the two superpowers agreed at the United Nations on a resolution banning weapons of mass destruction from outer space. Now both superpowers are intent on using space as a new military theatre, and the President has recently said that he is not interested in negotiating a ban on anti-satellite warfare and weapons.

Kennedy also made much of the Atlantic partnership and was hailed for that stand in 1963 in his visit to Berlin and other European capitals. Today that partnership, according to the experts in both parties and on both sides of the Atlantic, is in as sad a state of disrepair as it has ever been. The French government has said that it will help Nicaragua remove mines that we have helped to place in its harbors. The British government is still irate over the fact that it was not consulted when we invaded a British Commonwealth member. The Germans feel that a series, under at least two administrations if not more, of U.S. zig-zags and u-turns on the deployment of intermediate range nuclear weapons, and on the negotiations of limitations on such weapons, has left them in a politically impossible position with their own constituency.

One of Kennedy's proudest accomplishments in 1962, prior to the missile crisis, was the Trade Expansion Act. That led in time to the Kennedy round of negotiations at Tokyo and to a very wide and dramatic increase in the flow of trade, particularly among the industrialized countries. Now those same countries are on the verge of a trade war. Protectionism has become the moving force of the day in many capitals. Even President Kennedy's own party seems to be moving in the direction of protectionism with a domestic content bill, a steel quota and other such proposals. Despite the gains that have been made during these last twenty years, we could find ourselves set back by even more than two decades if this trend continues.

John Kennedy placed a great emphasis on the Alliance for Progress, an effort to focus U.S. attention and aid on economic and social institutions accompanied by political reforms in Central America and South America. Our focus now is almost totally on our military involvement in that part of the world.

The picture is equally discouraging on domestic policy. The Kennedy declaration of June 1963 on civil rights, unlike any declaration that any President had ever made in history regarding the legal and moral impropriety of racial segregation and discrimination, is not the kind of leadership that we receive from the White House or Department of Justice now.

The emphasis that Kennedy placed on attacking poverty and malnutrition—you will recall that his very first act in the White House was to order a distribution of federal surplus food—is evidence that he never forgot what he learned in the West Virginia primary about children who don't have enough food to even pay attention to their studies. As President, Kennedy revived food stamp programs and increased surplus food distribution programs and we were engaged in planning the war on poverty at the time of his death.

Now, and for the last several years, the number of people slipping below the poverty level has been steadily increasing. The cutbacks in many federally financed programs have simply cut some people off altogether from social concern.

Kennedy believed that it was possible to prevent inflation without a recession and to cure a recession without inflation and he did it. It took some rather emphatic presidential backing of the wage/price guidelines and some rather forceful presidential intervention on one occasion against price increases by big steel. Nevertheless he did it. The wholesale price index during the Kennedy administration actually declined. (It wasn't the rate of increase that slowed down, the index actually declined during those three years.) The consumer price index was virtually level. Now we seem to be back to the cyclical notion that the only way to cure inflation is through a recession and, as a result, we've come out of the worst recession since the Great Depression. There are some signs as well that we cannot come out of that recession without overheating the economy so that we will face a recurrence of the cycle all over again.

People forget that Kennedy was fiscally very conservative and paid more attention to the budget and budget deficit than any modern President before or after. I realize that the government has changed and that the dollar has changed in these last twenty-plus years. But they haven't changed as much as the increase in the annual federal budget deficit, which has risen from roughly eight billion dollars to two hundred billion dollars—or the budget itself, which Kennedy managed (partly for psychological and political reasons) to keep under one hundred billion dollars. Now it is an enormous multiple of that figure.

Finally, John Kennedy, as so many people have written since then, offered hope—hope to our own young people and minority population; hope to some of the oppressed peoples of the world; hope to the world in general that this country could fulfill its proper world leadership role, the destiny that its founders had originally intended. Today there is very little of that hope. There is very little confidence in our system. The opinion polls, for twenty years, with occasional upward blips when there is a new President elected or the economy is recovering, have shown a steady decline in the confidence of our citizens in our political institutions, our government, and the way we govern ourselves. And clearly the rest of the world has had all too little respect for us in recent years.

Nevertheless, I don't think that we should be totally discouraged. We should not feel that he had no impact at all. I think there is a Kennedy legacy that remains. It is not just style. Style was important to the Kennedy presidency. It helped him get elected. It helped him sell his program. It helped him communicate that program to the public and even to foreign leaders. But there was a great deal of substance that accompanied the style. The style, combined with the dramatic nature of his death, caused a good many people to exaggerate who John Kennedy was and what he did and to give us the myth of Camelot. But there was more than style; I think there is a legacy as well as the legend.

I'm not one of those who feels that all that Kennedy did would have happened anyway. I don't belong to that school of historians who say that the broad sweep of history really determines the progress of the world, that no individual can ever make a difference and that the pendulum swings back and forth regardless of individual leaders. I remember the events of 1960 all too clearly; I remember all too clearly how narrowly we won and, while there is lots of speculation on what would the world have been like had John F. Kennedy not been killed, I think it might be more useful to speculate on what the world would have been like had John F. Kennedy not been elected. I think that election made a difference then and I think it makes a difference now.

First of all, I think the election of Kennedy—followed by the policies of Kennedy during his administration—removed religion as a test for the presidency, an extra-constitutional bar that had previously told us that no Catholic (and presumably no member of any other religious minority) could serve in the White House. I say "his policies in the presidency" because he had been elected President by that narrow margin in which the religious issue did result in a very serious drain on his vote total. Had he done something to confirm the suspicions held by many—like sending an ambassador to the Vatican, or calling for government-sponsored prayer in the public schools—people would have said never again to a Catholic in the White House. But he did not; and a candidate's religion in that sense is no longer an issue.

Second, I come back to the Cuban missile crisis which I mentioned at the start. I'm not sure, none of us can be sure that we would be here discussing this topic had Kennedy blundered at the time of the missile crisis. The opportunities for blundering were immense. Many of his advisers urged a so-called surgical air strike upon the missiles—which upon further investigation by the President proved not to be "surgical" at all and ultimately would have required a full-fledged war in and over Cuba. Others urged that he do nothing at all or simply send a note to the Kremlin—but they were unable to persuade the President that this would not simply turn world initiative over to the Soviet Union and permit in time the erosion of our collective security, with our allies and the Third World convinced that we were giving in to intimidation. Ultimately, it was Kennedy's own decision, and his forceful implementation of that decision (for he tightly held the reins of command during the thirteen days of the missile crisis), that enabled the two superpowers to resolve that potential nuclear confrontation without the U.S. firing a shot. There has not been a comparable confrontation since—in part because both superpowers learned something from that lesson.

Third, despite some recent slippage on the civil rights front, the clock will never be turned back totally to where it was before John F. Kennedy's statements and legislation of mid-1963. We take for granted now that when we go into public places of accommodation that people of all races will be having lunch there or bowling there or whatever. We take it for granted now in the workplace that blacks and whites will be working side by side. We're not surprised to see black mayors and congressmen or black candidates for President. None of that was taken for granted twenty years ago. In fact, none of that was possible in many parts of the country twenty years ago. John F. Kennedy didn't start the civil rights revolution and could not have stopped it had he wanted to. But he was the first President to place his office at the front of that revolution, the first President to declare that all forms of discrimination and segregation would thereafter be illegal and contrary to American standards. He was the first President, then, in addition to his legislative program, to enlist the help of one group after another—the bar association, the educators' association, the medical association, all the interest groups and establishment groups in this country—to involve them, to tell them that times had changed and that there would have to be a new attitude on race in our society.

Still another tangible part of the Kennedy legacy are people in government and politics. There are not as many now, twenty-four years later, simply because of the passage of time. But countless numbers of people whom John Kennedy brought into public life for the first time went on to make enormous contributions in the federal agencies, or in international agencies such as the World Bank and the United Nations, or in Congress, or at the state and local level. This includes people who are not nationally known, and people who were not even known to John Kennedy, but who responded to his call that the public service should once again be a proud and noble career. They became excited about and interested in and therefore involved in politics—some in Kennedy's party and some in other parties, some in local elections and some in national elections. I might add this is true even in other countries. My law practice takes me abroad frequently, and I encounter leaders who tell me that they first were interested in public affairs because of the kind of example Kennedy set.

Finally, in addition to setting an example he set standards. High standards. Standards of excellence in how we govern ourselves. Standards of quality in the kinds of people attracted to government. Standards of eloquence, if I may say so. Standards of vision and hope. His critics have often said he raised expectations too high. I would plead John F. Kennedy guilty to that charge. He did raise expectations. I think a President ought to raise expectations instead of lowering them. As the poet said, "A man's grasp should exceed his reach or what's a heaven for." That's what a President is for, to lift our sights. Most Presidents of both parties since Kennedy have invoked his name and quoted his words and realized that they ought to try to reach that same standard.

I said in an op ed piece in the *Times* last fall that he was not an easy man to summarize. People mistakenly tend to put him into one category or another. The doves who like the fact that he negotiated the withdrawal of missiles from Cuba without firing a shot tend to downplay the fact that he was willing to invoke the potential use of American military force in Cuba and Laos and Berlin in order to obtain negotiated solutions. Those who hail the limited nuclear test ban treaty ought to remember that he was an advocate of deterrence as well as detente. Those who praise his programs for the poor, the hungry and the elderly should remember that he was the only President since Hoover never to incur a double digit deficit.

Some of the people in the Reagan administration point out that Kennedy had a tax cut at the same time that he increased defense spending. But he had a much smaller tax cut and it was accompanied by a much smaller budget deficit. That cut was allocated proportionately, with much more of its benefits going to the low income taxpayers. His first defense budget deleted some of the carry-over or proposed redundant weapons systems, including the forerunners of such first strike missiles as the MX.

Kennedy was in so many ways a remarkable combination. He was the first Catholic elected President; he was also the first President to support the population control efforts of the United Nations. He reduced tensions between the superpowers but he didn't reduce our vigilance or our military strength. He consulted our allies very carefully on Berlin but he didn't consult them at all on the Cuban missile crisis. He brought Congress in on many matters, such as international trade, but he brought them in only at the last moment, and not for their advice at the time of the Cuban missile crisis.

I think good friends of his, such as Bill Battle, would agree that while his public policies were made known to everyone, his private thoughts were made known to very few people. He often spoke lightly of those matters about which he cared very deeply. He poked fun at those whom he disdained, but he also poked fun at those whom he admired greatly, including himself. He would often conceal his liberal objectives in rather conservative rhetoric and he would often present limited proposals in visionary terms. He was a very down-to-earth pragmatist and yet he reached for the moon. He was an old-fashioned patriot but he was a hard-boiled politician. He brought into his administration many of the political opponents that irritated him the most; and yet he never forgot which stores in Boston refused to put his signs in their windows in his very first congressional campaign of 1946.

He was, as I say, a remarkable combination. He was, in short, a very remarkable President.

QUESTION: Do you think President Kennedy would have appointed a director of USIA who would allow a blacklist to be compiled of speakers?

MR. SORENSEN: No, I don't. I don't want to pretend that everyone whom we appointed to office was a gem. We made a few errors. Kennedy was not good at firing people. That was one of his weaknesses. Instead of firing some of those errors he promoted them. I have a federal judge or two in mind when I say that. Even an ambassador or two, but not in Australia. Nor can I say that Kennedy demonstrated goodwill toward everyone in the world. He never made an enemy list and was too smart to have one compiled, but I'm sure he had in his own mind some concept of who would not be an appropriate spokesman for the U.S. But he also took some steps to go in the opposite direction of blacklists and the line. Quite a list of people who, during the McCarthy era (which was less than a decade earlier), had been politically exiled, blacklisted, or otherwise condemned were honored or appointed to a high post or invited to serve on a White House commission or receive some other honor. That shows the difference between his way of thinking and the way of thinking that's so prevalent today.

QUESTION: Many of the sessions we've been having here on the presidency have led to a discussion of the role of the vice-president. One speaker even called for abolition of the office. He had even thought out the idea of having a President designate the vice-president as secretary of state and I know you have thoughts on the subject which you may be willing to share with us.

MR. SORENSEN: There are many facets to that question. Let me begin by saying that Kennedy's relations with his vice-president were better than advertised. Although there were some members of the White House staff who were somewhat disdainful of Johnson, that was not Kennedy's view. In fact he was often frustrated by his failure to get Johnson to participate. Johnson, whether out of antagonism, caution or whatever, would often fail or refuse to comment when Kennedy asked him for a comment. Johnson attended all the key formal meetings: the Cabinet meetings, the National Security Council meetings, the legislative leadership breakfasts, and the meetings that we had before the press conferences. Obviously a great deal of decisionmaking went on outside those formal meetings without Johnson being involved. But that's one of the reasons why I'm a little wary of proposals to mesh these offices. A President ultimately has to make decisions by himself. He may get advice from all kinds of advisers. But under our system, which I support, the President alone is accountable. He alone is responsible for the decisons that must be made and he has to make those decisions.

Ideally, we would have our vice-presidents chosen solely on the basis of their ability to succeed as President in case anything happened and to run the country effectively. I don't know of any vice-president who has been chosen on that basis. Lyndon Johnson was not chosen on that basis, although obviously Kennedy admired him and thought him a big man in every sense of the word. He was chosen because we thought it would help reunite the Democratic party, because we thought he would help carry southern states which were otherwise antagonistic to Kennedy's politics and religion, and because we thought there would probably be less wear and tear and tension having Johnson inside the executive branch than having him as the leader of the Senate in the legislative branch.

My new book examines a series of crises which I think this country is facing and suggests that there is a political stalemate in Washington now and has been for some time. It is reflected through a recurring cycle of ineffectiveness in the President. Each new President comes in with lots of hope and expectations and then in a year and a half or two years he's bogged down also. Given the serious nature of these crises—the nuclear arms race, the federal deficit escalation, the decline in our industrial competitiveness and so on—I felt obligated to present a solution, to get the debate underway. My solution was a one-term bipartisan government in which the President would select a vice-president from the other party and have a bipartisan Cabinet and a nonpartisan White House staff and so on. (I won't give it all away here—I want you to buy the book.)

It's an idea that is unlikely to be adopted this year but I don't rule it out altogether. If Reagan and Bush are reelected, and if some approaching crisis in the world becomes a real crisis, and then something should happen to Mr. Reagan, then I could see it as very possible that Mr. Bush, on becoming President and upon being required to go to a Democratic Congress for his vice-president under the new constitutional amendment, might be told at that point, by the Congress, that this is the time for a bipartisan administration. "We'll give you a Democrat for vice-president and we suggest that you have a bipartisan Cabinet and all the rest."

But, for now, it's hard to know what better use can be made of our vice-presidents. Fritz Mondale was saying that he was the most influential vice-president in history, played a very important role and had constant access to the President, but during the last six months or so he's been making it clear that he had nothing whatsoever to do with many Carter administration policies and has given us quite a long list of items he was against. As some vice-presidents have frankly recognized, it is a standby role. That's important; but as was said long ago, the vice-president really only has two duties under the Constitution; one is to preside over the Senate whenever he feels like it, and the other is to inquire each morning after the President's health.

QUESTION: Coming back to President Kennedy for a moment. Some Presidents leave what we might call an intellectual legacy alongside the other legacies. Maybe you could describe what Franklin Roosevelt left as a set of moral and social ideas, a social philosophy. You could describe the set of neoconservative/conservative currents that came into play in Ronald Reagan. Would you talk a little bit about the intellectual legacy of John Kennedy, if you can talk about him in so short a time in the same terms as these I've mentioned?

MR. SORENSEN: I think it can be done. I would like to give more thought to that before I try to spell it out. In many ways Kennedy's was a transition presidency. Before Kennedy was elected, the Gallup poll showed that the vast majority of the American people thought a nuclear war between the United States and the Soviet Union was inevitable. A Gallup poll the year after he died showed that a majority thought it could be avoided. I'm sure that a poll before Kennedy was elected regarding civil rights would have shown a majority against almost all of the legislation which with remarkably little difficulty was accepted as a given after the Kennedy presidency.

Kennedy, I believe, educated the country on our fiscal and economic policy. The fact that he proposed a tax cut at a time when the budget was not in balance was—it is ironic now that we think about it—attacked by the Republicans at that time as being irresponsible in the extreme. But he pointed out that the budget was really an instrument of the government, that budget deficits at a time when the country is not at full employment are a natural and even a desirable state of affairs, and that tax cuts could be viewed as an economic stimulus resulting in greater revenue, and not simply as a means of relieving somebody's tax burden.

There is a whole list of areas where Kennedy laid the groundwork in this transition presidency. You might also call it a "seed-planting presidency," seeds that later bore fruit. It was under Kennedy that we had the first public television legislation. I doubt that anyone between Theodore Roosevelt and Kennedy sent messages to the Congress on consumerism and on the environment. Kennedy appointed a commission on the status of women in America. That seems so archaic now that it's unbelievable but it was groundbreaking at the time.

The Kennedy acceleration of effort in our exploration of space has had a good many indirect benefits in medicine, science, industry and all the rest. Federal concern for the mentally retarded, which he cared personally very much about, represented a whole new legislative program. Physical fitness—again something that we all take for granted today—was brought to the nation's attention by Kennedy, with his talk about the fifty-mile hike and his introduction of the Physical Fitness Council in the White House. He was the first President to have a special adviser on the arts, the first to have a national council of the arts. Now we all assume that the federal government ought to play such a role.

In short, the Kennedy presidency was tragically brief in the sense that he had time merely to initiate that kind of legacy in a large number of areas. Yet the transitions over which he presided and for which he gets some credit—transitions in U.S./Soviet relations, in black/white relations, in our understanding of the economy—these seeds that he planted, I think, are all important parts of that legacy.

QUESTION: I wonder if you could say something about Kennedy's philosophy of the presidency. I seem to recall that about a year after he was in office he was asked at a press conference how the world looked from where he was in the presidency and he said, "It looks a lot less powerful than it did when I was in Congress." Other Presidents have said things like it is primarily a place of moral leadership. I wonder if you could give us some idea of what you sense to be Kennedy's essential philosophy of that office or his views toward it.

MR. SORENSEN: It is true that he remarked on more than one occasion that when he was in Congress he thought the President had all the power and when he was in the presidency he was astonished at how much power Congress had to block presidential power. It's also true that—and Kennedy has been criticized for this—he had no grand design. He did not take office saying, "This is what I am going to do in years one, two, three and four and this is where the world will be at the end of those four years." He felt, invoking Woodrow Wilson, that it was his responsibility to exercise the powers of the office to the fullest, to tackle each problem that arose (most of which could not be predicted in advance) with all of the vigor and skill at his command to advance the national interest. Because he had done a great deal of reading in American history he recognized that the office itself, the powers of the office, deserved respect and preservation.

He was not a man who talked much about "power." During the first few months that I stayed on and served with Lyndon Johnson, his people were always talking about power; and it struck me as odd, because I never remembered hearing Kennedy talk about power, certainly not power in the sense of ordering people to do this or that. Kennedy didn't shrink from responsibility, and he used all the tools that were in the office; but I don't think he sought power for the sake of power. He was one of those people who all his life was interested in and concerned with public affairs in this country, and with what kind of world we lived in. He wanted to make it a better country and better world, and he was determined to use his time in office to achieve that. It all sounds very vague and it was vague, but very real.

QUESTION: Does that mean that he would have disagreed with Gary Hart? In his *New Democracy* he was very detailed down to the pension plans and so forth and he makes a big deal of claiming to follow Kennedy's legacy. Would you say this claim is problematic?

MR. SORENSEN: No. Knowing quite a bit about both men, I would say that there are more similarities there in terms of approach than differences. I was not saying that Kennedy shied away from specific proposals. On the contrary, during the first hundred days in office I worked almost literally day and night, seven days a week, sending a series of some sixteen to twenty legislative messages to the Congress in which we spelled out in great detail what we regarded to be the agenda for the 1960s—not items that we expected Congress to adopt *in toto* immediately but what we wanted them to set their sights on. I'm simply saying that, in terms of philosophy of office, Kennedy didn't take office with a grand design for the country. But he certainly had a legislative program and he certainly sought to set high goals for the country. Yes, I would say that Hart and Kennedy are similar, not different.

QUESTION: Would you say a word or two about the relationship between the President and his brother Bobby and the extent to which he really depended upon him for advice?

MR. SORENSEN: The relationship was an extremely close one. In many ways President Kennedy felt Bobby was invaluable as an assistant, as a sounding board, as someone on whom he could totally rely and in whom he had complete confidence. In many areas of Justice Department jurisdiction he was willing to give Bobby a wider latitude than he gave to other Cabinet members. After the Bay of Pigs he asked Bobby (and me) to start attending National Security Council meetings because he felt that Bobby could give that extra set of skeptical eyes and ears that he felt he had not had during the limited meetings on the Bay of Pigs. In retrospect, it may have been an error to have Bobby as attorney general, but considering some of the attorney generals and attorney general designates we've had since, it doesn't look so bad.

It was an extremely close relationship. There were vast areas of government policy and presidential decisionmaking in which Bobby was not involved at all, so we should not exaggerate the role, but neither should we underestimate Bobby's importance on those matters in which he was involved.

QUESTION: Bobby was very influential during the Cuban missile crisis, was he not, in assisting and advising during that terribly tough time?

MR. SORENSEN: Yes, he was.

QUESTION: I wanted to pursue the matter of Kennedy and the Caribbean just a bit further. Certainly he deserves credit for the success of the missile crisis confrontation. But in that whole process of the Bay of Pigs there was the acceptance of Castro and the acceptance of a growing role of the Soviet Union in the Western Hemisphere. Could you elaborate a little further perhaps about his view of Castro and of the Soviets as a threat to U.S. security in the Caribbean invasion and in the Western Hemisphere generally?

MR. SORENSEN: He decided after the Bay of Pigs operation had gone awry, having been sold to him on a basis totally different from what actually proved to be the plan, that removing Castro by U.S. military efforts or separating Cuba from the Soviet Union by U.S. military efforts was not a feasible way to proceed, that it would only risk a war in which the potential gain would not be worth the potential cost. He then decided upon a variety of other steps. The first was to lessen the vulnerability of Latin America to penetration by Castro and Communism. The Alliance for Progress was an important part of that effort, providing assistance to strengthen the economies and to lessen the discontent and the political, social, economic and other miseries of those countries on which Castro hoped to play.

He also took steps to isolate Castro and Cuba in the hemisphere economically, politically, and diplomatically, although the cutoff of all diplomatic relations had been launched by Eisenhower. There was hope that in that fashion Castro would pay a price for his adherence to Soviet domination and that other members of the hemisphere would prefer to be a part of the Western Hemisphere community, and not easily choose to go Cuba's way. There was also military assistance to Venezuela and Colombia, who faced very serious problems from domestic insurgencies at the time. But if you are saying that the lack of military action in the Kennedy administration, including no attempt to use the missile crisis as an excuse to go in and conquer Cuba, represents an acceptance of a Soviet ally in the Western Hemisphere, then yes, in that sense, it did represent an acceptance, not because we liked or welcomed it but because the alternatives were deemed to be undesirable.

QUESTION: I recently gave a talk about the Vietnam War and in the early minutes of that lecture I quoted several passages from your book on Kennedy to the effect that Kennedy shared with you enormous doubts about the feasibility of getting involved in that part of the world.

So from that comes two questions. One is, if Kennedy had doubts, why did he still permit himself to be drawn gradually into that struggle and secondly, how would he have dealt with that war had he continued to live?

MR. SORENSEN: Well, let me combine the answers to both of those questions by saying this. The Vietnam conflict was not really a war at the time of the Kennedy administration or at least it wasn't so perceived. It was really a somewhat low-level civil insurrection. The government in South Vietnam was clearly under increasing pressure from the Viet Cong, and there wasn't much doubt that the Viet Cong was aided and abetted by the North but to the best of my recollection there were then no troop movements from north to south as there would later be.

As a result the conflict in Vietnam never received the attention it should have received in the Kennedy administration at the highest levels. It was a nagging pain, so to speak. But we had a lot of nagging pains in those days in all parts of the world—in Africa and Latin America and other parts of Asia. The so-called executive committee of the National Security Council, which was formally established at the time of the Cuban missile crisis, never had a meeting on Vietnam, for example. So, to begin with, Vietnam simply didn't get enough attention and maybe it should have gotten a lot more.

Second, Kennedy was, especially after the Bay of Pigs which fortunately happened early in his administration, suspicious of military solutions, suspicious that the premises on which they were being sold to him were not accurate, suspicious that their authors hadn't thought through the consequences of whether they could succeed and what would happen if they didn't succeed. In each of the crises that occurred thereafter—while he was, as I indicated in my opening remarks, prepared to use military strength, if necessary—he preferred to use that as a means of obtaining negotiations rather than fight first and negotiate later.

Next door to Vietnam in Laos is the best example. Eisenhower had told Kennedy on the day before the inauguration that the situation in Laos was impossible and that he was undoubtedly going to be required to send in American forces. And it *was* impossible if the objective was to maintain an anti-Communist regime with very little local support on the borders of China and North Vietnam. Ultimately Kennedy succeeded, including some threat of the use of force, in obtaining a negotiated solution in Laos for a neutral coalition government in which Communists served as well as pro-Americans, in which the king had his representatives and other groups in society had their representatives. That was obviously a risk. It was a neutral government, it wasn't a pro-United States government any longer. But I think it probably was the best that could be hoped for under those circumstances.

Later on the neutral government got swallowed up when the war in the late sixties broadened to cover the whole Indo-Chinese peninsula, but as a stop-gap solution at the time it wasn't bad. I've always thought that Kennedy might very well have looked for the opportunity to find a negotiated solution, including possibly a neutral coalition government in Vietnam as well as in Laos.

Nevertheless I don't want to omit the fact that the U.S. commitment to Vietnam expanded under Kennedy. The commitment had first been made by Eisenhower and not by Kennedy. The first troop deployments were sent by Johnson and not by Kennedy. The first bombing of the North was by Johnson and not by Kennedy. Nevertheless under Kennedy the number of advisers grew from about 3,500 to 15,000. Fifteen thousand is a long way from 500,000. Kennedy received advice as early as 1961 to send in combat troop units to the south. Walt Rostow, Lyndon Johnson and Maxwell Taylor were among those making that recommendation as well as to bomb the north. But he never did. The last official statement of the Kennedy administration on Vietnam was that the number of advisers was about to be reduced and that we looked forward to the day when they could be drastically reduced.

Moreover, Kennedy said on television, when asked about Vietnam, "It's their war, not our war." I thought that offers some hint of where he would have gone in the long run. My own view is that he would not have sent combat troop units, he would not have been dragged deep into a 500,000 man conflict, and he would have looked for an opportunity to negotiate his way out.

QUESTION: I also have two brief questions. To what do you attribute the worldwide distribution of pictures and a lot of other replicas of Kennedy in the homes of people througout the world?

The second question is when we look for your book, is it going to be fiction or nonfiction?

MR. SORENSEN: It's listed with those practical how-to-do-it books. Some of them are for cooking, some mechanical, but this is how to run the government and get something done.

I think as far the pictures go—and you are right, I've seen Kennedy's picture in remarkable places all over the world—there are many reasons for it. There are many reasons for the original worldwide hope in Kennedy. One was that he was a Catholic and there are a lot of Catholics around the world. Another was that he was young and most of the world outside of the advanced industrialized societies is young. A third reason is the one that I mentioned before—the element of hope. I think that John Kennedy, his personality, his speeches, his programs, his call for world peace, his avoidance of a nuclear confrontation over Cuba, his efforts to obtain some arms control agreements with the Soviet Union, his repeated interest in aiding the developing world (I might add that our aid to the Third World reached a peak under Kennedy and has been going down ever since, excluding military assistance), his role in the civil rights revolution (most of the world out there is not white)—I think that all those reasons gave people around the world, particularly in Africa and Asia and Latin America, a feeling that this was someone special. They had great hope in him and great hope in the United States. The tragic sudden nature of his death caused them to put up a picture and to keep it as a reminder of what once was.

NARRATOR: I hope there will be other ways that we can show our gratitude and that we can bring Ted Sorensen into the Virginia community. We cherish these few minutes and we know how much he has to give us as we think about the future.